# Divine Providence

*By Emmanuel Swedenborg*

**1764**

Divine Providence

Layout and Cover Copyright ©2010
All Rights Reserved
Printed in the USA

Published through CreateSpace

*[1]Swedenborg gave neither numbers nor brief captions to the chapters of the book. Nor did he prefix a recital of all the propositions and subsidiary propositions to come in the book; this was the work of the Latin editor. For this the above, giving the reader a succinct idea of the book's contents, is substituted. Tr.*

# Table of Contents

TRANSLATOR'S PREFACE ................................................................ 5

I. DIVINE PROVIDENCE IS GOVERNMENT BY THE LORD'S DIVINE LOVE AND WISDOM .................................................................... 12

II. THE LORD'S DIVINE PROVIDENCE HAS FOR ITS OBJECT A HEAVEN FROM THE HUMAN RACE ............................................. 30

III. IN ALL THAT IT DOES THE LORD'S DIVINE PROVIDENCE LOOKS TO WHAT IS INFINITE AND ETERNAL ........................................... 44

IV. THERE ARE LAWS OF PROVIDENCE THAT ARE UNKNOWN TO MEN ................................................................................................ 57

V. IT IS A LAW OF DIVINE PROVIDENCE THAT MAN SHALL ACT FROM FREEDOM ACCORDING TO REASON ................................ 59

VI. IT IS A LAW OF DIVINE PROVIDENCE THAT MAN SHALL REMOVE EVILS AS SINS IN THE EXTERNAL MAN OF HIMSELF, AND ONLY SO CAN THE LORD REMOVE THE EVILS IN THE INTERNAL MAN AND AT THE SAME TIME IN THE EXTERNAL ..... 83

VII. IT IS A LAW OF DIVINE PROVIDENCE THAT MAN SHALL NOT BE COMPELLED BY EXTERNAL MEANS TO THINK AND WILL, THUS TO BELIEVE AND LOVE WHAT PERTAINS TO RELIGION, BUT BRING HIMSELF AND AT TIMES COMPEL HIMSELF TO DO SO . 106

VIII. IT IS A LAW OF DIVINE PROVIDENCE THAT MAN SHALL BE LED AND TAUGHT BY THE LORD OUT OF HEAVEN BY MEANS OF THE WORD AND DOCTRINE AND PREACHING FROM IT, AND THIS TO ALL APPEARANCE AS OF HIMSELF .............................. 129

IX. IT IS A LAW OF DIVINE PROVIDENCE THAT MAN SHALL NOT PERCEIVE OR FEEL ANY OF THE ACTIVITY OF DIVINE

PROVIDENCE, AND YET SHOULD KNOW AND ACKNOWLEDGE PROVIDENCE ................................................................................ 148

X. THERE IS NO SUCH THING AS ONE'S OWN PRUDENCE; THERE ONLY APPEARS TO BE AND IT SHOULD SO APPEAR; BUT DIVINE PROVIDENCE IS UNIVERSAL BY BEING IN THE LEAST THINGS .. 163

XI. DIVINE PROVIDENCE LOOKS TO WHAT IS ETERNAL, AND TO THE TEMPORAL ONLY AS THIS ACCORDS WITH THE ETERNAL 181

XII. MAN IS NOT ADMITTED INWARDLY INTO TRUTHS OF FAITH AND GOODS OF CHARITY EXCEPT AS HE CAN BE KEPT IN THEM TO THE CLOSE OF LIFE ................................................................. 197

XIII. LAWS ON PERMISSION ARE ALSO LAWS OF DIVINE PROVIDENCE ................................................................................ 219

XIV. EVILS ARE TOLERATED IN VIEW OF THE END, WHICH IS SALVATION .................................................................................... 261

XV. DIVINE PROVIDENCE ATTENDS THE EVIL AND THE GOOD ALIKE ............................................................................................ 278

XVI. DIVINE PROVIDENCE APPROPRIATES NEITHER EVIL NOR GOOD TO ANYONE, BUT ONE'S OWN PRUDENCE APPROPRIATES BOTH ............................................................................................ 302

XVII. EVERY MAN CAN BE REFORMED, AND THERE IS NO PREDESTINATION [as commonly understood] .......................... 324

XVIII. THE LORD CANNOT ACT CONTRARY TO THE LAWS OF DIVINE PROVIDENCE BECAUSE TO DO SO WOULD BE TO ACT CONTRARY TO HIS DIVINE LOVE AND WISDOM, THUS CONTRARY TO HIMSELF ........................................................... 347

# TRANSLATOR'S PREFACE

### THE BOOK.

The reader will find in this book a firm assurance of God's care of mankind as a whole and of each human being. The assurance is rested in God's infinite love and wisdom, the love pure mercy, the wisdom giving love its ways and means. It is further grounded in an interpretation of the universe as a spiritual-natural world, an interpretation fully set forth in the earlier book, *Divine Love and Wisdom*, on which the present work draws heavily. As there is a world of the spirit, no view of providence can be adequate which does not take that world into account. For in that world must be channels for the outreach of God's care to the human spirit. There also any eternal goal—such as a heaven from the human race—must exist. A view of providence limited to the horizons of the passing existence can hardly resemble the care which the eternal God takes of men and women who, besides possessing perishable bodies, are themselves creatures of the spirit and immortal. The full title of the book, *Angelic Wisdom about Divine Providence*, implies that its author, in an other-world experience, had at hand the knowledge which men and women in heaven have of God's care. Who should know the divine guidance if not the men and women in heaven who have obviously enjoyed it? "The laws of divine providence, hitherto hidden with angels in their wisdom, are to be revealed now" (n. 70).

As it is presented in this book, providence seeks to engage man in its purposes, and to enlist all his faculties, his freedom and reason, his will and understanding, his prudence and enterprise. It acts first of all on his volitions and thinking, to align them with itself. That it falls directly on history, its events and our circumstances, is a superficial view. It is man's inner life which first feels the omnipresent divine influence and must do so. If we cannot be lifted to our best selves and if our aims and outlook cannot be modified for the better, how shall the world be bettered which we affect to handle? Paramount in God's presence with all men, if only in their possibilities, is His providential care.

This care, to which man's inner life is open, is alert every moment, not occasional. It is gentle and not tyrannical, constantly respecting man's freedom and reason, otherwise losing him as a human being. It has set this and other laws for itself which it pursues undeviatingly. The larger part of the book is an exposition of these laws in the conviction that by them the nature of providence is best seen. Is it not to be expected in a universe which has its laws, and in which impersonal forces are governed by laws, that the Creator of all should pursue laws in His concern with the lives of conscious beings? To fit a world of laws must not the divine care have its laws, too? Adjustment of thought about divine providence to scientific thought is not the overriding necessity, for scientific thought must keep adjusting to laws which it discerns in the physical world. In consonance, religious thought seeks to learn the lawful order in the guidance of the human spirit.

> Do not each and all things in tree or shrub proceed constantly and wonderfully from purpose to purpose according to the laws of their order of things? Why should not the supreme purpose, a heaven from the human race, proceed in similar fashion? Can there be anything in its progress which does not proceed with all constancy according to the laws of divine providence? (n 332)

Respecting the laws of providence, it is to be noted that there are more laws than those, five in number, which are stated at the heads of as many chapters in the book. Further laws are embodied in other chapters. At n. 249(2) we are told that further laws were presented in nn. 191-213, 214-220, and 221-233. In fact, at n. 243. there is a reference to laws which follow in even later chapters. In nn. 191-213 the law, partly stated in the heading over the chapter, comes to full sight particularly at n.

210(2), namely, that providence, in engaging human response, shall align human prudence with itself, so that providence becomes one's prudence (n. 311e). In nn. 214-220 the law is that providence employ the temporal goals of distinction and wealth towards its eternal goals, and perpetuate standing and wealth in a higher form, for a man will then have sought them not for themselves and handled them for the use they can be. To keep a person from premature spiritual experience, nn. 221-233, is obviously a law of providence, guarding against relapse and consequent profanation of what had become sacred to him.

The paradox of divine foreknowledge and human freedom, regularly discussed in studies of providence, receives an explanation which becomes more and more enlightening in the course of the book. The paradox, probably nowhere else discussed, of man's thinking and willing to all appearance all by himself, and of the fact that volition and thought come to him from beyond him, receives a similar, cumulative answer. The tension between the divine will and human self-will is a subject that pervades the book; to that subject the profoundest insights into the hidden activity of providence and into human nature are brought. On the question, "Is providence only general or also detailed?" the emphatic answer is that it cannot be general unless it takes note of the least things. On miracle and on chance conclusions unusual in religious thought meet the reader. The inequalities, injustices and tragedies in life which raise doubts of the divine care are faced in a long chapter after the concept of providence has been spread before the reader. What would be the point in considering them before what providence is has been considered? Against what manner of providence are the arguments valid? A chapter such as this, on doubts of providence and on the mentality which cherishes them, becomes a monograph on the subject, as the chapter on premature spiritual experience, with the risk of relapse and profanation, becomes a monograph on kinds of profanation.

Coming by revelation and by a lengthy other-world experience on Swedenborg's part (in which he learned of the incorrectness of some of his own beliefs, nn. 279(2), 290) the book, like others of his, nevertheless has for an outstanding feature a steady address to the reason. The profoundest truths of the spiritual life, among them the nature of God and the laws and ways of providence, are not beyond grasp by the reason. Sound reason Swedenborg credits with lofty insights.

*Divine Providence* is a book to be studied, and not merely read, and studied slowly. By its own way of proceeding, it extends an invitation to read, not straight through, but something like a chapter at a time. In a new chapter Swedenborg will recall for the reader what was said in the preceding chapter, as though the reader had mean-while laid the book down. The revelator proceeds at a measured pace, carries along the whole body of his thought, and places each new point in this larger context, where it receives its precise significance and its full force. It is an accumulation of thought and not a repetition of statements merely that one meets. "What has been written earlier cannot be as closely connected with what is written later as it will be if the same things are recalled and placed with both in view" (n. 193 (1)).

## THE TRANSLATION

This volume has been translated afresh from the Latin; it is not a revision of any earlier edition. Greater readableness has been striven for. In the past, it is generally recognized, Latin sentence structure and word order were clung to unnecessarily. "The defects in previous translations of Swedenborg have arisen mainly from too close an adherence to cognate words and to the Latin order of words and phrases." So wrote the Rev. John C. Ager in 1899 in his translator's note in the Library Edition of *Divine Providence*. Why, indeed, should English not be allowed its own sentence structure and word order? In addition, in this translation, long sentences, readily followed in an inflected language like Latin, have been broken up into short ones. English also uses fewer particles of logical relation than are at home in Latin. There is more paragraphing, aiding the eye, which both British and American translators have been doing for some years. Latin has neither a definite article nor an indefinite article, and a translator into English must decide when to use either or neither. The definite article, the present translator thinks, has been overused, perhaps in a dogmatic tendency to be as precise as can be. When, for instance, one is admitted into "truths of faith" he is certainly not admitted into "the truths of faith," as though he could comprehend them all. The very title of the book changes the impression which it makes as the definite article is inserted or omitted in it. "The divine providence" seems to single out a theological concept; "divine providence" seems more likely to lead the thought to God's actual care.

Swedenborg has his carefully chosen terms, of course, like "proprium," which are best kept, although in the present translation that term is sometimes rendered by an explanatory word and one which, in the particular context, is an equivalent. The verb "appropriate" presents a difficulty, but has been kept, partly because of the noun "proprium." One could translate rather wordily "make"—something good or evil—"one's own." The English word now means "take exclusive possession of," which one can hardly do of good or evil. Assimilation is the thought and the act, and with that in mind the verb "appropriate" and the noun "appropriation" can be retained. The unusual locution "affection of truth" or "of good," which Mr. Ager abandoned, translating "for truth" and "for good," has been returned to. Much is implied in that phrase which is not to be found in the other wording, namely, that we are affected by truth and by good, and that there is an influx of these into the human spirit. Similarly meaningful is another unusual way of speaking in English, of a person's being "in" faith or "in" charity, where we say that he has faith or exercises charity. The thought is that faith and charity, truth and goodness beckon to us, to be welcomed and entered into.

Latin sometimes has a number of words for an idea or an entity, and the English has not, but when English has the richer vocabulary, why not avail oneself of the variety possible? The Latin word "finis," for example, used in so many connections, can be rendered by one word in one connection and by another in another connection. The "goal" or the "object" of providence is plainer than the "end" of providence. The "close" of life is common speech. "Meritorious" has been kept in our translations, for in a restricted field of traditional theology it does mean that virtue, for example, earns a reward. To most readers the word will be misleading, for they will understand it in its usual meaning, that some act is well-deserving. The former is Swedenborg's meaning, which is that an act is done to earn merit, or is considered to have earned merit. We translate variously according to context to make that meaning clear (nn. 321(11), 326(8), 90).

As it is what Swedenborg has written that is to be translated, the Scripture passages which he quotes are translated without an effort to follow the Authorized Version, which he did not know. This is also done when he refers to the book which stands last in our Bibles; the name he knew it by, the Apocalypse, is retained.

## THE SUBJECT INDEX

The rewording in this translation would have necessitated revision of the index long used in editions of *Divine Providence*, which goes back to an index in French done by M. Le Boys des Guays. The opportunity was seized to compile a subject instead of a word index. It is based on an analysis of the contents of the book, and can serve as a reading guide. It does not usually quote the text, but sends the reader to it. Definitions of a number of terms are embodied in it.

The appearance that man thinks, wills, speaks and acts all of his own doing is the subject of much of the book, and this the index shows. The "life's love" deserves to be a separate entry, for little of a psychological nature in the book becomes more prominent than the love which forms in the way one actually lives, and which embodies one's actual belief and thought. Single words which have been scattered entries in the index long used—usually Scripture words of which the correspondential

## TRANSLATOR'S PREFACE

meaning is given—are assembled alphabetically under the entry "Correspondences."

A signal feature of Swedenborg's thought is the unities he perceives. Of love and wisdom he says that they can only be perceived as one (4(5)). So good and truth do not exist apart, nor charity and faith, nor affection and thought. These and other pairs of terms are therefore entered in the index; after references on the two together, references follow on each term alone.

The index, it is hoped, will do more than introduce the reader to statements made in the book, but will carry him into its stream of thought.

WM. F. WUNSCH

Divine Providence

## I. DIVINE PROVIDENCE IS GOVERNMENT BY THE LORD'S DIVINE LOVE AND WISDOM

1. To understand what divine providence is—namely, government by the Lord's divine love and wisdom—one needs to know what was said and shown earlier about divine love and wisdom in the treatise about them: "In the Lord divine love is of divine wisdom, and divine wisdom of divine love" (nn. 34-39); "Divine love and wisdom cannot but be in, and be manifested in, all else, created by them" (nn. 47-51); "All things in the universe were created by them" (nn. 52, 53, 151-156); "All are recipients of that love and wisdom" (nn. 55-60); "The Lord appears before the angels as a sun, the heat proceeding from it being love, and the light wisdom" (nn. 83-88, 89-92, 93-98, 296-301); "Divine love and wisdom, proceeding from the Lord, make one" (nn. 99-102); "The Lord from eternity, who is Jehovah, created the universe and everything in it from Himself, and not from nothing" (nn. 282-284, 290-295). This is to be found in the treatise entitled *Angelic Wisdom about Divine Love and Wisdom.*

2. Putting with these propositions the description of creation in that treatise, one may indeed see that what is called divine providence is government by the Lord's divine love and wisdom. In that treatise, however, creation was the subject, and not the preservation of the state of things after creation—yet this is the Lord's government. We now treat of this, therefore, and in the present chapter, of the preservation of the union of divine love and wisdom or of divine good and truth in what was created, which will be done in the following order:

    1. The universe, with each and all things in it, was created from divine love by divine wisdom.

## I. DIVINE PROVIDENCE IS GOVERNMENT BY THE LORD'S DIVINE LOVE AND WISDOM

2. Divine love and wisdom proceed as one from the Lord.
3. This one is in some image in every created thing.
4. It is of the divine providence that every created thing, as a whole and in part, should be such a one, and if it is not, should become such a one.
5. Good of love is good only so far as it is united to truth of wisdom, and truth of wisdom truth only so far as it is united to good of love.
6. Good of love not united to truth of wisdom is not good in itself but seeming good, and truth of wisdom not united to good of love is not truth in itself but seeming truth.
7. The Lord does not suffer anything to be divided; therefore it must be either in good and at the same time in truth, or in evil and at the same time in falsity.
8. That which is in good and at the same time in truth is something; that which is in evil and at the same time in falsity is not anything.
9. The Lord's divine providence causes evil and the attendant falsity to serve for equilibrium, contrast, and purification, and so for the conjunction of good and truth in others.

3. (1) *The universe, with each and all things in it, was created from divine love by divine wisdom.* In the work *Divine Love and Wisdom* we showed that the Lord from eternity, who is Jehovah, is in essence divine love and wisdom, and that He created the universe and all things in it from Himself. It follows that the universe, with each and all things in it, was created from divine love by means of divine wisdom. We also showed in that treatise that love can do nothing without wisdom, and wisdom nothing without love. For love apart from wisdom, or the will apart from understanding, cannot think anything, indeed cannot see, feel or say anything, so cannot do anything. Likewise, wisdom apart from love, or understanding apart from will, cannot think, see,

feel, or speak, therefore cannot do, anything. For if love is removed from wisdom or understanding, there is no willing and thus no doing. If this is true of man, for him to do anything, it was much more true of God—who is love itself and wisdom itself—when He created and made the world and all that it contains.

[2] That the universe, with each and all things in it, was created from divine love by divine wisdom may also be established from objects to be seen in the world. Take a particular object, examine it with some wisdom, and you will be convinced. Take the seed, fruit, flower or leaf of a tree, muster your wisdom, examine the object with a strong microscope, and you will see marvels. Even more wonderful are the more interior things which you do not see. Note the unfolding order in the growth of a tree from seed to new seed; reflect on the continuous effort in all stages after self-propagation—the end to which it moves is seed in which its reproductive power arises anew. If then you will think spiritually, as you can if you will, will you not see wisdom in all this? Furthermore, if you can think spiritually enough, you will see that this energy does not come from the seed, nor from the sun of the world, which is only fire, but is in the seed from God the Creator whose wisdom is infinite, and is from Him not only at the moment of creation but ever after, too. For maintenance is perpetual creation, as continuance is perpetual coming to be. Else it is quite as work ceases when you withdraw will from action, or as utterance fails when you remove thought from speech, or as motion ceases when you remove impetus; in a word, as an effect perishes when you remove the cause.

[3] Every created thing is endowed with energy, indeed, but this does nothing of itself but from Him who implanted it. Examine any other earthly object, like a silkworm, bee or other small creature. View it first naturally, then rationally, and at length spiritually, and if you can think deeply, you will be

## I. DIVINE PROVIDENCE IS GOVERNMENT BY THE LORD'S DIVINE LOVE AND WISDOM

astounded at all you see. Let wisdom speak in you, and you will exclaim in astonishment, "Who does not see the divine in such things? They are all of divine wisdom." Still more will you exclaim, if you note the uses of all created things, how they mount in regular order even to the human being, and from man to the Creator whence they are, and that the connection, and if you will acknowledge it, the preservation also of them all, depend on the conjunction of the Creator with man. That divine love created all things, but nothing apart from the divine wisdom, will be seen in what follows.

4. (2) Divine love and wisdom proceed as one from the Lord. This, too, is plain from what was shown in the work *Divine Love and Wisdom*, especially in the propositions: "Esse and existere are distinguishably one in the Lord" (nn. 14-17); "Infinite things are distinguishably one in Him" (nn. 17-22); "Divine love is of divine wisdom, and divine wisdom of divine love" (nn. 34-39); "Love not married to wisdom cannot effect anything" (nn. 401-403); "Love does nothing except in union with wisdom" (nn. 409, 410); "Spiritual heat and light, proceeding from the Lord as a sun, make one as divine love and wisdom make one in Him" (nn. 99-102). The truth of the present proposition is plain from these propositions, demonstrated in that treatise. But as it is not known how two distinct things can act as one, I wish now to show that there is no "one" apart from form, and that the form itself makes it a unit; then, that a form makes a "one" the more perfectly as the elements entering into it are distinctly different and yet united.

[2] There is no "one" apart from form, and the form itself makes it a unit. Everyone who brings his mind to bear on the matter can see clearly that there is no "one" apart from form, and if a thing exists at all, it is a form. For what exists at all derives from form what is known as its character and its predicates, its changes of state, also its relevance, and so on. A thing without form has no way of affecting us, and what has no power of affecting, has no reality. It is form which enables to all this. And

as all things have a form, then if the form is perfect, all things in it regard each other mutually, as link does link in a chain. It follows that it is form which makes a thing a unit and thus an entity of which character, state, affection or anything else can be predicated; each is predicated of it according to the perfection of the form.

[3] Such a unit is every object which meets the eye in the world. Such, too, is everything not seen with the eye, whether in interior nature or in the spiritual world. The human being is such a unit, human society is, likewise the church, and in the Lord's view the whole angelic heaven, too; in short, all creation in general and in every particular. For each and all things to be forms, He who created all things must be form itself, and all things made must be from that form. This, therefore, was also demonstrated in the work *Divine Love and Wisdom*, as that "Divine love and wisdom are substance and form" (nn. 40-43); "Divine love and wisdom are form itself, thus the one Self and the single independent existence" (nn. 44-46); "Divine love and wisdom are one in the Lord" (nn. 14-17, 18-22), "and proceed as one from Him" (nn. 99-102, and elsewhere).

[4] A form makes a one the more perfectly as the elements entering into it are distinctly different and yet united. This hardly falls into a comprehension not elevated, for the appearance is that a form cannot make a one except as its elements are quite alike. I have spoken with angels often on the subject. They said that this is a secret perceived clearly by their wiser men, obscurely by the less wise. They said it is the truth that a form is the more perfect as its constituents are distinctly different and yet severally united. They established the fact from the societies which in the aggregate constitute the form of heaven, and from the angels of a society, for as these are different and free and love their associates from themselves and from their own affection, the form of the society is more perfect. They also illustrated the fact from the marriage of good and truth, in that the more distinguishably two these are, the more perfectly do they make a one; similarly, of love and wisdom. The

## I. DIVINE PROVIDENCE IS GOVERNMENT BY THE LORD'S DIVINE LOVE AND WISDOM

indistinguishable is confusion, they said, whence comes imperfection of form.

[5] In various ways they went on to establish the manner in which perfectly distinct things are united and thus make a one, especially by what is in the human body, in which are innumerable things quite distinct and yet united, held distinct by coverings and united by ligaments. It is so with love, they said, and all its things, and wisdom and all its things, for love and wisdom are not perceived except as one. See further on the subject in *Divine Love and Wisdom* (nn. 14-22) and in the work *Heaven and Hell* (nn. 56 and 489). This has been adduced as part of angelic wisdom.

5. (3) This "one" is in some image in every created thing. It can be seen from what was demonstrated throughout the treatise *Divine Love and Wisdom* and especially at nn. 47-51, 55-60, 282-284, 290-295, 313-318, 319-326, 349-357, that divine love and wisdom which are one in the Lord and proceed as one from Him, are in some image in each created thing. It was shown that the divine is in every created thing because God the Creator, who is the Lord from eternity, produced the sun of the spiritual world from Himself, and all things of the universe through that sun. That sun, which is from Him and in which He is, is therefore not only the first but the sole substance from which are all things. As this is the one substance, it is in everything made, but with endless variety in accord with uses.

[2] In the Lord, then, are divine love and wisdom, and in the sun from Him divine fire and radiance, and from the sun spiritual heat and light; and in each instance the two make one. It follows that this oneness is in every created thing. All things in the world are referable, therefore, to good and truth, in fact to the conjunction of them. Or, what is the same, they are referable to love and wisdom and to the union of these; for good is of love and truth of wisdom, love calling all its own, "good," and wisdom calling all its own, "truth." It will be seen in what follows that there is a conjunction of these in each created thing.

6. Many avow that there is a single substance which is also the first, from which are all things, but what that substance is, is not known. The belief is that it is so simple nothing is more so, and that it can be likened to a point without dimensions, and that dimensional forms arose out of an infinite number of such points. But this is a fallacy, springing from an idea of space. To such an idea there seems to be such a least thing. The truth is that the simpler and purer a thing is, the more replete it is and the more complete. This is why the more interiorly a thing is examined, the more wonderful, perfect, and well formed are the things seen in it, and in the first substance the most wonderful, perfect and fully formed of all. For the first substance is from the spiritual sun, which, as we said, is from the Lord and in which He is. That sun is therefore the sole substance and, not being in space, is all in all, and is in the greatest and least things of the created universe.

[2] As that sun is the first and sole substance from which all things are, it follows that in it are infinitely more things than can possibly appear in substances arising from it, called substantial and lastly material. This infinity cannot appear in derivative substances because these descend from that sun by degrees of two kinds in accord with which perfections decline. For that reason, as we said above, the more interiorly a thing is regarded, the more wonderful, perfect and well formed are the things seen. This has been said to establish the fact that the divine is in some image in every created thing, but is less and less manifest with the descent over degrees, and still less when a lower degree, parted from the higher by being closed, is also choked with earthy matter. These concepts cannot but seem obscure unless one has read and understood what was shown in the treatise *Divine Love and Wisdom* about the spiritual sun (nn. 83-172), about degrees (nn. 173-281) and about the creation of the world (nn. 282-357).

7. (4) *It is of the divine providence that every created thing as a whole and in part should be such a one or should become such a one,* or that there be in it something of the divine love and wisdom, or what is the same, that there be good and truth in it, or

## I. DIVINE PROVIDENCE IS GOVERNMENT BY THE LORD'S DIVINE LOVE AND WISDOM

a union of them. (Inasmuch as good is of love and truth is of wisdom, as was said above (n. 5), in what follows we shall at times say good and truth instead of love and wisdom, and marriage of good and truth instead of union of love and wisdom.)

8. It is evident from the preceding proposition that divine love and wisdom, which are one in the Lord and proceed as one from Him, are in some image in everything created by Him. Something shall be said now specifically of the "one" or the union called the marriage of good and truth.

1. This marriage is in the Lord Himself—for, as we said, divine love and wisdom in Him are one.

2. This marriage is from Him, for in all that proceeds from Him love and wisdom are fully united. The two proceed from Him as a sun, divine love as heat, and divine wisdom as light.

3. These are received as two, indeed, by angels, likewise by men of the church, but are made one in them by the Lord.

4. In view of this influx of love and wisdom as one from the Lord with angels of heaven and men of the church, and in view of their reception of it, the Lord is spoken of in the Word as bridegroom and husband, and heaven and the church are called bride and wife.

5. An image and a likeness of the Lord are therefore to be found in heaven and in the church in general, and in an angel of heaven and a man of the church in particular, so far as they are in that union or in the marriage of good and truth. For good and truth in the Lord are one, indeed are the Lord.

6. Love and wisdom in heaven and in the church as a whole, and in an angel of heaven and a man of the church, are one when will and understanding, thus when good and truth, make one; or what is still the same, when doctrine from the Word and life according to doctrine make one.

7. How the two make one in man and in all that pertains to him was shown, moreover, in Part V of the treatise *Divine Love and Wisdom*, where the creation of man, and especially the correspondence of will and understanding with heart and lungs, were treated of (nn. 358-432).

9. How good and truth, however, make one in what is below or outside man, in both the animal and the vegetable kingdom, shall be told from time to time in what follows. Three points are premised. First, in the universe and in each and all things of it as created by the Lord, there was a marriage of good and truth. Second, after creation this marriage was severed in man. Third, it is the work of divine providence to unite what was severed, and so to restore the marriage of good and truth. As all three points were established by many things in the work *Divine Love and Wisdom*, there is no need to substantiate them further. Anyone can see from reason, moreover, that if there was a marriage of good and truth in each created thing and later it was severed, the Lord must be working constantly to restore it, and that the restoration of it, and hence the conjunction of the created world with the Lord through man, are of divine providence.

10. (5) *Good of love is good only so far as it is united to truth of wisdom, and truth of wisdom is truth only so far as it is united to good of love.* Good and truth have this from their origin, the one and the other originating in the Lord, who is good itself and truth itself and in whom the two are one. Hence in angels in heaven and men on earth, good is not good basically except so far as it is joined to truth, and truth is not truth basically except so far as it is joined to good. Granted that all good and truth are from the Lord, then inasmuch as good makes one with truth and truth with good in Him, good to be good in itself and truth to be truth in itself must make one in the recipient, that is, the angel in heaven or the man on earth.

11. It is indeed known that all things in the world are referable to good and truth. For by good is meant what universally embraces and involves all things of love; and by truth

## I. DIVINE PROVIDENCE IS GOVERNMENT BY THE LORD'S DIVINE LOVE AND WISDOM

what universally embraces and involves all things of wisdom. Still it is not known that good is nothing except when it is joined to truth, and truth nothing unless it is joined to good. Good apart from truth and truth apart from good still seem to be something; yet they are not. For love (to which all that is called good pertains) is the *esse* of a thing, and wisdom (to which all things called truths pertain) is a thing's *existere* from that *esse* (as was shown in the treatise *Divine Love and Wisdom*, nn. 14-16). Therefore, as *esse* is nothing apart from *existere*, or *existere* apart from *esse*, good is nothing apart from truth or truth from good. What, again, is good which has no relation to anything? Can it be called good if it is without affection and perception?

[2] That which is associated with good, permitting it to affect and to be perceived and felt, is referable to truth, since it has relation to what is in the understanding. Tell someone, not that a given thing is good, but simply say "good"—is good anything? It becomes something from what is perceived along with it. This is united with good only in the understanding, and all understanding has relation to truth. It is the same with willing. Apart from knowing, perceiving and thinking what one wills, to will is nothing actual; together with them it becomes something. All volition is of love and is referable to good; and all knowing, perceiving and thinking is of the understanding, and is referable to truth. It is clear, then, that to will is nothing actual, but to will this or that means something.

[3] So also with a use, inasmuch as a use is a good. Unless a use is addressed to something which makes one with it, it is not a use, and thus not anything. A use derives its something from the understanding, and what is thence conjoined or adjoined to it, has relation to truth. So a use gets its character.

[4] From these few things it is plain that good is nothing apart from truth, nor truth anything apart from good. But if good together with truth and truth together with good are something, evil with falsity and falsity with evil are not, for the latter are opposite to the former and the opposition destroys—that is, destroys the something. But of this in what follows.

12. Marriage of good and truth may, however, be found either in a cause or from the cause in an effect. In a cause the marriage of good and truth is one of will and understanding, or of love and wisdom. Such a marriage is in all that a man wills and thinks and in all his ensuing determinations and purposes. This marriage enters into and in fact produces the effect. But in producing the effect, good and truth seem distinct, for then the simultaneous turns successive. When, for example, a man wills and thinks about food, clothing, shelter, business or employment, or about his relationship to others, first he wills and thinks or comes to his conclusions and intentions all at the same time; but when these are determined to effects, truth follows on good, though in will and thought they continue to make one. In the effects the uses pertain to love or good, and the ways of performing the uses pertain to understanding or truth. Anyone can confirm these general truths by particular instances provided he perceives what is referable respectively to good of love and to truth of wisdom, and also how differently it is referable in cause and in effect.

13. We have said often that love constitutes man's life. This does not mean, however, love separate from wisdom or good from truth in the cause, for love separate or good separate is not an actuality. The love which makes man's inmost life—the life he has from the Lord—is therefore love and wisdom together; neither is the love which makes his life as a recipient being separate in the cause, but only in the effect. For love cannot be understood except from its quality, which is wisdom; and the quality or wisdom can exist only from its own esse, which is love; thence it is that they are one; it is the same with good and truth. Since truth is from good as wisdom is from love, it is the two taken together that are called good or love. For love has wisdom for its form, and good for its form truth, and form is the source, and the one source, of quality. It is plain from all this that good is good only so far as it has become one with its truth, and truth truth only so far as it has become one with its good.

14. (6) *Good of love not united to truth of wisdom is not good in itself but seeming good; and truth of wisdom not conjoined with good of love is not truth in itself but seeming truth.* The fact

## I. DIVINE PROVIDENCE IS GOVERNMENT BY THE LORD'S DIVINE LOVE AND WISDOM

is that no good, in itself good, can exist unless joined with its truth, and no truth, in itself truth, can exist unless it has become joined with its good. And yet good separate from truth is possible, and truth separate from good. They are found in hypocrites and flatterers, in evil persons of every sort, and in such as are in natural but not spiritual good. These can all do well by church, country, society, fellow-citizens, the needy, the poor, and widows and orphans. They can also comprehend truths, from understanding think them, and from thought speak and teach them. But the goods and truths are not interiorly such, that is, basically goods and truths, but only outwardly and seemingly such. For such good and truth look to self and the world, not to good itself and truth itself; they are not from good and truth; they are of the mouth and body only, therefore, and not of the heart.

[2] They may be likened to gold or silver which is spread on dross, rotten wood or mire. When uttered the truths may be likened to a breath exhaled and gone, or to a delusive light which dies away, though they appear outwardly like genuine truths. They are seeming truths in those who utter them; to those hearing and assenting, and unaware of this, they may be altogether different. For everyone is affected by what is external according to his internal. A truth, by whomsoever uttered, enters another's hearing and is taken up by his mind in keeping with the state or character of his mind.

Of those in natural good by inheritance, but in no spiritual good, nearly the same is true as of those described above. The internal of every good or truth is spiritual. The spiritual dispels falsities and evils, but the natural left to itself favors them. To favor evil and falsity does not accord with doing good.

15. Good can be separated from truth, and truth from good, and then still appear as good or truth, for the reason that the human being has a capacity to act which is called liberty, and a capacity of understanding called rationality. By abuse of these powers a man can appear in externals other than he is in internals; an evil man can do good and speak truth, and a devil

feign himself an angel of light. But on this see the following propositions in the treatise *Divine Love and Wisdom*: "The origin of evil is in the abuse of faculties proper to man, called liberty and rationality" (nn. 246-270); "These two faculties are to be found with the evil as well as with the good" (n. 425); "Love not married to wisdom, and good not married to truth, can effect nothing" (n. 401); "Love does nothing except in conjunction with wisdom or understanding, and it brings wisdom or the understanding reciprocally into conjunction with itself" (nn. 410-412); "From power given it by love, wisdom or understanding can be elevated and can perceive and receive the things of light from heaven" (n. 413); "Love can be raised similarly to receive the things of heat from heaven if it loves its mate, wisdom, in that degree" (nn. 414, 415); "Else love pulls wisdom or the understanding down from its elevation to act at one with itself" (nn. 416-418); "If the two are elevated, love is purified in the understanding" (nn. 419-421); "Purified by wisdom in the understanding, love becomes spiritual and celestial, but defiled in the understanding it become sensuous and corporeal" (nn. 422-424); "What is true of love and wisdom and their union is true of charity and faith and their conjunction" (nn. 427-430). What charity in heaven is, see n. 431.

16. (7) *The Lord does not suffer anything to be divided; it must be either in good and at the same time in truth, or in evil and at the same time in falsity.* The Lord's divine providence has for its goal, and to this end it labors, that man shall be in good and at the same time in truth. For then he is his own good and love and his own truth and wisdom; thereby the human being is human, for he is then an image of the Lord. But while he lives in the world he can be in good and at the same time in falsity, likewise in evil and at the same time in truth, indeed in evil and at the same time in good, and thus be double. As the cleavage destroys the Lord's image in him and thus the man, the Lord's divine providence takes care in every least act that this division shall not be. And as it is better for man to be in evil and at the same time in falsity than to be in good and at the same time in evil, the Lord permits it, not as one willing it, but as one unable

## I. DIVINE PROVIDENCE IS GOVERNMENT BY THE LORD'S DIVINE LOVE AND WISDOM

to resist because of the end sought, which is salvation.

[2] A man can be simultaneously in evil and in truth and the Lord be unable to prevent it in view of the end, which is salvation, for the reason that man's understanding can be raised into the light of wisdom and see truths, or acknowledge them when he hears them, while his love remains below. Thus a man can be in heaven as to understanding, while as to his love he is in hell. This is not denied him, because the two faculties of liberty and rationality, by virtue of which he is a human being and distinguished from beasts and by which alone he can be regenerated and thus saved, cannot be taken away. By means of them, he can act according to wisdom and at the same time according to an unwise love. From wisdom above he can view the love below and also the thoughts, intentions and affections, therefore the evils and falsities as well as the goods and truths of his life and doctrine, without a knowledge and recognition of which he cannot be reformed. We spoke of the two faculties before and shall say more in what follows. What has been said explains how man can be simultaneously in good and truth, or in evil and falsity, or in mixtures of them.

17. In this world a man can hardly come into one or the other conjunction or union, that is, of good and truth or of evil and falsity, for during his life in the world he is kept in a state of reformation or regeneration. After death, however, every man comes into the one union or the other, because he can then no longer be reformed or regenerated. He remains such as his life was in the world, that is, such as his reigning love was. If therefore his was a life of an evil love, all the truth acquired by him in the world from teacher, pulpit or Word is taken away. On the removal of it, he absorbs the falsity agreeing with his evil as a sponge does water. On the other hand, if his was the life of a good love, all the falsity is removed which he may have picked up in the world by hearing or from reading but did not confirm in himself, and in its place truth congruous with his good is given him. This is meant by the Lord's words:

> Take ... the talent from him, and give it to him that has ten talents. For to everyone who has, shall be given until he abounds but from him who has not, even what he has shall be taken away (Mt 25:28, 29; 13:12; Mk 4:25; Lu 8:18; 19:24-26).

18. After death everyone must be either in good and at the same time in truth or in evil and at the same time in falsity, for the reason that good and evil cannot be united, nor can good and the falsity of evil, nor evil and the truth of good. For these are opposites, and opposites contend until one destroys the other. Those who are at the same time in evil and in good are meant in the Apocalypse in these words of the Lord to the church of the Laodiceans:

> I know your works, that you are neither cold nor hot; would that you were cold or hot; but because you are lukewarm, I will spue you out of my mouth (3:15, 16):

also in these words of the Lord:

> No man can serve two masters, for either he will hate the one and love the other, or cleave to the one and not heed the other (Mt 6:24).

19. (8) *That which is in good and at the same time in truth is something; that which is in evil and at the same time in falsity is not anything.* See above (n. 11) that what is in good and at the same time in truth is something. It follows that what is at once evil and false is not anything. By not being anything is meant that it is without power and without spiritual life. Those at once in evil and in falsity (all of whom are in hell) have power indeed among themselves, for an evil man can do evil and does so in a thousand ways. Yet he can do evil to the evil only by reason of their evil; he cannot harm the good at all; if, as sometimes happens, he does, it is by conjunction with their evil.

[2] In this way temptations arise; they are infestations by evil spirits who are with a man; so combats ensue by which the good are freed from their evils. Since the wicked have no power, all hell in the Lord's sight is not only nothing, but nothing at all in point of power, as I have seen proved by much experience. But it

## I. DIVINE PROVIDENCE IS GOVERNMENT BY THE LORD'S DIVINE LOVE AND WISDOM

is remarkable that the evil all deem themselves powerful, and the good all think themselves powerless. This is because the evil ascribe everything to their own power or shrewdness and malice, and nothing to the Lord; whereas the good ascribe nothing to their own prudence, but all to the Lord who is almighty. Evil and falsity together are not anything for the further reason that they have no spiritual life. The life of the infernals is therefore called death, not life. Since life holds everything, death has nothing.

20. Men in evil and at the same time in truths may be likened to eagles flying aloft which, deprived of their wings, fall. For after death, on becoming spirits, men do the like who have understood and spoken and taught truths and yet have not looked to God in their lives. By means of things of the understanding they raise themselves aloft and even enter heaven at times and feign themselves angels of light. But when they are deprived of truths and are cast out, they fall down to hell. Eagles also signify rapacious men with intellectual acumen, and wings signify spiritual truths. Such, we said, are those who have not looked to God in their lives. To look to God in life means simply to think that a given evil is a sin against God, and for that reason not to commit it.

21. (9) *The Lord's divine providence causes evil and its falsity to serve for equilibrium, contrast, and purification, and so for the conjunction of good and truth in others.* It is obvious from the preceding that the Lord's divine providence continually operates in order that truth may be united in man with good and good with truth, because that union is the church and heaven. For that union is in the Lord and in all that proceeds from Him. From that union, heaven and the church are called a marriage, and the kingdom of God is likened in the Word to a marriage. Again, the Sabbath signified that union and was the holiest observance in the worship of the Israelitish Church. From that union also there is a marriage of good and truth in the Word and in each and all things of it (on this see *Doctrine of the New Jerusalem about Sacred Scripture*, nn. 80-90). The marriage of good and truth is from the marriage of the Lord with the church, and this in turn from the marriage of love and wisdom in Him, for good is of

love, and truth of wisdom. It is plain, then, that it is the constant aim of divine providence to unite good to truth and truth to good in a man, for so he is united to the Lord.

22. But many have severed and do sever this marriage, especially by separating faith from charity (for faith is of truth and truth is of faith, and charity is of good and good is of charity), and in so doing they conjoin evil and falsity in themselves and thus come into and continue in the opposite to good and truth. The Lord therefore provides that they shall nevertheless serve for uniting good and truth in others, through equilibrium, contrast and purification.

23. Conjunction of good and truth in others is provided by the Lord through equilibrium between heaven and hell. From hell evil and at the same time falsity constantly exhale, and from heaven good and at the same time truth. In equilibrium between them, and so in freedom to think, will, speak and act in which he can be reformed, every man is kept while he lives in the world. On the spiritual equilibrium from which the human being has freedom, see the work *Heaven and Hell*, nn. 589-596, 597-603.

24. Conjunction of good and truth is provided by the Lord through contrast. For the nature of good is not known except by contrast with what is less good and by its contrariety to evil. All perceptiveness and sensitivity arise so; their quality is thence. All pleasantness is perceived and felt over against the less pleasant and the unpleasant; all the beautiful by reference to the less beautiful and the unbeautiful; similarly all good of love by reference to lesser good and to evil; all truth of wisdom by a sense of lesser truth and of falsity. Everything inevitably varies from greatest to least, and with the same variation in its opposite and with equilibrium between them, there is contrast degree by degree, and the perception and sensation of a thing increase or diminish. But be it known that an opposite may either lower or exalt perceptions and sensitivities. It lowers them when it mingles in and exalts them when it does not mingle in, for which reason the Lord separates good and evil with man that they shall not mingle, as exquisitely as He does heaven and hell.

## I. DIVINE PROVIDENCE IS GOVERNMENT BY THE LORD'S DIVINE LOVE AND WISDOM

25. Conjunction of good and truth in others is provided by the Lord through purification in two ways; one through temptations, and the other through fermentations. Spiritual temptations are nothing else than combats against the evils and falsities exhaled from hell and affecting man. By these combats a man is purified from evils and falsities, and good and truth are united in him. Spiritual fermentations take place in many ways, and in heaven as well as on earth; but in the world it is not known what they are or how they come about. For evils and their falsities, let into societies, act as ferments do in meal or in must, separating the heterogeneous and conjoining the homogeneous until there is clarity and purity. Such fermentations are meant in the Lord's words:

> The kingdom of heaven is like leaven which a woman took and hid in three measures of meal until the whole was leavened (Mt 13:33; Lu 12:21).

26. The Lord provides these uses through the united evil and falsity of those in hell. The Lord's kingdom, which extends over hell as well as over heaven, is a kingdom of uses. It is the Lord's providence that there shall be no creature and no thing whereby a use is not performed.

## II. THE LORD'S DIVINE PROVIDENCE HAS FOR ITS OBJECT A HEAVEN FROM THE HUMAN RACE

27. Heaven does not consist of angels created such to begin with, nor does hell come from any devil created an angel of light and cast down from heaven. Both heaven and hell are from mankind, heaven consisting of those in the love of good and consequent understanding of truth, and hell of those in the love of evil and consequent understanding of falsity. This has been made known and sure to me by long-continued intercourse with angels and spirits. See what was said on the subject in the work *Heaven and Hell* (nn. 311-316); also in the little work *The Last Judgment* (nn. 14-27), and in *Continuation about the Last Judgment and the Spiritual World* (throughout).

[2] As heaven is from mankind and is an abiding with the Lord to eternity, it must have been the Lord's purpose in creation; being the purpose in creation, it is the purpose of His providence. The Lord created the world not for His own sake but for the sake of those with whom He would be in heaven. Spiritual love by nature desires to give its own to another, and so far as it can do so is in its esse, peace, and blessedness. Spiritual love derives this from the Lord's divine love which is such infinitely. It follows that the divine love and hence divine providence has for its object a heaven consisting of human beings who have become or are becoming angels, on whom the Lord can bestow all the blessings and felicities of love and wisdom and do so from Himself in men. It must be in this way, for the Lord's image and likeness are in men from creation, the image in them wisdom and the likeness love. Furthermore, the Lord in them is love united to wisdom and wisdom united to love

## II. THE LORD'S DIVINE PROVIDENCE HAS FOR ITS OBJECT A HEAVEN FROM THE HUMAN RACE

or (what is the same) is good united to truth and truth united to good (this union was treated of in the preceding chapter).

[3] What heaven is in general or with a number, and in particular or with an individual, is not known. Nor is it known what heaven is in the spiritual world and what it is in the natural world. Yet this knowledge is important, for heaven is the purpose of providence. I therefore desire to set the subject in some light in this order:

1. Heaven is conjunction with the Lord.
2. By creation the human being is such that he can be conjoined more and more closely to the Lord.
3. The more closely one is conjoined to the Lord the wiser one becomes.
4. The more closely one is conjoined to the Lord the happier one becomes.
5. The more closely one is conjoined to the Lord the more distinctly does he seem to himself to be his own, and the more plainly does he recognize that he is the Lord's.

28. (1) *Heaven is conjunction with the Lord.* Heaven is heaven, not from the angels but from the Lord. For the love and wisdom in which angels are and which make heaven are not theirs, but the Lord's, indeed are the Lord in them. And as love and wisdom are the Lord's, and are the Lord in heaven, and make the life of angels, it is plain that their life is the Lord's, indeed is the Lord. The angels themselves avow that they live from the Lord. Hence it is evident that heaven is conjunction with the Lord. But conjunction with Him is various and one man's heaven is not another's; therefore heaven is also according to the conjunction with the Lord. In the following proposition it will be seen that conjunction is more and more close or more and more remote.

[2] Here let something be said about how the conjunction takes place and what the nature of it is. It is a conjunction of the Lord with the angels and of the angels with Him, therefore is reciprocal. The Lord flows into the life's love of the angels, and

they receive Him in wisdom, thus in turn conjoining themselves with Him. It must be said, however, that it seems to the angels that they conjoin themselves to the Lord by wisdom; actually the Lord conjoins them to Himself by their wisdom, for the wisdom is also from the Lord. It is the same thing if we say that the Lord conjoins Himself to the angels by good and they in turn conjoin themselves to the Lord by truth, for all good is of love, and truth, of wisdom.

[3] This reciprocal conjunction is an arcanum, however, which few can understand unless it is explained. I want therefore to unfold it so far as it can be done by things within one's grasp. We showed in the treatise *Divine Love and Wisdom* (nn. 404, 405) how love unites itself with wisdom, namely, through affection for knowing from which comes an affection for truth, through affection for understanding from which comes perception of truth, and through affection for seeing what is known and understood, from which comes thought. Into all these affections the Lord flows, for they are all derivatives of one's life's love, and the angels receive the influx in perception of truth and in thought, for in these the influx becomes apparent to them, but not in the affections.

[4] As the perceptions and thoughts appear to the angels to be their own, although they arise from affections which are from the Lord, the appearance is that the angels reciprocally conjoin themselves to the Lord, when nevertheless the Lord conjoins them to Himself. The affection itself produces the perceptions and thoughts, for the affection, which is of love, is their soul. Apart from affection no one can perceive or think anything, and every one perceives and thinks according to his affection. It is evident that the reciprocal conjunction of the angels with the Lord is not from them, but as it were from them. Such, too, is the conjunction of the Lord with the church and of the church with Him, a union called celestial and spiritual marriage.

29. All conjunction in the spiritual world is effected by intent regard. When anyone there thinks of another with a desire to speak with him, the other is at once present, and the two come

## II. THE LORD'S DIVINE PROVIDENCE HAS FOR ITS OBJECT A HEAVEN FROM THE HUMAN RACE

face to face. Likewise, when one thinks of another from an affection of love; by this affection, however, there is conjunction, but by the other only presence. This is peculiar to the spiritual world; for there all are spiritual beings. It is otherwise in the natural world where all are physical beings. In the natural world something similar takes place in the affections and thoughts of the spirit; but as there is space here, while in the spiritual world space is appearance only, what takes place here in one's spirit occurs outwardly there.

[2] We have said so much to make known how conjunction of the Lord with angels and their seemingly reciprocal conjunction with Him is effected. All angels turn the face to the Lord; He regards them in the forehead, and they regard Him with the eyes. The reason is that the forehead corresponds to love and its affections, and the eyes correspond to wisdom and its perceptions. Still the angels do not of themselves turn the face to the Lord, but He faces them toward Himself, doing so by influx into their life's love, by this entering the perceptions and thoughts, and so turning the angels to Him.

[3] There is such a circuit from love to thoughts and under love's impulse from thoughts to love in all the mind's activity. It may be called the circling of life. On these subjects see some things also in the treatise *Divine Love and Wisdom*: as that "Angels constantly turn the face to the Lord as a sun" (nn. 129-134); "All the interiors of both the mind and the bodies of the angels are likewise turned to the Lord as a sun" (nn. 135-139); "Every spirit, whatever his character, turns himself likewise to his ruling love" (nn. 140-145); "Love conjoins itself to wisdom and causes wisdom to be conjoined reciprocally with it" (nn. 410-412); "Angels are in the Lord and He in them; and as the angels are only recipients, the Lord alone is heaven" (nn. 113-118).

30. The Lord's heaven in the natural world is called the church; an angel of this heaven is a man of the church who is conjoined to the Lord; on departure from this world he also becomes an angel of the spiritual heaven. What was said of the

angelic heaven is evidently to be understood, then, of the human heaven also which is called the church. The reciprocal conjunction with the Lord which makes heaven in the human being is revealed by the Lord in these words in John:

> Abide in Me, and I in you; ... he who abides in Me, and I in him, bears much fruit; for without Me ye can do nothing (15:4, 5, 7).

31. It is plain from this that the Lord is heaven not only in general with all in heaven, but in particular with each one there. For each angel is a heaven in least form; of as many heavens as there are angels, does heaven in general consist. In substantiation see *Heaven and Hell* (nn. 51-58). Since this is so, let no one cherish the mistaken idea, which first visits the thought of so many, that the Lord dwells in heaven among the angels or is among them like a king in his kingdom. To the sight He is above them in the sun there; He is in them in their life of love and wisdom.

32. (2) *By creation the human being is such that he can be conjoined more and more closely to the Lord.* This becomes evident from what was shown about degrees in the treatise *Divine Love and Wisdom*, Part III, especially in the propositions: "By creation there are three discrete degrees or degrees of height in the human being" (nn. 230-235); "These three degrees are in man from birth, and as they are opened, the man is in the Lord, and the Lord in him" (nn. 236-241); "All perfection increases and mounts with and according to the degrees" (nn. 199-204). Evidently, then, man is such by creation that he can be conjoined with the Lord more and more closely according to these degrees.

[2] But one must know well what degrees are and that there are two kinds —discrete degrees or degrees of height, and continuous degrees or degrees of breadth; also how they differ. It must be known, too, that every human being has by creation and hence from birth three discrete degrees or degrees of height, and that he comes at birth into the first degree, called natural, and can grow in this degree continuously until he becomes rational. He comes into the second degree, called spiritual, if he lives

## II. THE LORD'S DIVINE PROVIDENCE HAS FOR ITS OBJECT A HEAVEN FROM THE HUMAN RACE

according to spiritual laws of order, which are divine truths. He can also come into the third degree, called celestial, if he lives according to the celestial laws of order, which are divine goods.

[3] These degrees are opened in a person by the Lord according to his life and actually opened in the world, but not perceptibly and sensibly until after his departure from the world. As they are opened and later perfected a man is conjoined to the Lord more and more closely. This conjunction can grow to eternity in nearness to God and does so with the angels. And yet no angel can attain or touch the first degree of the Lord's love and wisdom, for the Lord is infinite and an angel is finite, and between infinite and finite no ratio obtains. Man's state and the state of his elevation and nearness to the Lord cannot be understood without a knowledge of these degrees; they have been specifically treated of, therefore, in the treatise *Divine Love and Wisdom*, nn. 173-281, which see.

33. We shall say briefly how man can be more and more closely conjoined to the Lord, and then how the conjunction seems closer and closer. How man is more and more closely conjoined to the Lord: this is effected not by knowledge alone, nor by intelligence alone, nor even by wisdom alone, but by a life conjoined to them. A man's life is his love, and love is manifold. In general there are love of good and love of evil. Love of evil is love of committing adultery, taking revenge, defrauding, blaspheming, depriving others of their possessions. In thinking and doing such things the love of evil finds its pleasure and joy. Of this love there are as many derivatives, which are affections, as there are evils in which it can find expression. And there are as many perceptions and thoughts of this love as there are falsities favoring and confirming such evils. The falsities make one with the evils as understanding makes one with will; they are mutually inseparable; the one is of the other.

[2] Inasmuch as the Lord flows into one's life's love and by its affections into the perceptions and thoughts, and not the other way about, as we said above, it follows that the Lord can conjoin Himself more closely to a man only as the love of evil is

removed along with its affections, which are lusts. These lusts reside in the natural man. What a man does from the natural man he feels that he does of himself. For his part, therefore, a man should remove the evils of that love; so far as he does, the Lord comes nearer and conjoins Himself to him. Anyone can see from reason that lusts with their pleasures block and close the door to the Lord and cannot be cast out by the Lord as long as the man himself keeps the door shut and presses and pushes from outside to keep it from being opened. It is plain from the Lord's words in the Apocalypse that a man must himself open the door:

> Behold, I stand at the door and knock; if anyone hears My voice and opens the door, I will come in to him, and sup with him, and he with Me (3:20).

[3] Plainly, then, so far as one shuns evils as diabolical and as obstacles to the Lord's entrance, he is more and more closely conjoined to the Lord, and he the most closely who abhors them as so many dusky and fiery devils. For evil and the devil are one and the same, and the falsity of evil and satan are one and the same. As the Lord's influx is into the love of good and into its affections and by these into the perceptions and thoughts, which have it from the good in which a man is that they are truths, so the influx of the devil, that is of hell, is into the love of evil and its affections, which are lusts, and by these into the perceptions and thoughts, which have it from the evil in which the man is that they are falsities.

[4] How the conjunction seems closer and closer. The more the evils in the natural man are removed by shunning and turning away from them, the more closely a man is conjoined to the Lord. Love and wisdom, which are the Lord Himself, are not in space, as affection which is of love, and thought which is of wisdom, have nothing in common with space. In the measure of the conjunction by love and wisdom, therefore, the Lord seems nearer; and, contrariwise, in the measure of the rejection of love and wisdom, more distant. There is no space in the spiritual world; distance and presence there are appearances according to similarity or dissimilarity of the affections. For, as we said, affections which are of love, and thoughts which are of wisdom,

## II. THE LORD'S DIVINE PROVIDENCE HAS FOR ITS OBJECT A HEAVEN FROM THE HUMAN RACE

in themselves spiritual, are not in space (on this see what was shown in the treatise *Divine Love and Wisdom*, nn. 7-10, 69-72, and elsewhere).

[5] The Lord's conjunction with a man in whom evils have been put away is meant by the Lord's words:

> The pure in heart shall see God (Mt 5:8);

and by the words:

> He who has my commandments and does them . . . with him will I make an abode (Jn 14:21, 23).

"To have the commandments" is to know and "to do them" is to love, for it is also said: "he who does my commandments, he it is that loves Me."

34. (3) *The more closely one is conjoined to the Lord the wiser one becomes.* As there are three degrees of life in man by creation and so from birth (see just above, n. 32), there are specifically three degrees of wisdom in him. These degrees it is that are opened in man according to conjunction, that is, according to love, for love is conjunction itself. Love's ascent by degrees, however, is only obscurely perceived by man; but wisdom's ascent is clearly perceived by those who know and see what wisdom is. The degrees of wisdom are perceived because love by its affections enters the perceptions and thoughts, and these present themselves to the internal mental sight, which corresponds to the external bodily sight. Thus wisdom appears, but not the affection of love which produces it. It is the same with all a man's deeds; he is aware how the body does them, but not how the soul does them. So he perceives how he meditates, perceives and thinks, but not how the soul of these mental activities, which is an affection of good and truth, produces them.

[2] There are three degrees of wisdom: natural, spiritual, and celestial. Man is in the natural degree of wisdom during his life in the world. This degree can be perfected in him to its height, but even so cannot pass into the spiritual degree, for the latter is not continuous with it, but conjoined to it by correspondences.

After death man is in the spiritual degree of wisdom. This degree also is such that it can be perfected to its height, and yet cannot pass into the celestial degree of wisdom, because neither is this continuous with the spiritual but conjoined to it by correspondences. Plainly, then, wisdom can be raised threefold, and in each degree can be perfected but only to its peak.

[3] One who understands the elevation and perfecting of these degrees can see to an extent why angelic wisdom is said to be ineffable. So ineffable, indeed, is it, that a thousand ideas in the thought of angels in their wisdom can present only a single idea in the thought of men in their wisdom, the other nine hundred and ninety-nine ideas being unutterable, because they are supernatural. Many a time have I been given to know this by living experience. But, as was said, no one can enter into the ineffable wisdom of the angels except by and according to conjunction with the Lord, for He alone opens spiritual and celestial degrees, and only in those who are wise from Him. Those are wise from the Lord who cast the devil, that is, evil, out of themselves.

35. But let no one believe that he has wisdom because he knows many things, perceives them in some light, and is able to talk intelligently about them, unless his wisdom is conjoined to love. For it is love that through its affections produces wisdom. Not conjoined to love, wisdom is like a meteor vanishing in the air and like a falling star. Wisdom united to love is like the abiding light of the sun and like a fixed star. A man has the love of wisdom when he is averse to the diabolical crew, that is, to the lusts of evil and falsity.

36. Wisdom that comes to perception is perception of truth from being affected by it, especially perception of spiritual truth. For there is civil, moral, and spiritual truth. Those who have some perception of spiritual truth from affection by it also have perceptions of moral and civil truth, for the affection of spiritual truth is the soul of those perceptions. I have spoken with angels at times about wisdom who said that wisdom is conjunction with the Lord because He is wisdom itself, and that the man who

## II. THE LORD'S DIVINE PROVIDENCE HAS FOR ITS OBJECT A HEAVEN FROM THE HUMAN RACE

rejects hell comes into this conjunction and comes into it so far as he rejects hell. They said that they picture wisdom to themselves as a magnificent and highly ornate palace into which one mounts by twelve steps. No one arrives at even the first step, they said, except from the Lord by conjunction with Him; and according to the measure of conjunction one ascends; also as one ascends, one perceives that no man is wise from himself but from the Lord. Furthermore, they said that the things in which one is wise are to those in which one is not wise like a few drops of water to a large lake. By the twelve steps into the palace of wisdom are meant goods united to truths and truths united to goods.

37. (4) *The more closely one is conjoined to the Lord the happier one becomes.* The like can be said of degrees of happiness as was said (nn. 32 and 34) of degrees of life and of wisdom according to conjunction with the Lord. Happiness, that is, blessedness and joy, also are heightened as the higher degrees of the mind, called spiritual and celestial, are opened with man. After his life in the world these degrees grow to eternity.

38. No one who is in the pleasures of the lusts of evil can know anything of the joys of the affections of good in which the angelic heaven is. These pleasures and joys are opposites in internals and hence inwardly in externals, though superficially they may differ little. Every love has its enjoyments; the love of evil with those in lusts also has, such as the love of committing adultery, of taking revenge, of defrauding, of stealing, of acting cruelly, indeed, in the worst men, of blaspheming the holy things of the church and of inveighing against God. The fountainhead of those enjoyments is the love of ruling from self-love. They come of lusts which obsess the interiors of the mind, from these flow into the body, and excite uncleannesses there which titillate the fibers. The physical pleasure springs from the pleasure which the mind takes in lusts.

[2] After death everyone comes to know in the spiritual world what the uncleannesses are which titillate the body's fibers in such persons and comes to know the nature of them. In general

they are things cadaverous, excrementitious, filthy, malodorous, and urinous; for their hells teem with such uncleannesses. These are correspondences, as may be seen in the treatise *Divine Love and Wisdom* (nn. 422-424). After one has entered hell, however, these filthy delights are turned into wretchedness. This has been told in order that it may be understood what heaven's felicity is and its nature, of which we are now to speak; for a thing is known from its opposite.

39. It is impossible to describe in words the blessedness, satisfaction, joy and pleasure, in short, the felicity of heaven, so sensibly perceived there. What is perceived solely by feeling, cannot be described, for it does not fall into ideas of thought nor, therefore, into words. For the understanding sees only and sees what is of wisdom or truth, but not what is of love or good. Those felicities are therefore inexpressible, but still they ascend in like degree with wisdom. They are infinitely various, and each is ineffable. I have heard this, also perceived it.

[2] These felicities enter when a man, of himself and yet from the Lord, casts out the lusts of the love of evil and falsity. For these felicities are the happinesses of the affections of good and truth, the opposites of the lusts of the love of evil and falsity. Those happinesses begin from the Lord, thus from the inmost, diffuse themselves thence into things lower even to lowermost things, and thus fill the angel, making him a body of delight. Such happinesses are to be found in infinite variety in every affection of good and truth, and eminently in the affection of wisdom.

40. There is no comparing the joys of the lusts of evil and the joys of the affections of good. Inwardly in the former is the devil, in the latter the Lord. If comparisons are to be ventured, the pleasures of the lusts of evil can only be compared to the lewd pleasures of frogs in stagnant ponds or to those of snakes in filth, while the pleasures of the affections of good must be likened to the delights which the mind takes in gardens and flower beds. For things like those which affect frogs and snakes affect those in the hells who are in lusts of evil; and things like

## II. THE LORD'S DIVINE PROVIDENCE HAS FOR ITS OBJECT A HEAVEN FROM THE HUMAN RACE

those which affect the mind in gardens and flower beds affect those in the heavens who are in affections of good. For, as was said above, corresponding uncleannesses affect the evil, and corresponding cleannesses the good.

41. Plainly, then, the more closely one is conjoined with the Lord the happier one is. This happiness rarely shows itself in the world, however; for man is then in a natural state, and the natural does not communicate with the spiritual by continuity, but by correspondence. The communication is felt only in a certain repose and peace of mind, especially after struggles against evil. But when a person puts off the natural state and enters the spiritual state, as he does on leaving the world, the happiness described above gradually manifests itself.

42. (5) The more closely one is conjoined to the Lord the more distinctly does he seem to himself to be his own, and the more plainly does he recognize that he is the Lord's. The appearance is that the more closely one is conjoined to the Lord the less one is one's own. This appearance prevails with all the evil. It also prevails with those who from religion believe that they are not under the yoke of the law and that no one can of himself do good. All these inevitably think that to be free only to do good and not to think and will evil is not to be one's own. Inasmuch as a man who is conjoined to the Lord does not will and cannot think or will evil, they conclude from the look that this is not to be one's own. Yet that is the opposite of the truth.

43. There is infernal freedom, and there is heavenly freedom. Thinking and willing evil and also speaking and doing it so far as civil and moral laws do not prevent, is from infernal freedom. But thinking and willing good and speaking and doing it so far as opportunity offers, is from heavenly freedom. A man perceives as his own what he thinks, wills, speaks and does in freedom. The freedom anyone has always comes from his love. The man in an evil love cannot but deem infernal freedom to be real freedom, and a man in love of the good perceives that heavenly freedom is real freedom; consequently each regards the opposite of his freedom as bondage. No one can deny that one or the other

must be freedom, for two kinds of freedom opposed to each other cannot both be freedom. Furthermore it cannot be denied that to be led by good is freedom and to be led by evil is bondage. For to be led by good is to be led by the Lord, but to be led by evil is to be led by the devil.

[2] Inasmuch as all he does in freedom appears to a man to be his own, coming as it does from what he loves, and to act from one's love, as was said, is to act freely, it follows that conjunction with the Lord causes a man to seem free and also his own, and the more closely he is conjoined to the Lord, to seem so much freer and so much more his own. He seems the more distinctly his own because it is the nature of the divine love to want its own to be another's, that is, to be the angel's or the man's. All spiritual love is such, preeminently the Lord's. The Lord, moreover, never coerces anyone. For nothing to which one is coerced seems one's own, and what seems not one's own cannot be done from one's love or be appropriated to one as one's own. Man is always led in freedom by the Lord, therefore, and reformed and regenerated in freedom. On this much more will be said in what follows; also see some things above, n. 4.

44. The reason why the more distinctly a man seems to be his own the more plainly he sees that he is the Lord's, is that the more closely he is conjoined to the Lord the wiser he becomes (as was shown, nn. 34-36), and wisdom teaches and recognizes this. The angels of the third heaven, as the wisest angels, perceive this and call it freedom itself; but to be led by themselves they call bondage. They give as the reason for this that the Lord does not flow immediately into the perceptions and thoughts of wisdom, but into the affections of the love of good and by these into the former, and this influx they perceive in the affection by which they have wisdom. Hence, they say, all that they think from wisdom seems to be from themselves, thus seemingly their own, and this gives reciprocal conjunction.

45. As the Lord's divine providence has for its object a heaven from mankind, it has for its object the conjunction of the human race with Him (see nn. 28-31). It also has for its object

## II. THE LORD'S DIVINE PROVIDENCE HAS FOR ITS OBJECT A HEAVEN FROM THE HUMAN RACE

that man should be more and more closely conjoined to Him (nn. 32, 33); for thus man possesses a more interior heaven. Further, it has for its object that by the conjunction man should become wiser (nn. 34-36) and happier (nn. 37-41), for he has heaven by and according to wisdom, and happiness by wisdom, too. Finally, providence has for its object that man shall seem more distinctly his own, yet recognize the more clearly that he is the Lord's (nn. 42-44). All these are of the Lord's divine providence, for all are heaven and heaven is its object.

## III. IN ALL THAT IT DOES THE LORD'S DIVINE PROVIDENCE LOOKS TO WHAT IS INFINITE AND ETERNAL

46. Christendom knows that God is infinite and eternal. The doctrine of the Trinity which is named for Athanasius says that God the Father is infinite, eternal and omnipotent, so also God the Son, and God the Holy Spirit, and that nevertheless there are not three who are infinite, eternal and omnipotent, but One. As God is infinite and eternal, only what is infinite and eternal can be predicated of Him. What infinite and eternal are, finite man cannot comprehend and yet can comprehend. He cannot comprehend them because the finite is incapable of what is infinite; he can comprehend them because there are abstract ideas by which one can see that things are, though not what they are. Of the infinite such ideas are possible as that God or the Divine, being infinite, is esse itself, is essence and substance itself, wisdom and love themselves or good and truth themselves, thus is the one Self, indeed is veritable Man; there is such an idea, too, in speaking of the infinite as "all," as that infinite wisdom is omniscience and infinite power omnipotence.

[2] Still these ideas turn obscure to thought and may meet denial for not being comprehended, unless what one's thought gets from nature is removed from the idea, especially what it gets from the two properties of nature, space and time. For these are bound to restrict the ideas and to make abstract ideas seem to be nothing. But if such things can be removed in a man, as they are in an angel, what is infinite can be comprehended by the means just mentioned. Then also it will be grasped that the human being is something because he was created by infinite God who is all; also that he is a finite substance, having been created by infinite God who is substance itself; further that man is wisdom

## III. IN ALL THAT IT DOES THE LORD'S DIVINE PROVIDENCE LOOKS TO WHAT IS INFINITE AND ETERNAL

inasmuch as he was created by infinite God who is wisdom itself; and so on. For were infinite God not all, and were He not substance and wisdom themselves, man would not be anything actual, thus would either be nothing or exist only in idea, as those visionaries think who are called idealists.

[3] It is plain from what was shown in the treatise *Divine Love and Wisdom* that the divine essence is love and wisdom (nn. 28-39); that divine love and wisdom are substance itself and form itself, the one Self and the sole underived being (nn. 40-46); and that God created the universe and its contents from Himself, and not from nothing (nn. 282-284 ). It follows that every creature and above all the human being and the love and wisdom in him, are real, and do not exist only in idea. For were God not infinite, the finite would not be; were the infinite not all, no particular thing would be; and had not God created all things from Himself, nothing whatever would be. In a word, we are because God is.

47. We are considering divine providence and at this point how it regards what is infinite and eternal in all that it does. This can be clearly told only in some order. Let this be the order:

1. The infinite and eternal in itself is the same as the Divine.
2. What is infinite and eternal in itself cannot but look to what is infinite and eternal from itself in finite things.
3. Divine providence looks to the infinite and eternal from itself in all that it does, especially in saving mankind.
4. An image of the infinite and eternal offers in an angelic heaven formed from a redeemed mankind.
5. The heart of divine providence is to look to what is infinite and eternal by fashioning an angelic heaven, for it to be like one human being before the Lord, an image of Him.

48. (1) *The infinite and eternal in itself is the same as the Divine*. This is plain from what was shown in many places in the

work *Divine Love and Wisdom*. The concept comes from the angelic idea. By the infinite, angels understand nothing else than the divine *esse* and by the eternal the divine *existere*. But men can see and cannot see that what is infinite and eternal in itself is the Divine. Those can see this who do not think of the infinite from space and of the eternal from time; those cannot see it who think of infinite and eternal in terms of space and time. Those, therefore, can see it who think at some elevation, that is, inwardly in the rational mind; those cannot who think in a lower, that is, more external way.

[2] Those by whom it can be seen reflect that a spatial infinite is an impossibility, so likewise a temporal eternity or an eternity from which the world has been. The infinite has no first or final limit or boundaries. They also reflect that there cannot be another infinite from it, for "from it" implies a boundary or beginning, or a prior source. They therefore think that it is meaningless to speak of an infinite and eternal from itself, for that is like talking of an esse from itself, which is a contradiction. An infinite from itself could only be an infinite from an infinite, and esse from itself only esse from esse. Such an infinite or esse would either be the same with the infinite or be finite. From these and like considerations, inwardly seen in the rational mind, it is plain that there is what is infinite in itself and eternal in itself, and that they are the Divine whence are all things.

49. I know that many will say to themselves, "How can anybody grasp anything inwardly and rationally apart from space and time, and think that it not only exists, but is also the all and the self from which are all things?" But think deeply whether love or any affection of love, or wisdom or any perception of wisdom, yes, whether thought is in space and time, and you will grasp the fact that they are not. The Divine, therefore, being love itself and wisdom itself, cannot be conceived of in space and time; neither, then, can the infinite. To see this more clearly ponder whether thought is in time and space. Suppose thought is sustained for ten or twelve hours; may not the length of time seem like one or two hours? May it not seem like one or two days? The seeming duration is according to the state of affection

## III. IN ALL THAT IT DOES THE LORD'S DIVINE PROVIDENCE LOOKS TO WHAT IS INFINITE AND ETERNAL

from which the thought springs. If the affection is a joyous one, in which time is not noticed, thought over ten or twelve hours seems as though it were one or two hours. The contrary is true if the affection is a sorrowful one, in which one watches the passage of time. It is evident from this that time is only an appearance according to the state of affection from which the thought springs. The same is true of one's thought of the distance on a walk or a journey.

50. Since angels and spirits are affections of love and thoughts thence they are not in space or time, either, but only in an appearance of them. Space and time appear to them in keeping with the states of their affections and their thoughts thence. When one of them, therefore, thinks with affection of another, intently desiring to see or speak with him, the other is at once present.

[2] Hence, too, present with every man are spirits who are in an affection like his—evil spirits with a man in an affection of similar evil, and good spirits with the man in an affection of similar good. They are as fully present as though he was one of their society. Space and time have nothing to do with their presence, for affection and thought therefrom are not in space and time, and spirits and angels are affections and thoughts therefrom.

[3] I have been given to know this by living experience over many years. For I have spoken with many on their death, some in different kingdoms of Europe, and some in different kingdoms of Asia and Africa, and all were near me. If space and time existed for them, a journey and time to make it would have intervened.

[4] Indeed, every man knows this by some instinct in him or in his mind, as has been verified to me by the fact that nobody has thought of distances when I have reported that I had spoken with some person who died in Asia, Africa or Europe, for example with Calvin, Luther, or Melancthon, or with some king, governor or priest in a far region. The thought occurred to no one, "How could he speak with those who had lived there, and how could they come and be present with him, when lands and

seas lay between?" So it was plain to me that in thinking of those in the spiritual world a man does not think of space and time. For those there, however, there is an appearance of time and space; see the work *Heaven and Hell*, nn. 162-169, 191-199.

51. From these considerations it may now be plain that the infinite and eternal, thus the Lord, are to be thought of apart from space and time and can be so thought of; plain, likewise, that they are so thought of by those who think interiorly and rationally; and plain that the infinite and eternal are identical with the Divine. So think angels and spirits. In thought withdrawn from space and time, divine omnipresence is comprehended, and divine omnipotence, also the Divine from eternity, but these are not at all grasped by thought to which an idea of space and time adheres. Plain it is, then, that one can conceive of God from eternity, but never of nature from eternity. So one can think of the creation of the world by God, but never of its creation from nature, for space and time are proper to nature, but the Divine is apart from them. That the Divine is apart from space and time may be seen in the treatise *Divine Love and Wisdom* (nn. 7-10, 69-72, 73-76, and other places).

52. (2) *What is infinite and eternal in itself cannot but look to what is infinite and eternal from itself in finite things.* By what is infinite and eternal in itself the Divine itself is meant, as was shown in the preceding section. By finite things are meant all things created by the Lord, especially men, spirits, and angels. By looking to the infinite and eternal from itself is meant to look to the Divine, that is to Himself, in these, as a person beholds his image in a mirror. This was shown in several places in the treatise *Divine Love and Wisdom*, particularly where it was demonstrated that in the created universe there is an image of the human being and that this is an image of the infinite and eternal (nn. 317, 318), that is, of God the Creator, namely, the Lord from eternity. But be it known that the Divine-in-itself is in the Lord; whereas the divine-from-itself is the divine from the Lord in things created.

## III. IN ALL THAT IT DOES THE LORD'S DIVINE PROVIDENCE LOOKS TO WHAT IS INFINITE AND ETERNAL

53. But for better comprehension let this be illustrated. The Divine can look only to the divine, and can do so only in what has been created by it. This is evident from the fact that no one can regard another except from what is his own in himself. One who loves another regards him from his own love; a wise man regards another from his own wisdom. He can note whether the other loves him or not, is wise or not; but this he does from the love and wisdom in himself. Therefore he unites himself with the other so far as the other loves him as he loves the other, or so far as the other is wise as he is wise; for thus they make one.

[2] It is the same with the Divine-in-itself. For the Divine cannot look to itself from another, that is, from man, spirit, or angel. For there is nothing in them of the Divine-in-itself from which are all things, and to look to the Divine from another in whom there is nothing of the Divine would be to look to the Divine from what is not divine, which is an impossibility. Hence the Lord is so conjoined to man, spirit, or angel that all which is referable to the Divine is not from them but from the Lord. For it is known that all good and truth which anyone has are not from him but from the Lord; indeed that no one can name the Lord or speak His names Jesus and Christ except from Him.

[3] Consequently the infinite and eternal, which is the same as the Divine, looks to all things in finite beings infinitely and conjoins itself with them in the degree in which they receive love and wisdom. In a word, the Lord can have His abode and dwell with man and angel only in His own, and not in what is solely theirs, for this is evil; if it is good, it is still finite, which in and of itself is incapable of the infinite. Plainly, the finite cannot possibly look to what is infinite, but the infinite can look to the infinite-from-itself in finite beings.

54. It seems as if the infinite could not be conjoined to the finite because no ratio is possible between them and because the finite cannot compass the infinite. Conjunction is possible, nevertheless, both because the Infinite created all things from Himself (as was shown in the work *Divine Love and Wisdom*, nn. 282-284), and because the Infinite cannot but look in things

finite to what is infinite from Him, and this infinite-from-Him in finite beings can appear as if it were in them. Thereby a ratio is possible between finite and infinite, not from the finite, indeed, but from the infinite in the finite. Thereby, too, the finite is capable of the infinite, not the finite being in himself, but as if in himself from the infinite-from-itself in him. But of this more in what follows.

55. (3) Divine providence looks to the infinite and eternal from itself in all that it does, especially in saving mankind. The infinite and eternal in itself is the Divine itself, or the Lord in Himself; the infinite and eternal from itself is the proceeding Divine or the Lord in others created by Him, thus in men and angels. This Divine is identical with divine providence, for by the divine from Himself the Lord provides that all things shall be held together in the order in which and into which they were created. This the Divine in the act of proceeding accomplishes and consequently all this is divine providence.

56. That divine providence in all that it does looks to what is infinite and eternal from itself is evident from the fact that every created thing proceeds from a first, which is the infinite and eternal, to things last, and from things last to the first whence it is (as was shown in the work *Divine Love and Wisdom*, in the part in which the creation of the world is treated of). But the first whence anything is, is inmostly in all the progression, and therefore the proceeding Divine or divine providence in all that it does has in view some image of the infinite and eternal. It does so in all things, in some obviously so that it is perceptible, in others not. It makes that image evident to perception in the variety, and in the fructification and multiplication, of all things.

[2] An image of the infinite and eternal is apparent in the variety of all things, in that no one thing is the same as another nor can be to eternity. The eye beholds this in the variety of human faces ever since creation; in the variety of minds, of which faces are types; and in the variety of affections, perceptions and thoughts, for of these the mind consists. In all heaven, therefore, no two angels or spirits are the same, nor can

## III. IN ALL THAT IT DOES THE LORD'S DIVINE PROVIDENCE LOOKS TO WHAT IS INFINITE AND ETERNAL

be to eternity. The same is true of every object to be seen in either the natural or the spiritual world. Plainly, the variety is infinite and eternal.

[3] An image of the infinite and eternal is manifest in the fructification and multiplication of all things, in the vegetable kingdom in the capacity implanted in seeds, and in the animal kingdom in reproduction, especially in the family of fishes. Were the seeds to bear fruit and the animals to multiply in the measure of ability, they would fill all the world, even the universe, in a generation. Obviously there is latent in that ability an endeavor after self-propagation to infinity. And as fructification and multiplication have not failed from the beginning of creation and never will, plainly there is in that ability an endeavor after self-propagation to eternity also.

57. The like is true of human beings as to their affections, which are of love, and their perceptions, which are of wisdom. The variety of either is infinite and eternal; so, too, is their fructification and multiplication, which is spiritual. No person enjoys an affection and perception so like another's as to be identical with it, nor ever will. Affections, moreover, may be fructified and perceptions multiplied without end. Knowledge, it is well known, is inexhaustible. This capacity of fructification and multiplication without end or to infinity and eternity exists in natural things with men, in spiritual with the spiritual angels, and in celestial with the celestial angels. Affections, perceptions and knowledges have this endless capacity not only in general, but in every least particular. They have it because they exist from the infinite and eternal in itself through what is infinite and eternal from itself. But as the finite has in it nothing of the Divine, nothing of the kind, not the least, is in the human being as his own. Man or angel is finite and only a receptacle, by itself dead. Whatever is living in him is from the proceeding Divine, joined to him by contact, and appearing in him as if it were his. The truth of this will be seen in what follows.

58. Divine providence regards what is infinite and eternal from itself especially in saving mankind because its object is a

heaven from mankind (as was shown, nn. 27-45), and therefore it is man's reformation and regeneration or salvation to which it especially looks, since heaven consists of the saved or regenerate. To regenerate man, moreover, is to unite good and truth or love and wisdom in him, as they are united in the Lord's proceeding Divine; to this especially, therefore, providence looks in saving the race. The image of the infinite and eternal is not to be found elsewhere in man than in the marriage of good and truth. This marriage the proceeding Divine effects. Men filled by the proceeding Divine, which is called the Holy Spirit, have prophesied, as we know from the Word; men enlightened by it see divine truths in heaven's light; above all, angels sensibly perceive the presence, influx and conjunction, though they are aware that the conjunction is no more than can be termed adjunction.

59. It has not been known that divine providence in all its procedure with man looks to his eternal state. It can look to nothing else because the Divine is infinite and eternal, and the infinite and eternal or the Divine is not in time; therefore all future things are present to it. It follows that there is eternity in all that the Divine does. But those who think from time and space perceive this with difficulty, not only because they love temporal things, but also because they think from what is on hand in the world and not from what is at hand in heaven; this is as remote to them as the ends of the earth. Those, however, who are in the Divine, inasmuch as they think from the Lord, think from what is eternal as well as from what is at present, asking themselves, "What is that which is not eternal? Is not the temporal relatively nothing and does it not become nothing when it is past?" The eternal is not so; it alone is; its esse has no end. To think thus is to think both from the present and the eternal, and when a man not only thinks so but lives so, the proceeding Divine with him or divine providence looks in all its procedure to the state of his eternal life in heaven and guides to it. In what follows it will be seen that the Divine looks to the eternal in everybody, in an evil as well as in a good person.

## III. IN ALL THAT IT DOES THE LORD'S DIVINE PROVIDENCE LOOKS TO WHAT IS INFINITE AND ETERNAL

60. (4) *An image of the infinite and eternal offers in an angelic heaven.* Among things we need to know about is the angelic heaven. Everyone who has any religion thinks about heaven and wishes to go there. Yet heaven is granted only to those who know the way to it and walk in that way. We can know the way to an extent by knowing the character of those who constitute heaven and by knowing that no one becomes an angel or comes into heaven unless he brings with him from the world what is angelic. In what is angelic there is a knowledge of the way from walking in it, and a walking in the way through a knowledge of it. In the spiritual world, moreover, there are actually ways leading to every society of heaven or of hell. Each sees his own way as if for himself. He does so because a way is there for every love; the love discloses the way and takes a man to his fellows. No one sees other ways than the way of his love. Plain it is from this that angels are nothing but heavenly loves; otherwise they would not have seen the ways tending to heaven. This will be plainer still when heaven is described.

61. Every man's spirit is affection and thought therefrom. And as all affection is of love, and thought is of the understanding, every spirit is his own love and his own understanding therefrom. When a man is thinking solely from his own spirit, therefore, as he does in private meditation at home, he thinks from the affection belonging to his love. It is clear, then, that when a man becomes a spirit, as he does after death, he is the affection of his own love and has no other thought than that of his affection. If his love has been one of evil, he is an evil affection, which is a lust; if his love has been one of good, he is a good affection. Everyone has a good affection so far as he has shunned evils as sins, and an evil affection so far as he has not shunned evils as sins. As all spirits and angels, then, are affections, the whole angelic heaven is nothing but the love of all the affections of good and the attendant wisdom of all the perceptions of truth. Since all good and truth are from the Lord and He is love itself, the angelic heaven is an image of Him. Furthermore, as divine love and wisdom are human in form, it

also follows that the angelic heaven must be in that form. Of this we shall say more in the following section.

62. The angelic heaven is an image of the infinite and eternal, then, because it is an image of the Lord, who is infinite and eternal. The image of His infinity and eternity is manifest in heaven's being constituted of myriads and myriads of angels, and in its consisting of as many societies as there are general affections of heavenly love; manifest, again, in every angel's being distinctly his own affection; manifest further in that the form of heaven—a unit in the divine sight just as man is a unit—is assembled from so many affections, general and particular; also manifest in that this form is perfected to eternity with the increase in numbers, the greater the number of those entering into the form of the divine love which is the form of forms, the more perfect the resulting unity. It is plain from all this that the angelic heaven presents an image of the infinite and eternal.

63. From the knowledge of heaven to be had from this brief description it is evident that it is an affection of the love of good that makes heaven in a man. But who knows this today? Who knows even what an affection of the love of good is, or that these affections are innumerable, in fact, infinite? For, as was said, each angel is his own particular affection; and the form of heaven is the form of all the affections of the divine love there. Only one Being can combine all affections into this form—only He who is love and wisdom itself and who is at once infinite and eternal. For throughout that form is what is infinite and eternal; the infinite is in its unity and the eternal in its perpetuity; were they removed the form would instantly collapse. Who else can combine affections into a form? Who else can bring about this unity? The unity can be accomplished only in an idea of the total, and the total realized only in thought for each single part. Myriads on myriads compose that form; annually myriads enter it and will do so to eternity. All infants enter it and all adults who are affections of the love of good. Again from all this the image of the infinite and eternal in the angelic heaven is to be seen.

## III. IN ALL THAT IT DOES THE LORD'S DIVINE PROVIDENCE LOOKS TO WHAT IS INFINITE AND ETERNAL

64. (5) *The heart of divine providence is to look to what is infinite and eternal by fashioning an angelic heaven for it to be like one human being before the Lord, an image of Him.* See in the work *Heaven and Hell* (nn. 59-86) that heaven as a whole is like one man in the Lord's sight; that each society of heaven also is; that as a result each angel is a human being in perfect form; and that this is because God the Creator, who is the Lord from eternity, is Man; also (nn. 87-102) that as a result there is a correspondence of all things of heaven with all things in the human being. The entire heaven as one man has not been seen by me, for only the Lord can so behold it; but that an entire society, whether large or small, can appear as one man, I have seen. I was then told that the largest society of all, which is heaven in its entirety, so appears, but to the Lord alone; and that this causes every angel to be in full form a human being.

65. As all heaven is like one man in the Lord's view, it is divided into as many general societies as there are organs, viscera and members in man, and each general society into as many less general or particular societies as there are larger divisions in each of the viscera and organs. This makes evident what heaven is. Because the Lord is very Man and heaven is His image, to be in heaven is called "being in the Lord." See in the work *Divine Love and Wisdom* that the Lord is very Man (nn. 11-13, 285-289).

66. From all this the arcanum, well called angelic, can in a measure be seen, that each affection of good and at the same time of truth is human in form. For whatever proceeds from the Lord gets from His divine love that it is an affection of good and from His divine wisdom that it is an affection of truth. An affection of truth proceeding from the Lord appears in angel and man as perception and consequent thought of truth. For we are aware of perception and thought, but little aware of the affection whence they are, although all come as one from the Lord.

67. Man, then, is by creation a heaven in least form and hence an image of the Lord; heaven consists of as many affections as there are angels; and each affection in its form is man. It must

then be the constant striving of divine providence that a man may become a heaven in form and an image of the Lord, and as this is effected by means of an affection of the good and true, that he may become such an affection. This is therefore the unceasing effort of divine providence. But its inmost aim is that a man may be here or there in heaven or in the divine heavenly man, for so he is in the Lord. But this is accomplished with those whom the Lord can lead to heaven. As He foresees who can be led He also provides continually that a man may become amenable; for thus everyone who suffers himself to be led to heaven is prepared for his own place there.

68. We have said that heaven is divided into as many societies as there are organs, viscera and members in man; and in these no part can be in any place but its own. As angels are the parts in the divine heavenly man, and none become angels who were not men in the world, the man who suffers himself to be led to heaven is continually prepared by the Lord for his own place there. This is done by the affection of good and truth which corresponds with that place. To this place every angel-man is also assigned on his departure from the world. This is the inmost of divine providence touching heaven.

69. On the other hand, a man who does not permit himself to be led to heaven and allotted a place there is prepared for his own place in hell. Of himself a man tends constantly to the depths of hell but is continually withheld by the Lord. He who cannot be withheld is prepared for a given place in hell, to which he is assigned on departure from the world. This place is opposite one in heaven; for hell is the opposite of heaven. So, as the angel-man according to his affection of good and truth is allotted his place in heaven, the devil-man according to his affection of evil and falsity is allotted his in hell. The two opposites, set exactly over against each other, are kept in connection. This is the inmost of divine providence touching hell.

## IV. THERE ARE LAWS OF PROVIDENCE THAT ARE UNKNOWN TO MEN

70. Men know there is divine providence, but not what its nature is. This is not known because its laws are arcana, hitherto hidden in the wisdom of angels. These laws are to be revealed now in order that what belongs to the Lord may be ascribed to Him, and nothing ascribed to man that is not man's. For very many in the world attribute everything to themselves and their prudence, and what they cannot so attribute they call fortuitous and accidental, not knowing that human prudence is nothing and that "fortuitous" and "accidental" are idle words.

[2] We say that the laws of divine providence are arcana "hidden until now in the wisdom of the angels." They have been hidden because the understanding has been closed in Christendom in religion's name on divine things, and has been rendered so dull and averse in these matters that man has not been able because he has not been willing, or has not been willing because he has not been able, to understand anything about providence beyond the mere fact that it exists, or to do more than argue whether it exists or not, also whether it is only general or also detailed. Closed up on divine things in the name of religion, understanding could advance no further.

[3] But it is acknowledged in the church that man cannot of himself do good which is in itself good or of himself think truth which is in itself truth. This acknowledgment is at one with divine providence; these are interdependent beliefs. Lest therefore one be affirmed and the other denied and both fail, what divine providence is must by all means be revealed. It cannot be revealed unless the laws by which the Lord oversees and governs the volitions and thoughts of the human being are disclosed. The laws enable one to know the nature of providence,

and only one who knows its nature can acknowledge providence, for then he beholds it. The laws of divine providence, hitherto hidden with angels in their wisdom, are therefore to be revealed now.

# V. IT IS A LAW OF DIVINE PROVIDENCE THAT MAN SHALL ACT FROM FREEDOM ACCORDING TO REASON

71. As is known, man is free to think and will as he wishes, but not to speak whatever he thinks or to do whatever he wills. The freedom meant here, therefore, is spiritual freedom and natural freedom only as they make one; for thinking and willing are spiritual, and speaking and acting are natural. The two are readily distinguishable in man, for he can think what he does not utter and will what he does not do; plainly, spiritual and natural are discriminated in him. He can pass from the former to the latter therefore only on a decision to do so—a decision which can be likened to a door that must first be unfastened and opened. This door, it is true, stands open, as it were, in those who think and will from reason in accord with the civil laws of the land and the moral laws of society, for they speak what they think and do what they will to do. But in those who think and will contrary to those laws, the door stands shut, as it were. One who watches his volitions and subsequent deeds knows that such a decision intervenes, sometimes more than once in a single utterance or action. This we have premised for it to be understood that by acting from freedom according to reason is meant to think and will freely and thence to speak and do freely what is according to reason.

72. Since few know, however, that the law above can be a law of divine providence, principally because a man is also free then to think evil and falsity (still divine providence is continually leading him to think and will what is good and true), for clearer perception we must proceed step by step and shall do so in this order:

1. The human being has reason and freedom or rationality and liberty, and has these two faculties from the Lord.
2. Whatever a man does in freedom, whether with reason or not, provided it is according to his reason, seems to him to be his.
3. Whatever a man does in freedom according to his thought, is appropriated to him as his and remains.
4. A man is reformed and regenerated by the Lord by means of the two faculties and cannot be reformed and regenerated without them.
5. A man can be reformed and regenerated by means of the two faculties so far as he can be led by them to acknowledge that all truth and good which he thinks and does are from the Lord and not from himself.
6. The conjunction of the Lord with man, and man's reciprocal conjunction with the Lord, is effected by means of these two faculties.
7. In all the procedure of His divine providence the Lord safeguards the two faculties in man unimpaired and as sacred.
8. It is therefore of the divine providence that man shall act in freedom according to reason.

73. (1) *The human being has reason and freedom or rationality and liberty, and has these two faculties from the Lord.* Man has a faculty of understanding, which is rationality, and a faculty of thinking, willing, speaking and doing what he understands, which is liberty; and he has these two faculties from the Lord (see the work *Divine Love and Wisdom*, nn. 264-270, 425, and above, nn. 43, 44). But many doubts may arise about either of the two faculties when thought is given to them; therefore I want to say something at this point just about man's freedom to act according to reason.

[2] First, it should be known that all freedom is of love, so much so that love and freedom are one. As love is man's life, freedom is of his life, too. For man's every enjoyment is from some love of his and has no other source, and to act from the

## V. IT IS A LAW OF DIVINE PROVIDENCE THAT MAN SHALL ACT FROM FREEDOM ACCORDING TO REASON

enjoyment of one's love is to act in freedom. Enjoyment leads a man as the current bears an object along on a stream. But loves are many, some harmonious, others not; therefore freedoms are many. In general there are three: natural, rational, and spiritual freedom.

[3] Natural freedom is man's by heredity. In it he loves only himself and the world: his first life is nothing else. From these two loves, moreover, all evils arise and thus attach to love. Hence to think and will evil is man's natural freedom, and when he has also confirmed evils in himself by reasonings, he does them in freedom according to his reason. Doing them is from his faculty called liberty, and confirming them from his faculty called rationality.

[4] For example, it is from the love into which he is born that he desires to commit adultery, to defraud, to blaspheme, to take revenge. Confirming these evils in himself and by this making them allowable, he then, from his love's enjoyment in them, thinks and wills them freely and as if according to reason, and so far as civil laws do not hinder, speaks and does them. It is of the Lord's divine providence that man is allowed to do so, for freedom or liberty is his. This natural freedom is man's by nature because by heredity, and those are in this freedom who have confirmed it in themselves by reasonings from enjoyment in self-love and love of the world.

[5] Rational freedom is from the love of good repute for the sake of standing or gain. The delight of this love is to seem outwardly a moral person. Loving this reputation, the man does not defraud, commit adultery, take revenge, or blaspheme; and making this his reasoned course, he also does in freedom according to reason what is sincere, just, chaste, and friendly; indeed from reason can advocate such conduct. But if his rational is only natural and not spiritual, his freedom is only external and not internal. He does not love these goods inwardly at all, but only outwardly for reputation's sake, as we said. The good deeds he does are therefore not in themselves good. He can also say that they should be done for the sake of the general

welfare, but he speaks out of no love for that welfare, but from love of his own standing or gain. His freedom therefore derives nothing from love of the public good, nor does his reason, which complies with his love. This rational freedom, therefore, is inwardly natural freedom. The Lord's divine providence leaves everyone this freedom too.

[6] Spiritual freedom is from love of eternal life. Into this love and its enjoyment only he comes who regards evils as sins and therefore does not will them, and who also looks to the Lord. Once a man does this he is in this freedom. One can refuse to will and do evils for the reason that they are sins, only from an interior or higher freedom, belonging to his interior or higher love. This freedom does not seem at first to be freedom, yet it is. Later it does seem freedom, and the man acts in real freedom according to true reason, thinking, willing, speaking and doing the good and the true. This freedom grows as natural freedom decreases and serves it; and it unites with rational freedom and purifies it.

[7] Anyone can come into this freedom if he is willing to think that there is a life eternal, and that the joy and bliss of life in time and for a time is like a passing shadow to the joy and bliss of life in eternity and for eternity. A man can think so if he will, for he has rationality and liberty, and the Lord, from whom he has the two faculties, constantly enables him to do so.

74. (2) Whatever a man does in freedom, whether with reason or not, provided it is according to his reason, seems to him to be his. Nothing makes so clear what rationality and liberty are, which are proper to the human being, as to compare man and beast. Beasts do not have any rationality or faculty of understanding, or any liberty or faculty of willing freely. They do not have understanding or will, therefore, but instead of understanding they have knowledge and instead of will affection, both of these natural. Not having the two faculties, animals do not have thought, but instead an internal sight which makes one with their external sight by correspondence.

## V. IT IS A LAW OF DIVINE PROVIDENCE THAT MAN SHALL ACT FROM FREEDOM ACCORDING TO REASON

[2] Every affection has its mate, its consort, so to speak. An affection of natural love has knowledge, one of spiritual love has intelligence, and one of celestial love, wisdom. Without its mate or consort an affection is nothing, but is like esse apart from existere or substance without form, of which nothing can be predicated. Hence there is in every created thing something referable to the marriage of good and truth, as we have shown several times. In beasts it is a marriage of affection and knowledge; the affection is one of natural good, and the knowledge is knowledge of natural truth.

[3] Affection and knowledge in beasts act altogether as one. Their affection cannot be raised above their knowledge, nor the knowledge above the affection; if they are raised, they are raised together. Nor have animals a spiritual mind into which, or into the heat and light of which, they can be raised. Thus they have no faculty of understanding or rationality, or faculty of freely willing or liberty, and nothing more than natural affection with its knowledge. Their natural affection is that of finding food and shelter, of propagating, of avoiding and guarding against injury, together with the knowledge needed for this. As this is their kind of existence, they cannot think, "I will this but not that," or "I know this but not that," still less, "I understand this" or "I love that." They are borne along by affection and its knowledge without rationality and liberty. It is not from the natural world that they are borne along so, but from the spiritual world. Nothing can exist in the natural world that does not have its connection with the spiritual world: thence is every cause that accomplishes an effect. On this see also some things below (n. 96).

75. It is otherwise with man, who has affections not only of natural love, but also of spiritual and celestial loves. For man's mind is of three degrees, as was shown in Part III of the treatise *Divine Love and Wisdom*. Man can be raised therefore from natural knowledge into spiritual intelligence and on into celestial wisdom. From the two, intelligence and wisdom, he can look to the Lord, be conjoined with Him, and thereby live to eternity. This elevation as to affection would not be possible did he not

from rationality have the power to raise the understanding, and from liberty the power to will this.

[2] By means of the two faculties man can think in himself about what he perceives outside him through the senses, and can also think on high about what he thinks below. Anyone can say, "I have thought and I think so and so," "I have willed and I will so and so," "I understand that this is a fact," "I love this for what it is," and so on. Obviously, man thinks above his thought, and sees it, as it were, below him. This comes to him from rationality and liberty; from rationality he can think on high, and from liberty he can will so to think. Unless he had liberty to think so, he would not have the will, nor the thought from it.

[3] Those, therefore, who will to understand only what is of the world and nature and not what moral and spiritual good and truth are, cannot be raised from knowledge into intelligence, still less into wisdom, for they have stifled those faculties. They render themselves no longer men except that they can understand if they wish, and can also will, by virtue of the implanted rationality and liberty; from the two capacities it is that one can think and from thought speak. In other respects, they are not men but beasts, and some, in their abuse of those faculties, are worse than beasts.

76. From an unclouded rationality anyone can see or grasp that without the appearance that it is his own a man cannot be in any affection to know or to understand. Every joy and pleasure, thus everything of the will, is from an affection of some love. Who can wish to know or to understand anything except that an affection of his takes pleasure in it? Who can feel this pleasure unless what he is affected by seems to be his? Were it not his, but another's altogether, that is, if another from his affection should infuse something into his mind when he himself felt no affection for knowing or grasping it, would he receive it? Indeed, could he receive it? Would he not be like one called a dullard or a clod?

[2] It should be manifest then that although everything that a man perceives, thinks, knows and, according to perception, wills

## V. IT IS A LAW OF DIVINE PROVIDENCE THAT MAN SHALL ACT FROM FREEDOM ACCORDING TO REASON

and does, flows into him, nevertheless it is of the Lord's divine providence that it seems to be the man's. Otherwise, as we said, a man would not receive anything and so could be given no intelligence or wisdom. It is known that all good and truth are the Lord's and not man's, and yet appear to be man's. As good and truth so appear, so do all things of the church and of heaven, and all things of love and wisdom, and all things of charity and faith; yet none of them is man's. No one can receive them from the Lord unless it seems to him that he perceives them for himself. Plainly, the truth of the matter is that whatever a man does in freedom, whether with reason or not, provided only that it accords with his reason, seems to him to be his.

77. Who cannot from his faculty called rationality understand that a given good is serviceable to society, and a given evil harmful to society? That, for example, justice, sincerity, the chastity of marriage are serviceable to it, and injustice, insincerity, and misconduct with the wives of others, harmful? Consequently that these evils are in themselves injuries, and those goods in themselves benefits? Who then cannot make this a matter of his reason if only he will? He has rationality and he has liberty; the two faculties are bared, show, take charge and enable him to perceive and do in the measure that he avoids those evils because they are evils. So far as a man does this he looks on those goods as a friend looks on friends.

[2] By his faculty called rationality a man can conclude from this what goods are useful to society in the spiritual world and what evils are hurtful there, if instead of evils he sees sins and instead of goods works of charity. This he can also make a matter of his reason if he will, since he has liberty and rationality. His rationality and liberty emerge, become manifest, take charge and give him perception and power so far as he shuns evils as sins. So far as he does this he regards the goods of charity as neighbor regards neighbor in mutual love.

[3] For the sake of reception and union the Lord wills that whatever a man does freely according to reason shall seem to him to be his; this agrees with reason itself. It follows that a man

can from his reason will something on the ground that it means his eternal happiness and can perform it by the Lord's divine power, implored by him.

78. (3) *Whatever a man does in freedom according to his thought is appropriated to him as his and remains.* The reason is that a man's own and his freedom make one. His proprium is of his life, and what he does from his life he does in freedom. His proprium is also of his love, for love is one's life, and what he does from his life's love he does in freedom. We speak of his acting in freedom "according to his thought" because what is of his life or love he also thinks and confirms by thought, and what is so confirmed he does in freedom then according to thought. What a man does, he does from the will by the understanding; freedom is of the will and thought is of the understanding.

[2] A man can also act freely contrary to reason, likewise not freely in accord with reason: then nothing is appropriated to him—what he does is only of the mouth and body, not of the spirit or heart; only what is of the spirit and heart, when it is also of the mouth and body, is appropriated. The truth of this can be illustrated by many things, but this is not the place.

[3] By being appropriated to man is meant entering his life and becoming part of it, consequently becoming his own. It will be seen in what follows that there is nothing, however, which is man's very own; it only seems to him as if it were. Only this now: all the good a man does in freedom according to reason is appropriated to him as if it were his because it seems to be his in that he thinks, wills, speaks and does it. Good is not man's, however, but the Lord's with man (above, n. 76). How evil is appropriated to man will appear in a section of its own.

79. We said that what a man does in freedom in accord with his thought also remains. For nothing that a man has appropriated to himself can be eradicated; it has been made part of his love and at the same time of his reason, or of his will and at the same time of his understanding, and so of his life. It can be put aside indeed, but not cast out; put aside, it is borne from

## V. IT IS A LAW OF DIVINE PROVIDENCE THAT MAN SHALL ACT FROM FREEDOM ACCORDING TO REASON

center to periphery, where it stays; this is what we mean by its remaining.

[2] If, for example, in boyhood or youth, a man appropriated an evil to himself by doing it with enjoyment from love of it—a fraud, blasphemy, revenge, or fornication—having done it freely with the assent of thought, he made it his; but if later he repents, shuns it and considers it a sin to be averse from, and so desists from it freely according to reason, then the opposite good is appropriated to him. Good then takes the center and removes evil to the periphery, farther according to his aversion and abhorrence for it. Still the evil cannot be so thrust out that one can say it is extirpated; it may indeed in that removal seem extirpated. What occurs is that the man is withheld from the evil by the Lord and held in good. This can happen with all inherited evil and all a man's actual evil.

[3] I have seen this verified by the experience of some in heaven who thought they were without evil, being held in good as they were by the Lord. Lest they should believe that the good in which they were was their own, they were let down from heaven and let into their evils until they acknowledged that of themselves they were in evil, and in good only from the Lord. Upon this acknowledgment they were returned to heaven.

[4] Be it known, therefore, that goods are appropriated to man only in that they are constantly with him from the Lord, and that as a man acknowledges this the Lord grants that good shall seem to be the man's, that is, that it shall seem to him that he loves the neighbor or has charity, believes or has faith, does good and understands truth, thus is wise, of himself. From this an enlightened person may see the nature and the strength of the appearance in which the Lord wills man to be. The Lord wills it for salvation's sake, for without that appearance no one can be saved. Also see what was shown above on the subject (nn. 42-45).

80. Nothing that a person only thinks, not even what he thinks to will, is appropriated to him unless he also wills it so that he does it when opportunity offers. For when a man then does it, he

does it from the will by the understanding or from affection of the will by thought of the understanding. If it is something thought only, it cannot be appropriated, for the understanding does not conjoin itself to the will, or the thought of the understanding to the affection of the will, but the latter with the former, as we have shown many times in the treatise *Divine Love and Wisdom*, Part V. This is meant by the Lord's words,

> Not that which enters the mouth renders a man unclean, but that which goes forth from the heart by the mouth renders a man unclean ( Mt 15:11, 17, 18, 19).

In the spiritual sense thought is meant by "mouth," for thought is spoken by it; affection which is of love is meant by "heart"; if the man thinks and speaks from this he makes himself unclean. In Luke 6:45 also by "heart" an affection of love or of the will is meant, and by "mouth" the thought of the understanding.

81. Evils which a man believes are allowable, though he does not do them, are also appropriated to him, for the licitness in thought is from the will, as there is assent. When a man deems an evil allowable he loosens the internal bond on it and is kept from doing it only by external bonds, which are fears. As his spirit favors the evil, he commits it when external bonds are removed as allowable, and meanwhile is committing it in spirit. But on this see *Doctrine of Life for the New Jerusalem*, nn. 108-113.

82. (4) *A man is reformed and regenerated by the Lord by means of the two faculties and cannot be reformed or regenerated without them.* The Lord teaches that,

> Unless one is born anew, he cannot see the kingdom of God (Jn 3:3,5,7).

Few know what it is to be born anew or regenerated. For most do not know what love and charity are, therefore what faith is, either. One who does not know what love and charity are cannot know what faith is because charity and faith make one as good and truth do, and as affection which is of the will, and thought which is of the understanding, do. On this union see the treatise

## V. IT IS A LAW OF DIVINE PROVIDENCE THAT MAN SHALL ACT FROM FREEDOM ACCORDING TO REASON

*Divine Love and Wisdom*, nn. 427-431; also Doctrine for the New Jerusalem, nn. 13-24; and above, nn. 3-20.

83. No one can enter the kingdom of God unless he has been born anew for the reason that by heredity from his parents he is born into evils of every kind, with the capacity of becoming spiritual through removal of the evils; unless he becomes spiritual, then, he cannot enter heaven. To become spiritual from being natural is to be born again or regenerated. Three things need to be considered if one is to know how man is regenerated: the nature of his first state, which is one of damnation; the nature of his second state, which is one of reformation; and the nature of his third state, which is one of regeneration.

[2] Man's first state, which is one of damnation, is every one's state by heredity from his parents. For man is born thereby into self-love and love of the world, and from these as fountains into evils of every kind. By the enjoyments of those loves he is led, and they keep him from knowing that he is in evil, for the enjoyment of any love is felt to be good. Unless he is regenerated, therefore, a man knows no otherwise than that to love himself and the world above all things is good itself, and to rule over others and possess their riches is the supreme good. So comes all evil. For only oneself is regarded with love. If another is regarded with love it is as devil loves devil or thief thief when they are in league.

[3] Those who confirm these loves with themselves and the evils flowing from them, from enjoyment in them, remain natural and become sensuous-corporeal, and in their own thinking, which is that of their spirit, are insane. And yet, as long as they are in the world they can speak and act rationally and wisely, for they are human beings and so have rationality and liberty, though they still do this from self-love and love of the world. After death and on becoming spirits, they can enjoy nothing that they did not enjoy in the world. Their enjoyment is that of an infernal love and is turned into the unpleasant, sorrowful and dreadful, meant in the Word by torment and hell-fire. Plain it is, then, that man's first state is one of damnation

and that they are in it who do not suffer themselves to be regenerated.

[4] Man's second state—of reformation—is his state when he begins to think of heaven for the joy there, thus of God from whom he has heaven's joy. But at first the thought comes from the enjoyment of self-love; to him heaven's joy is that enjoyment. While the enjoyments of that love and of the evils flowing from it rule, moreover, he cannot but think that to gain heaven is to pour out prayers, hear sermons, observe the Supper, give to the poor, help the needy, make offerings to churches, contribute to hospitals, and the like. In this state a man is persuaded that merely to think about what religion teaches, whether this is called faith or called faith and charity, is to be saved. He is so minded because he gives no thought to the evils in the enjoyments of which he is. While those enjoyments remain, the evils do. The enjoyments of the evils are from the lust for them which continually inspires them and, when no fear restrains, brings them to pass.

[5] While evils remain in the lusts of love for them and so in one's enjoyments, there is no faith, piety, charity or worship except in externals, which seem real in the world's sight, but are not. They may be likened to waters flowing from an impure fountain, which one cannot drink. While a man is such that he thinks about heaven and God from religion but gives no thought to evils as sins, he is still in the first state. He comes into the second state, which is one of reformation, when he begins to think that there is such a thing as sin and still more when he thinks that a given evil is a sin, explores it somewhat in himself, and does not will it.

[6] Man's third state, which is one of regeneration, sets in and continues from the former. It begins when a man desists from evils as sins, progresses as he shuns them, and is perfected as he battles against them. Then as he conquers from the Lord he is regenerated. The order of his life is changed; from natural he becomes spiritual; the natural separated from the spiritual is in disorder and the spiritual is in order. The regenerated man acts

## V. IT IS A LAW OF DIVINE PROVIDENCE THAT MAN SHALL ACT FROM FREEDOM ACCORDING TO REASON

from charity and makes what is of his faith a part of his charity. But he becomes spiritual only in the measure in which he is in truths. Everyone is regenerated by means of truths and of a life in accord with them; by truths he knows life and by his life he does the truths. So he unites good and truth, which is the spiritual marriage in which heaven is.

85. Man is reformed and regenerated by means of the two faculties called rationality and liberty, and cannot be reformed or regenerated without them, because it is by means of rationality that he can understand and know what is evil and what is good, and hence what is false and true, and by means of liberty that he can will what he understands and knows. But while the enjoyment of an evil love rules him he cannot will good and truth freely or make them a matter of his reason, and therefore cannot appropriate them to him. For, as was shown above, what a man does in freedom from reason is appropriated to him as his, and unless it is so appropriated, he is not reformed and regenerated. He acts from the enjoyment of a love of good and truth for the first time when the enjoyment of love for the evil and false has been removed. Two opposite kinds of enjoyments of love at one and the same time are impossible. To act from the enjoyment of love is to act freely and is also to act according to reason, inasmuch as the reason favors the love.

86. Because an evil man as well as a good man has rationality and liberty, the evil man as well as the good can understand truth and do good. The evil man cannot do this in freedom according to reason, while a good man can; for the evil man is in the enjoyment of a love of evil, the good man in the enjoyment of a love of good. The truth which an evil man understands and the good he does are therefore not appropriated to him, as they are to the good man, and aside from appropriation there is no reformation or regeneration. With the evil man evils with their falsities occupy the center, as it were, and goods with their truths the circumference, but goods with their truths the center with the good man and evils with their falsities the periphery. In each case what is at the center is diffused to the circumference, as heat is from a fiery center and cold from an icy one. Thus with the

wicked the good at the circumference is defiled by evils at the center, and with the good evils at the circumference grow mild from the good at the center. For this reason evils do not condemn a regenerating man, nor do goods save the unregenerate.

87. (5) *A man can be reformed and regenerated by means of the two faculties so far as he can be led by them to acknowledge that all truth and good which he thinks and does are from the Lord and not from himself.* What reformation and regeneration are has been told just above, likewise that man is reformed and regenerated by means of the two faculties of rationality and liberty. Because it is done by those faculties, something more is to be said of them. From rationality a man can understand and from liberty he can will, doing each as of himself. Yet he does not have the ability to will good in freedom and to do it in accord with reason unless he is regenerated. An evil man can will only evil in freedom and do it according to his thinking, which by confirmations he has made to be his reasoning. For evil can be confirmed as well as good, but is confirmed by fallacies and appearances which then become falsities; evil so confirmed seems to accord with reason.

88. Anyone thinking from interior understanding can see that the power to will and the power to understand are not from man, but from Him who has power itself, that is, power in its essence. Only think whence power is. Is it not from Him who has it in its full might, that is, who possesses it in and from Himself? Power in itself, therefore, is divine. All power must have a supply on which to draw and direction from an interior or higher self. Of itself the eye cannot see, nor the ear hear, nor the mouth speak, nor the hand do; there must be supply and direction from the mind. Nor can the mind of itself think or will this or that unless something more interior or higher determines the mind to it. The same is true of the power to understand and the power to will. These are possible only from Him who has in Himself the power of willing and understanding.

[2] It is plain, then, that the two faculties called rationality and liberty are from the Lord and not from man. Man can

## V. IT IS A LAW OF DIVINE PROVIDENCE THAT MAN SHALL ACT FROM FREEDOM ACCORDING TO REASON

therefore will or understand something only as if of himself, and not of himself. Anyone can confirm the truth of this for himself who knows and believes that the will to good and the understanding of truth are wholly from the Lord, and not from man. The Word teaches that man can take nothing of himself and do nothing of himself (Jn 3:27; 15:5).

89. As all willing is from love and all understanding is from wisdom, the ability to will is from divine love, and the ability to understand is from divine wisdom; thus both are from the Lord who is divine love itself and divine wisdom itself. Hence to act in freedom according to reason has no other source. Everyone acts in freedom because, like love, freedom cannot be separated from willing. But there is interior and exterior willing, and a man can act upon the exterior without acting at the same time on the interior willing; so hypocrite and flatterer act. Exterior willing, however, is still from freedom, being from a love of appearing other than one is, or from love of an evil which the person intends in the love of his inner will. An evil man, however, as has been said, cannot in freedom according to reason do anything but evil; he cannot do good in freedom according to reason; he can do good, to be sure, but not in the inner freedom which is his own, from which the outer freedom has its character of not being good.

90. A person can be reformed and regenerated, we have said, in the measure in which he is led by the two faculties to acknowledge that all good and truth which he thinks and does are from the Lord and not from himself. A man can make this acknowledgment only by means of the two faculties, because they are from the Lord and are the Lord's in him, as is plain from what has been said. Man can make this acknowledgment, therefore, only from the Lord and not from himself; he can make it as if of himself; this the Lord gives everyone to do. He may believe that it is of himself, but when wiser acknowledge that it is not of himself. Otherwise the truth he thinks and the good he does are not in themselves truth and good, for the man and not the Lord is in them. Good in which the man is and which is done

by him for salvation's sake is self-righteous, but not that in which the Lord is.

91. Few can grasp with understanding that acknowledgment of the Lord, and acknowledgment that all good and truth are from Him, cause one to be reformed and regenerated. For a person may think, "What does the acknowledgment effect when the Lord is omnipotent and wills the salvation of all? This He wills and can accomplish if only He is moved to mercy." One is not thinking then from the Lord, nor from the interior sight of the understanding, that is, from enlightenment. Let me say briefly what the acknowledgment accomplishes.

[2] In the spiritual world where space is appearance only, wisdom brings about presence and love union, or the contrary happens. One can acknowledge the Lord from wisdom, and one can acknowledge Him from love. The acknowledgment of Him from wisdom (viewed in itself this is only knowledge) is made by doctrine; acknowledgment from love is made in a life according to doctrine. This effects union, the other, presence. Those, therefore, who reject instruction about the Lord remove themselves from Him, and as they also refuse life they part from Him. Those who do not reject instruction, but do refuse life, are present but still separated—like friends who converse but do not love each other, or like two one of whom speaks as a friend with the other, although as his enemy he hates him.

[3] The truth of this is commonly recognized in the idea that one who teaches and lives well is saved but not one who teaches well but lives wickedly, and in the idea that one who does not acknowledge God cannot be saved. This makes plain what kind of religion it is only to think about the Lord from faith, so called, and not to do something from charity. Therefore the Lord says,

Why do you call Me Lord, Lord, and do not do what I say? Everyone who comes to Me and hears my words and does them ... is like a house-builder who has placed the foundation on a rock, but the man who hears and does not do, is like a man building a house on the ground without a foundation (Lu 6:46-49).

## V. IT IS A LAW OF DIVINE PROVIDENCE THAT MAN SHALL ACT FROM FREEDOM ACCORDING TO REASON

92. (6) *The conjunction of the Lord with man and man's reciprocal conjunction with the Lord is effected by these two faculties.* Conjunction with the Lord and regeneration are one and the same thing, for a man is regenerated in the measure that he is conjoined with the Lord. All that we have said above about regeneration can be said therefore of the conjunction, and all we said about conjunction can be said about regeneration. The Lord Himself teaches in John that there is a conjunction of the Lord with man and a reciprocal conjunction of man with the Lord.

> Abide in Me, and I in you. . . . He that abides in Me and I in him, brings forth much fruit (15:4, 5).

In that day you will know that you are in Me and I in you (14:20).

[2] From reason alone anyone can see that there is no conjunction of minds unless it is reciprocal, and that what is reciprocal conjoins. If one loves another without being loved in return, then as he approaches, the other withdraws; but if he is loved in return, as he approaches, the other does also, and there is conjunction. Love also wills to be loved; this is implanted in it; and so far as it is loved in return it is in itself and in its delight. Thence it is plain that if the Lord loves man and is not in turn loved by man, the Lord advances but man withdraws; thus the Lord would be constantly willing to meet with man and enter him, but man would be turning back and departing. So it is with those in hell, but with those in heaven there is mutual conjunction.

[3] Since the Lord wills conjunction with man for salvation's sake, He also provides something reciprocal with man. This consists in the fact that the good a man wills and does in freedom and the truth he thinks and speaks from the will according to reason seem to be from himself, and that the good in his will and the truth in his understanding seem to be his—indeed they seem to the man to be from himself and to be as completely his as though they really were; there is no difference; does anyone perceive otherwise by any sense? See above (nn. 74-77) on the appearance as of self, and (nn. 78-81) on appropriation as of

oneself. The only difference is the acknowledgment which a man ought to make, that he does good and thinks truth not of himself but from the Lord, and hence that the good he does and the truth he thinks are not his. So to think from some love of the will because it is the truth makes conjunction; for then a man looks to the Lord and the Lord looks on the man.

93. I have been granted both to hear and see in the spiritual world what the difference is between those who believe that all good is from the Lord and those who believe that good is from themselves. Those who believe that good is from the Lord turn their faces to Him and receive the enjoyment and blessedness of good. Those who think that good is from themselves look to themselves and think they have merit. Looking to themselves, they perceive only the enjoyment of their own good which is the enjoyment not of good but of evil, for man's own is evil, and enjoyment of evil perceived as good is hell. Those who have done good but believed it was of themselves, and who after death do not receive the truth that all good is from the Lord, mingle with infernal spirits and finally join them. Those who receive that truth, however, are reformed, though no others receive it than those who have looked to God in their life. To look to God in one's life is nothing else than to shun evils as sins.

94. The Lord's conjunction with man and man's reciprocal conjunction with the Lord is effected by loving the neighbor as one's self and the Lord above all. To love the neighbor as one's self consists simply in not acting insincerely or unjustly with him, not hating him or avenging one's self on him, not cursing and defaming him, not committing adultery with his wife, and not doing other like things to him. Who cannot see that those who do such things do not love the neighbor as themselves? Those, however, who do not do such things because they are evils to the neighbor and at the same time sins against the Lord, deal sincerely, justly, amicably and faithfully by the neighbor; as the Lord does likewise, reciprocal conjunction takes place. And when conjunction is reciprocal, whatever a man does to the neighbor he does from the Lord, and what he does from the Lord is good. The neighbor to him then is not the person, but the good

## V. IT IS A LAW OF DIVINE PROVIDENCE THAT MAN SHALL ACT FROM FREEDOM ACCORDING TO REASON

in the person. To love the Lord above all is to do no evil to the Word, for the Lord is in the Word, or to the holy things of the church, for He is in these, too, and to do no evil to the soul of another, for everyone's soul is in the Lord's hand. Those who shun these evils as monstrous sins against the Lord love Him above all else. None can do this except those who love the neighbor as themselves, for the two loves are conjoined.

95. In view of the fact that there is a conjunction of the Lord with man and of man with the Lord, there are two tables of the Law, one for the Lord and the other for man. So far as man as of himself keeps the laws of his table, the Lord enables him to observe the laws of the Lord's table. A man, however, who does not keep the laws of his table, which are all referable to love for the neighbor, cannot do the laws of the Lord's table, which are all referable to love for the Lord. How can a murderer, thief, adulterer, or false witness love God? Does reason not insist that to be any of these and to love God is a contradiction? Is not the devil such? Must he not hate God? But a man can love God when he abhors murder, adultery, theft and false witness, for then he turns his face away from the devil to the Lord; turning his face to the Lord he is given love and wisdom—these enter him by the face, and not by the back of the neck. As conjunction is accomplished only so, the two tables are called a covenant, and a covenant exists between two.

96. (7) *In all the procedure of His divine providence the Lord safeguards the two faculties in man unimpaired and as sacred.* The reasons are that without those two faculties man would not have understanding and will and thus would not be human; likewise that without them he could not be conjoined to the Lord and so be reformed and regenerated; and because without them he would not have immortality and eternal life. The truth of this can be seen from what has been said about the two faculties, liberty and rationality, but not clearly seen unless the reasons just given are brought forward as conclusions. They are, therefore to be clarified.

[2] (a) *Without those two faculties man would not have understanding and will and thus would not be human.* Man has will only in that he can will freely as of himself, and to will freely as of oneself is from the faculty called liberty, steadily imparted by the Lord. Man has understanding only in that he can understand as of himself whether a thing is of reason or not, and so to understand is from the other faculty, called rationality, steadily imparted to him by the Lord. These faculties unite in man as will and understanding do, for because a man can will, he can also understand; willing is impossible without understanding; understanding is its partner and mate apart from which it cannot exist. With the faculty called liberty there is therefore given the faculty called rationality. If, too, you take willing away from understanding, you understand nothing.

[3] In the measure that you will, you can understand provided the helps, called knowledges, are present or available, for these are like tools to a workman. We say, in the measure you will you can understand, meaning, so far as you love to understand, for will and love act as one. This seems like a paradox, but it appears so to those who do not love or hence will to understand. They say they cannot understand, but in the following section we shall tell who cannot understand, and who can hardly understand.

[4] It is plain without confirmation that unless man had will from the faculty called liberty, and understanding from the faculty called rationality, he would not be human. Beasts do not have these faculties. Beasts seem to be able to will and to understand, but cannot do so. They are led and moved to do what they do solely by a natural affection, in itself desire, which has knowledge for its mate. Something civil and moral there is in their knowledge, but it does not transcend the knowledge, for they have nothing spiritual enabling them to perceive or to think analytically of what is moral. They can indeed be taught to do something, but this is natural only, is assimilated to their knowledge and at the same time to their affection, and reproduced through sight or hearing, but never becomes with

## V. IT IS A LAW OF DIVINE PROVIDENCE THAT MAN SHALL ACT FROM FREEDOM ACCORDING TO REASON

them anything of thought, still less of reason. On this see some things above, n. 74.

[5](b) *Without those two faculties man could not be conjoined to the Lord or reformed and regenerated.* This has been shown above. The Lord resides with men, whether evil or good, in these two faculties and conjoins Himself by them to every man. Hence an evil man as well as a good man can understand and has the will of good and the understanding of truth potentially—that he does not possess them actually is owing to abuse of those faculties. The Lord resides in those faculties in everyone by the influx of His will, namely, to be received by man and to have an abode with him, and to give him the felicities of eternal life; all this is of the Lord's will, being of His divine love. It is this will of the Lord which causes what a man thinks, speaks, wills and does, to seem to be his own.

[6] That the influx of the Lord's will effects this can be confirmed by much in the spiritual world. Sometimes the Lord fills an angel with His divine so that the angel does not know but that he is the Lord. Thus inspired were the angels who appeared to Abraham, Hagar, and Gideon, and who therefore spoke of themselves as Jehovah; of whom the Word tells. So also one spirit may be filled by another so that he does not know but that he is the other; I have seen this often. In heaven it is general knowledge that the Lord operates all things by willing, and that what He wills takes place.

From all this it is plain that it is by those two faculties that the Lord conjoins Himself to man and causes the man to be reciprocally conjoined. We told above and shall say more below about how man is reciprocally conjoined by the two faculties and how, consequently, he is reformed and regenerated by means of them.

[7](c) *Without those two faculties man would not have immortality or eternal life.* This follows from what has been said: that by the two faculties there is conjunction with the Lord and also reformation and regeneration. By conjunction man has immortality, and through reformation and regeneration he has

## Divine Providence

eternal life. As every man, evil as well as good, is conjoined to the Lord by the two faculties every man has immortality. Eternal life, or the life of heaven, however, only that man has with whom there is reciprocal conjunction from inmosts to outmosts.

The reasons may now be clear why the Lord, in all the procedure of His divine providence, safeguards the two faculties in man unimpaired and as sacred.

97. (8) *It is therefore [a law] of divine providence that man shall act in freedom from reason.* To act in freedom according to reason, to act from liberty and rationality, and to act from will and understanding, are the same. But it is one thing to act in freedom according to reason, or from liberty and rationality, and another thing to act from freedom itself according to reason itself or from liberty and rationality themselves. The man who does evil from love of evil and confirms it in himself acts indeed from freedom according to reason, but his freedom is not in itself freedom or very freedom, but an infernal freedom which in itself is bondage, and his reason is not in itself reason, but is either spurious or false or plausible through confirmations. Still, either is of divine providence. For if freedom to will evil and do it as of the reason through confirmation of it were taken from the natural man, liberty and rationality and at the same time will and understanding would perish, and he could not be withdrawn any longer from evils, be reformed or united with the Lord, and live to eternity. The Lord therefore guards man's freedom as a man does the apple of his eye. Through that freedom the Lord steadily withdraws man from evils and so far as He can do this implants goods, thus gradually putting heavenly freedom in place of infernal freedom.

98. We said above that every man has the faculty of volition called liberty and the faculty of understanding called rationality. Those faculties, moreover, it should be known, are as it were inherent in man, for humanness itself is in them. But as was just said, it is one thing to act from freedom in accord with reason, and another thing to act from freedom itself and according to reason itself. Only those do the latter who have suffered

## V. IT IS A LAW OF DIVINE PROVIDENCE THAT MAN SHALL ACT FROM FREEDOM ACCORDING TO REASON

themselves to be regenerated by the Lord; others act in freedom according to thought which they make seem like reason. Unless he was born foolish or supremely stupid, every person can attain to reason itself and by it to liberty itself. Many reasons why all do not do so will be disclosed in what follows. Here we shall only tell to whom freedom itself or liberty itself, and at the same time reason itself or rationality itself cannot be given and to whom they can hardly be given.

[2] True liberty and rationality cannot be given to those foolish from birth or to those who become foolish later, while they remain so. Nor can they be given to those born stupid and dull or to any made so by the torpor of idleness, or by a disease which perverts or entirely closes the interiors of the mind, or by love of a bestial life.

[3] Genuine liberty and rationality cannot be given to those in Christendom who utterly deny the Divine of the Lord and the holiness of the Word, and have kept that denial confirmed to life's close. For this is meant by the sin against the Holy Spirit which is not forgiven in this world or in the world to come (Mt 12:31, 32).

[4] Liberty itself and rationality itself cannot be given to those who ascribe all things to nature and nothing to the Divine, and have made this a conviction by reasonings from visible things; for these are atheists.

[5] True liberty and rationality can hardly be given to those who have confirmed themselves much in falsities of religion; for a confirmer of falsity is a denier of truth. But they can be given to those, in whatever religion, who have not so confirmed themselves. On this see what is adduced in Doctrine for the New Jerusalem about Sacred Scripture, nn. 91-97.

[6] Infants and children cannot attain to essential liberty and rationality before they grow up. For the interiors of the mind of man are opened gradually, and meanwhile are like seeds in unripe fruit, without ground in which to sprout.

99. We have said that true liberty and rationality cannot be given to those who have denied the Divine of the Lord and the holiness of the Word; to those who have confirmed themselves in favor of nature and against the Divine; and hardly to those who have strongly confirmed themselves in falsities of religion; still none of these have destroyed the faculties themselves. I have heard atheists, who had become devils and satans, understand arcana of wisdom quite as well as angels, but only while they heard them from others; on returning into their own thought, they did not understand them, for the reason that they did not will to do so. They were shown that they could also will this, did not the love and enjoyment of evil turn them away. This they understood, too, when they heard it. Indeed they asserted that they could but did not will to be able to do so, for then they could not will what they did will, namely, evil from enjoyment in the lust of it. I have often heard such astonishing things in the spiritual world. I am fully persuaded therefore that every man has liberty and rationality, and that every man can attain true liberty and rationality if he shuns evils as sins. But the adult who has not come into true liberty and rationality in the world can never do so after death, for the state of his life remains to eternity what it was in the world.

# VI. IT IS A LAW OF DIVINE PROVIDENCE THAT MAN SHALL REMOVE EVILS AS SINS IN THE EXTERNAL MAN OF HIMSELF, AND ONLY SO CAN THE LORD REMOVE THE EVILS IN THE INTERNAL MAN AND AT THE SAME TIME IN THE EXTERNAL

100. Anyone can see from reason alone that the Lord who is good itself and truth itself cannot enter man unless the evils and falsities in him are removed. For evil is opposed to good, and falsity to truth, and two opposites cannot mingle, but as one approaches the other, combat arises which lasts until one gives way to the other; what gives way departs and the other takes its place. Heaven and hell, or the Lord and the devil, are in such opposition. Can anyone reasonably think that the Lord can enter where the devil reigns, or heaven be where hell is? By the rationality with which every sane person is endowed, who cannot see that for the Lord to enter, the devil must be cast out, or for heaven to enter, hell must be removed?

[2] This opposition is meant by Abraham's words from heaven to the rich man in hell:

> Between us and you a great gulf is fixed, so that those who would cross from us to you cannot, nor those over there cross to us (Lu 16:26).

Evil is itself hell, and good is itself heaven, or what is the same, evil is itself the devil, and good itself the Lord. A person in whom evil reigns is a hell in least form, and one in whom good reigns is a heaven in least form. How, then, can heaven enter hell when a gulf is fixed between them so great that there is no crossing from one to the other? It follows that hell must by all means be removed for the Lord to enter with heaven.

101. But many, especially those who have confirmed themselves in faith severed from charity, do not know that they are in hell when they are in evils. In fact, they do not know what evils are, giving them no thought. They say that they are not under the yoke of the law and so the law does not condemn them; likewise, that as they cannot contribute to their salvation, they cannot remove any evil of themselves and furthermore cannot do any good of themselves. It is these who neglect to give some thought to evil and therefore keep on in evil. They are meant by the Lord under "goats" in Matthew 25:32, 33; 41-46, as may be seen in Doctrine of the New Jerusalem on Faith, nn. 61-68; to them it is said in verse 41, "Depart from Me, you accursed, into everlasting fire prepared for the devil and his angels."

[2] Persons who give no thought to the evils in them, and who do not examine themselves and then desist from the evils, cannot but be ignorant what evil is, and cannot but love it then from delighting in it. For one who is ignorant of it loves it, and one who fails to give it thought, goes on in it, blind to it. Thought sees good and evil as the eye sees beauty and ugliness. One who thinks and wills evil is in evil, and so is a person who thinks that it does not come to God's sight, or if it does is forgiven by Him; he supposes then that he is without evil. If such persons refrain from doing evil, they do so not because it is a sin against God, but for fear of the law and for their reputation's sake. In spirit they still do evil, for it is man's spirit that thinks and wills. As a result, what a man thinks in his spirit in the world, he commits when he becomes a spirit on his departure from the world.

[3] In the spiritual world, into which everyone comes after death, the question is not asked what your belief has been or your doctrine, but what your life has been. Was it such or such? For, as is known, such as one's life is, such is one's belief, yes, one's doctrine. For life fashions a doctrine and a belief for itself.

102. From all this it is plain that it is a law of divine providence that evils be removed by man, for without the

## VI. IT IS A LAW OF DIVINE PROVIDENCE THAT MAN SHALL REMOVE EVILS AS SINS IN THE EXTERNAL MAN OF HIMSELF, AND ONLY SO CAN THE LORD REMOVE THE EVILS IN THE INTERNAL MAN AND AT THE SAME TIME IN THE EXTERNAL

removal of them the Lord cannot be conjoined to man and from Himself lead man to heaven. But it is not known that man ought to remove evils in the external man as of himself and that unless he does so the Lord cannot remove the evils in his internal man. This is to be presented, therefore, to the reason in light of its own in this order:

1. Every man has an external and an internal of thought.
2. His external of thought is in itself such as his internal is.
3. The internal cannot be purified from the lusts of evil as long as the evils in the external man have not been removed, for these impede.
4. Only with the man's participation can evils in the external man be removed by the Lord.
5. Therefore a man ought to remove evils from the external man as of himself.
6. The Lord then purifies him from the lusts of evil in the internal man and from the evils themselves in the external.
7. The continuous effort of the Lord in His divine providence is to unite man to Himself and Himself to man, in order to be able to bestow the felicities of eternal life on him, which can be done only so far as evils, along with their lusts, are removed.

103. (1) *Every man has an external and an internal of thought.* By external and internal of thought the same is meant here as by external and internal man, and by this nothing else is meant than external and internal of will and understanding, for will and understanding constitute man, and as they both manifest themselves in thoughts, we speak of external and internal of thought. And as it is man's spirit and not his body which wills and understands and consequently thinks, external and internal are external and internal of his spirit. The body's activity in speech or deed is only an effect from the external and internal of man's spirit, for the body is so much obedience.

104. As he grows older, every person has an external and an internal of thought, or an external and an internal of will and understanding or of his spirit, identical with external and internal man. This is evident to anyone who observes another's thoughts and intentions as they are revealed in speech or deed, or who observes his own when he is in company and when he is by himself. For from the external thought one can talk amicably with another and yet in internal thought be hostile. From external thought and from its affection, too, a man can talk about love for the neighbor and for God when in his internal thought he cares nothing for the neighbor and does not fear God. From external thought together with its affection he can talk about the justice of civil laws, the virtues of the moral life, and matters of doctrine and the spiritual life, and yet in private and from his internal thought and its affection speak against the civil laws, the moral virtues, and matters of doctrine and spiritual life. So those do who are in lusts of evil but want to appear to the world not to be in them.

[2] Many also, as they listen to others, think to themselves, "Do those speaking think inwardly in themselves as they think in utterance? Are they to be believed or not? What do they intend?" Flatterers and hypocrites notoriously possess a twofold thought. They can be self-restrained and guard against the interior thought's being disclosed, and some can hide it more and more deeply and bar the door against its appearing. That a man possesses external and internal thought is also plain in that from his interior thought he can behold the exterior thought, can reflect on it, too, and judge whether or not it is evil. The human mind is such because of the two faculties, called liberty and rationality, which one has from the Lord. Unless he possessed internal and external of thought from these faculties, a man could not perceive and see an evil in himself and be reformed. In fact, he could not speak but only make sounds like a beast.

105. The internal of thought comes out of the life's love, its affections and the perceptions from them. The external of thought is from what is in the memory, serving the life's love for confirmation and as means to its end. From childhood to early

## VI. IT IS A LAW OF DIVINE PROVIDENCE THAT MAN SHALL REMOVE EVILS AS SINS IN THE EXTERNAL MAN OF HIMSELF, AND ONLY SO CAN THE LORD REMOVE THE EVILS IN THE INTERNAL MAN AND AT THE SAME TIME IN THE EXTERNAL

manhood a person is in the external of thought from an affection for knowledge, which is then his internal; from the life's love born in one from parents something of lust and hence of disposition issues, too. Later, however, his life's love is as he lives, and its affections and the perceptions from them make the internal of his thought. From his life's love comes a love of means; the enjoyments of these means and the information drawn thereby from the memory make his external of thought.

106. (2) *Man's external of thought is in itself such as his internal is.* We showed earlier that from head to foot a man is what his life's love is. Something must be said about his life's love, for until this is done nothing can be said about the affections which together with perceptions make the internal of man, or about the enjoyments of the affections together with thoughts which make his external. Loves are many, but two—heavenly love and infernal love—are like lords or kings. Heavenly love is love to the Lord and the neighbor; infernal love is love of self and the world. These are opposite to each other as heaven and hell are. For a man in love of self and the world wishes well only to himself; a man in love to the Lord and the neighbor wishes well to all. These two are the loves of man's life, though with much variety. Heavenly love is the life's love of those whom the Lord leads, and infernal love the life's love of those whom the devil leads.

[2] No one's life's love can be without derivatives, called affections. The derivatives of infernal love are affections of evil and falsity —lusts, properly speaking; and those of heavenly love are affections of good and truth—loves, strictly. Affections, or strictly lusts, of infernal love are as numerous as evils are, and affections, or properly loves, of heavenly love are as many as there are goods. Love dwells in its affections like a lord in his domain and a king in his realm; its domain or realm is over the things of the mind, that is, of the will and understanding and thence of the body. By its affections and the perceptions from them and by its enjoyments and the thoughts therefrom, the life's

love of man rules him completely, the internal of the mind by the affections and perceptions from them, and the external by the enjoyments of the affections and of the thoughts from them.

107. The manner of this rule may be seen to some extent from comparisons. Heavenly love with its affections of good and truth and the perceptions from them, together with the enjoyments of such affections and the thoughts from these, may be compared to a tree, notable for its branches, leaves and fruit. The life's love is the tree; the branches with their leaves are the affections of good and truth with their perceptions; and the fruits are the enjoyments of the affections with their thoughts. Infernal love, however, with its affections or lusts of evil and falsity, together with the enjoyments of the lusts and the thinking from those enjoyments, may be compared to a spider and the web spun about it. The love itself is the spider; the lusts of evil and falsity together with their subtle cunning are the net of threads nearest the spider's post; and the enjoyments of the lusts together with their crafty schemes are the more remote threads where flies are snared on the wing, enveloped and eaten.

108. These comparisons may help one to see the connection of all things of the will and understanding or of man's mind with his life's love, and yet not to see it rationally. Rationally it may be seen in this way. Everywhere there are three which make one, called end, cause and effect. Here the life's love is end; the affections with their perceptions are cause; and the enjoyments of the affections and consequent thoughts are effect. For as an end passes into effect through a cause, love passes by its affections to its enjoyments and by its perceptions to its thoughts. The effects are in the enjoyments of the mind and the thoughts thence when the enjoyments are from the will and the thoughts from the attendant understanding, that is, when all fully agree. The effects are then part of man's spirit and although they do not come into bodily act are still a deed there when there is this agreement. At the same time they are in the body, dwelling there with man's life's love and longing for the deed, which occurs when nothing hinders. The same is true of lusts of evil and evil deeds with those who make evils allowable in spirit.

## VI. IT IS A LAW OF DIVINE PROVIDENCE THAT MAN SHALL REMOVE EVILS AS SINS IN THE EXTERNAL MAN OF HIMSELF, AND ONLY SO CAN THE LORD REMOVE THE EVILS IN THE INTERNAL MAN AND AT THE SAME TIME IN THE EXTERNAL

[2] As an end unites itself with a cause and by the cause with an effect, the life's love unites itself with the internal of thought and by this with its external. It is plain then that man's external of thought is in itself what his internal is, for an end imparts all of itself to the cause and through the cause to the effect. Nothing essential is present in an effect which is not in the cause and through the cause in the end, and as the end is what essentially enters cause and effect, these are called "mediate end" and "final end" respectively.

109. Sometimes the external of thought seems to be different in itself from the internal. This is because the life's love with its internals about it sets a vicar under it called the love of means, and directs it to watch and guard against anything of its lusts appearing. This vicar, with the cunning of its chief, the life's love, therefore speaks and acts in accordance with the laws of a kingdom, the ethical demands of reason, and the spiritual requirements of the church, so cunningly, too, and cleverly that no one sees that persons are other than they say and act, and finally the persons themselves, so disguised, scarcely know otherwise. Such are all hypocrites. Such are priests, also, who at heart care nothing for the neighbor and do not fear God, yet preach about love of the neighbor and of God. Such are judges who judge by gifts and friendships while affecting zeal for justice and speaking with reason about judgment. Such are traders who at heart are insincere and fraudulent while dealing honestly for the sake of profit. Such are adulterers when, from the rationality every man possesses, they talk about the chastity of marriage; and so on.

[2] The same persons, when they strip the love of means, the vicar of their life's love, of the purple and linen which they have thrown around it and put its house dress on it, then think exactly the contrary, and exchanging thought with their best friends who are in a similar life's love, they speak so. It may be believed that when they have spoken so justly, honestly and piously from the love of means, the character of the internal of thought was not in

the external of their thought; yet it was; hypocrisy is in them, and love of self and the world is in them, the cunning of which aims to capture a reputation for the sake of standing or gain through just the outward appearance. This, the nature of the internal, is in the external of their thought when they speak and act so.

110. With those in a heavenly love, however, internal and external of thought or internal and external man make one when they speak, and they are aware of no difference. Their life's love, with its affections of good and the perceptions of truth from these, is like a soul in what they think and then say and do. If they are priests, they preach out of love to the neighbor and to the Lord; if judges, they judge from justice itself; if tradesmen, they deal with honesty; if they are husbands, they love the partner with true chastity; and so on. Their life's love also has a love of the means for vicar, which it teaches and leads to act with prudence and clothes with garments of a zeal for both truths of doctrine and goods of life.

111. (3) *The internal cannot be purified from the lusts of evil as long as evils in the external man are not removed, for these impede.* This follows from what has been said above, that the external of man's thought is in itself what the internal of his thought is and that they cohere as what is not only in the other but also from the other; one cannot be removed, therefore, unless the other is at the same time. This is true of any external which is from an internal, and of anything subsequent from what is prior, and of every effect from a cause.

[2] As lusts together with slynesses make the internal of thought with evil persons, and the enjoyments of the lusts together with scheming make the external of thought in them, and the two are joined into one, it follows that the internal cannot be purified from the lusts as long as the evils in the external man are not removed. It should be known that man's internal will is in the lusts; his internal understanding in the slynesses; his external will in the enjoyments of the lusts; and his external understanding in the sly scheming. Anyone can see that lusts and their enjoyments make one, that slynesses and scheming also do,

## VI. IT IS A LAW OF DIVINE PROVIDENCE THAT MAN SHALL REMOVE EVILS AS SINS IN THE EXTERNAL MAN OF HIMSELF, AND ONLY SO CAN THE LORD REMOVE THE EVILS IN THE INTERNAL MAN AND AT THE SAME TIME IN THE EXTERNAL

and that the four are one series and as it were make a single bundle. From this again it is evident that the internal, consisting of lusts, cannot be cast out except on the removal of the external, consisting of evils. Lusts produce evils by their enjoyments, and when evils are deemed allowable, as they are when will and understanding agree on it, the enjoyments and the evils make one. It is well known that assent is deed; this is also what the Lord said:

> If anyone looks on the woman of another to lust after her, he has already committed adultery with her in his heart (Mt 5:28). 111-1

The same is true of all other evils.

112. From this it may now be evident that for a person to be purified from the lusts of evil, evils must by all means be removed from the external man, for the lusts have no way out before. If no outlet exists, they remain within and breathe out enjoyments and so incite man to consent, thus to deed. Lusts enter the body by the external of thought; when there is consent, therefore, in the external of thought they are instantly in the body; the enjoyment felt is bodily. See in the treatise *Divine Love and Wisdom* (nn. 362-370) that the body, thus the whole man, is what the mind is. This can be illustrated by comparisons, and by examples.

[2] By comparisons: lusts with their enjoyments can be compared to a fire which blazes the more, the more it is nursed; the freer its way the more widely it spreads until in a city it consumes houses and in a woods the trees. In the Word, moreover, lusts are compared to fire, and the evils from them to a conflagration. The lusts of evil with their enjoyments also appear as fires in the spiritual world; hellfire is nothing else. Lusts may also be compared to floods and inundations as dikes or dams give way. They may also be likened to gangrene and abscesses which bring death to the body as they run their course or are not healed.

[3] By examples: it is obvious that when evils are not removed in the external man, the lusts with their enjoyments grow and flourish. The more he steals the more a thief lusts to steal until he cannot stop; so with a defrauder, the more he defrauds; it is the same with hatred and vengeance, luxury and intemperance, whoredom and blasphemy. It is notorious that the love of ruling from the love of self increases when left unbridled; so also the love of possessing things from love of the world; they seem to have no limit or end. Plain it is then that so far as evils are not removed in the external man, lusts for them intensify; also that in the degree that evils are given free rein, the lusts increase.

113. A person does not see the lusts of his evil; he sees their enjoyments, to be sure, but still he reflects little on them, for they divert thought and drive off reflection. Unless he learned from elsewhere that they are evils he would call them goods and give them expression freely according to his thought's reasoning; doing so, he appropriates them to himself. So far as he confirms them as allowable he enlarges the court of his ruling love, which is his life's love. Lusts constitute its court, being its ministers and retinue, as it were, by which it governs the exteriors of its realm. But such as is the king, such are the ministers and retinue, and such is the kingdom. If the king is diabolic, his ministers and the retinue are insanities, and the people of his realm are falsities of every kind. The ministers (who are called wise although they are insane) cause these falsities to appear as truths by reasonings from fallacies and by fantasies and cause them to be acknowledged as truths. Can such a state in a man be changed except by the evils being removed in the external man? Then the lusts which cling to the evils are also removed. Otherwise no outlet offers for the lusts; they are shut in like a besieged city or like an indurated ulcer.

114. (4) *Only with man's participation can evils in the external man be removed by the Lord.* In all Christian churches it is an accepted point of doctrine that before coming to the Holy Communion a person should examine himself, see and confess his sins, and do penitence, desisting from his sins and rejecting

## VI. IT IS A LAW OF DIVINE PROVIDENCE THAT MAN SHALL REMOVE EVILS AS SINS IN THE EXTERNAL MAN OF HIMSELF, AND ONLY SO CAN THE LORD REMOVE THE EVILS IN THE INTERNAL MAN AND AT THE SAME TIME IN THE EXTERNAL

them because they are from the devil; and that otherwise the sins are not forgiven him and he is damned. The English, despite the fact that they are in the doctrine of faith alone, nevertheless in the exhortation to the Holy Communion openly teach self-examination, acknowledgment, confession of sins, penitence and renewal of life, and warn those who do not do these things with the words that otherwise the devil will enter into them as he did into Judas, fill them with all iniquity, and destroy both body and soul. Germans, Swedes and Danes, who are also in the doctrine of faith alone, teach the same in the exhortation to the Holy Communion, also warning that otherwise the communicants will make themselves liable to infernal punishments and eternal damnation for mixing sacred and profane together. These words are read out by the priest in a deep voice to all who are about to observe the Holy Supper, and are listened to by them in full acknowledgment that they are true.

[2] Nevertheless, after hearing a sermon on the same day about faith alone and to the effect that the law does not condemn them because the Lord has fulfilled it for them, and that of themselves they cannot do any good which is not self-righteous and thus that one's works have nothing saving in them, only faith alone has, these same persons return home completely forgetting their earlier confession and rejecting it so far as they think along the lines of the sermon. But which is true, the latter or the former? Contrary to each other, both cannot be true. Which is? That there can be no forgiveness of sins, thus no salvation but only eternal damnation, apart from self-examination, the knowledge and acknowledgment, confession and breaking off of sins, that is, apart from repentance? Or that such things effect nothing towards salvation inasmuch as full satisfaction for all the sins of men has been made by the Lord through the passion of the cross for those who have faith, and that those in faith alone with trust that it is so and with confidence in the imputation of the Lord's merit, are sinless and appear before God like men with shining faces for having washed?

# Divine Providence

[3] It is plain from this that the religion common to all churches in Christendom is that one shall examine himself, see and acknowledge his sins and then desist from them, and that otherwise there is no salvation, but damnation. This, moreover, is divine truth itself, as is plain from passages in the Word in which man is bidden to do penitence, as from the following:

> John said, Do . . . fruits worthy of repentance . . . this moment the axe is at the root of the tree; every tree not giving good fruit will be cut down and cast into the fire (Lu 3:8, 9).
>
> Jesus said, Unless you do repentance, you shall all . . . perish (Lu 13:3,5).
>
> Jesus preached the gospel of the kingdom of God; . . . do repentance, and believe the gospel (Mk 1:14, 15).
>
> Jesus sent out the disciples who on going out were to preach that men should repent (Mk 6:12).
>
> Jesus told the apostles that they were to preach repentance and the remission of sins to all peoples (Lu 24:27).
>
> John preached the baptism of repentance for the remission of sins (Mk 1:4; Lu 3:3).

Think about this also with some degree of understanding; if you have religion, you will see that repentance of one's sins is the way to heaven, that faith apart from repentance is not faith, and that those in no faith for lack of repenting are in the way to hell.

115. Those in faith severed from charity who have confirmed themselves in it by Paul's saying to the Romans that a man is justified by faith without the works of the law (3:28) worship that saying quite like men who worship the sun. They become like those who fix their gaze steadily on the sun with the result that the blurred vision sees nothing in normal light. For they fail to see what is meant in the passage by "works of the law," namely, the rituals described by Moses in his books, called "law" in them everywhere, and not the precepts of the Decalog. Lest it be thought these are meant, Paul explains, saying at that point,

## VI. IT IS A LAW OF DIVINE PROVIDENCE THAT MAN SHALL REMOVE EVILS AS SINS IN THE EXTERNAL MAN OF HIMSELF, AND ONLY SO CAN THE LORD REMOVE THE EVILS IN THE INTERNAL MAN AND AT THE SAME TIME IN THE EXTERNAL

> Do we not then make the law void through faith? Far from it, rather we establish the law (verse 31 of the same chapter).

Those who have confirmed themselves by that saying in faith severed from charity, looking on it as on the sun, do not see the passages in which Paul lists the laws of faith and that these are the very works of charity. What indeed is faith without its laws? Nor do they see the passages in which he lists evil works, declaring that those who do them cannot enter heaven. What blindness has been brought about by this one passage badly understood!

116. Evils in the external man cannot be removed without man's cooperation for the reason that it is by divine providence that whatever a man hears, sees, thinks, wills, speaks and does shall seem to him to be his own doing. Apart from that appearance (as was shown above, nn. 71-95 ff.) there would be no reception of divine truth on man's part, nor determination to do what is good, nor any appropriation of love and wisdom or of charity and faith, hence no conjunction with the Lord, no reformation therefore or regeneration, and thus no salvation. Without that appearance, repentance for sins would clearly be impossible and in fact faith would; without that appearance, likewise, man is not man but is devoid of rational life like the beasts. Let him who will, consult his reason whether it appears otherwise than that man thinks from himself about good and truth, spiritual as well as moral and civil; then accept the doctrine that all good and truth are from the Lord and none from man. Must he not then acknowledge as a consequence that man is to do good and think truth of himself, yet always acknowledge that these are from the Lord? And acknowledge further that man is to remove evils of himself, but still acknowledge that he does so from the Lord?

117. Many are unaware that they are in evils since they do not do them outwardly, fearing the civil law and the loss of reputation. Thus by custom and habit they practice to avoid evils

as detrimental to their standing and interests. But if they do not shun evils on religious principle, because they are sins and against God, the lusts of evil with their enjoyments remain in them like impure waters stopped up or stagnant. Let them probe their thoughts and intentions and they will come on the lusts provided they know what sins are.

[2] Many such, who have confirmed themselves in faith separated from charity and who believe that the law does not condemn, pay no attention to sins. Some doubt there are sins, or if so, that they exist in God's sight, having been pardoned. Such also are natural moralists, who believe that civil and moral life with its prudence accomplishes all things and divine providence nothing. Such are those, also, who strive with great care after a reputation and a name for honesty and sincerity for the sake of standing and preferment. But those who are such and who at the same time have spurned religion become lustful spirits after death, appearing to themselves like men indeed, but to others at a distance like priapi; and they see in the dark and not at all in the light, like night-owls.

118. (5) *Proposition v, that a man ought to remove evils from the external man of himself*, is substantiated then. Further explanation may be seen in *Doctrine of Life for the New Jerusalem* under three propositions: 1. No one can flee evils as sins so as to be averse to them inwardly except by combats against them (nn. 92-100); 2. A man ought to shun evils as sins and fight against them as of himself (nn. 101-107); and 3. If he shuns evils for any other reason than that they are sins, he does not shun them, but only keeps them from appearing to the world.

119. (6) *The Lord then purifies man from the lusts of evil in the internal man and from the evils themselves in the external.* The Lord purifies man from the lusts of evil only when man as of himself removes the evils because He cannot do so before. For the evils are in the external man and the lusts in the internal man, and they cling together like roots and a trunk. Unless the evils are removed, therefore, no outlet offers; they block the way and shut the door, which the Lord can open only with a man's

## VI. IT IS A LAW OF DIVINE PROVIDENCE THAT MAN SHALL REMOVE EVILS AS SINS IN THE EXTERNAL MAN OF HIMSELF, AND ONLY SO CAN THE LORD REMOVE THE EVILS IN THE INTERNAL MAN AND AT THE SAME TIME IN THE EXTERNAL

participation, as was shown just above. When the man as of himself opens the door, the Lord then roots out the lusts.

[2] A second reason why the Lord cannot do so sooner is that He acts upon man's inmost and by that on all that follows even to outmosts where man himself is. While outmosts, therefore, are kept closed by man, no purification can take place, but only that activity of the Lord in interiors which is His activity in hell, of which the man who is in lusts and at the same time in evils is a form—an activity which is solely provision lest one thing destroy another and lest good and truth be violated. It is plain from words of the Lord in the Apocalypse that He constantly urges and prompts man to open the door to Him:

> Behold, I stand at the door, and knock; if anyone hears my voice and opens the door, I will come in to him, and sup with him, and he with Me (3:20).

120. Man knows nothing at all of the interior state of his mind or internal man, yet infinite things are there, not one of which comes to his knowledge. His internal of thought or internal man is his very spirit, and in it are things as infinite and innumerable as there are in his body, in fact, more numerous. For his spirit is man in its form, and all things in it correspond to all things of his body. Now, just as man knows nothing by any sensation about how his mind or soul operates on all things of the body as a whole or severally, so he does not know, either, how the Lord works on all things of his mind or soul, that is, of his spirit. The divine activity is unceasing; man has no part in it; still the Lord cannot purify a man from any lust of evil in his spirit or internal man as long as the man keeps the external closed. Man keeps his external closed by evils, each of which seems to him to be a single entity, although in each are infinite things. When a man removes what seems a single thing, the Lord removes infinite things in it. So much is implied in the Lord's purifying man from the lusts of evil in the internal man and from the evils themselves in the external.

## Divine Providence

121. Many believe that a person is purified from evils merely by believing what the church teaches; some, by doing good; others by knowing, speaking and teaching what is of the church; others by reading the Word and books of devotion; others by going to church, hearing sermons and especially by observing the Holy Supper; still others, by renouncing the world and devoting oneself to piety; others still by confessing oneself guilty of all sins; and so on. And yet none of these things purifies man at all unless he examines himself, sees his sins, acknowledges them, condemns himself on account of them, and repents by desisting from them, and does all this as of himself, yet with the acknowledgment in heart that he does so from the Lord.

[2] Until this is done, the things mentioned above do not avail, being either self-righteous or hypocritical. Such persons appear to the angels in heaven either like pretty courtesans smelling badly of their corruption, or like unsightly women painted to appear handsome, or like masked clowns and mimics in the theater, or like apes in men's clothes. But when evils have been removed, then all that has just been mentioned becomes the expression of love in such persons, and they appear as beautiful human beings to the sight of the angels in heaven and as partners and companions of theirs.

122. But it should be rightly known that in repenting a man ought to look to the Lord alone. He cannot be purified if he looks to God the Father alone, or to the Father for the sake of the Son, or to the Son as a man only. For there is one God and the Lord is He, for His Divine and Human is one Person, as we have shown in *Doctrine of the New Jerusalem about the Lord*. In order that the intending penitent may look to Him alone, the Lord instituted the Holy Supper, which confirms the remission of sins in those who repent, and does so because everyone is kept looking to the Lord alone in it.

123. (7) *The perpetual effort of the Lord in His divine providence is to conjoin man with Himself and Himself with man, in order to be able to bestow the felicities of eternal life on him, which can be done only so far as evils with their lusts have*

## VI. IT IS A LAW OF DIVINE PROVIDENCE THAT MAN SHALL REMOVE EVILS AS SINS IN THE EXTERNAL MAN OF HIMSELF, AND ONLY SO CAN THE LORD REMOVE THE EVILS IN THE INTERNAL MAN AND AT THE SAME TIME IN THE EXTERNAL

*been removed.* It was shown above (nn. 27-45) that it is the unceasing effort of the Lord in His divine providence to conjoin man to Himself and Himself to man; that this conjunction is what is called reformation and regeneration; and that by it man has salvation. Who does not see that conjunction with God is life eternal and salvation? Everyone sees this who believes that men by creation are images and likenesses of God (Ge 1:26, 27) and who knows what an image and likeness of God is. [2] What man of sound reason, thinking from his rationality and wanting to think in freedom, can believe that there are three Gods equal in essence and that divine being or essence can be divided? One can conceive and comprehend a Trine in the one God, however, just as soul, body and outgoing life in angel and man are comprehensible. As this Trine in One exists only in the Lord, conjunction must be with Him. Use your power of reason together with your liberty of thought, and you will see this truth in its own light; but admit first that God is, and heaven, and eternal life.

[3] As, then, God is one, and the human being was made by creation an image and likeness of Him, and inasmuch as by infernal love and its lusts and enjoyments man has come into a love of all evils and thus destroyed the image and likeness of God in him, it follows that it is the continuous effort of the Lord's divine providence to conjoin man to Himself and Himself to man and thus make him an image of Himself. It also follows that this is to the end that the Lord may be able to bestow on him the felicities of eternal life, for such is divine love.

[4] He cannot bestow them, however, nor make man an image of Himself, unless man removes sins in the external man as of himself, because the Lord is not only divine love but also divine wisdom, and divine love does nothing except by its divine wisdom and in consonance with it. It is according to divine wisdom that man cannot be conjoined to the Lord and thus reformed, regenerated and saved unless he is allowed to act in freedom according to reason, for so man is man. Whatever is

according to the Lord's divine wisdom is also of His divine providence.

124. To this let me append two arcana of angelic wisdom showing further what divine providence is like. One is that the Lord never acts on one thing by itself in man, but on all things at the same time, and the other is that He acts at once from inmosts and outmosts. He never acts on some one thing by itself but on all things together because all things in man are in such connection and from this in such form that they act not as a number but as one. We know that there is such connectedness and by it such organization in man's body. The human mind is in similar form as a result of the connection of all things, for the mind is the spiritual man and truly the man. Hence man's spirit or the mind in the body in its entire form is man. Consequently man is man after death equally as he was in the world with the sole difference that he has thrown off the clothing which made up his body in the world.

[2] As the human form, then, is such that all its parts form a community which acts as a whole, some one thing cannot be moved out of place or altered in state except with adaptation of the rest, for if it were, the form which acts as a whole would suffer. Hence it is plain that the Lord never acts on any one thing without acting on all. So He acts on the total angelic heaven since in His view it is like one man; so He acts on each angel, for each angel is heaven in least form; so He acts also on each man, most nearly on all things of man's mind and by these on all things of his body; for man's mind is his spirit and in the measure of conjunction with the Lord is an angel, and the body is obedience.

[3] It is to be well noted, however, that the Lord does act on each particular thing in man singly, singularly so, when acting on all things in man's organization; even so He does not alter the state of any part or of any one thing except suitably to the whole form. But more will be said of this in following numbers where we shall show that divine providence is general because it extends to particulars, and particular because it is general.

## VI. IT IS A LAW OF DIVINE PROVIDENCE THAT MAN SHALL REMOVE EVILS AS SINS IN THE EXTERNAL MAN OF HIMSELF, AND ONLY SO CAN THE LORD REMOVE THE EVILS IN THE INTERNAL MAN AND AT THE SAME TIME IN THE EXTERNAL

[4] The Lord acts from inmosts and outmosts at the same time because only in this way are all things held in connection, for the intermediate things depend one upon another from inmosts to outmosts and are assembled in outmosts (it was shown in Part III of the treatise *Divine Love and Wisdom* that all things from the inmost onward are present simultaneously in what is outmost ). For this reason the Lord from eternity or Jehovah came into the world and assumed and bore human nature in outmosts. He could thus be at once from firsts in lasts, and from firsts by lasts govern the whole world and so save whom He could save according to the laws of His divine providence, which are also the laws of His divine wisdom. For it is true, as Christendom knows, that no mortal could have been saved had the Lord not come into the world (see Doctrine for the New Jerusalem on Faith, n. 35). For the same reason the Lord is called "The First and the Last."

125. These angelic arcana have been premised in order that it may be comprehended how the Lord's divine providence operates to unite man to Him and Himself to man. It does not act upon a particular thing by itself in man, but on all things together and from man's inmost and outmosts simultaneously. Man's inmost is his life's love; the outmosts are in the external of thought; what is intermediate is in the internal of thought (what external and internal are like with the wicked was shown earlier); from which it is plain again that the Lord cannot act by inmosts and outmosts simultaneously except together with man, for in the outmosts man and the Lord are together. Wherefore, as the man acts in outmosts, which are in his determination, being within the range of his freedom, so the Lord acts from man's inmosts and in what follows from them to the outmosts. Man does not know at all what is in the inmosts and in what follows to the outmosts, therefore is unaware of how the Lord acts there or what He effects there. But as all these things cohere as one with the outmosts, man does not need to know more than that he should shun evils as sins and look to the Lord. Only so can his life's

love, which by birth is infernal, be removed by the Lord and a heavenly life's love be implanted in its place.

126. When a heavenly life's love has been implanted by the Lord in place of an infernal life's love, affections of good and truth are implanted in place of lusts of evil and falsity; enjoyments of affections of good are implanted instead of enjoyments of lusts of evil and falsity, and goods of heavenly love in place of evils of infernal love; prudence is implanted in place of cunning, wise thinking in place of malevolent. So a man is born again and becomes a new man. What goods replace evils you may see in *Doctrine of Life for the New Jerusalem*, nn. 67-73, 74-79, 80-86, 87-91; likewise that so far as man shuns and is averse to evils as sins so far he loves truths of wisdom, nn. 32-41, and has faith and is spiritual, nn. 42-52.

127. From the exhortations read aloud in all Christian churches before Holy Communion we showed that it is the common religion of all Christendom that a man should examine himself, see his sins, avow them, confess them before God, and desist from them; and that this is repentance, remission of sins and hence salvation. This is also evident from the Creed named after Athanasius and received throughout Christendom which concludes with the words:

> The Lord will come to judge the living and the dead; at whose coming those who have done good will enter into life eternal, and those who have done evil, into everlasting fire.

128. Who does not know from the Word that everyone is allotted a life after death according to his deeds? Open the Word, read it, and you will see this clearly, but the while remove the thoughts from faith and justification by faith alone. The few passages following are testimony that the Lord teaches so everywhere in His Word:

> Every tree which does not yield good fruit shall be cut down and cast into the fire. By their fruits therefore shall you know them (Mt 7:19, 20).
>
> Many will say to Me in that day, Lord . . . have we not prophesied in your name, . . . and in your name done many

## VI. IT IS A LAW OF DIVINE PROVIDENCE THAT MAN SHALL REMOVE EVILS AS SINS IN THE EXTERNAL MAN OF HIMSELF, AND ONLY SO CAN THE LORD REMOVE THE EVILS IN THE INTERNAL MAN AND AT THE SAME TIME IN THE EXTERNAL

mighty things? But I shall confess to them then, I know you not, depart from Me, you who work iniquity (Mt 7:22, 23).

Everyone who hears my words and does them I shall liken to a prudent man who built a house on a rock: . . . but everyone who hears my words but does not do them shall be likened to a foolish man who built his house on the ground without a foundation (Mt 7:24, 26; Lu 6:46-49).

[2] The Son of man will come in the glory of His Father .. . and render then to everyone according to his deeds (Mt 16:27).

The kingdom of God shall be taken away from you, and given to a people bringing forth its fruits (Mt 21:43).

Jesus said, These are My mother and brothers who hear the Word of God and do it (Lu 8:21).

Then shall you begin to stand . . . and knock at the door, saying, Lord, . . . open to us, but replying He will say to them, I know not whence you are; depart from Me, all you workers of iniquity (Lu 13:25-27).

Those who have done good shall go out into the resurrection of life, but those who have done evil into the resurrection of judgment (Jn 5:29).

[3] We know . . . that God does not hear sinners, but if a man worships God and does His will, him He hears (Jn 9:31).

If you know these things, blessed are you if you do them (13:17).

He who has My commandments and does them, he it is who loves Me, ... and I will love him, . . . and I will come to him, and make an abode with him (14:15, 21-24).

You are My friends, if you do whatsoever I command you... . I have chosen you . . . that you may bear fruit and that your fruit may remain (15:14, 16).

[4] The Lord said to John, Write to the angel of the Ephesian church, I know your works: . . . I have against you that you have left an earlier charity; . . . repent, and do the

former works; else . . . I shall remove your candlestick from its place (Apoc 2:1, 2, 4, 5).

To the angel of the church of the Smyrneans write, I know your works (2:8, 9).

To the angel of the church in Pergamos write, . . . I know your works, repent (2:12, 13, 16).

To the angel of the church in Thyatira write, . . . I know your works and charity, . . . and your later works are more than the first (2:18, 19).

To the angel of the church in Sardis write, . . . I know your works, that you have a name that you are alive, but you are dead; . . . I have not found your works perfect before God; . . . repent (3:1-3).

To the angel of the church in Philadelphia write, I know your works (3:7, 8).

To the angel of the church of the Laodiceans write, I know your works; . . . repent (3:14, 15, 19).

I heard a voice from heaven saying, Write, blessed are the dead who die in the Lord from now on; ... their works follow them (14:13).

A book was opened, which is the book of life, and the dead were judged, ... all according to their works (20:12, 13).

Lo, I come quickly, and My reward is with Me, to give to everyone according to his work (22:12).

These are passages in the New Testament;

[5] there are still more in the Old, from which I shall quote only this one:

Stand in the gate . . . of Jehovah, and proclaim this word there: Thus says Jehovah Zebaoth the God of Israel, Make your ways good, and your works; . . . put not your trust in lying words, saying, The temple, the temple, the temple of Jehovah is this. . . . Thieving and killing and committing adultery and swearing falsely . . . will you then come to stand before Me in this house which is called by My name and say, We are delivered? When you do those abominable things? Has not this house been made a den of robbers?

## VI. IT IS A LAW OF DIVINE PROVIDENCE THAT MAN SHALL REMOVE EVILS AS SINS IN THE EXTERNAL MAN OF HIMSELF, AND ONLY SO CAN THE LORD REMOVE THE EVILS IN THE INTERNAL MAN AND AT THE SAME TIME IN THE EXTERNAL

Even I, lo, I have seen it, is the word of Jehovah (Je 7:2-4, 9-11).

## VII. IT IS A LAW OF DIVINE PROVIDENCE THAT MAN SHALL NOT BE COMPELLED BY EXTERNAL MEANS TO THINK AND WILL, THUS TO BELIEVE AND LOVE WHAT PERTAINS TO RELIGION, BUT BRING HIMSELF AND AT TIMES COMPEL HIMSELF TO DO SO

129. This law of divine providence follows from the preceding two, namely: man is to act in freedom according to reason (nn. 71-99); and is to do this of himself and yet from the Lord, thus as of himself (nn. 100-128). Inasmuch as being compelled is not to act in freedom according to reason and also not to act of oneself, but to act from what is not freedom and from someone else, this law of divine providence follows in due order on the first two. Everyone knows that no one can be forced to think what he is unwilling to think or to will what he decides not to will, thus to believe what he does not believe, least of all what he wills not to believe, or to love what he does not love and still less what he wills not to love. For the spirit or mind of man enjoys complete freedom in thinking, willing, believing and loving. It does so by influx which is not coercive from the spiritual world (for the human spirit or mind is in that world); and not by influx from the natural world, received only when the two agree.

[2] A man can be driven to say that he thinks and wills, believes and loves what is religious, but if this is not a matter of his affection and reasoning or does not become so, he does not think, will, believe or love it. A man may also be compelled to speak in favor of religion and to act according to it, but he cannot

## VII. IT IS A LAW OF DIVINE PROVIDENCE THAT MAN SHALL NOT BE COMPELLED BY EXTERNAL MEANS TO THINK AND WILL, THUS TO BELIEVE AND LOVE WHAT PERTAINS TO RELIGION, BUT BRING HIMSELF AND AT TIMES COMPEL HIMSELF TO DO SO

be compelled to think in its favor from any faith or to will in its favor out of love for it. In countries in which justice and judgment are guarded, one is indeed compelled not to speak or act against religion, but still no one can be compelled to think and will in its favor. For everyone has freedom to think and to will along with, and in favor of, hell or along with, and in favor of, heaven. Reason, however, teaches what either course is like and what lot awaits it, and by reason the will has the choice and decision.

[3] Plainly, then, what is external cannot coerce what is internal; nevertheless it happens sometimes, but that it works harm will be shown in this order:

1. No one is reformed by miracles and signs, for they coerce.
2. No one is reformed by visions and communication with the dead, for they coerce.
3. No one is reformed by threats and penalties, as these coerce.
4. No one is reformed in states of no rationality or no freedom.
5. Self-compulsion is not contrary to rationality and freedom.
6. The external man is to be reformed through the internal, and not the other way about.

130. (1) *No one is reformed by miracles and signs, for they coerce.* We have shown above that man has an internal and an external of thought, and that the Lord acts into the external by the internal in man and so teaches and leads him; also that it is of the Lord's divine providence that man is to act in freedom according to reason. Either action would perish in man if miracles were done and he were driven by them to believe. That this is so can be seen rationally in this way: undeniably miracles induce belief and powerfully persuade a person that what the miracle-doer says and teaches is true, and at first this engages

man's external of thought, virtually holding it spellbound. But one is deprived by this of the two faculties called rationality and liberty, thus cannot act in freedom according to reason, nor can the Lord then inflow into the external of man's thought through the internal save only to leave man to confirm from his rationality what has been made a matter of his belief by the miracle.

[2] The state of man's thought is such that from the internal of thought he can see a piece in the external of his thought as in a mirror—for as was said above, one can behold one's own thought, which is possible only from more interior thought. Beholding the item as in a mirror he can turn it this way and that and shape it to look attractive to him. If there is truth in it, it may be likened to an attractive and animated maiden or youth. But if a man cannot turn it this way and that and shape it, but only believe it persuaded of it by a miracle, then if there is truth in it, it may be likened to a maiden or youth carved in stone or wood, in which is nothing alive. It may also be compared to an object which is constantly in view and looked at alone, keeps one from seeing what is to either side and behind it. It can also be compared to a continual sound in the ear, which does away with perceiving the harmony of many sounds. Such are the blindness and deafness induced on the mind by miracles. It is the same with anything confirmed but not regarded from rationality before it is confirmed.

131. Plain it is from this that a faith induced by miracles is not faith, but persuasion. For it has nothing rational in it, still less anything spiritual, as it is only external without an internal. This is true of everything a man does from such persuasive faith, whether he is acknowledging God, worshiping Him at home or in church, or doing good deeds. When only a miracle leads a person to acknowledgment of God and to adoration and piety, he acts from the natural and not the spiritual man. For a miracle infuses belief by an external and not an internal way, thus from the world and not from heaven. The Lord enters man by an internal way, by the Word and by doctrine and preaching from it. As miracles close this way, no miracles are done today.

## VII. IT IS A LAW OF DIVINE PROVIDENCE THAT MAN SHALL NOT BE COMPELLED BY EXTERNAL MEANS TO THINK AND WILL, THUS TO BELIEVE AND LOVE WHAT PERTAINS TO RELIGION, BUT BRING HIMSELF AND AT TIMES COMPEL HIMSELF TO DO SO

132. That miracles are of this nature can be clearly established from those performed in the presence of the people of Judah and Israel. Although they beheld many miracles in the land of Egypt and later at the Red Sea and others in the Wilderness and particularly on Mt. Sinai when the Law was promulgated, nevertheless, in a month's time while Moses tarried on that mountain, they made themselves a golden calf and hailed it as Jehovah who had led them out of the land of Egypt (Ex 32:4-6). Again, it is plain from the miracles done later in the land of Canaan; nevertheless the people fell away time and again from the prescribed worship. It is equally plain from the miracles which the Lord did before their eyes when He was in the world; yet they crucified Him.

[2] Miracles were done among the Jews and Israelites because they were altogether external men and had been brought into the land of Canaan merely to represent a church and its eternal verities by the externalities of worship—something a bad man as well as a good man can do. For the externals are rituals which with that people signified spiritual and celestial things. Indeed Aaron, although he made the golden calf and ordered worship of it (Ex 32:2-5, 35 ), could still represent the Lord and His work of salvation. As the people could not be brought by the internal things of worship to represent them, they were brought to do so by miracles—in fact, were driven and forced to it.

[3] They could not be led by internals of worship because they did not acknowledge the Lord although the entire Word which they had treats of Him alone. One who does not acknowledge the Lord cannot receive anything internal in worship. But miracles ceased after the Lord had manifested Himself and was received and acknowledged as eternal God in the churches.

133. The effect of miracles on the good and on the evil differs, however. The good do not desire miracles, but believe those in the Word. If they hear of some miracle, they regard it

only as a slight indication confirming their faith; for they draw their thought from the Word and thus from the Lord, and not from a miracle. It is different with the evil. They can be driven and compelled, of course, to belief, to worship, too, and to piety, but only for a little while. For their evils are enclosed, and the lusts of those evils and the enjoyments of the lusts continually press against the outward worship and piety; and in order that the evils may come out of their confinement and burst forth, the wicked ponder the miracle, finally call it ridiculous and a ruse or a natural phenomenon, and so return to their evils. One who returns to his evils after having worshiped profanes the truths and goods of worship, and the lot of profaners after death is the worst of all fates. They are meant by the Lord's words in Matthew (12:43-45) about those whose last state is worse than the first. Besides, if miracles were to be done for those who have no faith from the miracles in the Word, they would have to be done constantly and before their eyes. It may be plain from all this why miracles are not done at this day.

134. (2) No one is reformed by visions or by communication with the dead, for they coerce. Visions are of two kinds, divine and diabolic. Divine visions are effected by representations in heaven; diabolic by magic in hell. There are also phantasmal visions, which are illusions of an estranged mind. Divine visions, produced as we said by representative things in heaven, are such as the prophets had who at the time were not in the body but in the spirit, for visions cannot appear to anyone in bodily wakefulness. When these came to the prophets, therefore, it is remarked that they were "in the spirit," as is plain from the following:

> Ezekiel said, The Spirit picked me up and carried me to Chaldea to the captivity in a vision of God, in the spirit of God; so the vision rose over me which I saw (11:1, 24).
>
> Again that the Spirit bore him between earth and heaven and brought him to Jerusalem in visions of God (8:3, 4).
>
> He was likewise in visions of God or in the spirit when he saw four beasts which were cherubim (1 and 10).

## VII. IT IS A LAW OF DIVINE PROVIDENCE THAT MAN SHALL NOT BE COMPELLED BY EXTERNAL MEANS TO THINK AND WILL, THUS TO BELIEVE AND LOVE WHAT PERTAINS TO RELIGION, BUT BRING HIMSELF AND AT TIMES COMPEL HIMSELF TO DO SO

>So, too, when he saw a new temple and a new earth, and an angel measuring them (40-48).

That he was in "visions of God" then, he says at 40:2, 26, and that he was "in the spirit" at 43:5.

[2] Zechariah was in a similar state when he saw

>a horseman among myrtle trees (1:8 ff)

>four horns (1:18) and a man with a measuring line in his hand (2:1-3 ff)

>a candlestick and two olive trees (4:1 ff)

>a flying roll and an ephah (5:1, 6)

>four chariots coming out between two mountains, and horses (8:1 ff).

In a like state was Daniel when he saw

>four beasts coming up from the sea (7:1 ff)

>a combat between a ram and a he-goat (8:1 ff).

That he saw these things "in the vision of his spirit" is stated at 7:1, 2, 7, 13; 8:2; 10:1, 7, 8, and that the angel Gabriel was seen by him in a "vision" at 9:21.

[3] John was also in the vision of the spirit when he beheld what he has described in the Apocalypse, as when he saw

>seven candlesticks and the Son of man in the midst of them (1:12-16)

>a throne in heaven, and One sitting on the throne, and around it four beasts, which were cherubim (4)

>the book of life taken by the Lamb (5)

>horses coming out from the book (6)

>seven angels with trumpets (8)

>the pit of the abyss opened, and locusts coming out a dragon, and its battle with Michael (12)

two beasts, rising, one from the sea and the other from the land (13)

a woman seated on a scarlet beast (17)

Babylon destroyed (18)

a white horse, and One seated on it (19)

a new heaven and a new earth, and the holy Jerusalem descending from heaven (21)

the river of the water of life (22).

That he saw these "in the vision of the spirit" is said 1:10; 4:2; 5:1; 6:1; 21:1, 2.

[4] Such were the visions which appeared from heaven to the sight of the spirit of these men, but not to their bodily sight. Such visions do not occur at this day because if they did, they would not be understood inasmuch as they are produced by representations the details of which signify internal things of the church and arcana of heaven. Daniel also foretold (9:24) that they would cease when the Lord came into the world.

Diabolic visions, however, have occurred at times, incited by fanatical and visionary spirits who in their delirium called themselves the Holy Spirit. But those spirits have now been gathered together by the Lord and cast into a hell separate from the hells of others. There are also phantasmal visions which are merely the illusions of an estranged mind.

All this makes clear that no one can be reformed by any visions other than those in the Word.

134r. The fact that no one is reformed by communication with the dead is plain from the Lord's words about the rich man in hell and Lazarus in Abraham's bosom.

For the rich man said, I ask you, father Abraham, to send Lazarus to my father's house, for I have five brothers, to testify to them lest they also come into this place of torment. Abraham said to him, They have Moses and the prophets; let them hear them. But he said, No, father Abraham, but if some one will go to them from the dead, they will repent. He replied, If they do

## VII. IT IS A LAW OF DIVINE PROVIDENCE THAT MAN SHALL NOT BE COMPELLED BY EXTERNAL MEANS TO THINK AND WILL, THUS TO BELIEVE AND LOVE WHAT PERTAINS TO RELIGION, BUT BRING HIMSELF AND AT TIMES COMPEL HIMSELF TO DO SO

not hear Moses and the prophets, they will not be persuaded either if one should arise from the dead (Lu 16:27-31).

Communication with the dead would have the same result as miracles (of which just above), namely, that a man would be influenced and driven into worship for a short time. But as this deprives a man of rationality and at the same time shuts his evils in, as was said above, the captivation or the inward bond is undone, and the imprisoned evils break out, with blasphemy and profanation; this last occurs, however, only when spirits introduce something dogmatic from religion, which is never done by a good spirit, still less by an angel of heaven.

135. Nevertheless, speech with spirits—rarely with angels of heaven—is possible and has been granted to many for ages. When it is granted, spirits speak with a man in his native tongue and briefly. And those who speak with the Lord's permission never say anything that takes away the freedom of the reason, nor do they instruct, for the Lord alone teaches man, doing so by means of the Word to the man's enlightenment (of this in numbers to come). I have been given to know this in my own experience. I have spoken with spirits and angels for many years now. No spirit has dared and no angel has wished to tell me, still less to instruct me, about things in the Word or about any of its doctrine. The Lord alone has taught me, who revealed Himself to me and afterwards continued to appear to me as He does now, as the Sun in which He is, as He appears to the angels, and He has enlightened me.

136. (3) *No one is reformed by threats or penalties, as these coerce.* It is known that the external cannot compel the internal, but the internal can compel the external; also that the internal refuses to be coerced by the external and turns away. It is likewise known that external enjoyments entice the assent and love of the internal; and it may also be known that there is a forced internal and a free internal. But all this, though known, needs to be lighted up, for much on being heard is perceived at

once to be so, because it is truth and hence is affirmed, but if it is not confirmed by reasons, it can be weakened by arguments from fallacies and finally denied. What we have said is known, is therefore to be taken up afresh and established rationally.

[2] *First: The external cannot compel the internal, but the internal can compel the external.* Who can be forced to believe or love? One can no more be compelled to believe than he can be compelled to think that something is so when he thinks it is not so, or to love than to will something that he does not will; belief attaches to thought, and love to the will. The internal can be compelled, however, by what is external not to speak improperly against the laws of a kingdom, the morals of life or the sanctities of the church. The internal can be compelled to this by threats and penalties and is compelled and should be. But this is not the specifically human internal, but one which the human being shares with beasts; they can also be compelled. The human internal resides above this animal internal. Here the human internal which cannot be coerced is meant.

[3] *Second: The internal refuses to be coerced by the external and turns away.* The reason is that the internal wills to be in freedom and loves freedom. For, as was shown, freedom attaches to man's love and life. When the internal feels it is being subjected to compulsion, therefore, it withdraws as it were into itself, averts itself, and regards the compulsion as its enemy. For the love which makes man's life is irritated and causes him to think that he is then not himself and has no life of his own. The internal of the human being is of this nature by the law of the Lord's divine providence that he shall act from freedom in accord with reason.

[4] Plainly, then, it does harm to compel men to divine worship by threats and penalties. Some permit themselves to be forced to religion, some do not. Many who do are adherents of Catholicism; but this is the case with those in whom there is nothing internal in worship, but all is external. Among those who do not allow themselves to be coerced are many of the English nation, and as a result there is what is internal in their worship

## VII. IT IS A LAW OF DIVINE PROVIDENCE THAT MAN SHALL NOT BE COMPELLED BY EXTERNAL MEANS TO THINK AND WILL, THUS TO BELIEVE AND LOVE WHAT PERTAINS TO RELIGION, BUT BRING HIMSELF AND AT TIMES COMPEL HIMSELF TO DO SO

and what is external is from the internal. Their interiors in respect to religion appear in the light of the spiritual world like bright clouds, but those of the former like dark clouds. The one and the other appearance is to be seen in that world, and one who wishes may see it when he enters that world on death. Furthermore, enforced worship shuts one's evils in, which are hidden then like fire in wood under ashes which keeps stirring and spreading until it bursts into flame. But worship, not enforced but spontaneous, does not shut evils in; these are therefore like a fire that flares up and goes out. Thence it is plain that the internal refuses to be forced by the external and turns away. The internal can compel the external because it is like a master and the external like a servant.

[5] *Third: External enjoyments entice assent and love from the internal.* Enjoyments are of two kinds, of the understanding or of the will. Enjoyments of the understanding are also enjoyments of wisdom, and those of the will also enjoyments of love; for wisdom belongs to the understanding and love to the will. Enjoyments of the body or of the senses, which are external pleasures, act as one with the internal enjoyments, which are enjoyments of the understanding and the will. Therefore, just as the internal is so averse to compulsion by the external as to turn away, it looks so kindly on enjoyment in the external that it turns to it. Assent follows on the part of the understanding, and love on the part of the will.

[6] In the spiritual world all children are introduced by the Lord into angelic wisdom and through this into heavenly love by delightful and charming means, first by pretty things in the home and the charms of a garden; then by representations of spiritual things affecting the interiors of their minds with pleasure; and finally by truths of wisdom and goods of love. Thus they are steadily led by enjoyments in due order, first by the enjoyments of a love of the understanding and of its wisdom, and then by the enjoyments of the love of the will which is their life's love, to

which all else that has entered through enjoyment is kept subordinate.

[7] This is done because the will and understanding must all be formed by what is external before they are formed by what is internal, for they are formed first by what enters by the physical senses, chiefly the sight and the hearing; then when a first will and understanding have been formed, the internal of thought regards them as the externals of its thinking, and either joins itself to them or separates itself from them, as they are or are not enjoyable to it.

[8] It should be well understood, however, that the internal of the understanding does not unite itself to the internal of the will, but it is the latter that unites itself to the former and causes reciprocal union. This is done by the internal of the will, not at all by the internal of the understanding. Hence it is that man cannot be reformed by faith alone, but by the love of the will which makes a faith for itself.

[9] *Fourth: There is a forced internal and a free one.* A forced internal is found in those who are in external worship only and in none that is internal. Their internal consists of thinking and willing what the external is coerced to. Such are persons who worship living or dead men or idols, or who rest their faith on miracles. No internal is possible with them which is not at the same time external. And yet a forced internal is possible with persons in internal worship; it may be forced by fear or compelled by love. That forced by fear is found in those who worship for fear of the torment and fire of hell. This internal is not the internal of thought of which we have treated, however, but an external of thought called internal here because it partakes of thought. The internal of thought of which we have treated cannot be forced by any fear; it can be compelled by love and by fear of failing to love. In the true sense fear of God is nothing else. To be compelled by love and by the fear of failing in it is self-compulsion, and self-compulsion, it will be seen in what follows, is not contrary to freedom and rationality.

## VII. IT IS A LAW OF DIVINE PROVIDENCE THAT MAN SHALL NOT BE COMPELLED BY EXTERNAL MEANS TO THINK AND WILL, THUS TO BELIEVE AND LOVE WHAT PERTAINS TO RELIGION, BUT BRING HIMSELF AND AT TIMES COMPEL HIMSELF TO DO SO

137. It is plain then what forced worship and unforced worship are like. Forced worship is corporeal, inanimate, obscure and sad—corporeal because it is of the body and not of the mind; inanimate because it has no life in it; obscure for lack of understanding in it; and sad because it does not have the joy of heaven in it. But worship not forced and real is spiritual, living, seeing and joyful—spiritual, because spirit from the Lord is in it; living, because life from Him is in it; seeing because wisdom from Him is in it; and joyful because heaven from Him is in it.

138. (4) *No one is reformed in states of no liberty or rationality.* We showed above that only what a man does in freedom according to reason is made his. This is because freedom belongs to the will and reason to the understanding; acting in freedom in accord with reason a man acts from the will by the understanding and what is done in the union of the two is appropriated. Now, since the Lord wills that a man be reformed and regenerated in order that eternal life or the life of heaven may be his, and none can be reformed or regenerated unless good is appropriated to his will and truth to his understanding as if they were his, and only that can be appropriated which is done in freedom of the will and in accord with the reason of the understanding, no one is reformed in states of no freedom or rationality. There are many such states, but they may be summarized as states of fear, misfortune, mental illness, physical disease, ignorance, and intellectual blindness. Something will be said of each.

139. No one is reformed in a state of fear because fear takes away freedom and reason or liberty and rationality. Love opens the mind's interiors but fear closes them, and when they are closed man thinks little and only what comes to the lower mind or to the senses. All fears that assail the lower mind have this effect.

[2] We showed above that man has an internal and an external of thought. Fear can never invade the internal of thought; this is always in freedom, being in a man's life-love. But it can invade the external of thought. When it does, the internal of thought is closed and thereupon man can no longer act in freedom in accord with his reason, nor be reformed.

[3] The fear which invades the external of thought and closes the internal is chiefly fear of losing standing or profit. Fear of civil penalties or of outward ecclesiastical penalties does not close the internal, for the laws respecting them pronounce penalties only on those who speak and act contrary to the civil requirements of the kingdom and the spiritual of the church, but not on those who think contrary to them.

[4] Fear of infernal punishment invades the external of thought, to be sure, but only for some moments, hours or days; it is soon restored to its freedom by the internal of thought, which is man's spirit and life-love and is called thought of the heart.

[5] Fear of losing one's standing or wealth, however, does invade man's external of thought, and when it does, closes the internal of thought above to influx from heaven and makes it impossible for man to be reformed. This is because everyone's life-love from birth is love of self and the world, and self-love is at one with the love of position, and love of the world with the love of wealth. When a man has position or wealth, therefore, for fear of losing them he strengthens the means at hand—whether civil or churchly and in either case means to power—which serve him for position and wealth. The man who does not yet have standing or wealth but aspires to them, does the same, but for fear he will lose the reputation they give.

[6] It was said that this fear seizes on the external of thought and closes the internal above to heaven's inflowing. The internal is said to be closed when it makes one completely with the external, as it is then not in itself but in the external.

[7] But as the loves of self and the world are infernal loves and the fountain-heads of all evils, it is plain what the internal of

## VII. IT IS A LAW OF DIVINE PROVIDENCE THAT MAN SHALL NOT BE COMPELLED BY EXTERNAL MEANS TO THINK AND WILL, THUS TO BELIEVE AND LOVE WHAT PERTAINS TO RELIGION, BUT BRING HIMSELF AND AT TIMES COMPEL HIMSELF TO DO SO

thought in itself is like with men in whom those loves reign and are their life's loves, namely, that it is full of lusts of evils of every kind.

[8] This men do not know who fear loss of place and opulence and are strongly persuaded of their special religion, most particularly if this promises that they may be worshiped as holy and also as governors of hell; they can blaze, as it were, with zeal for the salvation of souls and yet this is from infernal fire. As this fear especially takes away rationality itself and liberty itself, which have a heavenly origin, plainly it makes against the possibility that a man may be reformed.

140. No one is reformed in a state of misfortune if he thinks about God and implores help only then, for it is a coerced state; wherefore, on coming into a free state he returns to his former state when he thought little if at all about God. It is different with those who feared God in a state of freedom previously. For by "fearing God" is meant fearing to offend Him, and by "offending Him" to sin, and this comes not from fear but from love. Does not one who loves another fear to hurt him? And the more he loves him, the more he fears hurting him? Lacking this fear, love is insipid and superficial, of the mind only and not of the will. By states of misfortune states of despair in danger are meant, in battles, for example, duels, shipwreck, falls, fires, threatening or unexpected loss of property, also of office or standing, and similar mishaps. To think about God only then is not to think from God but from self. For then the mind is as it were imprisoned in the body, so is not in freedom nor possessed then of rationality, and without these reformation is impossible.

141. No one is reformed in a state of mental illness because such illness takes away rationality and thus the liberty of acting in accord with reason. The whole mind is sick and not sane; the sane mind is rational, but not a sick one. Such disorders are melancholy, a spurious or a false conscience, fantasies of different kinds, mental grief over misfortune, anxiety and

anguish of the mind over a bodily defect. Sometimes these are regarded as temptations, but they are not. Genuine temptations have spiritual objects in view and in them the mind is wise, but these states are concerned with natural objects and in them the mind is disordered.

142. No one is reformed in a state of bodily sickness because his reason is not then in a state of freedom; the state of the mind depends on that of the body. When the body is sick, the mind is also, if for no other reason because it is withdrawn from the world. Withdrawn from the world it thinks indeed about God but not from Him, for it is not possessed of freedom of the reason. Man has this freedom in being midway between heaven and the world, thus can think from heaven and from the world, likewise from heaven about the world and from the world about heaven. So when he is ill and thinks about death and the state of his soul after death, he is not in the world but is withdrawn in spirit. In this state by itself no one can be reformed, but he can be strengthened in it if he was reforming before he fell ill.

[2] It is similar with those who renounce the world and all occupation in it and give themselves only to thoughts about God, heaven and salvation; on this further elsewhere. If those of whom we were speaking have not been reformed before their illness, then if they die they become such as they were before their illness. It is vain, therefore, to suppose that one can repent or receive some faith in illness; for no deed accompanies the repentance, and there is no charity in the faith; each is oral only and not at all from the heart.

143. No one is reformed in a state of ignorance, for all reformation is by truths and a life according to them. Therefore those who do not know truths cannot be reformed, but if they long for them with affection for them, after they die they undergo reformation in the spiritual world.

144. Nor can one be reformed in a state of blindness of the understanding. These also have no knowledge of truths or consequently of life, for the understanding must teach truths and the will must do them; when the will does what the

## VII. IT IS A LAW OF DIVINE PROVIDENCE THAT MAN SHALL NOT BE COMPELLED BY EXTERNAL MEANS TO THINK AND WILL, THUS TO BELIEVE AND LOVE WHAT PERTAINS TO RELIGION, BUT BRING HIMSELF AND AT TIMES COMPEL HIMSELF TO DO SO

understanding teaches, a man has life in accord with truths. When the understanding is blind, however, the will also is indifferent and acts in freedom according to one's reason only to do the evil confirmed in the understanding, and the confirmation is falsity. Besides ignorance, a religion which teaches a blind faith also blinds the understanding; so does a false doctrine. For just as truths open the understanding, falsities close it. They close it above and open it below, and opened only below, the understanding cannot see truths but only confirm what a man wills, falsity especially. The understanding is also blinded by lusts of evil. As long as the will is in these, it moves the understanding to confirm them, and so far as they are confirmed, the will cannot be in affections of good, from these see truths, and so be reformed.

[2] Take, for instance, one who is in the lust of adultery: his will, which is in the enjoyment of his love, moves his understanding to confirm it, saying, "What is adultery? Is there any evil in it? Does not the like occur between husband and wife? Cannot offspring be born of it, too? Cannot a woman receive more than one without harm? How does anything spiritual enter into this?" So thinks the understanding which is then the courtesan of the will. So stupid is it made by debauchery with the will that it is unable to see that marital love is spiritual and heavenly love itself, a reflection of the love between the Lord and the church from which it is derived; is in itself sacred and chastity itself, purity and innocence; causes men to be forms of love, since partners can love each other from inmosts and so form themselves into loves; nor can it see that adultery destroys this form and with it the Lord's image; and what is abhorrent, that the adulterer mingles his life with that of the husband in the wife, for a man's life is in the seed.

[3] Because this is profane, hell is called adultery, and heaven on the other hand is called marriage. Furthermore, the love of adultery communicates with the lowest hell, but true marital love with the inmost heaven; the reproductive organs of both sexes

also correspond to societies of the inmost heaven. These things are adduced so that it may be known how blinded the understanding is when the will is in the lust of evil, and that no one can be reformed in a state of blindness of the understanding.

145. (5) *Self-compulsion is not contrary to rationality and liberty.* We have shown that man has an internal and an external of thought; that they are distinguishable as prior and subsequent or higher and lower; and that being so distinct they can act separately and also jointly. They act separately when a man speaks and acts from the external of his thought otherwise than he thinks and wills inwardly; they act jointly when he speaks and acts as he thinks and wills. The latter is common with the sincere, the former with the insincere.

[2] Inasmuch as the internal and the external of the mind are so distinct, the internal can even fight with the external and by combat drive it to compliance. Conflict arises when the man deems evils to be sins and resolves to desist from them. When he desists, a door is opened and the lusts of evil which have occupied the internal of thought are cast out by the Lord and affections of good are implanted in their place. This occurs in the internal of thought. But the enjoyments of evil lust which occupy the external of thought cannot be cast out at the same time; conflict arises therefore between the internal and the external of thought. The internal wants to cast out those enjoyments because they are enjoyments of evil and do not agree with the affections of good in which the internal now is, and wants to introduce in their place enjoyments of good which do agree. These are what are called goods of charity. From the disagreement comes the conflict which, if it grows severe, is called temptation.

[3] Now as man is man by virtue of the internal of his thought, for this is his very spirit, obviously he compels himself when he compels the external of his thought to comply or to receive the enjoyments of his affections or the goods of charity. Plainly this is not contrary to rationality and liberty but in accord with them; rationality starts the combat and liberty follows it up;

## VII. IT IS A LAW OF DIVINE PROVIDENCE THAT MAN SHALL NOT BE COMPELLED BY EXTERNAL MEANS TO THINK AND WILL, THUS TO BELIEVE AND LOVE WHAT PERTAINS TO RELIGION, BUT BRING HIMSELF AND AT TIMES COMPEL HIMSELF TO DO SO

liberty itself resides with rationality in the internal man and from that in the external.

[4] Accordingly, when the internal conquers, which it does when it has reduced the external to compliance and obedience, man is given liberty itself and rationality itself by the Lord, for he is delivered by the Lord then from infernal freedom which in itself is enslavement, is brought into heavenly freedom which is freedom in itself, and is given association with angels. The Lord Himself teaches ( John 8:31-36) that those who are in sins are enslaved and that He delivers those who receive truth from Him through the Word.

146. Let an example serve for illustration. A man who has taken pleasure in defrauding and deceiving sees and inwardly acknowledges it to be sin and resolves to desist from it; with this a battle begins of his internal with the external. The internal man is in an affection for honesty, but the external still in the enjoyment of defrauding. This enjoyment, utterly opposed to enjoyment in honesty, does not give way unless forced to do so and can be forced to do so only by combat with it. When the fight is won, the external man comes into the enjoyment of a love of honesty, which is charity. Then the pleasure of defrauding gradually turns unpleasant to him. It is the same with all other sins, with adultery and whoredom, revenge and hatred, blasphemy and lying. The most difficult battle of all is with the love of ruling from self-love. A person who subdues this love, easily subdues all other evil loves, for this is their summit.

147. Let it be told briefly how the Lord casts out lusts of evil occupying the internal man from birth and in their place bestows affections of good when a man on his part removes the evils as sins. It was shown earlier that man possesses a natural, a spiritual and a celestial mind, that he is only in the natural mind as long as he is in lusts of evil and their enjoyments, and that during this time the spiritual mind is closed. But as soon as a man on self-examination confesses evils to be sins against God because they

are contrary to divine laws and accordingly resolves to desist from them, the Lord opens the spiritual mind, enters the natural by affections of truth and good, enters the reason, and by the reason puts into order what is disordered below in the natural. It is this that strikes the man as a battle, and strikes those who have indulged much in enjoyments of evil as temptation, for when the order of its thinking is inverted the lower mind suffers pain.

Inasmuch as the battle is against what is in the man himself and what he feels to be his, and no one can fight against himself except from a more interior self and from freedom in it, it follows that the internal man fights against the external and does so from freedom, and compels the external to obey. This, then, is compelling oneself, and, clearly, it is not contrary to liberty and rationality, but in accord with them.

148. Everyone desires to be free, moreover, and to be rid of the unfree or servitude. The boy under a master wishes to be his own master and thus free; so every man-servant under his master or maid under her mistress. Every girl wishes to leave the paternal home and marry, to do freely in a home of her own; and every boy who desires to work, enter business, or hold some position wishes to be released from his subordination to others and to be at his own disposal. All of these who serve willingly in order to be free compel themselves, and in doing so act from freedom according to reason but from an inner freedom, by which outward freedom is regarded as servant. We add this to confirm the fact that self-compulsion is not contrary to rationality and liberty.

149. One reason why man does not wish in like manner to come out of spiritual servitude into spiritual freedom is that he does not know what either is; he does not have the truths to teach this, and without them spiritual servitude is believed to be freedom and spiritual freedom to be servitude. A second reason is that the religion of Christendom has closed the understanding, and "faith alone" has sealed it shut. Each has built an iron wall around itself in the dogma that theological matters transcend and cannot be approached by the reason, but are for the blind and not

## VII. IT IS A LAW OF DIVINE PROVIDENCE THAT MAN SHALL NOT BE COMPELLED BY EXTERNAL MEANS TO THINK AND WILL, THUS TO BELIEVE AND LOVE WHAT PERTAINS TO RELIGION, BUT BRING HIMSELF AND AT TIMES COMPEL HIMSELF TO DO SO

the seeing. So truths that would teach what spiritual liberty is have been hidden. A third reason is that few examine themselves and see their sins, and one who does not see and quit them is in the freedom that sins have, which is infernal freedom, in itself enslavement. To view heavenly freedom, which is genuine freedom, from that freedom is like trying to see daylight in pitch darkness or sunshine from under a black cloud. So it happens that it is not known what heavenly freedom is, or that the difference between it and infernal freedom is like the difference between what is living and what is dead.

150. (6) *The external man is to be reformed by the internal, and not the other way about.* By internal and external man the same is meant as by external and internal of thought, of which frequently before. The external must be reformed by the internal because the internal flows into the external and not the reverse. The learned world knows that what is spiritual flows into what is natural and not the reverse, for reason dictates it; the church knows that the internal man must first be cleansed and made new and the external by it then, because the Lord teaches it. He does so in the words:

> Woe to you . . . hypocrites, for you make the outside of the cup and platter clean, but the inside is full of extortion and excess. Blind Pharisee, cleanse first the inside of the cup and platter that the outside may also be made clean (Mt 23:25, 26).

We have shown in a number of places in the treatise *Divine Love and Wisdom* that reason dictates this. For what the Lord teaches He grants man to see rationally. This a man does in two ways: in one, he sees in himself that something is so upon hearing it; in the other, he grasps it by reasons for it. Seeing in oneself takes place in the internal man, and understanding through reasoning in the external man. Who does not perceive it within himself when he hears that the internal man is to be purified first and the external by it? But one who does not receive the general idea of this by influx from heaven may go astray when he consults the external of this thought; from it alone no one sees but that outward works of charity and piety are saving apart from the internal. It is so in other things, as that sight and hearing flow into thought, and smell and taste into perception, that is, that the external flows into the internal, when the contrary is true. The appearance that what is seen and heard flows into the thought is a fallacy, for the understanding does the seeing in the eye and the hearing in the ear, and not the other way about. So it is in all else.

(Footnote: 111-1 The Greek is simply "on a woman" and does not have the word here rendered "of another." Though Swedenborg quotes the verse several times in his works he seems not to have checked as he usually did beyond the rendering of the Schmidius Latin Bible which he used.)

151. But something should be said here on how the internal man is reformed and by it the external. The internal man is not reformed solely by knowing, understanding and being wise, consequently not by thinking only; but by willing what these teach. When a person knows, understands and has the wisdom to see that heaven and hell exist and that all evil is from hell and all good from heaven, and if he then does not will evil because it is from hell but good because it is from heaven, he has taken the first step in reformation and is on the threshold from hell to heaven. When he advances farther and resolves to desist from evils, he is at the second step in reformation and is out of hell but not yet in heaven; this he beholds above him. There must be this internal for man to be reformed, but he is not reformed unless the external is reformed as well as the internal. The external is reformed by the internal when the external desists from the evils which the internal sets its will against because they are infernal, and still further reformed when the external shuns and fights against the evils. Thus the internal provides the will, the external the deed. For unless a man does the deed he wills, inwardly he does not will it, and finally he wills not to do it.

## VII. IT IS A LAW OF DIVINE PROVIDENCE THAT MAN SHALL NOT BE COMPELLED BY EXTERNAL MEANS TO THINK AND WILL, THUS TO BELIEVE AND LOVE WHAT PERTAINS TO RELIGION, BUT BRING HIMSELF AND AT TIMES COMPEL HIMSELF TO DO SO

[2] One can see from these few considerations how the external man is reformed by the internal. This is also meant by the Lord's words to Peter:

> Jesus said, If I do not wash you, you have no part with Me. Peter said to Him, not my feet only but my hands and head. Jesus said to him, he who has been washed has no need except to have his feet washed, and is entirely clean (Jn 13:8-10).

By "washing" spiritual washing is meant, which is purification from evils; by "washing head and hands" purifying the internal man is meant, and by "washing the feet" purifying the external. That when the internal man has been purified, the external must be, is meant by this: "He who has been washed has no need except to have his feet washed." That all purification from evils is the Lord's doing, is meant by this, "If I do not wash you, you have no part with Me." We have shown in many places in *Arcana Caelestia* that with the Jews washing represented purification from evils, that this is signified by "washing" in the Word, and that purification of the natural or external man is signified by the "washing of feet."

152. Since man has an internal and an external and each must be reformed for the man to be reformed, and since no one can be reformed unless he examines himself, sees and admits his evils, and then quits them, not only the external is to be examined, but the internal as well. If a man examines only the external he sees only what he has committed to deed, and that he has not murdered or committed adultery or stolen or borne false witness, and so on. He examines bodily evils and not those in his spirit; yet evils of the spirit are to be examined if one is to be capable of reformation. Man lives as a spirit after death and all the evils in his spirit persist. The spirit is examined only when a man attends to his thoughts, above all to his intentions, for these are thoughts from the will. There the evils exist at their source and roots, that is, in their lusts and enjoyments. Unless they are seen and acknowledged, a man is still in evils though he may not have

committed them outwardly. That to think with intention is to will and do, is plain from the Lord's words:

> If any one has looked on another's woman to lust after her, he has already committed adultery with her in his heart (Mt 5:28). 152-1

Such self-examination is of the internal man, and from it the external man is truly examined.

153. I have often marveled that although all Christendom knows that evils must be shunned as sins and otherwise are not forgiven, and that if they are not forgiven there is no salvation, yet scarcely one person among thousands understands this. Inquiry was made about this in the spiritual world, and it was found to be so. Anyone in Christendom knows it from the exhortations, read out to those who attend the Holy Supper, in which it is publicly stated; and yet when asked whether they know it, they reply that they do not know it and have not known it. The reason is that they have paid no attention to it, and most say they have thought only about faith and salvation by faith alone. I have also marveled that "faith alone" has closed their eyes so that those who have confirmed themselves in it do not see anything in the Word when they read it about love, charity and works. It is as though they spread "faith" all over the Word, as red lead is spread over writing so that nothing underneath shows; if anything does show, it is absorbed by faith and declared to be faith.

## VIII. IT IS A LAW OF DIVINE PROVIDENCE THAT MAN SHALL BE LED AND TAUGHT BY THE LORD OUT OF HEAVEN BY MEANS OF THE WORD AND DOCTRINE AND PREACHING FROM IT, AND THIS TO ALL APPEARANCE AS OF HIMSELF

154. The appearance is that man is led and taught by himself; in reality he is led and taught by the Lord alone. Those who confirm the appearance in themselves and not the reality at the same time are unable to remove evils from themselves as sins, but those who confirm the appearance and at the same time the reality can do so; for evils are removed as sins apparently by the man, but really by the Lord. The latter can be reformed, but the former cannot.

[2] All who confirm the appearance in themselves and not the reality also, are idolaters inwardly, for they are worshipers of self and the world. If they have no religion they become worshipers of nature and thus atheists; if they have some religion they become worshipers of men and of images. Such are meant now in the first commandment of the Decalog under those who worship other gods. Those, however, who confirm in themselves the appearance and also the reality become worshipers of the Lord, for He raises them out of what is their own, in which the appearance is, conducts them into the light in which the reality is and which is the reality, and gives them to perceive inwardly that they are not led and taught by themselves but by Him.

[3] The rational capacity of the two may seem much the same to many, but it differs. In those who are at once in the appearance and the reality, it is a spiritual reasoning ability, but

in those in the appearance but not at the same time in the reality it is a natural reasoning ability; this can be likened to a garden in winter light, and the spiritual reasoning capacity to a garden in springtime light. But If these things more in what follows, in this order:

i. Man is led and taught by the Lord alone. ii. He is led and taught by the Lord alone through and from the angelic heaven. iii. He is led by the Lord through influx and taught through enlightenment. iv. Man is taught by the Lord through the Word and doctrine and preaching from it, thus immediately by Him alone. v. Man is led and taught in externals by the Lord to all appearance as of himself.

155. (1) *Man is led and taught by the Lord alone.* This flows as a general consequence from all that was demonstrated in the treatise *Divine Love and Wisdom*; from what was said in Part I about the Lord's divine love and wisdom; in Part II about the sun of the spiritual world and the sun of the natural world; in Part III about degrees; in Part IV about the creation of the universe; and in Part V about the creation of the human being.

156. Man is led and taught by the Lord alone in that he lives from the Lord alone; for his life's will is led, and his life's understanding is taught. But this is contrary to the appearance, for it seems to man that he lives of himself, and yet the truth is that he lives from the Lord and not from himself. Man cannot, however, be given a sense-perception of this while he is in the world (the appearance that he lives of himself is not taken away, for without it man is not man). This must be established by reasons, therefore, which are then to be confirmed from experience and finally from the Word.

157. That the human being has life from the Lord alone and not of himself is established by these considerations:

1. There is an only essence, substance and form from which all the essences, substances, and forms exist that have been created.

## VIII. IT IS A LAW OF DIVINE PROVIDENCE THAT MAN SHALL BE LED AND TAUGHT BY THE LORD OUT OF HEAVEN BY MEANS OF THE WORD AND DOCTRINE AND PREACHING FROM IT, AND THIS TO ALL APPEARANCE AS OF HIMSELF

2. The one essence, substance and form is divine love and wisdom from which is all that is referable to love and wisdom in man.
3. It is also good itself and truth itself to which all things are referable.
4. Likewise it is life, from which is the life of all and all things of life.
5. Again the only One and very Self is omnipresent, omniscient and omnipotent.
6. This only One and very Self is the Lord-from-eternity or Jehovah.

[2] 1. *There is an only essence, substance and form from which all the essences, substances, and forms exist that have been created.* This was demonstrated in the treatise *Divine Love and Wisdom* (nn.44-46). In Part II it was shown that the sun of the angelic heaven, which is from the Lord and in which He is, is the one sole substance and form from which all that has been created exists, also that nothing can exist or come into existence except from it. In Part III it was shown that all things arise from that sun by derivations according to degrees.

[3] Who does not perceive by the reason and acknowledge that there is some one essence from which is all essence, or one being from which is all being? What can exist apart from being, and what can being be from which is all other being except being itself? Being itself is also unique and is being in itself. Since this is so (and anyone perceives and acknowledges it by reason, or if not, can do so), what else follows than that this Being, the Divine itself, Jehovah, is all in all in what is or comes to be?

[4] It is the same if we say there is an only substance from which all things are, and as there is no substance without form there is a single form from which all things are. We have shown in the treatise mentioned above that the sun of the angelic heaven

is that substance and form, also shown how that essence, substance and form is varied in things created.

[5] (b) *The one essence, substance and form is divine love and wisdom from which is all that is referable to love and wisdom in man.* This also was fully demonstrated in the treatise *Divine Love and Wisdom.* Whatever appears to live in man is referable to will and understanding in him; any-one can perceive by the reason and acknowledge that these two constitute his life. What else is "This I will," or "This I understand," or "I love this," or "I think this"? And as man wills what he loves, and thinks what he understands, all things of the will relate to love and those of the understanding to wisdom. As no one has love or wisdom from himself but only from Him who is love itself and wisdom itself, they are from the Lord-from-eternity or Jehovah. If they were not, man would be love itself and wisdom itself, thus God-from-eternity, at which the human reason itself is horrified. Can anything exist except from a prior self? Or the prior self exist except from one prior to it? And finally from a first or from underived being?

[6] (c). *It is also good itself and truth itself, to which all things are referable.* Everyone possessed of reason agrees and acknowledges that God is good itself and truth itself, likewise that all good and truth are from Him, therefore that any good and truth can come only from good itself and truth itself. All this is acknowledged by every rational person when he first hears it. When it is said, then, that everything of the will and understanding, of love and wisdom, or of affection and thought in a man who is led by the Lord relates to good and truth, it follows that all that such a man wills and understands or loves and has for his wisdom, or is affected by and thinks, is from the Lord. Hence anyone in the church knows that whatever good and truth a man has in himself is not good and truth except as it is from the Lord. Since this is true, all that such a man wills and thinks is from the Lord. It will be seen in following numbers that an evil man can will and think from no other source.

## VIII. IT IS A LAW OF DIVINE PROVIDENCE THAT MAN SHALL BE LED AND TAUGHT BY THE LORD OUT OF HEAVEN BY MEANS OF THE WORD AND DOCTRINE AND PREACHING FROM IT, AND THIS TO ALL APPEARANCE AS OF HIMSELF

[7] (d). *The one essence, substance and form is likewise life, from which is the life of all and all things of life.* This we have shown in many places in the treatise *Divine Love and Wisdom*. At the first hearing the human reason also agrees and acknowledges that all man's life is that of the will and understanding, for if these are taken away he ceases to live, or what is the same, that all his life is one of love and thought, for if these are taken away he does not live. Inasmuch as all of the will and understanding or all of love and thought in man is from the Lord, all of his life, as we said above, is from Him.

[8] (e) *This only One and very Self is omnipresent, omniscient and omnipotent.* This also every Christian acknowledges from his doctrine and every gentile from his religion. In consequence, wherever he is, a man thinks that God is there and that he prays to God at hand; thinking and praying so, men cannot but think that God is everywhere, that is, omnipresent; likewise omniscient and omnipotent. Everyone praying to God, therefore, implores Him from the heart to lead him because He can lead him; thus he acknowledges the divine omnipresence, omniscience and omnipotence, doing so in turning his face to the Lord; thereupon the truth flows in from the Lord.

[9] (f) This only One and very Self is the Lord-from-eternity or Jehovah. In *Doctrine of the New Jerusalem about the Lord* it was shown that God is one in essence and in person and that He is the Lord, and that the Divine itself, called Jehovah Father, is the Lord-from-eternity; that the Divine Human is the Son conceived by His Divine from eternity and born in the world; and that the proceeding Divine is the Holy Spirit. He is called "very Self" and "only One" because, as was said, the Lord-from-eternity or Jehovah is life itself, being love itself and wisdom itself or good itself and truth itself, from which are all things. That the Lord created all things from Himself and not from nothing may be seen in the treatise *Divine Love and Wisdom* nn. 282-284, 349-357. So the truth that the human being is led and taught by the Lord alone is established by reasons.

158. This same truth is established in angels not only by reasons but also by living perceptions, especially with angels of the third heaven. They perceive the influx of divine love and wisdom from the Lord. Perceiving it and in their wisdom aware that love and wisdom are life, they declare that they live from the Lord and not of themselves, and not only say so but love and will it so. Yet they are in the full appearance that they live of themselves, yes, more strongly in the appearance than other angels. For as was shown above (nn. 42-45) the more nearly one is united with the Lord, the more distinctly does he seem to himself to be his own, and the more plainly is he aware that he is the Lord's. For many years now it has been granted me to be in a similar simultaneous perception and appearance, and I am fully convinced that I will and think nothing from myself but that it only appears to be from myself; it has also been granted to love and will it so. The same truth may be established by much else from the spiritual world, but these two references must suffice now.

159. It is plain from the following passages in the Word that life is the Lord's alone.

> I am the resurrection and the life; he who believes in Me, though he die, shall live (Jn 11:25).

> I am the way and the truth and the life (Jn 14:6).

> The Word was God . . . and in Him was life; and the life was the light of men (Jn 1:1, 4).

"The Word" in this passage is the Lord.

> As the Father has life in Himself, so has he given the Son to have life in Himself (Jn 5:26).

From the following it is clear that man is led and taught by the Lord alone:

> Without Me you can do nothing (Jn 15:5).

> A man cannot receive anything unless it is given him from heaven (Jn 3:27).

> A man cannot make one hair white or black (Mt 5:36).

## VIII. IT IS A LAW OF DIVINE PROVIDENCE THAT MAN SHALL BE LED AND TAUGHT BY THE LORD OUT OF HEAVEN BY MEANS OF THE WORD AND DOCTRINE AND PREACHING FROM IT, AND THIS TO ALL APPEARANCE AS OF HIMSELF

By "hair" in the Word the least of all is signified.

160. It will be shown in what follows in an article of its own that the life of the wicked has the same source; now this will merely be illustrated by a comparison. Heat and light flow in from the sun of the world alike to trees bearing bad fruit and to trees bearing good fruit, and they are alike quickened and grow. The forms into which the heat flows make the difference, not the heat in itself. It is the same with light, which is turned into various colors according to the forms into which it flows. The colors are beautiful and gay or ugly and sombre, and yet it is the same light. It is so with the influx of spiritual heat which in itself is love, and with spiritual light which in itself is wisdom, from the sun of the spiritual world. The forms into which they flow cause diversity, but not in itself that heat which is love or that light which is wisdom. The forms into which these flow are human minds. It is clear from these considerations that man is led and taught by the Lord alone.

161. What the life of animals is, however, was shown above (nn. 74, 96), namely that it is a life of merely natural affection with its attendant knowledge, and a mediated life corresponding to the life of human beings in the spiritual world.

162. (2) *Man is led and taught by the Lord alone through the angelic heaven and from it.* We say "through" the angelic heaven and from it, but that He does so "through" the angelic heaven is the apparent fact, while "from it" is the reality. The Lord seems to lead and teach through the angelic heaven because He appears above that heaven as a sun, but the reality is that He does so from heaven because He is in heaven as the soul is in man. For the Lord is omnipresent and not in space, as was shown above. Therefore distance is an appearance according to conjunction with Him, and the conjunction is according to the reception of love and wisdom from Him. Since no one can be conjoined to the Lord as He exists in Himself He appears to angels at a distance as a sun; nevertheless He is in the angelic heaven as the

soul is in man. He is similarly in every society of heaven and in every angel, for man's soul is not only the soul of man as a whole but also of every part of him.

[2] It is according to the appearance that the Lord governs all heaven and through it the world from the sun which is from Him and in which He is (about the sun see Part II of the treatise *Divine Love and Wisdom*), and everyone is allowed to speak according to the appearance, cannot, in fact, do otherwise. Everyone who is not in wisdom itself is also allowed to think that the Lord rules each and all things from His sun and rules the world through the angelic heaven. Angels of the lower heavens think from the appearance, but those of the higher heavens speak indeed in keeping with the appearance but think from the reality, namely, that the Lord rules the universe from the angelic heaven, that is, from Himself.

[3] One can illustrate by the sun of the world that simple and wise speak alike but do not think alike. All speak from the appearance that the sun rises and sets. Despite speaking so the wise think it stands still, which is again the reality, as the other is the appearance. The same thing can be illustrated from appearances in the spiritual world, for space and distance appear there but are dissimilarities of affections and of resulting thoughts. The same is true of the Lord's appearing in His sun.

163. We shall say briefly how the Lord leads and teaches everyone from the angelic heaven. In the treatise *Divine Love and Wisdom* and above in the present treatise, also in the work *Heaven and Hell*, published in London in the year 1758, it has been made known from things seen and heard that the angelic heaven appears before the Lord as one man, and each society of heaven likewise, and it is from this that each angel or spirit is a human being in complete form. It was also shown in the treatises mentioned that heaven is not heaven from anything belonging to the angels but from their reception of divine love and wisdom from the Lord. Hence it may be evident that the Lord rules the whole angelic heaven as one man, and since heaven is itself man, it is the very image and likeness of the Lord and the Lord rules it

## VIII. IT IS A LAW OF DIVINE PROVIDENCE THAT MAN SHALL BE LED AND TAUGHT BY THE LORD OUT OF HEAVEN BY MEANS OF THE WORD AND DOCTRINE AND PREACHING FROM IT, AND THIS TO ALL APPEARANCE AS OF HIMSELF

as the soul rules its body. Since all mankind is ruled by the Lord, it is ruled by the Lord not through heaven, but from heaven, consequently by Him, for He is heaven, as we have said.

164. This is an arcanum of angelic wisdom, however, and therefore cannot be comprehended by man unless his spiritual mind has been opened; for such a man, who is united with the Lord, is an angel. From what has preceded he can comprehend the following:

1. Men as well as angels are in the Lord and the Lord in them according to their conjunction with Him, or, what is the same, according to their reception of love and wisdom from Him.
2. Each of them has a place allotted to him in the Lord, thus in heaven, according to the nature of the conjunction or the reception of Him.
3. Each in his place has a state of his own distinct from that of others and draws his portion from what is had in common according to his situation, function and need, quite as each part does in the human body.
4. Everyone is brought into his place by the Lord according to his life.
5. Every human being is introduced from infancy into this divine man whose soul and life is the Lord, and within it and not outside of it is led and taught from His divine love according to His divine wisdom; but as a man is not deprived of freedom, he can be led and taught only in the measure of his receptiveness as of himself.
6. Those who are receptive are conducted to their places through an infinite maze by winding paths, much as the chyle is carried through the mesentery and the lacteal vessels there to its cistern, and from this into the blood by the thoracic duct, and so to its place.

7. Those who are not receptive are parted from those within the divine man, as excrement and urine are removed from man.

These are arcana of angelic wisdom which man can comprehend to some extent; there are many more which he cannot.

165. (3) *Man is led by the Lord through influx and taught through enlightenment.* Man is led through influx by the Lord because "being led" and "flowing in" are spoken of love and the will; and he is taught by the Lord through enlightenment because "being taught" and "enlightened" are spoken of wisdom and the understanding. It is known that every person is led by himself from his own love and according to it by others, and not by his understanding. He is led by his understanding and according to it only as his love or his will prompts the understanding, and then it can be said that his understanding is led also. Even then the understanding is not led, but the will which prompts it.

The term "influx" is used because it is commonly said that the soul flows into the body; influx is spiritual and not physical, as we showed above, and man's soul or life is his love or will. For another reason, influx is comparatively like the flow of the blood into the heart and from the heart into the lungs. We showed in the treatise *Divine Love and Wisdom* that the heart corresponds to the will and the lungs correspond to the understanding, and that the conjunction of the will with the understanding is like the flowing of the blood from the heart to the lungs.

166. Man is taught, however, through enlightenment; being taught and being enlightened are said of the understanding. For the understanding or man's internal sight is enlightened by spiritual light quite as the eye or man's external sight is by natural light. The two are also taught similarly; the internal sight, however, which is that of the understanding, by spiritual objects, and the external sight or the sight of the eye by natural objects. There is spiritual light and natural light, one like the other in outward appearance, but dissimilar in internal appearance. For natural light comes from the sun of the natural world and so is in

## VIII. IT IS A LAW OF DIVINE PROVIDENCE THAT MAN SHALL BE LED AND TAUGHT BY THE LORD OUT OF HEAVEN BY MEANS OF THE WORD AND DOCTRINE AND PREACHING FROM IT, AND THIS TO ALL APPEARANCE AS OF HIMSELF

itself dead, but spiritual light, which is from the sun of the spiritual world, is in itself living. This light, not nature's, enlightens the human intellect. Natural and rational light comes from it and not from nature's light, and is here called natural and rational because it is spiritual-natural.

[2] There are three degrees of light in the spiritual world: celestial, spiritual and spiritual-natural. Celestial light is a flaming, ruddy light and is the light of those who are in the third heaven; spiritual light is a gleaming white light and is the light of those in the middle heaven; and spiritual-natural light is like daylight in our world. This is the light of those who are in the lowest heaven and of those in the world of spirits, which is intermediate between heaven and hell; with the good in that world it is like the light of summer on earth and with the evil like winter's light.

It should be known, however, that light in the spiritual world has nothing in common with light in the natural world; they are as different as what is living and what is lifeless. It is plain, then, from what has been said that it is spiritual light and not the natural light before our eyes that enlightens the understanding. Man does not know this, not having known anything hitherto about spiritual light. In the work *Heaven and Hell* we have shown (nn. 126-140) that spiritual light has its origin in divine wisdom and truth.

167. Having spoken about the light of heaven, we should say something about the light of hell. This also is of three degrees. The light in the lowest hell is like that from fiery coals; in the middle hell like that from the flame of a hearth; and in the highest hell like that from candles and to some like moonlight at night. All this is spiritual light and not natural, for all natural light is dead and extinguishes the understanding. As has been shown, those in hell possess the faculty of understanding called rationality; rationality itself comes from spiritual light and not from natural light. The spiritual light which they have in

rationality is turned, however, into infernal light, as the light of day is into the dark of night.

[2] Nevertheless, all those in the spiritual world, whether in the heavens or the hells, see in their own light as clearly as man sees in his by day. This is because everyone's eyesight is formed to receive the light in which it finds itself. Thus the eyesight of the angels of heaven is formed to receive the light in which they see, and the sight of the spirits of hell is formed to receive their light; this is comparatively like that of birds of night and bats, which see objects at night and in the evening as clearly as other birds see them by day, for their eyes are formed to receive their light.

[3] The difference between the one light and the other appears very clearly, however, to those who look from one to the other. When, for instance, an angel of heaven looks into hell he sees only thick darkness, and when a spirit of hell looks into heaven he sees only thick darkness there. For heavenly wisdom is like thick darkness to those in hell; in turn, infernal insanity is like thick darkness to those in heaven. It is plain from all this that such as a man's understanding is, such is the light he has, and that after death everyone comes into his own light, for he sees in no other. In the spiritual world, moreover, where all are spiritual even to the body, the eyes of all are formed to see by their own light. Everyone's life-love fashions an understanding for itself and thus a light, also, for love is like the fire of life and from this comes the light of life.

168. As few know anything about the enlightenment in which the understanding of a man is who is taught by the Lord, something will be said of it. There is inner and outer enlightenment from the Lord, and inner and outer enlightenment from oneself. Inner enlightenment from the Lord consists in man's perceiving on first hearing something whether it is true or not; outer enlightenment consists in thought from this. Inner enlightenment from oneself is simply from confirmation and outer enlightenment merely from information. We will say something of each.

## VIII. IT IS A LAW OF DIVINE PROVIDENCE THAT MAN SHALL BE LED AND TAUGHT BY THE LORD OUT OF HEAVEN BY MEANS OF THE WORD AND DOCTRINE AND PREACHING FROM IT, AND THIS TO ALL APPEARANCE AS OF HIMSELF

[2] By inner enlightenment from the Lord a rational person perceives about many things the moment he hears them whether they are true or not; for example, that love is the life of faith or that faith lives by love. By interior enlightenment a person also perceives that a man wills what he loves and does what he wills, consequently that to love is to do; again, that a man wills and does whatever he believes from love, and therefore to have faith is also to do; and that the impious man cannot have love for God or faith then in Him. By inner enlightenment a rational man also perceives the following truths at once on hearing them: God is one; He is omnipresent; all good is from Him; all things have relation to good and truth; all good is from good itself and all truth from truth itself. A man perceives these and other similar truths inwardly in himself on hearing them and does so because he possesses a rationality which is in heaven's enlightening light.

[3] Outer enlightenment is enlightenment of one's thought from this inner enlightenment. One's thought is in this enlightenment so far as it remains in the perception it has from inner enlightenment and so far as it possesses knowledge of good and truth, for it gets from this knowledge reasons confirming it. Thought from outer enlightenment sees a matter on both sides; on the one, it sees reasons which confirm it, and on the other, the appearances that weaken it; it dispels these and assembles the reasons.

[4] Inner enlightenment from oneself, however, is quite different. By it one regards a matter on one side only, and having confirmed it sees it in light apparently like that just spoken of, but it is a wintry light. For example, a judge who judges unjustly in view of gifts or gain, once he has confirmed the judgment by law and reason sees in it nothing but justice. Some judges see the injustice but not wanting to see it, they keep it out of sight and blind themselves and so do not see. The same is true of a judge who renders judgments out of friendship, or to gain favor, or on account of relationship.

[5] Such persons act in the same way in anything they have from a man in authority or from the mouth of a celebrity or have hatched from self-intelligence; they are blind reasoners, for they see from the falsities which they confirm; falsity closes the sight, just as truth opens it. They do not see any truth in the light of truth nor justice from a love for it but from the light of confirmation, which is an illusory light. They appear in the spiritual world like headless faces or like faces resembling human faces on wooden heads, and are called reasoning animals for rationality is potential in them. Those have outer enlightenment from themselves who think and speak solely from information impressed on the memory; of themselves they can hardly confirm anything.

169. Such are the differences in enlightenment and consequently in perception and thought. There is actual enlightenment by spiritual light, but it is not manifest to one in the natural world because natural light has nothing in common with spiritual light. This enlightenment has sometimes been manifested to me in the spiritual world, however, visible in those enlightened by the Lord as a luminosity around the head, aglow with the color of the human face. With those in enlightenment from themselves the luminosity was not around the head but around the mouth and over the chin.

170. Besides these kinds of enlightenment there is another in which it is revealed to one in what faith, intelligence and wisdom he is; he perceives this in himself, such is the revelation. He is admitted into a society where there is genuine faith and true intelligence and wisdom. There his interior rationality is opened, from which he sees the nature of his own faith, intelligence and wisdom, even to avowing it. I have seen some as they returned and heard them confessing that they had no faith although in the world they had believed they had much faith and markedly more than others; they said the same of their intelligence and wisdom. Some were in faith alone and in no charity, and some in self-intelligence.

## VIII. IT IS A LAW OF DIVINE PROVIDENCE THAT MAN SHALL BE LED AND TAUGHT BY THE LORD OUT OF HEAVEN BY MEANS OF THE WORD AND DOCTRINE AND PREACHING FROM IT, AND THIS TO ALL APPEARANCE AS OF HIMSELF

171. (4) *Man is taught by the Lord through the Word and doctrine and preaching from it, thus immediately by the Lord alone.* We said and showed above that man is led and taught by the Lord alone, and from heaven but not through heaven or any angel there. As it is by the Lord alone, it is done immediately and not mediately. How this takes place will be told now.

172. It was shown in Doctrine of the New Jerusalem about the Sacred Scripture that the Lord is the Word and that all the doctrine of the church is to be drawn from the Word. Inasmuch as the Lord is the Word the man who is taught from the Word is taught by the Lord alone. This is comprehended with difficulty and will be clarified in this order:

1. The Lord is the Word because the Word is from Him and about Him.
2. Also because the Word is divine truth together with divine good.
3. To be taught from the Word is to be taught from Him, therefore.
4. That this is done mediately through preaching does not take away its immediacy.

[2] *First: The Lord is the Word because it is from Him and about Him.* No one in the church denies that the Word is from the Lord, but that it is about Him alone, while not denied, is not known. This was shown in *Doctrine of the New Jerusalem about the Lord*, nn. 1-7, 37-44, and in Doctrine of the New Jerusalem about the Sacred Scripture, nn. 62-69, 80-90, 98-100. Inasmuch as the Word is from the Lord alone and treats of Him alone, a man is taught by the Lord when he is taught from the Word, for it is the divine Word. Who can communicate what is divine and implant it in the heart except the Divine Himself from whom it is and of whom it treats? Therefore, in speaking of His union with His disciples He says that they are to abide in Him and His words in them (Jn 15:7), that His words are spirit and life (Jn 6:63), and that He makes His abode with those who keep His

Divine Providence

words (Jn 14:20-24). To think from the Lord therefore is to think from the Word, and as it were, through the Word. It was shown in Doctrine of the New Jerusalem about the Sacred Scripture from beginning to end that all things of the Word have communication with heaven, and as the Lord is heaven, this means that all things of the Word have communication with the Lord Himself. The angels of heaven indeed have communication; this, too, is from the Lord.

[3] *Second: The Lord is the Word because it is divine truth together with divine good.* The Lord teaches that He is the Word by these words in John:

> In the beginning was the Word, and the Word was with God, and the Word was God . . . and the Word was made flesh and dwelt among us (1:1, 14).

This passage has been understood hitherto to mean only that God teaches men through the Word and has been explained as an hyperbole, with the implication that the Lord is not the Word itself. This is because expositors did not know that the Word is divine truth together with divine good or, what is the same, divine wisdom together with divine love. That these are the Lord Himself was shown in the treatise *Divine Love and Wisdom*, Part I, and that they are the Word in Doctrine of the New Jerusalem about the Sacred Scripture, nn. 1-86.

[4] We will say briefly in what way the Lord is divine truth together with divine good. Each human being is human not because of face and body but from the good of his love and the truths of his wisdom; and because a man is a man from these, he is also his own good and his own truth or his own love and his own wisdom; without these he is not a human being. But the Lord is good itself and truth itself or, what is the same, love itself and wisdom itself; and these are the Word which in the beginning was with God and was God and which was made flesh.

[5] *Third: To be taught from the Word, then, is to be taught by the Lord Himself.* For it means that one is taught from good itself and truth itself or from love itself and wisdom itself, and,

## VIII. IT IS A LAW OF DIVINE PROVIDENCE THAT MAN SHALL BE LED AND TAUGHT BY THE LORD OUT OF HEAVEN BY MEANS OF THE WORD AND DOCTRINE AND PREACHING FROM IT, AND THIS TO ALL APPEARANCE AS OF HIMSELF

as we have said, these are the Word. But everyone is taught according to an understanding agreeing with his love; what goes beyond this does not remain. All who are taught by the Lord in the Word are instructed in a few truths while in the world but in many when they become angels. For the interiors of the Word, which are divine spiritual and divine celestial, are implanted at the time, but are not consciously possessed until a man on his death is in heaven where he is in angelic wisdom which, compared with human wisdom, thus his earlier wisdom, is ineffable. That divine spiritual and divine celestial things which constitute angelic wisdom are present in each and all things of the Word see Doctrine of the New Jerusalem about the Sacred Scripture, nn. 5-26.

[6] *Fourth: That this teaching is done mediately through preaching does not take away the immediacy.* Inevitably the Word is taught mediately by parents, teachers, preachers, books and particularly by reading. Still it is not taught by them but by the Lord through them. Preachers, aware of this, say that they speak not from themselves but from the spirit of God and that all truth like all good is from God. They can speak it and bring it to the understanding of many, but not to anyone's heart; and what is not in the heart passes away from the understanding; by "heart" a man's love is meant. From this it is plain that man is led and taught by the Lord alone and immediately by Him when he is taught from the Word. This is a supreme arcanum of angelic wisdom.

173. We have shown in *Doctrine of the New Jerusalem about the Sacred Scripture* (nn. 104-113) that those outside the church who do not have the Word still have light by means of it. Man has light by means of the Word and from the light has understanding, and both the wicked and the good have understanding. It follows that from light in its origin there is light in its derivatives which are perceptions and thoughts on whatever subject. The Lord says that without Him men can do nothing (Jn 15:5); that a man can receive nothing unless it is

given him from heaven (Jn 3:27); and that the Father in the heavens makes His sun to rise on the evil and the good, and sends rain on the just and on the unjust (Mt 5:45). In the Word in its spiritual sense by "sun" here, as elsewhere, is meant the divine good of divine love and by "rain" the divine truth of divine wisdom. These are extended to the evil and the good, to the unjust and the just, for if they were not, no one would possess perception and thought. It was shown above that there is only one Life from which all have life. But perception and thought are part of life; they are therefore from the same fountain from which life springs. It has been shown many times before that all the light which forms the understanding is from the sun of the spiritual world, which is the Lord.

174. (5) *Man is led and taught in externals by the Lord to all appearance as of himself.* This is so of man's externals, but not inwardly. No one knows how the Lord leads and teaches man inwardly, just as no one knows how the soul operates so that the eye sees, the ear hears, the tongue and mouth speak, the heart circulates the blood, the lungs breathe, the stomach digests, the liver and the pancreas distribute, the kidneys secrete, and much else. These processes do not come to man's perception or sensation. The same is true of what the Lord does in the infinitely more numerous interior substances and forms of the mind. The Lord's activity in these is not apparent to man, but many of the effects are, as well as some of the causes producing the effects. It is in the externals that man and the Lord are together, and as the externals make one with the internals, cohering as they do in one series, no disposition can be made by the Lord except in keeping with the disposition made in the externals with man's participation.

[2] Everyone knows that man thinks, wills, speaks and acts to all appearance as of himself, and everyone can see that without this appearance man would have no will and understanding, thus no affection and thought, also no reception of any good and truth from the Lord. It follows that without this appearance there would be no rational conception of God, no charity and no faith, consequently no reformation and regeneration, and therefore no

## VIII. IT IS A LAW OF DIVINE PROVIDENCE THAT MAN SHALL BE LED AND TAUGHT BY THE LORD OUT OF HEAVEN BY MEANS OF THE WORD AND DOCTRINE AND PREACHING FROM IT, AND THIS TO ALL APPEARANCE AS OF HIMSELF

salvation. Plainly, this appearance is granted to man by the Lord for the sake of all these uses and particularly that he may have the power to receive and reciprocate so that the Lord may be united to him and he to the Lord, and that through this conjunction the human being may live forever. This is "appearance" as it is meant here.

## IX. IT IS A LAW OF DIVINE PROVIDENCE THAT MAN SHALL NOT PERCEIVE OR FEEL ANY OF THE ACTIVITY OF DIVINE PROVIDENCE, AND YET SHOULD KNOW AND ACKNOWLEDGE PROVIDENCE

175. The natural man who does not believe in divine providence thinks to himself, "What can divine providence be when the wicked are promoted to honors and gain wealth more than the good, and many such things go better with those who do not believe in divine providence than with the good who believe in it? Indeed, infidels and the impious can inflict injuries, loss, misfortune and sometimes death on the believing and pious, doing so, too, by cunning and malice." He thinks therefore, "Do I not see in full daylight, as it were, in actual experience that crafty schemes prevail over fidelity and justice if only a man can make them seem trustworthy and just by a clever artfulness? What is left except necessities, consequences and the fortuitous in which there is no semblance of divine providence? Does not nature have its necessities, and are not consequences causes arising from natural or civil order, while the fortuitous comes, does it not, from unknown causes or from none?" So the natural man thinks to himself who attributes all things to nature and nothing to God, for one who ascribes nothing to God ascribes nothing to divine providence either; God and divine providence make one.

[2] But the spiritual man speaks and thinks within himself quite otherwise. Although he does not perceive the course of divine providence by any thought or feel it from any sight of it, he still knows and acknowledges providence. Inasmuch as the appearances and resulting fallacies just mentioned have blinded the understanding, and this can receive sight only when the

## IX. IT IS A LAW OF DIVINE PROVIDENCE THAT MAN SHALL NOT PERCEIVE OR FEEL ANY OF THE ACTIVITY OF DIVINE PROVIDENCE, AND YET SHOULD KNOW AND ACKNOWLEDGE PROVIDENCE

fallacies which have induced the blindness and the falsities which have induced the darkness are dispelled, and since this can be done only by truths which have the power to dispel falsities, these truths are to be disclosed, and for distinctness let it be in this order:

1. If man perceived or felt the activity of divine providence he would not act in freedom according to reason, nor would anything appear to be his own doing. It would be the same if he foreknew events.
2. If man saw divine providence plainly, he would inject himself into the order and tenor of its course, and pervert and destroy them.
3. If man beheld divine providence plainly he would either deny God or make himself god.
4. Man can see divine providence on the back and not in the face; also in a spiritual, not a natural state.

176. (1) *If man perceived or felt the activity of divine providence he would not act in freedom according to reason, nor would anything appear to be his own doing.* It would be the same if he foreknew events. In given articles we made evident to the understanding that it is a law of providence that man should act in freedom according to reason; also that all which a man wills, thinks, speaks and does shall seem to be his own doing; that without this appearance a man would have nothing of his own nor be his own man. He would thus have no selfhood and nothing could be imputed to him, and in that case whether he did good or evil would not matter, and whether he believed in God or was under the persuasion of hell would be immaterial; in a word, he would not be a human being.

[2] We have now to show that man would have no liberty to act according to reason and there would be no appearance of self-activity if he perceived or felt the activity of divine providence, for if he did he would also be led by it. The Lord leads all men by His divine providence and man only seemingly

leads himself, as was shown above. If, therefore, man had a lively perception or sense of being led, he would not be conscious of living life and would be moved to make sounds and act much like a graven image. If he were still conscious of living he would be led like one bound in manacles and fetters or like a yoked animal. Who does not see that man would have no freedom then? And without freedom he would be without reason, for one thinks from and in freedom; whatever he does not so think seems to him to be not from himself but from someone else. Indeed if you consider this interiorly you will perceive that he would not possess thought, still less reason, and hence would not be a human being.

177. The Lord's divine providence is constantly seeking to withdraw man from evils. If a man perceived or felt this constant activity and yet was not led like one bound, would he not struggle against it continually and then either quarrel with God or mingle himself in divine providence? If he did the latter he would also make himself God; if he did the former he would free himself from constraint and deny God. Manifestly two forces would constantly be acting then against each other, the force of evil from man and the force of good from the Lord. When two opposites act against each other, one of them conquers or they both perish. In this instance if one conquers they both perish. For the evil, which is man's, does not let in good from the Lord in a moment, nor does good from the Lord cast out evil from man in a moment; if either was done in a moment no life would be left to man. These and many other harmful results would follow if man manifestly perceived or felt the operation of divine providence. This will be demonstrated clearly by examples in what follows.

178. Man is not given a foreknowledge of events for the same reason, namely, that he may be able to act in freedom according to reason. It is well known that man wants what he loves effected, and he guides himself to this end by reasoning. It is also known that what a man meditates in his reason comes from his love of giving it effect through thought. If, then, he knew the effect or the eventuality by divine prediction, his reason would

## IX. IT IS A LAW OF DIVINE PROVIDENCE THAT MAN SHALL NOT PERCEIVE OR FEEL ANY OF THE ACTIVITY OF DIVINE PROVIDENCE, AND YET SHOULD KNOW AND ACKNOWLEDGE PROVIDENCE

become inactive and with it his love; for love along with reasoning ends with the effect, to begin anew. It is reason's very enjoyment to envision with love the effect in thought, not after it is attained but before it is, not in the present but as future. So man has what is called hope, which rises and declines in the reason as he beholds or awaits the event. The enjoyment is fulfilled in the event and then is forgotten along with thought about the event. The same thing would occur with an event that was foreknown.

[2] The human mind dwells always in the trine called end, cause and effect. If one of these is lacking, the mind is not possessed of its life. An affection of the will is the initiating end; the thought of the understanding is the efficient cause; and bodily action, utterance or external sensation is the effect from the end by means of the thought. Anyone sees that the human mind is not possessed of its life when it is only in an affection of the will and in naught besides, or when it is only in an effect. The mind has no life from one of these separately, therefore, but from the three together. The life of the mind would diminish and depart if an event were foretold.

179. As a foreknowledge of future events takes away humanness itself, which is action in freedom in accord with one's reason, no one is given to know the future; but everyone is allowed to form conclusions by the reason about the future; the reason is then fully in its own life. Accordingly man does not know his lot after death or know any event until he is on it. For if he knew, he would no longer think from his inner self how he should act or live so as to meet it, but would think only from his exterior self that he was meeting it. This state closes the interiors of his mind where the two faculties of his life, liberty and reason, especially reside. A desire to know the future is born with most persons but has its origin in a love of evil. It is taken away, therefore, from those who believe in divine providence; and trust that the Lord disposes their lot is given them. Therefore they do not desire to know it beforehand lest they inject themselves in

some way into divine providence. The Lord teaches this in many sayings in Luke (12:14-48).

[2] Much from the world of the spirit can confirm that this is a law of divine providence. On entering that world after death most persons desire to know their lot. The answer they receive is that if they have lived well their lot is in heaven and if wickedly it is in hell. But as all, including the wicked, fear hell they ask what they should do and believe to get into heaven. They are answered that they are to do and believe as they will, but know that one does not do good or believe truth in hell, only in heaven. "As you can, seek what is good and true, thinking truth and doing good." Everyone is thus left to act in freedom according to reason in the spiritual world as he is in the natural world; but as one has acted in this world he acts in that, for everyone's life remains to him and so his lot awaits him, for this is his life's lot.

180. (2) *If man saw divine providence plainly he would inject himself into the order and tenor of its course and pervert and destroy them.* To bring this distinctly to the perception of the rational man and also of the natural man, it will be illustrated by examples in this order:

1. External things are so connected with internal things that they make one in all that is done.
2. The human being joins the Lord only in some external things and if he did in internal things also, he would pervert and destroy the whole order and tenor of the course of divine providence.

As we said, these points will be illustrated by examples.

[2] *First: External things are so connected with internal things that they make one in all that is done.* Let this be illustrated by examples from several things in man's body. Everywhere in it are things external and internal. The external are called skins, membranes and coverings; the internal are forms variously composed and woven of nerve fibres and blood vessels. The covering over these enters into them by extensions from itself even to the inmost, so that the external or the

## IX. IT IS A LAW OF DIVINE PROVIDENCE THAT MAN SHALL NOT PERCEIVE OR FEEL ANY OF THE ACTIVITY OF DIVINE PROVIDENCE, AND YET SHOULD KNOW AND ACKNOWLEDGE PROVIDENCE

covering unites with the internals or the organic forms of fibres and vessels. It follows that the internals act and are acted on as the external acts or is acted on. For they are all constantly bound up together.

[3] Take such a common covering in the body as the pleura, for example, which covers the chest cavity and the heart and lungs. Examine it in an anatomical view, or if you do not know anatomy consult anatomists, and you will learn that this general covering by various circumvolutions and finer and finer extensions from itself enters into the inmost parts of the lungs, even into the smallest bronchial branches and into the sacs themselves which are the beginnings of the lungs, not to mention its subsequent progress by the trachea into the larynx and toward the tongue. From this it is plain that there is a constant connection of the outmost with inmosts; the interiors from the inmosts on therefore act and are acted upon as the external acts or is acted on. For this reason when that outmost covering, the pleura, is congested, inflamed or ulcerated, the lungs labor from their inmost parts; if the disease grows worse, all action of the lungs ceases and the man dies.

[4] The same is true everywhere else in the body. For instance it is true of the peritoneum, the general covering of all the abdominal viscera, also of the coverings on such organs severally as the stomach, liver, pancreas, spleen, intestines, mesentery, kidneys, and the organs of generation in both sexes. Choose any one of these viscera, examine it yourself or consult those skilled in the science, and you will see or hear. Take the liver, for example; you will find there is a connection between the peritoneum and that organ and by its covering with its inmost parts. For the covering puts out constant extensions from itself and insertions towards the interiors and thus continues to inmosts and as a result the whole is bound together. The entire form acts or is acted upon in such manner as the covering acts or is acted upon. The same is true of the rest of the organs. For what is

general and what is particular or the universal and the singular in a form act together by a marvelous connection.

[5] You will see below that what occurs in natural forms and their processes, which relate to motion and actions, occurs similarly in spiritual forms and in the changes and variations of their state, which relate to activities of the will and the understanding. Inasmuch as man joins the Lord in certain external activities and no one is deprived of the liberty of acting according to reason, the Lord can act in internals only as, together with man, He does in externals. If man does not shun and turn away from evils as sins, therefore, the external and at the same time the internal of his thought and will are infected and destroyed, comparatively as the pleura is by the disease in it called pleurisy, of which the body dies.

[6] *Second: If man were in internals at the same time he would pervert and destroy the whole order and tenor of divine providence.* Examples from the human body will illustrate this also. If man knew all the workings of the two brains into the fibres, of the fibres into the muscles and of the muscles into actions, and by this knowledge were to have the disposition of them as he disposes his deeds, would he not pervert and destroy all?

[7] If man knew how the stomach digests, and how the surrounding organs take their portion, work the blood and distribute it where needed for life, and if he had the disposing of these as he has of external activities, such as eating and drinking, would he not pervert and destroy all? When he cannot handle the external, seemingly a single thing, without destroying it by luxury and intemperance, what would he do if he had the disposal of the internals, infinite in number? Lest man enter into them by any volition and have control of them, things internal are therefore taken entirely away from the will except for the muscles, which are a covering; moreover, how these act is not known, only that they do.

[8] The same can be said of other organs. To give examples: if man had the disposing of the interiors of the eye for seeing,

## IX. IT IS A LAW OF DIVINE PROVIDENCE THAT MAN SHALL NOT PERCEIVE OR FEEL ANY OF THE ACTIVITY OF DIVINE PROVIDENCE, AND YET SHOULD KNOW AND ACKNOWLEDGE PROVIDENCE

those of the ear for hearing, or the tongue for tasting, those of the skin for feeling, those of the heart for systolic action, of the lungs for breathing, of the mesentery to distribute the chyle, or of the kidneys for secretion, the interiors of the organs of generation for propagation, or those of the womb for perfecting an embryo, and so on, would he not pervert and destroy the ordered course of the divine providence in them in innumerable ways? As we know, man is in externals, for example sees with the eye, hears with the ear, tastes with the tongue, feels with the skin, breathes with the lungs, impregnates a wife, and so on. Is it not enough for him to know the externals and dispose them for health of body and mind? When he cannot do this, what would happen if he disposed internals also? It may be plain from this that if man saw divine providence plainly, he would inject himself into the order and tenor of its course and pervert and destroy them.

181. The like occurs in the spiritual things of the mind to what occurs in the natural things of the body for the reason that all things of the mind correspond to all things of the body. For the same reason the mind actuates the body in externals and generally does so completely. It moves the eyes to see, the ears to hear, the mouth and tongue to eat and drink, also to speak, the hands to do, the feet to walk, the generative organs to propagate. The mind not only moves the externals in these ways but the internals, too, in their whole series, outmosts from inmosts and inmosts from outmosts. Thus while moving the mouth to speak, it moves lungs, larynx, glottis, tongue and lips at the same time, each separately to its especial function, and the face suitably also.

[2] It is clear then that the same can be said of the spiritual forms of the mind as was said of the natural forms of the body, and the same can be said of the spiritual activities of the mind as was said of the natural activities of the body. Consequently the Lord orders the internals as a man does the externals, in one way if the man orders the externals of himself and in another if he

orders them under the Lord and at the same time as of himself. The mind of man is also in its total organization a man, for it is his spirit which appears after death altogether as a human being as in the world; hence there are similar things in mind and body. Thus what has been said about the conjunction of externals with internals in the body is to be understood of the conjunction of externals with internals in the mind, with the sole difference that the latter is spiritual and the former is natural.

182. (3) *If man beheld divine providence plainly he would either deny God or make himself god.* The merely natural man says to himself, "What is divine providence? Is it anything else or more than an expression which people get from a priest? Who sees anything of it? Is it not by prudence, wisdom, cunning and malice that all things are done in the world? Is not all else necessity or consequence? And does not much happen by chance? Does divine providence lie concealed in this? How can it do so in deceptions and schemes? Yet it is said that divine providence effects all things. Then let me see it and I will believe in it. Can one believe in it until he sees it?"

[2] So speaks the merely natural man, but the spiritual man speaks differently. Acknowledging God he also acknowledges divine providence and sees it, too. He cannot make it manifest, however, to anyone whose thought is on nature only and from nature, for such a person cannot raise his mind above nature, see anything of divine providence in its phenomena, or come to conclusions about providence from nature's laws, which are also laws of divine wisdom. If, therefore, he beheld divine providence plainly, he would sink it in nature and thus not only enshroud it in fallacies but profane it. Instead of acknowledging it he would deny it, and one who denies divine providence in his heart denies God also.

[3] Either one thinks that God governs all things or that nature does. He who thinks that God does thinks that they are ruled by love itself and wisdom itself, thus by life itself; but he who thinks that nature governs all, thinks that all things are ruled by nature's heat and light, although these in themselves are dead,

## IX. IT IS A LAW OF DIVINE PROVIDENCE THAT MAN SHALL NOT PERCEIVE OR FEEL ANY OF THE ACTIVITY OF DIVINE PROVIDENCE, AND YET SHOULD KNOW AND ACKNOWLEDGE PROVIDENCE

coming as they do from a dead sun. Does not what is itself alive govern what is lifeless? Can what is dead govern anything? If you think that what is lifeless can give life to itself, you are mad; life must come from life.

183. It does not seem likely that if a man saw divine providence and its activity plainly he would deny God; it would seem that he could not but acknowledge it and thus acknowledge God. Yet the contrary is true. Divine providence never acts in keeping with the love of man's will, but constantly against it. For the human being by force of his hereditary evil is ever panting for the lowest hell, but the Lord in His providence is constantly leading him away and withdrawing him from it, first to a milder hell, then away from hell, and finally to Himself in heaven. This activity of divine providence is perpetual. If, then, man saw or felt this withdrawing and leading away, he would be angered, consider God his enemy, and deny Him on account of the evil of his selfhood. In order that man may not know of it, therefore, he is held in freedom and thereby does not know but that he leads himself.

[2] But let examples serve for illustration. By heredity man wants to become great and also rich. In the measure in which these loves are not checked he wants to become still greater and richer and finally the greatest and richest; even so he would not rest, but would want to become greater than God Himself and possess heaven itself. This lust is hidden deep in hereditary evil and consequently in man's life and in the nature of his life. Divine providence does not remove this evil in a moment; if it were removed in a moment man would cease to live; but divine providence removes it quietly and gradually without man's knowing of it. It does this by letting man act according to the thinking which he deems rational; then by various means, rational and also civil and moral, it leads him away and withdraws him so far as he can be withdrawn in freedom. Nor can evil be removed from anyone unless it comes out and is seen

## Divine Providence

and acknowledged; it is like a wound which heals only when opened.

[3] If, therefore, man knew and saw that the Lord in His divine providence works in this way against his life's love, the source of his highest enjoyment, he could not but go in the opposite direction, be enraged, rebel, say harsh things, and finally, on account of his evil, brush aside the activity of divine providence, denying it and so denying God. He would do this especially if he saw success thwarted or saw himself lowered in standing or deprived of wealth.

[4] But it is to be known that the Lord in no wise leads man away from seeking position and acquiring wealth, but leads him away from the lust of seeking position solely for the sake of eminence or for his own sake, and also from acquiring wealth for its own sake or just to have it. Leading the man away, He introduces him into the love of uses so that he may regard eminence not for his own sake but for the sake of uses, thus as attached to uses and only so to himself, and not as attached to him and then to the uses; the same applies to wealth. At many places in the Word the Lord Himself teaches that He continually humbles the proud and exalts the humble; what He teaches in it is also of His divine providence.

184. Any other evil in which man is by heredity is dealt with in like manner, such as adultery, fraud, vengeance, blasphemy and other similar evils, none of which can be removed except as freedom to think and will them is left to man for him to remove them as if of himself. Nevertheless he can do this only as he acknowledges divine providence and prays that it may be done by it. Apart from this freedom and from divine providence at the same time, the evils would be like poison shut in and not driven out, which would spread quickly and consign all parts to death, or would be like disease of the heart itself, from which the whole body soon dies.

185. The truth of what has been said cannot be better known than from human lives after death in the spiritual world. Very many who had become great or wealthy in the natural world and

## IX. IT IS A LAW OF DIVINE PROVIDENCE THAT MAN SHALL NOT PERCEIVE OR FEEL ANY OF THE ACTIVITY OF DIVINE PROVIDENCE, AND YET SHOULD KNOW AND ACKNOWLEDGE PROVIDENCE

in their eminence or riches had regarded themselves alone, at first speak of God and divine providence as though they had acknowledged them at heart, but seeing divine providence clearly then and their final lot under it, namely, for them to enter hell, they unite with devils there and not only deny God then but also blaspheme Him. Finally they reach such madness that they acknowledge the more powerful among devils as their gods and desire nothing more ardently than to become gods themselves.

186. Man would go contrary to God and also deny Him if he saw the activities of God's divine providence plainly, for the reason that man is in the enjoyment of self-love and this enjoyment constitutes his very life. Therefore when man is held in the enjoyment of his life he is in his freedom, for freedom and the enjoyment make one. If, then, he should perceive that he is continually being led away from his enjoyment, he would be enraged as against one who wanted to destroy his life and would hold him to be an enemy. Lest it happen, the Lord in His divine providence does not appear manifestly, but leads man by it as silently as a hidden stream or favorable current does a vessel. Consequently man does not know but that he is steadily in his own, for his freedom and his proprium make one. Hence it is plain that freedom appropriates to him what divine providence introduces, which would not take place if providence were manifest. To be appropriated means to become of one's life.

187. (4) *Man can see divine providence on the back and not in the face; also in a spiritual state but not in a natural.* To see divine providence on the back but not in the face means after it acts and not before. To see it in a spiritual state and not in a natural is to see it from heaven and not from the world. All who receive influx from heaven and acknowledge divine providence, especially those who have become spiritual through reformation, on beholding events taking a wonderful course see providence as it were from an interior acknowledgment and confess it. These do not wish to see it in the face, that is, before it eventuates,

fearing that their volition may intrude on something of its order and tenor.

[2] It is otherwise with those who do not admit any influx from heaven but only from the world, especially with those who have become natural by confirming appearances in themselves. They do not see anything of divine providence on the back, that is, after it eventuates, but wish to behold it in the face or before it eventuates; and as divine providence works by means, and these are provided through man or the world, they attribute providence, whether they look it in the face or on the back, to man or to nature, and so confirm themselves in the denial of it. They make this ascription of it because their understanding is closed above, that is, to heaven, and open only below, that is, to the world; one cannot see divine providence in a worldly outlook, only in a heavenly. I have wondered sometimes whether they would acknowledge divine providence if their understanding was opened above and they were to see as in the light of day that nature in itself is dead, and human intelligence in itself nothing, and that it is by influx that either appears to have being. I perceived that those who have confirmed themselves in favor of nature and of human prudence would not make the acknowledgment because the natural light flowing in from below would immediately extinguish the spiritual light flowing in from above.

189. The man who has become spiritual by acknowledgment of God, and wise by rejection of the proprium, sees divine providence in the world as a whole and in each and all things in it. Looking at natural things, he sees it; at civil things, he sees it; at spiritual things, he sees it; and in things simultaneous as well as successive. He sees it in ends, causes, effects, uses, forms, things great and small. Above all he sees it in the salvation of men, as that Jehovah gave the Word, taught men by it about God and about heaven and hell and eternal life, and Himself came into the world to redeem men and save them. Man sees these and many other things and divine providence in them from spiritual light in natural light.

## IX. IT IS A LAW OF DIVINE PROVIDENCE THAT MAN SHALL NOT PERCEIVE OR FEEL ANY OF THE ACTIVITY OF DIVINE PROVIDENCE, AND YET SHOULD KNOW AND ACKNOWLEDGE PROVIDENCE

[2] The merely natural man, however, sees none of these things. He is like a man who sees a magnificent temple and hears a preacher enlightened in divine things, but once home asserts that he saw only a stone building and heard nothing but sounds made. Again, he is like a near-sighted man who steps into a garden remarkable for fruits of every sort and who reports on getting home that he saw only woods and trees. Moreover, when such persons, having become spirits after death, are taken up into the angelic heaven where all objects are in forms representative of love and wisdom, they see none of them, not even that they exist. I have seen this happen with a number who denied the Lord's divine providence.

190. Many constant things exist, created that inconstant things may exist. Such constants are the ordained changes in the rising and setting of sun, moon and stars; their obscurations by interpositions called eclipses; the heat and light from them; the seasons of the year, called spring, summer, autumn and winter; the times of the day, morning, noon, evening and night; also atmospheres, waters and lands, viewed in themselves; the vegetative force in the plant kingdom, that and the reproductive in the animal kingdom; likewise what is constantly produced when these forces are set in action in accord with the laws of order. These and many more things existing from the creation are provided so that infinitely varying things may exist, for what varies can exist only in what is constant, fixed and certain.

[2] Examples will illustrate this. The varieties of vegetation would not be possible unless sunrise and sunset and the resulting heat and light were constant. Harmonies are infinitely varied, and would not exist unless the atmospheres were constant in their laws and the ear in its form. Varieties of vision, which are also infinite, would not exist unless the ether in its laws and the eye in its organization were constant; equally so, colors, unless light was constant. The same is true of thoughts, words and actions, which are of infinite variety too; they could not exist, either, unless the organic forms of the body were constant. Must

not a house be steady for a variety of things to be done in it by a person? So must a temple be for the various acts of worship, preaching, instruction and devout meditation to be possible in it. So in much else.

[3] As for the varieties found in the constant, fixed and certain, they go on to infinity and have no end; no one thing in the whole universe or in any part of it is ever precisely the same as another, nor can be in the progress of things to eternity. Who disposes these varieties which proceed to infinity and eternity so that they have order unless it is He who created what is constant to the end that they may exist in it? And who can dispose the infinite varieties of life among men but He who is life itself, that is, love itself and wisdom itself? Except by His divine providence, which is like a continual creation, can the infinite affections of men and their thoughts thence and thus the men themselves be disposed so as to make one? Evil affections and the thoughts from them to make one devil which is hell, and good affections and the thoughts from them one Lord in heaven? We have said and shown several times before that the whole angelic heaven is like one man in the Lord's sight, an image and likeness of Him, and all hell over against it like one monstrous man. This has been said because some natural men seize on arguments for their madness in favor of nature and of one's own prudence from even the constant and fixed which must exist for the variable to exist in it.

## X. THERE IS NO SUCH THING AS ONE'S OWN PRUDENCE; THERE ONLY APPEARS TO BE AND IT SHOULD SO APPEAR; BUT DIVINE PROVIDENCE IS UNIVERSAL BY BEING IN THE LEAST THINGS

191. That there is no such thing as one's own prudence is contrary to appearances and therefore to the belief of many. Because it is, one who believes, on the strength of the appearance, that human prudence does all things, cannot be convinced except by reasons to be had from a more profound investigation and to be gathered from causes. The appearance is an effect, and causes disclose how it arises. By way of introduction something will be said about the common faith on the subject. Contrary to the appearance the church teaches that love and faith are not from man but from God, so also wisdom and intelligence, therefore prudence also, and in general all good and truth. When this teaching is accepted, one must also agree that there is no such thing as one's own prudence, but there only appears to be. Prudence comes only from intelligence and wisdom and both of these only from the understanding and its grasp of truth and good. All this is accepted and believed by those who acknowledge divine providence, but not by those who only acknowledge human prudence.

[2] Now, either what the church teaches is true, that all wisdom and prudence are from God, or what the world teaches, that they are from man. Can these views be reconciled in any other way than this, that what the church teaches is the truth, and what the world teaches is the appearance? For the church establishes its teaching from the Word, but the world its teaching from the proprium; and the Word is God's, and the proprium is

man's. Because prudence is from God and not from man a Christian in his devotions, prays God to lead his thoughts, purposes and actions, and also adds that by himself he cannot. Again, seeing someone doing good, he says the person has been led to it by God; and so about much else. Can anyone speak so unless he inwardly believes it? To believe it inwardly comes from heaven. But when a man deliberates and gathers arguments in favor of human prudence he can believe the contrary, and this is from the world. The internal faith prevails with those who acknowledge God in their hearts; the external faith with those who do not acknowledge Him at heart, however much they may with the lips.

192. We said that a person who believes, on the strength of the appearance, that human prudence does all things, can be convinced only by reasons to be had from a more profound investigation and gathered from causes. In order, then, that the reasons gathered from causes may be plain to the understanding, let them be put forward in due order as follows:

1. All man's thoughts are from affections of his life's love; there are and can he no thoughts apart from them.
2. The affections of the life's love are known to the Lord alone.
3. Through His divine providence the Lord leads the affections of the life's love of man and at the same time the thoughts, too, from which human prudence comes.
4. By His divine providence the Lord assembles the affections of all mankind into one form—the human form.
5. Heaven and hell, which are from mankind, are therefore in such a form.
6. Those who have acknowledged nature alone and human prudence alone make up hell, and those who have acknowledged God and His divine providence make up heaven. vii. All this can be effected only as

## X. THERE IS NO SUCH THING AS ONE'S OWN PRUDENCE; THERE ONLY APPEARS TO BE AND IT SHOULD SO APPEAR; BUT DIVINE PROVIDENCE IS UNIVERSAL BY BEING IN THE LEAST THINGS

it appears to man that he thinks from himself and disposes by himself.

193. (1) *All man's thoughts are from affections of his life's love; there are and can be no thoughts apart from them.* It has been shown above in this treatise and also in the one entitled *Angelic Wisdom about Divine Love and Wisdom*, Parts I and V particularly, what the life's love and the affections and the thoughts from them are essentially, and what the sensations and actions arising from them in the body are. Inasmuch as these are the causes from which human prudence issues as an effect, something needs to be said about them here also. For what has been written earlier elsewhere cannot be as closely connected with what is written later as it will be if the same things are recalled and placed with both in view.

[2] Earlier in this treatise, and in that just mentioned about *Divine Love and Wisdom*, it was shown that in the Lord are divine love and wisdom; that these two are life itself; that from the two man has will and understanding, will from the divine love and understanding from the divine wisdom; that heart and lungs in the body correspond to these two; that this may make plain that as the pulsation of the heart along with the respiration of the lungs rules the whole man as to the body, so the will together with the understanding rules him as to his mind; that thus there are two principles of life in everyone, one natural and the other spiritual, and that the natural principle of life is the heartbeat, and the spiritual is the will of the mind; that each adjoins a consort to itself with which it cohabits and performs the functions of life; and that the heart joins the lungs to itself, and the will the understanding to itself.

[3] Now, as the soul of the will is love, and the soul of the understanding is wisdom, both of them from the Lord, love is the life of everyone and is such life as it has in union with wisdom; or what is the same, the will is the life of everyone and is such life as it has in conjunction with the understanding. More on the

subject may be seen above in this treatise and especially in *Angelic Wisdom about Divine Love and Wisdom*, Parts I and V.

194. It was also demonstrated in the treatises mentioned that the life's love produces subordinate loves from itself, called affections; that these are exterior and interior; and that taken together they make one dominion or kingdom as it were, in which the life's love is lord or king. It was also shown that these subordinate loves or affections adjoin consorts to themselves, each its own, the interior affections consorts called perceptions, and the exterior consorts called knowledges, and each cohabits with its consort and performs the functions of its life. In each instance, it was shown, the union is like that of life's very being with life's coming forth, which is such that the one is nothing without the other; for what is life's being unless it is active and what is life's activity if it is not from life's very being? The conjunction in life, it was likewise shown, is like that of sound and harmony, of sound and utterance, too, in general like that of the heart's pulsation and the respiration of the lungs, a union, again, such that one without the other is nothing and each becomes something in union with the other. Union must either be in them or come about by them.

[2] Consider, for example, sound. One who thinks that sound is something if there is nothing distinctive in it is much mistaken. It also corresponds to affection in man, and as something distinctive is always in it the affection of a person's love is known from the sound of his voice in speaking, and his thought is known from the varied sounds which speech is. Hence the wiser angels perceive just from the sound of his voice a man's life's love together with some of the affections which are its derivatives. This has been remarked that it may be known that no affection is possible without its thought, and no thought without its affection. More on the subject can be seen above in this treatise and in *Angelic Wisdom about Divine Love and Wisdom*.

195. Inasmuch as the life's love has its enjoyment, and its wisdom its pleasure, and likewise every affection, which is essentially a lesser love derived from the life's love like a stream

## X. THERE IS NO SUCH THING AS ONE'S OWN PRUDENCE; THERE ONLY APPEARS TO BE AND IT SHOULD SO APPEAR; BUT DIVINE PROVIDENCE IS UNIVERSAL BY BEING IN THE LEAST THINGS

from its source or a branch from a tree or an artery from the heart, therefore every affection has its enjoyment and the perception or thought from it its pleasure. Consequently these enjoyments and pleasures make man's life. What is life without joy and pleasure? It is not animated at all, but inanimate. Reduce enjoyment and pleasure and you grow cold and torpid; take them away and you expire and die. Vital heat comes from the enjoyments of the affections and the pleasures of the perceptions and thoughts.

[2] As every affection has its enjoyment and the thought thence its pleasure, it may be plain whence good and truth are and what they are essentially. Whatever is the enjoyment of one's affection is one's good, and one's truth is what is pleasant to the thought from that affection. For everyone calls that good which he feels in the love of his will to be enjoyable, and calls that truth which he then perceives in the wisdom of his understanding to be pleasant. The enjoyable and the pleasant both flow out from the life's love as water does from a spring or blood from the heart; together they are like an element or the atmosphere in which man's whole mind is.

[3] The two, enjoyment and pleasure, are spiritual in the mind and natural in the body, and in each make man's life. From this it is plain what it is in man that is called good, and what it is that is called truth; likewise what it is in man that is called evil and false; whatever destroys the enjoyment of his affection is evil to him, and what destroys the pleasure of his thought thence is false to him. It is plain, moreover, that evil on account of the enjoyment in it and falsity on account of the pleasure in it may be called good and truth and believed to be good and truth. Goods and truths are indeed changes and variations of state in the forms of the mind, but they are perceived and have life only through the enjoyments and pleasures they have to give. This is noted to make known what affection and thought are in their life.

196. Inasmuch as it is not the body but man's mind that thinks and that does so from the enjoyment of one's affection, and

inasmuch as man's mind is his spirit which lives after death, man's spirit is nothing else than affection and thought therefrom. It is altogether plain from spirits and angels in the spiritual world that thought cannot exist apart from affection, for they all think from the affections of their life's love; the enjoyments of these affections attend each as his atmosphere, and all are united by these spheres exhaled from the affections by their thoughts. The character of each one is known also by the sphere of his life. It may be seen from this that all thought is from an affection and is the form of that affection. The same applies to the relationship between will and understanding, good and truth, and charity and faith.

197. (2) The affections of the life's love of man are known to the Lord alone. Man knows his thoughts and his intentions in them because he sees them in himself, and as all prudence is from them, he sees this, too, within him. Then if his life's love is self-love, he comes to take pride in his own intelligence, ascribes prudence to himself, gathers arguments in support of it, and thus recedes from acknowledging divine providence. Much the same happens if love of the world is his life's love, but he does not then recede to the same extent. It is plain from this that these two loves ascribe all things to man and to his prudence and when interiorly examined ascribe nothing to God and to His providence. When persons who do this happen to hear that the reality is that there is no such thing as human prudence, but that divine providence alone governs all things, they laugh at this if they are outright atheists; if they hold something of religion in remembrance and are told that all wisdom is from God, they assent on first hearing it, but inwardly in their spirit deny it. Such especially are priests who love themselves more than God, and the world more than heaven, or what is the same, worship God for position's or riches' sake, and yet have been preaching that charity and faith, all good and truth, all wisdom, too, and in fact prudence are from God and none of them from man.

[2] In the spiritual world I once heard two priests debating with a certain royal ambassador about human prudence whether it is from God or from man, and the debate was heated. The three

## X. THERE IS NO SUCH THING AS ONE'S OWN PRUDENCE; THERE ONLY APPEARS TO BE AND IT SHOULD SO APPEAR; BUT DIVINE PROVIDENCE IS UNIVERSAL BY BEING IN THE LEAST THINGS

believed alike at heart, namely, that human prudence does all and divine providence nothing, but the priests in their theological zeal at the moment asserted that there was nothing of wisdom and prudence from man. When the ambassador retorted that there was nothing of thought then, either, they said "yes, nothing of thought." But as angels perceived that the three believed alike, they bade the ambassador, "Put on priestly robes, believe yourself to be a priest, and then speak." He robed himself, believed he was a priest, and thereupon declared in a deep voice that never could there be wisdom or prudence in man save from God. He defended this with the customary eloquence filled with rational arguments. Then the two priests were told, "Put off your robes, put on those of political ministers, and believe that that is what you are." They did so, thought then from their interior selves, and gave voice to the arguments they had entertained inwardly before in favor of human prudence and against divine providence. Upon this the three, believing alike, became warm friends and set out together on the path of one's own prudence, which leads to hell.

198. It was shown above that man can have no thought except from some affection of his life's love and that the thought is nothing other than the form of the affection. Now, man sees his thought but cannot see his affection, which he feels; it is therefore from sight which dwells on the appearance, and not from affection which does not come into sight but into feeling, that he concludes that one's own prudence does all things. For affection shows itself only in a certain enjoyment of thought and in pleasure ever reasoning about it. This pleasure and enjoyment make one with the thought in those who, from self-love or love of the world, believe in one's own prudence. The thought glides along in its enjoyment like a ship in a river current to which the skipper does not attend, attending only to the sails he spreads.

199. Man can indeed reflect on what his external affection finds enjoyable when it is also an enjoyment of a bodily sense, but he still does not reflect that that enjoyment comes from the enjoyment of his affection in thought. For example, when a

lecher sees a lewd woman his eyes light with a lascivious fire and from this he feels a physical pleasure; he does not, however, feel his affection's enjoyment or that of the lust in his thought, only a strong desire more nearly physical. The same is true of the robber in a forest at sight of travelers and of the pirate at sea on sighting vessels, and so on. Obviously a man's enjoyments govern his thoughts, and the thoughts are nothing apart from them; but he thinks he has only the thoughts, when nevertheless these are affections put into forms by his life's love so that they appear in the light; for all affection has heat for its element and thought has light.

[2] The external affections of thought manifest themselves in bodily sensation, and sometimes in the thought of the mind, but the internal affections of the thought from which the external exist never make themselves manifest to man. Of these he knows no more than a rider asleep in a carriage does of the road or than one feels the rotation of the earth. Now, when man knows nothing of the things beyond number that take place in the interiors of his mind, and the few external things which come to the sight of his thought are produced from the interiors, and the interiors are governed by the Lord alone through His divine providence and the few external by the Lord also together with man, how can anyone assert that one's own prudence does all things? Were you to see just one idea laid open, you would see astounding things, more than tongue can tell.

[3] It is clear from the endless things in the body that there are so many things in the mind's interiors that the number cannot be given, and nothing of them comes to sight or sense except only a much simplified action. Yet to the action thousands of motor or muscular fibres contribute, and thousands of nerve fibres, thousands of blood-vessels, thousands of cells in the lungs which must cooperate in every action, thousands in the brains and in the spinal cord, and many more things still in the spiritual man which is the human mind, in which all things are forms of affections and of perceptions and thoughts from the affections. Does not the soul, which disposes the interiors, dispose the actions also which spring from them? Man's soul is nothing else

## X. THERE IS NO SUCH THING AS ONE'S OWN PRUDENCE; THERE ONLY APPEARS TO BE AND IT SHOULD SO APPEAR; BUT DIVINE PROVIDENCE IS UNIVERSAL BY BEING IN THE LEAST THINGS

than the love of his will and the resulting love of his understanding; such as this love is the whole man is, becoming so according to the disposition he makes of his externals in which he and the Lord are together. Therefore, if he attributes all things to himself and to nature, self-love becomes the soul; but if he attributes all things to the Lord, love to the Lord becomes the soul; this love is heavenly, the other infernal.

200. Inasmuch as the enjoyments of his affections, from inmosts down through interiors to exteriors and finally to outermost things in the body, bear man along as wave and wind bear a ship; and inasmuch as nothing of this is apparent to man except what takes place in the outermost things of the mind and the body, how can he claim for himself what is divine on the strength merely of the fact that those few outermost things seem to be his own? Even less should he claim what is divine for himself, knowing from the Word that a man can receive nothing of himself unless it is given by heaven; and knowing from reason that this appearance has been granted him in order to live as a human being, see what is good and evil, choose between them, and appropriate his choice to himself that he may be united reciprocally with the Lord, be reformed, regenerated and saved, and live forever. It has been stated and shown above that this appearance has been granted to man in order that he may act in freedom according to reason, thus as of himself, and not drop his hands and await influx. From all this it follows that proposition iii to be demonstrated has been confirmed: Through His divine providence the Lord leads the affections of the life's love of man and at the same time the thoughts, too, from which human prudence comes.

(Footnote: 152-1 See footnote at n. 111.)

201. (4) *By His divine providence the Lord assembles the affections of all mankind into one form—the human form.* In a subsequent paragraph it will be seen that this is the universal effort of divine providence. Those who ascribe everything to nature deny God at heart, and those who ascribe everything to

human prudence, at heart deny divine providence; the one cannot be separated from the other. Yet both groups for their reputation's sake and for fear of losing it profess in words that divine providence is universal, but say its details fall to man and in their aggregate are grasped by human prudence.

[2] But consider: what is universal providence when the details are taken from it? Is it anything but just an expression? For that is called universal which consists of the total of details as what is general does of particulars. If, then, you remove details, what is the universal except something empty, thus like a surface with nothing underneath or an aggregate without content? If it should be said that divine providence is a universal government but nothing is governed but only held in connection and items of the government are handled by others, can this be called a universal government? No king has such a government. For if a king gave his subjects the government of everything in his kingdom, he would no longer be king, but would only be called king; he would have the standing in name only and not in fact. In the case of such a king one cannot speak of government, still less of universal government.

[3] God's providence is called man's prudence. As universal prudence cannot be said of a king who has only kept the name so that the kingdom may be called a kingdom and be held together, so one cannot speak of universal providence if human beings provide everything by their own prudence. The same is true of the terms "universal providence" and "universal government" in reference to nature when they mean that God created the universe but endowed nature to produce everything from herself. What is "universal providence" then but a metaphysical term, and nothing but a term? Many of those who attribute everything produced to nature and everything accomplished to human prudence and yet profess orally that God created nature, regard divine providence as an empty expression. But the reality is that divine providence is in the least things of nature and of human prudence also and is thereby universal.

## X. THERE IS NO SUCH THING AS ONE'S OWN PRUDENCE; THERE ONLY APPEARS TO BE AND IT SHOULD SO APPEAR; BUT DIVINE PROVIDENCE IS UNIVERSAL BY BEING IN THE LEAST THINGS

202. The Lord's divine providence is universal by being in the least things in that He created the universe in order that an infinite and eternal creation might come about from Him, and it does as He forms a heaven from mankind which in His sight is like one humanity, His image and likeness. We showed above (nn. 27-45) that heaven formed of human beings is such in His sight; that this was the purpose of creation; and that the divine regards what is infinite and eternal in all that it does (nn. 46-69). The infinite and eternal to which the Lord looks in forming His heaven from mankind is the growth of it to infinity and eternity and thus His dwelling constantly in the purpose of His creation. This infinite and eternal creation the Lord provided for in creating the universe and He pursues it steadily in His divine providence.

[2] Can anyone who knows and believes from the church's doctrine 202-1 that God is infinite and eternal be so lacking in reason that he does not agree on hearing it that God can then regard only what is infinite and eternal in the great work of His creation? To what else can He look from His infinite being? To what else in mankind of which He forms His heaven? What else can divine providence then have for its end than the reformation and salvation of mankind? No one can be reformed by himself through his prudence; he is reformed by the Lord through His divine providence. Consequently, unless the Lord leads man every least moment the man lapses from the way of reformation and perishes.

[3] Every change or variation in the state of the human mind means a change or variation in a series of things present and to come; what then of progress to eternity? The situation is like that of an arrow shot from a bow, which if it deviated from the target in the least on being aimed would deviate widely at a thousand feet or more. The like would happen if the Lord did not lead the states of the human mind every least moment. The Lord does so according to the laws of His divine providence; it is according to them that it seems to man he leads himself; but the Lord foresees how he leads himself and constantly acts in adaptation. In what

follows it will be seen that laws of tolerance are also laws of divine providence, that every man can be reformed and regenerated, and that no other predestination is possible.

203. Since every man lives forever after death and is allotted a place either in heaven or in hell according to his life, and heaven and hell must each be in a form to act as a unit, as we said before, and since no one can be allotted a place in that form other than his own, humanity in all the world is under the Lord's guidance and everyone is led by the Lord from infancy to the close of life in the least things, and his place is foreseen and provided.

[2] Clearly then, the Lord's divine providence is universal by being in the least things, and it is an infinite and eternal creation that He has provided for Himself in creating the world. Man does not espy this universal providence, and if he did, it would look to him like scattered heaps and collections of material for building a house such as passersby see, while the Lord beholds rather a magnificent palace, constantly building and enlarging.

204. (5) *Heaven and hell are in the form described.* That heaven is in the human form has been made known in the work *Heaven and Hell*, published in London in 1758 (nn. 59-102), also in the treatise *Divine Love and Wisdom*, and here and there in the present treatise. I therefore omit further confirmation. Hell is said to be in the human form also, but it is in a monstrous human form, like that of the devil, by whom hell in its entirety is meant. Hell is in the human form inasmuch as those who are in it were born human beings too; they also possess the two human faculties of liberty and rationality, though they have misused liberty by willing and doing evil, and rationality by thinking and confirming evil.

205. (6) *Those who have acknowledged nature alone and human prudence alone make up hell, and those who have acknowledged God and His divine providence make up heaven.* All who lead an evil life, inwardly acknowledge nature and human prudence alone. This acknowledgment lies hidden in all evil, however the evil may be veiled by good and truth, which

## X. THERE IS NO SUCH THING AS ONE'S OWN PRUDENCE; THERE ONLY APPEARS TO BE AND IT SHOULD SO APPEAR; BUT DIVINE PROVIDENCE IS UNIVERSAL BY BEING IN THE LEAST THINGS

are borrowed raiment, or like wreaths of perishable flowers, put around the evil lest it appear in its nakedness. That all who lead an evil life, inwardly acknowledge nature and human prudence alone is not known because of this general covering hiding it from view. The source and cause of their acknowledgment, however, may make clear that they acknowledge nature and one's own prudence. We shall say, therefore, whence man's own prudence is and what it is; then whence divine providence is and what it is; next who they are respectively, and of what character, who acknowledge divine providence and who acknowledge man's own prudence; and lastly show that those who acknowledge divine providence are in heaven and that those who acknowledge man's own prudence are in hell.

206. Whence man's own prudence is and what it is. It is from man's proprium, which is his nature and is called his soul from his parent. This proprium is self-love and the accompanying love of the world, or it is love of the world and the accompanying self-love. Self-love by nature regards self only and others as cheap or of no account. If it regards any it does so as long as they honor and do it homage. Inmostly in that love, like the endeavor in seed to fructify and propagate, there lies hidden the desire to become great and if possible a king and then possibly a god. A devil is such, for he is self-love itself; he adores himself and favors no one unless he also adores him; another devil like himself he hates, because he in turn wants alone to be adored. Since no love is possible without its consort and the consort of love or of the will in man is called the understanding, when self-love breathes itself into its consort, the understanding, it becomes pride there, which is the pride of self-intelligence, and from this comes man's own prudence.

[2] Inasmuch as self-love wants to be the one lord of the world and thus a god, the lusts of evil which are derived from it have their life from it, so have the perceptions of the lusts, which are schemes; likewise the enjoyments of the lusts, which are evils, and the thoughts of the lusts, which are falsities. All these are like slaves and ministers of their lord, responding to his every

nod, unaware that they do not act but are acted upon; they are actuated by self-love through the pride of self-intelligence. Hence man's own prudence because of its origin lies concealed in every evil.

[3] The acknowledgment of nature alone is also hidden in it, for self-love has closed the window overhead through which heaven is plain and the side windows, too, in order not to see or hear that the Lord alone governs all things, that nature in herself is lifeless, and that man's proprium is infernal and consequently love of it is diabolical. With the windows shuttered, self-love is in darkness, builds itself a hearth fire at which it sits with its consort, and the two reason amicably in favor of nature as against God and in favor of man's own prudence as against divine providence.

207. Whence and what divine providence is. It is the divine activity in the man who has removed self-love. For, as was said, self-love is the devil, and lusts with their enjoyments are the evils of his kingdom, which is hell. On the removal of self-love the Lord enters with the affections of neighborly love, opening the overhead window and then the side windows, thus enabling man to see that there is a heaven, a life after death and eternal happiness. By the spiritual light and at the same time the spiritual love which then flow in, the Lord causes him to acknowledge that God governs all things by His divine providence.

208. Who and of what nature those in each group are. Those who acknowledge God and His divine providence are like the angels of heaven, who are averse to being led by themselves and love to be led by the Lord. It is a sign that they are led by the Lord that they love the neighbor. Those, however, who acknowledge nature and one's own prudence are like the spirits of hell, who are averse to being led by the Lord and love to be led by themselves. If they were powerful persons in a kingdom or prelates in the church they want to dominate all things. If they were judges, they pervert judgment and exercise power over the laws. If they were learned, they apply scientific information to confirm nature and man's proprium. If they were merchants they

## X. THERE IS NO SUCH THING AS ONE'S OWN PRUDENCE; THERE ONLY APPEARS TO BE AND IT SHOULD SO APPEAR; BUT DIVINE PROVIDENCE IS UNIVERSAL BY BEING IN THE LEAST THINGS

act like robbers, and if husbandmen like thieves. All are enemies of God and scoffers at divine providence.

209. It is amazing that when heaven is opened to such men and they are told that they are insane, and this is made plain to their very perception by influx and enlightenment, still they angrily shut heaven away from them and look to the earth beneath which is hell. This is done with such men while they are still outside hell. It makes plain how mistaken those are who think, "If I see heaven and hear angels speaking with me, I shall acknowledge." Their understanding makes the acknowledgment, but if the will does not at the same time, they still do not acknowledge. For the love of the will inspires in the understanding what it wills (it is not the other way about); indeed, it destroys everything in the understanding which is not from itself.

210. (7) *All this can be effected only as it appears to man that he thinks from himself and disposes by himself.* In what precedes we have shown fully that unless it seemed to man that he lives of himself and thus thinks and wills, speaks and acts of himself, he would not be man. Consequently, unless he could in his own prudence make the disposition of all pertaining to his function and life, he could not be led and guided by divine providence. He would be like one with his hands hanging limp, his mouth open, his eyes shut, holding his breath in expectation of influx. He would divest himself of the human which he has from the perception and sensation that he thinks, wills, speaks and acts as it were of himself. At the same time he would divest himself of the two faculties, liberty and rationality, distinguishing him from the beasts. Above in this treatise and in the treatise *Divine Love and Wisdom* it was shown that without this appearance a man would not have the power to receive or reciprocate nor have immortality then.

[2] If then you desire to be led by divine providence, use prudence as a servant and minister that faithfully dispenses his master's goods. This prudence is the talent given to the servants

to trade with, of which they were to give account (Lu 19:13-28; Mt 25:14-31). It seems to man to be his own, and he believes it is his own as long as he holds shut up within him the bitterest enemy God and divine providence have, the love of self. This dwells in the interiors of every man by birth; if you do not recognize it (and it wishes not to be recognized), it dwells securely and guards the door lest man open the door and the Lord cast it out. The door is opened by man through shunning evils as sins as if of himself with the acknowledgment that he does so from the Lord. With this prudence divine providence acts as one.

211. Divine providence operates so secretly that scarcely anyone is aware it exists in order that man may not perish. For man's proprium, which is his will, never acts at one with divine providence, against which it has an inborn enmity. The proprium is the serpent which seduced the race's parents of which it is said,

> I will put enmity between you and the woman, and between your seed and her Seed, and It shall bruise your head (Ge 3:15).

The serpent is evil of every sort; its head is self-love. The seed of the woman is the Lord, and the enmity set is between the love of man's proprium and the Lord, thus between man's own prudence and the Lord's divine providence. For man's own prudence is constantly exalting that head, and divine providence is constantly abasing it.

[2] If man felt this, he would be enraged and wrought-up against God and would perish. While he does not feel it, he may be enraged and wrought-up against others or himself or against fortune without perishing. Therefore the Lord leads man by His divine providence in freedom always, and the freedom seems to man to be utterly his own. To lead a man freely in opposition to himself is like raising a heavy and resisting weight from the ground by means of screws through the power of which weight and resistance are not felt. And it is as though someone is unknowingly with an enemy who means to kill him and a friend

## X. THERE IS NO SUCH THING AS ONE'S OWN PRUDENCE; THERE ONLY APPEARS TO BE AND IT SHOULD SO APPEAR; BUT DIVINE PROVIDENCE IS UNIVERSAL BY BEING IN THE LEAST THINGS

leads him away quietly and only afterwards tells him the enemy's intention.

212. Who does not talk of fortune? Who does not acknowledge it by speaking of it and know something of it by experience? Yet who knows what it is? One cannot deny that it is something, for it exists and occurs, and a thing cannot exist and occur without being caused; but the cause of this something, fortune, is not known. Lest fortune be denied merely because the cause is unknown, consider dice or playing cards and play yourself or ask the players; do any deny that fortune exists? For they play with it and it plays with them surprisingly. Who can repulse it if it opposes him? Does it not laugh then at prudence and wisdom? When you shake the dice or shuffle the cards, does fortune not seem to know and direct the turns and twists of the wrists in favor of one player rather than another for some cause? Can the cause have any other source than divine providence in outermost things where it works along with human prudence in a wonderful way, constant or changeful, concealing itself at the same time?

[2] We know that pagans of old acknowledged Fortune and built a temple to her, as Italians did at Rome. It has been granted me to learn many things which I am not permitted to make public about this fortune, which, as was said, is divine providence in outmosts. These made it plain to me that fortune is not an illusion of the mind nor a sport of nature nor something without a cause, for this has no reality, but is visible evidence that divine providence is over the least things in human thought and action. As divine providence occurs in these least things which are insignificant and trifling, why should it not in the significant and important matters of peace and war in the world and of salvation and life in heaven?

213. I know, however, that human prudence bears the rational faculty its way more than divine providence does its way, for the latter does not show itself and the former does. It can be accepted more readily that there is only one life, namely God,

and that all men are recipients of life from Him, as we have shown many times, yet this amounts to saying that prudence is from Him, for prudence is part of life. What man, speaking in favor of nature and of human prudence in his reasoning, is not speaking from the natural or external man? And what man, speaking in favor of divine providence and of God in his reasoning, is not speaking from the spiritual or internal man? But, "Pray, write two books," I say to the natural man, "and fill them with plausible, likely and lifelike reasons which in your judgment are solid ones, the one book in favor of one's own prudence, and the other in favor of nature. Then hand them to any angel. I know he will write down on them these few words: `All this is appearance and fallacy.'"

# XI. DIVINE PROVIDENCE LOOKS TO WHAT IS ETERNAL, AND TO THE TEMPORAL ONLY AS THIS ACCORDS WITH THE ETERNAL

214. That divine providence looks to what is eternal and to the temporal only so far as this makes one with the eternal, will be demonstrated in this order:

1. The temporal has to do with distinction and wealth, thus with standing and gain, in the world.
2. The eternal has to do with spiritual standing and abundance, of love and wisdom, in heaven.
3. The temporal and the eternal are separated by man, but are united by the Lord.
4. The uniting of temporal and eternal is the Lord's divine providence.

215. (1) *The temporal has to do with distinction and wealth, thus with standing and gain, in the world.* Many things are temporal, but they are all related to distinction and wealth. By the temporal is meant all that either perishes in time or at least comes to an end with man's life in the world. By the eternal is meant all that does not perish or come to an end in time and thus not with life in the world. Since, as we said, all that is temporal concerns distinction and wealth, it is important to know the following: what, and whence, distinction and wealth are; the nature of the love of them for themselves and the nature of the love of them for the sake of use; that these two loves are distinct from each other, as hell and heaven are; and that man hardly knows the difference between them. But of these points one by one.

[2] First: *What, and whence, distinction and wealth are.* Distinction and wealth in the most ancient times were quite

different from what they gradually became later. Distinction in those times existed only in the relation of parents and children and was one of love, a love full of respect and veneration, accorded the parents not because of birth from them, but because of the instruction and wisdom received from them, which was a second birth of the children, in itself spiritual, being of their spirit. This was the sole distinction in most ancient days because tribes, families, and households dwelt separately and not like today under governments. The distinction attached to the head of the family. Men of old called the times golden ages.

[3] But after those times the love of ruling, just out of enjoyment of that love, crept in by stages, and as enmity and hostility did so at the same time towards those who were unwilling to submit, tribes, families, and households congregated of necessity in communities and set over themselves one whom they called judge at first, then prince, and finally king and emperor. They also began to protect themselves by towers, earthworks and walls. The lust of ruling spread like a contagion to many from the judge, prince, king or emperor as from the head into the body, and as a result degrees of distinction arose and prestige according to them, and self-love also and pride in one's own prudence.

[4] The same thing happened with the love of riches. In the most ancient days when tribes and families lived by themselves, there was no other love of riches than to possess the necessaries of life which they provided for themselves from flocks and herds and from the lands, fields and gardens which supplied their food. Suitable houses, furnished with useful articles of every kind, and clothing were also among their necessities of life. Parents, children and male and female servants, making up the household, engaged in the care and labor for all these necessities.

[5] But after the love of dominion entered and destroyed this state of society, the love of having means beyond what was needed crept in also and grew to the extreme of wanting to possess the wealth of all other men. The two loves are like blood relatives, for one who wants to rule over all things, also wants to

## XI. DIVINE PROVIDENCE LOOKS TO WHAT IS ETERNAL, AND TO THE TEMPORAL ONLY AS THIS ACCORDS WITH THE ETERNAL

possess all things; for then all others become servants, and they alone masters. This is clearly evident from those in the papist world who have exalted their dominion even into heaven, to the Lord's throne, on which they have placed themselves, and who at the same time seek the wealth of the whole earth and want to enlarge their treasury endlessly.

[6] Second: *The nature of the love of distinction and wealth for their own sake and for usefulness' sake respectively.* The love of distinction and standing for their own sake is self-love—strictly, the love of ruling from self-love; and the love of riches and wealth for their own sake is love of the world—more precisely, the love of possessing the goods of others by whatever device. But the love of distinction and riches for usefulness' sake is love of the use, which is the same as love to the neighbor; for that for the sake of which a man acts is the purpose from which he acts, and is first or primary, and all else is means and secondary.

[7] As for the love of distinction and standing, identical with self-love and strictly with the love of ruling from self-love, it is the love of the proprium; and man's proprium is all evil. Hence it is said that man is born into all evil and that what he has by heredity is nothing but evil. What he has by heredity is his proprium in which he is and into which he comes through self-love and especially through the love of ruling from self-love; for one who is in that love regards only himself and thus immerses his thoughts and affections in his proprium. Hence a love of evil-doing is present in self-love. The reason is that he does not love the neighbor but only himself; and one who loves himself only, sees others as outsiders or as mean or nothing worth, despises them, and does not hesitate to do them injury.

[8] For this reason one who is in the love of ruling from the love of self thinks nothing of defrauding his neighbor, committing adultery with his wife, slandering him, breathing vengeance on him even to the death, treating him cruelly, and other such deeds. This a man gets from the fact that the devil himself, with whom he is conjoined and by whom he is led, is

nothing else than the love of ruling from self-love. One who is led by the devil, that is, by hell, is led into all these evils and is constantly led by enjoyments of these evils. Hence all who are in hell want to do evil to all, but those in heaven want to do well by all. From this opposition there results the intermediate state in which man is and in it is in equilibrium, as it were, so that he can turn towards hell or towards heaven. So far as he favors the evils of self-love he turns towards hell, and so far as he removes them from him he turns towards heaven.

[9] It has been granted me to feel the nature and also the strength of the enjoyment of ruling from the love of self. I was let into it that I might know. It was such as to exceed all worldly enjoyments. It was an enjoyment of the whole mind from its inmosts to its outmosts, but felt in the body only as pleasure and gratification, making the chest swell. It was also granted me to perceive that there issued from this enjoyment as from their fountainhead the enjoyments of evils of all kinds, such as adultery, revenge, fraud, slander, and evil-doing in general. There is a similar enjoyment in the love of possessing the wealth of others by whatever ruse, and from this love in the lusts derived from it; yet not the same degree of enjoyment unless this love is conjoined with self-love. As for distinction and riches sought not for themselves but for usefulness' sake, this is not love of them but love of uses; distinction and wealth serve it as means. This love is heavenly. But of it more in what follows.

[10] Third: *These two loves are distinct from each other, as heaven and hell are.* This is plain from what has just been said, to which I will add the following. All who are in the love of ruling from self-love, whoever they are and whether they are great or small, are in hell in spirit. They are also in the love of all evils. If they do not commit them, still in their spirit they believe that they are allowable, and when honor, standing, or fear of the law do not deter, they commit them physically. What is more, the love of ruling from self-love hides hatred of God deeply within itself, consequently of divine things which are of the church and especially of the Lord. If such men acknowledge God it is with the lips only, and if they acknowledge the divine things of the

## XI. DIVINE PROVIDENCE LOOKS TO WHAT IS ETERNAL, AND TO THE TEMPORAL ONLY AS THIS ACCORDS WITH THE ETERNAL

church, it is for fear of losing standing. This love hides hatred of the Lord deeply within it because deep in it is the desire to be God, for it worships and adores itself alone. Hence if anyone honors it, even to saying that it possesses divine wisdom and is the god of the world, it loves him with all the heart.

[11] It is otherwise with the love of distinction and wealth for usefulness' sake; this love is heavenly, for, as was said, it is the same as love of the neighbor. By uses goods are meant, and by doing uses doing good is meant, and by doing uses or good, serving and helping others is meant. Although those doing so may possess distinction and wealth, they regard these only as means for doing uses, thus for serving and helping. They are meant in these words of the Lord:

> Whoever would be great among you, must be your minister; and whoever would . . . be first, must be your servant (Mt 20:26, 27).

It is these also whom the Lord entrusts with ruling in heaven. For ruling is to them the means of doing uses or good, thus of serving; and when uses or good deeds are their purpose and their love, they do not rule; the Lord does, from whom is all that is good.

[12] Fourth: Man hardly knows the difference between the two loves. For most men of distinction and wealth also perform uses, yet do not know whether they do so for their own sake or for the sake of usefulness. They know this the less because love of self and the world has more fire and ardor for doing uses than have those who are not in love of self and the world. The former do uses, however, for the sake of fame or gain, thus for their own benefit; but the latter, doing so for the sake of usefulness and what is beneficial, act not from themselves but from the Lord.

[13] The difference between the two loves can scarcely be recognized by man, for he is ignorant whether he is being led by the devil or by the Lord. Led by the devil he does uses for his own sake or the world's; led by the Lord, he does them for the sake of the Lord and of heaven. All who shun evils as sins do uses from the Lord; all who do not shun evils as sins do uses

from the devil, for evil is the devil, and use or good is the Lord. Only so is the difference in question recognizable. Outwardly the two loves look the same; inwardly they are wholly unlike. One is like gold with dross in it, the other like gold with pure gold in it. One is like artificial fruit, looking outwardly like the fruit of a tree, but is colored wax with dust or pitch in it; the other is like noble fruit, flavorsome and fragrant, with seeds in it.

216. (2) The eternal has to do with spiritual standing and wealth, of love and wisdom, in heaven. As the natural man calls the enjoyments of self-love, which are also the enjoyments of the lusts of evil, good, and confirms that they are goods, he calls distinction and wealth divine blessings. But when the natural man sees the wicked as well as the good raised to distinction and prospered, and still more when he beholds the good despised and poorly off and the wicked honored and affluent, he thinks to himself, "Why is this? It cannot be by divine providence. For if providence governed everything, it would lavish distinction and wealth on the good and inflict contempt and poverty on the wicked, and thus drive the wicked to acknowledge there is a God and divine providence."

[2] But unless he is enlightened by the spiritual man, that is, is at the same time spiritual, the natural man does not see that distinction and wealth can be blessings but also curses, and that when they are from God they are blessings, and when they are from the devil they are curses. It is well known, moreover, that the devil bestows distinction and wealth; it is on this account that he is called the prince of the world. As it is not known when distinction and wealth are blessings and when they are curses, let it be told in this order:

1. Distinction and wealth are blessings and are curses.
2. When they are blessings they are spiritual and eternal; when they are curses they are temporal and ephemeral.
3. Distinction and wealth which are curses, compared with those which are blessings, are as nothing

## XI. DIVINE PROVIDENCE LOOKS TO WHAT IS ETERNAL, AND TO THE TEMPORAL ONLY AS THIS ACCORDS WITH THE ETERNAL

compared with everything or as that which has no existence in itself compared with that which has.

217. The three points are now each to be clarified.

1. Distinction and wealth are blessings and are curses. Common experience attests that both the pious and the impious, or the just and the unjust, that is, the wicked and the good, gain distinction and wealth, and yet it is undeniable that the impious and unjust, that is, the wicked, enter hell, and the pious and just, that is, the good, enter heaven. As this is true, distinction and wealth or standing and means are either blessings or curses, blessings with the good and curses with the evil. It was shown in the work *Heaven and Hell*, published in London in the year 1758, that rich and poor and great and small are found in both heaven and hell (nn. 357-365). It is plain from this that distinction and wealth with those now in heaven were blessings in the world, and with those now in hell were curses in the world.

[2] If he will think about the matter with reason, anyone can know when distinction and wealth are blessings or curses, namely, that they are blessings with those who do not set their heart on them, and curses with those who do. One sets the heart on them in loving oneself in them, and one does not set the heart on them when he loves uses and not himself in them. Above (n. 215) we told what the difference between the two loves, and the nature of it, is. It is to be added that distinction and wealth seduce some and not others. They do so when they excite the loves in man's proprium, that is, self-love, which is the love found in hell and is called the devil (as remarked above), and they do not seduce if they do not excite that love.

[3] Both the wicked and the good come to distinction and are prospered in means because the wicked as well as the good perform uses. The wicked perform uses for the sake of their personal standing and gain; the good do so for the sake of the standing and profit of the work which they do. The good regard the standing and profit of their work as principal causes of action, and personal standing and gain as instrumental causes;

but the wicked regard their personal standing and gain as the main incentives and the standing and gain of their work as the instrumental. Yet who does not see that a person, whatever his function or standing, is to serve the affairs which he administers, and not they him? Who does not see that a judge is to serve justice, a magistrate the common welfare, a king his kingdom, and that it is not to be the other way around? According to the laws of a kingdom, a man is invested therefore with distinction and standing in keeping with the eminence of the work he does. Moreover, who does not see that the difference between the two loves is like that between what is principal and what is instrumental? One who ascribes to himself personally the eminence of a position appears in the spiritual world, when this inversion is pictured, as himself inverted, feet up and head down.

[4] Second: When distinction and wealth are blessings they are spiritual and eternal, but when they are curses they are temporal and ephemeral. There are distinction and wealth in heaven as there are in the world. For governments and hence administrations and functions exist there, trade also and hence wealth, for there are societies and communities. All heaven is divided into two kingdoms, one called the celestial kingdom and the other the spiritual kingdom. Each kingdom is divided into innumerable societies, larger and smaller, all of which with all in them are arranged according to differences of love and of wisdom thence, the societies of the celestial kingdom according to differences of celestial love, which is love to the Lord, and the societies of the spiritual kingdom according to differences of spiritual love, which is love to the neighbor. Inasmuch as there are such societies, and all who are in them were men in the world and hence retain the loves they cherished in the world, with the one difference that they are spiritual beings now, and that distinction and wealth are spiritual in the spiritual kingdom and celestial in the celestial kingdom, therefore those have greater distinction and abundance than others who have greater love and wisdom. And to them distinction and wealth in the world were blessings.

## XI. DIVINE PROVIDENCE LOOKS TO WHAT IS ETERNAL, AND TO THE TEMPORAL ONLY AS THIS ACCORDS WITH THE ETERNAL

[5] The nature of spiritual distinction and wealth may then be plain—they attach to one's function and not to one's person. The distinguished person in the spiritual world indeed enjoys magnificence and glory like those of kings on earth, yet does not regard the distinction itself as anything but rather the uses in the administration and discharge of which he is engaged. Each also receives the honors of his high post but ascribes them not to himself but to the uses, and as all uses are from the Lord, he ascribes the honors to the Lord as their source. Such are the spiritual distinction and wealth which are eternal.

[6] It is quite otherwise with those to whom eminence and wealth were curses in the world. Having attributed these to themselves and not to uses, and not wanting the uses to control them but wanting to control the uses, which they regarded as uses only as they served their own standing and honor, they are in hell and are base slaves, despised and wretched. Their distinction and wealth are gone, therefore are called temporal and fleeting. The Lord teaches about both sorts in the words:

> Do not lay up treasures for yourselves on earth, where moth and rust corrupt and thieves break through and steal; but lay up treasures for yourselves in heaven, where neither moth nor rust corrupts and where thieves do not break through and steal; for where your treasure is . . . your heart also is (Mt 6:19-21).

[7] Third: The distinction and wealth which are curses, compared with those which are blessings, are as nothing compared with everything or as that which has no existence in itself compared with that which has. Everything that perishes and comes to nothing is inwardly nothing in itself. Outwardly, indeed, it is something and appears to be much and to some everything while it lasts; but inwardly in itself it is not. It is like a surface with nothing beneath or like an actor in kingly robes when the play is over. But what remains to eternity is something in itself perpetually, thus everything, and it truly is, for it does not cease to be.

218. (3) *The temporal and the eternal are separated by man, but are united by the Lord.* For all that is man's is temporal, and

## Divine Providence

he may therefore be called temporal, but all things that are the Lord's are eternal, and so the Lord is called eternal. Temporal things are such as come to an end and perish, eternal things are such as do not. Anyone can see that the two can be united only by the infinite wisdom of the Lord, thus by Him and not by man. To make it known, however, that the two are separated by man and united by the Lord, this is to be demonstrated in the following order:

1. What temporal things are and what eternal are.
2. The human being is in himself temporal and the Lord in Himself eternal, and only the temporal can proceed from man, and only the eternal from the Lord.
3. Temporal things separate eternal things from themselves, while eternal things join temporal things to themselves.
4. The Lord joins man to Himself by means of appearances.
5. He does so by correspondences also.

219. These points will be clarified and established one by one. First: *What temporal things are and what eternal are.* The temporal are all things that are proper to nature and from nature proper to man. Space and time especially are proper to nature, both of them having a limit or termination. Things thence derived and proper to man are all things of his own will and understanding, thus of his affection and thought and especially of his prudence; it is well known that these are finite and limited. Eternal things, however, are all that are proper to the Lord and from Him seemingly proper to man. What is proper to the Lord is all of it infinite and eternal, thus timeless, endless and without limit; what is seemingly proper to man thence is also infinite and eternal; but nothing of this is actually proper to man, but the Lord's alone in him.

[2] Second: *The human being is in himself temporal and the Lord in Himself eternal, and only the temporal can proceed from man, and from the Lord only the eternal.* Man, we said, is in himself temporal and the Lord in Himself eternal. Since only

## XI. DIVINE PROVIDENCE LOOKS TO WHAT IS ETERNAL, AND TO THE TEMPORAL ONLY AS THIS ACCORDS WITH THE ETERNAL

what is in a person can proceed from him, nothing can proceed from man except what is temporal, and nothing from the Lord except what is eternal. For the infinite cannot proceed from the finite; that it can is a contradiction. The infinite, however, can proceed from the finite, still not from the finite but from the infinite by the finite. In turn, what is finite cannot proceed from the infinite; this is also a contradiction; it can be produced from the infinite and this is creation and not proceeding. On this subject see *Angelic Wisdom about Divine Love and Wisdom*, from beginning to end. If then the finite proceeds from the Lord, as it does in many ways with man, it proceeds not from the Lord but from man, and can be said to do so from the Lord by man, because it so appears.

[3] This may be clarified by these words of the Lord:

> Let your communication be, Yea, yea, Nay, nay, what is more than these comes of evil (Mt 5:37).

Such is the speech of all in the third heaven. For they never reason about divine things whether a thing is so or not, but see in themselves from the Lord whether or not it is. To reason about divine things whether they are so or not comes from the reasoner's not seeing them from the Lord, but wanting to see them from himself, and what one sees from oneself is evil. But still the Lord desires man to think and speak about things divine, also to reason about them, in order that he may see whether or not they are so. Such thought, speech and reasoning may be said to be from the Lord in man provided the end is to see the truth, although they are from the man until he sees and acknowledges the truth. Meanwhile it is from the Lord alone that he can think, speak and reason; for he does so from the two faculties, called liberty and rationality, which are his from the Lord alone.

[4] *Third: Temporal things separate eternal things from themselves, while eternal things join temporal things to themselves.* That temporal things separate eternal things from themselves means that man, who is temporal, does so from the temporal in himself; and that eternal things join temporal things to themselves means that the Lord, who is eternal, does so from

what is eternal in Himself, as was said above. In what precedes we showed that there is a conjunction of the Lord with man and a conjunction in turn of man with the Lord, but the reciprocal conjunction of man with the Lord is not man's doing but the Lord's; also that man's will goes counter to the Lord's will or, what is the same, man's own prudence goes counter to divine providence. From these circumstances it follows that man puts the eternal things of the Lord aside by force of the temporal things in him, but the Lord joins His eternal things to man's temporal, that is, Himself to man and man to Him. As these points have been treated many times in what precedes, there is no need to confirm them further.

[5] Fourth: *The Lord joins man to Himself by means of appearances.* For it is an appearance that of himself man loves the neighbor, does good, and speaks truth. Unless this appeared to man to be so, he would not love the neighbor, do good, or speak truth, and therefore would not be conjoined with the Lord. Since love, good and truth are from the Lord, plainly the Lord joins man to Himself by means of the appearance. This appearance, and the Lord's conjunction with man and man's with the Lord, have been treated above at length.

[6] Fifth: *The Lord unites man to Himself by means of correspondences.* He does this by means of the Word, the sense of the letter of which consists wholly of correspondences. In *Doctrine of the New Jerusalem about Sacred Scripture*, from beginning to end, it was shown that by means of that sense there is a conjunction of the Lord with man and a reciprocal conjunction of man with the Lord.

220. (4) The conjunction of the temporal and the eternal in man is the Lord's divine providence. As this cannot come at once to the perception of the understanding or before being reduced to order and then unfolded and demonstrated according to that order, let this be the order in considering it:

1. It is by divine providence that man puts off the natural and temporal through death and puts on the spiritual and eternal.

## XI. DIVINE PROVIDENCE LOOKS TO WHAT IS ETERNAL, AND TO THE TEMPORAL ONLY AS THIS ACCORDS WITH THE ETERNAL

2. Through His divine providence the Lord joins Himself with natural things by means of spiritual and to temporal by means of eternal in accordance with uses.
3. The Lord joins Himself to uses by means of correspondences, and so by means of appearances according as man confirms these.
4. This conjunction of temporal and eternal is divine providence.

All this will be placed in clearer light by explanation.

[2] First: *It is of divine providence that man puts off the natural and temporal through death and puts on the spiritual and eternal.* Natural and temporal things are the outermost and lowest things which man first enters, as he does on being born, to the end that he may be introduced then into interior and higher things; for the outmost and lowest things are containants, and these are in the natural world. For this reason no angel or spirit was created such at once, but all were born as men first and then were introduced into interior and higher things. Thus they have an outmost and lowest which in itself is fixed and stable, within and by which the interiors can be held in connection.

[3] Man first puts on the grosser substances of nature; his body consists of them; but he puts these off by death, retaining the purer substances of nature nearest to the spiritual, which then are his containants. Moreover, all interior or higher things are together in the outmost and lowermost, as was shown earlier in passages on the subject. Every activity of the Lord is therefore from topmost and outmost simultaneously and so is in fullness. But as the farthest and outmost things of nature as they are in themselves cannot receive the spiritual and eternal things for which the human mind was formed, and yet man was born to become spiritual and live forever, man puts them off and retains only those interior natural things which suit and harmonize with the spiritual and celestial and serve to contain them. This is effected by the rejection of the temporal and natural outmosts, which is the death of the body.

[4] Second: *Through His divine providence the Lord joins Himself with natural things by means of spiritual things and to temporal by means of eternal in accordance with uses.* Natural and temporal things are not only those proper to nature, but also those proper to men in the natural world. At death man puts off both of these and puts on the spiritual and eternal things corresponding to them. That he puts these on according to uses has been shown in much that precedes. The natural things proper to nature relate in general to time and space and in particular to things visible on earth. These man leaves behind at death and instead receives spiritual things which are similar in outward aspect or appearance but not in their inward aspect and actual essence. This also was considered above.

[5] Temporal things proper to men in the natural world in general are related to distinction and wealth and in particular to human needs such as food, clothing and habitation. These are also put off at death and left behind; things are put on and received that are similar in outward aspect or appearance but not in their internal aspect and essence. All these get their inward aspect and essence from the uses made of temporal things in the world. Uses are the goods which are called goods of charity. It is evident, then, that the Lord through His divine providence unites spiritual and eternal things to natural and temporal things according to uses.

[6] Third: *The Lord joins Himself to uses by means of correspondences, and thus by means of appearances according as man confirms these.* As this must seem obscure to those who have not yet acquired a clear idea of correspondence and appearance, what these are must be illustrated by examples and explained. All the sayings of the Word are outright correspondences of spiritual and celestial things, and being correspondences are also appearances, that is, are all divine goods of divine love and divine truths of divine wisdom which in themselves are naked, but are clothed upon by the Word's literal meaning. They therefore appear as a man would clothed, if his clothing corresponded to the state of his love and wisdom. Obviously, then, if one confirms appearances in himself, he

## XI. DIVINE PROVIDENCE LOOKS TO WHAT IS ETERNAL, AND TO THE TEMPORAL ONLY AS THIS ACCORDS WITH THE ETERNAL

mistakes the clothing for the man, whereupon appearance becomes fallacy. It is otherwise if he seeks truths and sees them in the appearances.

[7] Inasmuch as all uses or truths and goods of charity, which a man renders to the neighbor may be rendered either according to the appearance or according to the verities of the Word, he is in fallacies if he renders them according to the appearances he has confirmed, but renders them as he should if he does so in accord with the verities. This may make plain what is meant when the Lord is said to join Himself to uses through correspondences and thus through appearances according to the confirmation of these by man.

[8] Fourth: *This conjunction of temporal and eternal is divine providence.* This is to be illustrated by two instances in order to bring it before the understanding in some light. The one instance is that of eminence and standing, and the other that of riches and wealth. These are all natural and temporal in outward form but spiritual and eternal in inward form. Distinction with its standing is natural and temporal when a man has regard in them only to himself personally and not to the common welfare and to the uses. For he is bound then to think inwardly that the community exists for his sake and not he for its sake. It is like a king's thinking that the kingdom and all its members exist for his sake, and not he for the sake of kingdom and people.

[9] The identical distinction, however, along with the standing it brings, is spiritual and eternal when man considers that he exists for the sake of the common well-being and for uses, and not these for his sake. Doing this, he is in the truth and essence of the distinction and of the standing it brings. But doing as described above, he is in the correspondence and appearance; if then he confirms these, he is in fallacies and has conjunction with the Lord only as those have who are in falsities and evils therefrom, for fallacies are falsities with which evils unite themselves. Such men have indeed done uses and good but from themselves and not from the Lord, thus have put themselves in the Lord's place.

[10] The same is true of riches and wealth; for these also are natural and temporal, and spiritual and eternal. They are natural and temporal with those who have regard only to them and to themselves in them and who find all their pleasure and enjoyment in them. But they are spiritual and eternal with those who regard good uses in them and take an interior pleasure and enjoyment in uses. The outward pleasure and enjoyment in such men also becomes spiritual, and the temporal becomes eternal. They are therefore in heaven after death and in palaces there, the useful designs of which are resplendent with gold and precious stones. They look on these things, however, as the shining and translucent external of inward things, namely, of uses, in which they take a pleasure and enjoyment which are the happiness and joy of heaven. The opposite is the lot of those who have looked on riches and wealth just for the sake of riches and wealth and for their own sake, thus on the externalities and on nothing inward; thus on appearance and not on the essential reality. When they put off the externalities, as they do on dying, they come into their internals, and as these are not spiritual, they cannot but be infernal; they must be one or the other and cannot be spiritual and infernal at the same time. The lot of these men then is poverty instead of riches and wretchedness instead of wealth.

[11] By uses not only the necessities of life are meant, such as food, raiment and habitation for oneself and one's own, but also the good of one's country, community and fellow-citizens. Business is such a good when it is the end-love and money is a mediate, subservient love, as it is only when the businessman shuns and is averse to fraud and bad practices as sin. It is otherwise when money is the end-love and business the mediate, subservient love. For this is avarice, which is a root of evils (on this see Lu 12:15 and the parable on it, verses 16-21).

## XII. MAN IS NOT ADMITTED INWARDLY INTO TRUTHS OF FAITH AND GOODS OF CHARITY EXCEPT AS HE CAN BE KEPT IN THEM TO THE CLOSE OF LIFE

221. It is well known in Christendom that the Lord wills the salvation of all, and also is almighty. From this many conclude that He can save everyone and saves those who implore His mercy, especially those who implore it by the formula of the received faith that God the Father may be merciful for the sake of the Son, particularly if they pray at the same time that they may receive this faith. That it is quite otherwise, however, will be seen in the last chapter of this treatise where it will be explained that the Lord cannot act contrary to the laws of His divine providence because that would be acting against His divine love and wisdom, thus against Himself. There, too, it will be seen that such immediate mercy is impossible, for man's salvation is effected by means, and he can be led in accordance with these means only by Him who wills the salvation of all and is at the same time almighty, thus by the Lord. These means are what are called laws of divine providence. Among them is this, that man is not admitted inwardly into truths of wisdom and goods of love except as he can be kept in them to the close of life. To make this plain to the reason, it is to be explained in this order:

1. Man may be admitted into wisdom about spiritual things and also into love of them and still not be reformed.
2. If he recedes from them afterwards and turns to what is the contrary, he profanes holy things.

3. There are many kinds of profanation, but this kind is the worst of all.
4. The Lord therefore does not admit man interiorly into truths of wisdom and at the same time into goods of love except as man can be kept in them to the very close of life.

222. (1) *Man may be admitted into wisdom about spiritual things and also into love of them and still not be reformed.* This is because he possesses rationality and liberty; by rationality he can be raised into an almost angelic wisdom, and by liberty into love not unlike angelic love. But such as the love is, such is the wisdom; if the love is celestial and spiritual, the wisdom becomes so, but if the love is diabolical and infernal, the wisdom is likewise. Outwardly, and so to others, it may seem to be celestial and spiritual, but in inward form, namely in its essence, it is diabolical and infernal; not as manifested, but as it is within one. That it is of this nature men do not see, for they are natural, see and hear naturally, and the outward form is natural; but angels do see it, for they are spiritual, see and hear spiritually, and the inward form is spiritual.

[2] From this it is plain that man can be admitted into wisdom about spiritual things and also into love of them and still not be reformed; he is admitted only into a natural love of them, not into a spiritual. This is for the reason that man can admit himself into a natural love, but the Lord alone can admit him into a spiritual love, and those admitted into this are reformed, but those admitted only into the natural love are not. For the most part the latter are hypocrites, and many are of the Order of Jesuits who inwardly do not believe in the divine at all, but play outwardly with divine things like actors.

223. It has been granted me by much experience in the spiritual world to know that man possesses in himself the faculty of apprehending arcana of wisdom like the angels themselves. For I have seen fiery devils who not only understood arcana of wisdom when they heard them, but who spoke them, too, out of their rationality. But the moment they returned to their diabolical

## XII. MAN IS NOT ADMITTED INWARDLY INTO TRUTHS OF FAITH AND GOODS OF CHARITY EXCEPT AS HE CAN BE KEPT IN THEM TO THE CLOSE OF LIFE

love they did not understand them, but in place of them the contrary, which was insanity, and this they called wisdom. In fact, I was allowed to hear them laugh at their insanity when they were in a state of wisdom, and at wisdom when they were in an insane state. One who has been of this character in the world, on becoming a spirit after death is usually brought into states of wisdom and insanity by turns, for him to distinguish the one from the other. But although such men see from the wisdom that they are insane, when the choice is given them, as it is to each, they betake themselves into the state of insanity, love it and feel hatred for the state of wisdom. The reason is that their inward nature has been diabolical and their outward seemingly divine. They are meant by devils who affect to be angels of light, and by the man in the house of the nuptials who was not dressed in a wedding garment and was cast into outer darkness (Mt 22:11-13).

224. Who cannot see that it is the internal from which the external exists and that consequently the external has its essence from the internal? And who does not know by experience that the external can appear out of accord with the essence it has from the internal? It does so obviously with hypocrites, flatterers and dissemblers. That a person can outwardly feign to be other than himself is manifest from actors and mimics. They know how to represent kings, emperors and even angels in tone of voice, speech, face and gesture as though they were really such, when they are nevertheless only actors. We allude to this because man can similarly act the deceiver in spiritual things as well as civil and moral, and that many do is well known.

[2] When the internal in its essence is infernal, and the external in its form appears to be spiritual and yet has its essence, as we said, from the internal, the question arises where in the external that essence is hidden. It does not show in gesture, voice, speech or face, yet is interiorly hidden in all four. That it is, is plain from the same in the spiritual world. For when man passes from the natural world to the spiritual, as he does at death, he leaves his externals behind along with his body and retains his

internals, which he has stored up in his spirit. If his internal was infernal, he then appears as a devil, such as he was as to his spirit during life in the world. Who does not acknowledge that everyone leaves external things behind with the body and enters into internal things on becoming a spirit?

[3] To this I will add that in the spiritual world there is a communication of affections and of thoughts from them, which results in no one's being able to speak except as he thinks; likewise, everyone changes facial expression and reflects his affection, and thus shows in his face what he is. Hypocrites are allowed sometimes to speak otherwise than they think, but the tone of the voice sounds utterly out of harmony with their interior thoughts, and they are recognized by the discord. It may be evident from this that the internal lies hidden in the tone of voice, the speech, the face and gesture of the external, and that it is not perceived by men in the world, but plainly by angels in the spiritual world.

225. It is plain from this that while he lives in the natural world man may be admitted into wisdom about spiritual things and into love of them also, and that this happens or can happen with the merely natural as well as with those who are spiritual, with this difference, however, that the latter are reformed by these means and the former are not. It may seem, also, that the former love wisdom, but they do so only as an adulterer loves a noble woman, that is, as mistress, speaking caressingly to her and giving her beautiful garments, but saying of her privately to himself, "She is only a vile harlot whom I will make believe that I love because she gratifies my lust; if she should not, I would cast her away." The internal man of the unreformed lover of wisdom is this adulterer; his external man is the woman.

226. (2) *If man recedes from these later and turns to what is contrary, he profanes holy things.* There are many kinds of profanation of what is holy, of which in the following section, but this is the gravest of all. Those who profane in this way become no longer human beings after death; they live indeed, but are continually in wild fantasies. They seem to themselves to

## XII. MAN IS NOT ADMITTED INWARDLY INTO TRUTHS OF FAITH AND GOODS OF CHARITY EXCEPT AS HE CAN BE KEPT IN THEM TO THE CLOSE OF LIFE

soar aloft and while they remain there they sport with fantasies which they see as realities. No longer human, they are referred to not as "he" or "she" but "it." In fact, when they come to view in heaven's light they look like skeletons, some like skeletons of the color of bone, others like fiery skeletons, and still others like charred ones. The world does not know that profaners of this kind become like this after death, and the reason is that the cause is unknown. The real cause is that when man first acknowledges and believes divine things and then lapses and denies them, he mixes the holy with the profane. Once they are mixed, they cannot be separated without destroying the whole. That these things may be perceived more clearly, they are to be disclosed in due order as follows:

1. Whatever a man thinks, speaks and does from the will, whether good or evil, is appropriated to him and remains.
2. The Lord in His divine providence constantly foresees and disposes that evil shall be by itself and good by itself, and thus may be separated.
3. This cannot be done, however, if man first acknowledges and lives according to truths of faith and afterwards recedes and denies them.
4. Then he mixes good and evil to the point that they cannot be separated.
5. Since good and evil in anyone must be separated, and in such a person cannot be, he is destroyed in all that is truly human.

227. These are the causes that lead to such enormity, but as they are obscure as a result of ignorance of them, they are to be explained so that they will be plain to the understanding.

(a). *Whatever man thinks, speaks and does from the will, whether good or evil, is appropriated to him and remains. This was explained above (nn. 78-81); for man has an external or natural memory and an internal or spiritual memory.* On the latter memory are written each and all things that he thought, spoke or did from his will in the world, so fully that nothing is lacking. This memory is his book of life, which is opened after death and according to which he is judged. Much more about this memory is reported from experience in the work *Heaven and Hell* (nn. 461-465).

[2] (b) *The Lord in His divine providence constantly foresees and disposes that evil shall be by itself and good by itself, and thus may be separated.* Everyone is both in evil and in good, for he is in evil from himself and in good from the Lord; he cannot live without being in both. If he were in himself alone and thus in evil alone, he would not possess anything living; nor would he if he were in the Lord alone and thus in good alone. In the latter case he would be like one suffocated and gasping for breath or like one dying in agony; in the former case he would be devoid of life, for evil apart from good is dead. Therefore everyone is in both, with the difference that in the one instance he is inwardly in the Lord and outwardly as if in himself, and in the other inwardly in himself and outwardly as if in the Lord. The latter man is in evil, the former in good, and yet each is in good and evil both. The wicked man is in both because he is in the good of civil and moral life and outwardly, in some measure, in the good of spiritual life, too, besides being kept by the Lord in rationality and liberty, making it possible for him to be in good. This is the good by means of which everyone, even a wicked man, is led by the Lord. It may then be seen that the Lord keeps evil and good apart, so that one is interior and the other exterior, and thus provides against their being mingled.

[3] (c). *This cannot be done, however, if man first acknowledges and lives according to truths of faith and then later recedes and denies them.* This is plain from what has just been said, that all which a man thinks, speaks and does from the will is appropriated to him and remains; and that the Lord in His divine providence constantly foresees and disposes that good shall be by itself and evil by itself, and so can be separated. They are also separated by the Lord after death. Those who are inwardly evil and outwardly good are deprived of the good and left to their evil. The reverse occurs with the inwardly good who

## XII. MAN IS NOT ADMITTED INWARDLY INTO TRUTHS OF FAITH AND GOODS OF CHARITY EXCEPT AS HE CAN BE KEPT IN THEM TO THE CLOSE OF LIFE

outwardly like other men have acquired wealth, sought distinction, delighted in the mundane, and indulged some lusts. Good and evil have not been commingled by them, however, but are separate, like internal and external; they have resembled the evil in many ways outwardly but not inwardly. Evil is separate from good in the evil, too, who have appeared outwardly like the good for piety, worship, speech and deeds, although wicked inwardly. With those, however, who have first acknowledged and lived by truths of faith and then lived contrary to them and rejected them and particularly if they have denied them, good and evil are no longer separate, but mixed. Such a person has appropriated both good and evil to himself, and thus combined and mixed them.

[4] (d). *He then mixes good and evil to a point where they cannot be separated.* This follows from what has just been said. And if evil cannot be separated from good and good from evil, a person can be neither in heaven nor in hell. Everyone must be in one or the other; he cannot be in both; for so he would be now in heaven and now in hell; and in heaven he would act in hell's favor and in hell act in heaven's favor. He would thus destroy the life of all around him, heavenly life among the angels and infernal life among the devils; as a result everyone's life would perish. For everyone must live his own life; no one lives a life foreign to his own, still less one opposed to it. Hence, in every man after death, when he becomes a spirit or a spiritual being, the Lord separates good from evil and evil from good, good from evil in those who are inwardly in evil, and evil from good in those inwardly in good. This accords with His own words:

> To everyone who has, shall be given, that he may abound, and from him who has not, shall even what he has be taken away (Mt 13:12; 25:29; Mk 4:25; Lu 8:18; 19:26).

[5] (e). Since good and evil in anyone must be separated and in such a person cannot be, he is destroyed in all that is truly human. As was shown earlier, everyone has what is truly human from rationality, in that he can see and know what is true and good if he wishes, and from liberty, enabling him to will, think,

speak and do it. But this liberty has been destroyed along with their rationality in those who have commingled good and evil in themselves, for they cannot from good see evil, nor from evil recognize good; the two make one in them. Hence they no longer possess rationality in any efficacy or power, nor any liberty. For this reason they are like the sheerest wild fantasies, as we said above, and no longer look like men but like bones covered with skin, and therefore when mentioned are referred to not as "he" or "she" but "it." Such is the lot of those who have commingled sacred and profane in the manner we have described. There are several kinds of profanation which are not of this character, however; of them in a later section.

228. No one can profane holy things in the way described who is ignorant of them. For one who is ignorant of them cannot acknowledge them and then deny them. Those, therefore, who are outside Christendom and know nothing of the Lord or of redemption and salvation at His hands do not profane the holiness of this in not accepting it or even by speaking against it. The Jews do not profane its sanctity, for from infancy they have no desire to receive and acknowledge it. It would be otherwise if they received and acknowledged it and afterwards denied it. This seldom occurs, however; for many among them acknowledge it outwardly but deny it inwardly and are like hypocrites. But those who first accept and acknowledge and later lapse and deny, are the ones who profane holy things by mingling them with profane.

[2] It is beside the point here that holy things are accepted and acknowledged in infancy and childhood, as they are by every Christian. For what pertains to faith and charity is not accepted and acknowledged at that age from any rationality and liberty, that is, in the understanding from the will, but only by the memory and from confidence in the teacher; and if the life is in accord it is so by blind obedience. If, however, on coming into the exercise of his rationality and freedom, which one does gradually in growing up to youth and manhood, a man acknowledges truths and lives by them only later to deny them, he does mingle the holy with the profane and (as was said above)

## XII. MAN IS NOT ADMITTED INWARDLY INTO TRUTHS OF FAITH AND GOODS OF CHARITY EXCEPT AS HE CAN BE KEPT IN THEM TO THE CLOSE OF LIFE

from being human becomes a monster. On the other hand, if a man is in evil after attaining rationality and freedom, that is, after becoming his own master, even in his early manhood, but later acknowledges truths of faith and lives by them and remains in them also to the close of life, he does not commingle the holy and the profane. The Lord then severs the evils of his earlier life from the good of his later life, as is done with all who repent. Of this more will be said in what follows.

229. (3) *There are many kinds of profanation of what is holy, but this kind is the worst of all.* In the widest sense by profanation all impiety is meant, and by profaners, therefore, all the impious who at heart deny God, the holiness of the Word, and consequently the spiritual things of the church which are essentially holy, and who also speak of them impiously. We are not now treating of such profaners but of those who profess God, uphold the holiness of the Word, and acknowledge the spiritual things of the church (yet most persons do so with the lips only). These commit profanation for the reason that holiness from the Word is in them and with them, and this which is in them, part of their understanding and will, they profane. But in the impious who deny the Divine and divine things, there is nothing holy which they can profane; they are profaners, of course, but still not profane as the others are.

230. The profanation of what is holy is meant in the second precept of the Decalog, "You shall not profane the name of your God," and that it ought not to be profaned is meant in the Lord's Prayer by "Hallowed be Thy name." Hardly anyone in Christendom understands what is meant by God's name. The reason for this is that in the spiritual world names are not what they are in this world; everyone has a name in accord with the character of his love and wisdom. As soon as he enters a society or into fellowship with others he is named according to his character. This can be done in spiritual language, which is such that it can give a name to everything, for each letter in the alphabet signifies some one thing, and the several letters combined in a word, making a person's name, involve the whole

state of the subject. This is among the wonders in the spiritual world.

[2] From this it is plain that by "the name of God" in the Word, God with all the divine in Him and proceeding from Him is signified. And as the Word is the divine proceeding, it is God's name, and as all the divine things which are called the spiritual things of the church are from the Word, they, too, are God's name. It may be seen then what is meant in the second commandment of the Decalog by

> You shall not profane the name of God (Ex 20:7);

and in the Lord's Prayer by

> Hallowed be Thy name (Mt 6:9).

The name of God and of the Lord has a like signification in many passages in the Word of either Testament, as in Mt 7:22; 10:22; 18:5, 20; 19:29; 21:9; 24:9, 10; Jn 1:12; 2:23; 3:17, 18; 12:13, 28; 14:14-16; 16:23, 24, 26, 27; 17:6; 20:31; besides other passages, and in very many in the Old Testament.

[3] One who knows this significance of "name" can know what is signified by these words of the Lord:

> Whoever receives a prophet in the name of a prophet will receive a prophet's reward; whoever receives a righteous man in the name of a righteous man will receive a righteous man's reward . . . and whoever will give one of these little ones to drink a cup of cold water only in the name of a disciple . . . shall not lose a reward (Mt 10:41, 42).

One who understands by the name of a prophet, of a righteous man and of a disciple only a prophet, a righteous man and a disciple knows only the sense of the letter in that passage. Nor does he know what is signified by a prophet's reward, a righteous man's reward, or by the reward given a disciple for a cup of cold water, when yet by the name and reward of a prophet the state and happiness of those who are in divine truths is meant; by the name and reward of a righteous man is meant the state and happiness of those in divine goods; by a disciple is meant the state of those who are in a measure of the spiritual

## XII. MAN IS NOT ADMITTED INWARDLY INTO TRUTHS OF FAITH AND GOODS OF CHARITY EXCEPT AS HE CAN BE KEPT IN THEM TO THE CLOSE OF LIFE

things of the church, and by a cup of cold water is meant a measure of truth.

[4] That the nature of a state of love and wisdom or of good and truth is meant by "name" is also made evident by these words of the Lord:

> He who enters in by the door is the shepherd of the sheep; the porter opens to him, and the sheep hear his voice; he calls his own sheep by name, and leads them out (Jn 10:2, 3).

To "call the sheep by name" is to teach and lead everyone who is in the good of charity according to the state of his love and wisdom; by the "door" the Lord is meant, as verse 9 makes plain:

> I am the door; if a man enters by Me, he will be saved (Jn 10:9).

It is clear from this that for one to be saved the Lord Himself is to be approached; one who does so is a "shepherd of the sheep" and one who does not is a "thief" and a "robber" (so the first verse of the chapter).

231. Profanation of what is holy is predicated of those who know truths of faith and goods of charity from the Word and also acknowledge them in some measure, not of those who do not know them, nor of those who impiously reject them altogether. Therefore what now follows is said of the former, not of the latter; by the former many kinds of profanation, lighter and graver, are committed, but they may be summed up in the seven following.

A first kind of profanation on their part is making jokes from the Word or about the Word, or of and about the divine things of the church. Some do this from a bad habit, picking names or expressions from the Word and mingling them with unseemly and sometimes filthy speech. This cannot be done without some contempt being added for the Word. Yet the Word in each and all things is divine and holy; every expression in it stores in its bosom something divine and by means of it gives communication with heaven. This kind of profanation is lighter or more grave according to one's acknowledgment of the sacredness of the Word and to the unseemliness of the comment into which it is brought by those who jest about it.

[2] A second kind of profanation by those under discussion is that while they understand and acknowledge divine truths, they live contrary to them. Those who only understand profane more lightly, and those who also acknowledge profane more seriously; for the understanding only teaches quite as a preacher does, but does not of itself unite with the will, but acknowledgment does, for one cannot acknowledge anything without the consent of the will. Still this union with the will varies and the profanation is according to the measure of it in living contrary to acknowledged truths. Thus if one acknowledges that revenge and hatred, adultery and fornication, fraud and deceit, blasphemy and lying are sins against God and yet commits them, he is therefore in the more grievous of this kind of profanation. For the Lord says:

> The servant who knows his lord's will and does not do it, shall be beaten with many strokes (Lu 12:47).

And again,

> If you were blind, you would not have sin, but you say, We see; therefore your sin remains (Jn 9:41).

But it is one thing to acknowledge apparent truths and another to acknowledge genuine truths. Those who acknowledge genuine truths and yet do not live by them appear in the spiritual world to be without the light and warmth of life in voice and speech, as though they were so much inertness.

[3] A third kind of profanation is committed by those who apply the sense of the letter of the Word to confirm evil loves and false principles. This is because the confirmation of falsity is the denial of truth, and the confirmation of evil is a rejection of good. In its bosom the Word is nothing but divine truth and good. But this does not appear in the lowest sense or sense of the letter in genuine truths, except where the Lord and the very way

## XII. MAN IS NOT ADMITTED INWARDLY INTO TRUTHS OF FAITH AND GOODS OF CHARITY EXCEPT AS HE CAN BE KEPT IN THEM TO THE CLOSE OF LIFE

of salvation are taught, but in clothed truths, called appearances of truth.

That sense can therefore be seized upon to confirm heresies of many kinds. But one who confirms evil loves does violence to divine goods, and one who confirms false principles does violence to divine truths. The latter violence is called falsification of truth and the former adulteration of good; both are meant by "bloods" 231-1 in the Word. For a spiritual holiness, which is also the spirit of truth proceeding from the Lord, is in every particular of the sense of the letter of the Word. This holiness is injured when the Word is falsified and adulterated. It is plain that this is profanation.

[4] A fourth kind of profanation is committed by those who utter pious and holy things and also counterfeit affections of a love for them in tone and manner, and yet at heart do not believe and love them. Most of these are hypocrites and Pharisees who are deprived after death of all truth and good and thereupon are sent into outer darkness. Those who have confirmed themselves by this kind of profanation against the Divine and against the Word and thus against the spiritual things of the Word, sit in outer darkness dumb, unable to speak, wanting to babble pious and holy things as they did in the world, but unable to do so. For in the spiritual world everyone is compelled to speak as he thinks. A hypocrite, however, wants to speak otherwise than he thinks, but there is impediment in the tongue as a result of which he can only mumble. Hypocrisies are lighter or more grave in the measure of the confirmation against God and of the outward rationalizing in favor of God.

[5] A fifth kind of profanation is committed by those who ascribe to themselves what is divine. These are meant by Lucifer in Isaiah 14; and by Lucifer Babylon is meant, as is plain from verses 4 and 24 of that chapter, where the fate, too, of such profaners is described. The same profaners are also meant and described in the Apocalypse (chapter 17) under the harlot seated on the scarlet beast. Babylon and Chaldea are mentioned at many

places in the Word; by Babylon profanation of good is meant and by Chaldea profanation of truth; the one and the other committed by those who ascribe to themselves what is divine.

[6] A sixth kind of profanation is committed by those who acknowledge the Word but deny the divine of the Lord. In the world they are called Socinians and some Arians. The lot of both is that they invoke the Father and not the Lord and keep praying the Father, some of them for the sake of the Son, that they may be admitted to heaven, but in vain, until they lose hope of salvation. They are then sent down to hell among deniers of God. They are meant by those who blaspheme the Holy Spirit and who will not be forgiven in this world or that to come (Mt 12:32). For God is one in person and essence, in Him is the Trinity, and this God is the Lord. Since the Lord is heaven also and thus those in heaven are in the Lord, those who deny the divine of the Lord cannot be admitted to heaven and be in the Lord. It was shown above that the Lord is heaven and that those in heaven are therefore in Him.

[7] The seventh kind of profanation is committed by those who first acknowledge and live by divine truths and then recede from them and deny them. This is the worst kind of profanation because holy things are mixed by them with profane to the point where they cannot be separated. Yet they must be separated for one to be either in heaven or in hell, and as this cannot be accomplished with them, all that is human, either of the understanding or of the will, is rooted out, and they become, as we said, no longer human beings. Almost the same occurs with those who acknowledge the divine things of the Word and of the church at heart but immerse them entirely in their proprium, which is a love of ruling over all things, of which much has been said before. After death, when they become spirits, they do not want to be led by the Lord but by themselves. When loose rein is given their love, they want to rule not only over heaven but over the Lord, too; and as they cannot do this, they deny the Lord and become devils. It should be known that the life's love, which is one's reigning love, remains with everyone after death and cannot be taken away.

## XII. MAN IS NOT ADMITTED INWARDLY INTO TRUTHS OF FAITH AND GOODS OF CHARITY EXCEPT AS HE CAN BE KEPT IN THEM TO THE CLOSE OF LIFE

[8] Profaners of this class are meant by the lukewarm, of whom it is written in the Apocalypse:

> I know your works, that you are neither cold nor hot; would that you were cold or hot; but because you are lukewarm, and neither cold nor hot, I will spue you out of my mouth (3:14, 15, 16).

This manner of profanation is also described by the Lord in Matthew:

> When the unclean spirit goes out from a man, he walks through dry places, seeking rest but finds none. Then he says, I will return to the house whence I came out. When he returns and finds it empty, swept and garnished for him, he goes and gathers to him seven other spirits worse than himself, and they enter and dwell there; and the last state of the man is worse than the first (12:43-45).

The conversion of the man is described by the unclean spirit's going out of him; his reverting to his former evils when things good and true have been cast out, is described by the return of the unclean spirit with seven worse than himself into the house garnished for him; and the profanation of the holy by what is profane is described by the last state of that man being worse than the first. The same is meant by this passage in John,

> Jesus said to the man healed in the pool of Bethesda: Sin no more, lest something worse befall you (5:14).

[9] That the Lord provides that man shall not acknowledge truths inwardly and afterwards leave them and become profane, is meant by these words:

> He has blinded their eyes and hardened their heart, that they should not see with their eyes and understand with their heart, and be converted, and I should heal them (Jn 12:40).

"Lest they should be converted, and I should heal them" signifies lest they should acknowledge truths and then depart from them and thus become profane. For the same reason the Lord spoke in parables, as He Himself says (Mt 13:13). The Jews were forbidden to eat fat and blood (Lev 3:17, 7:13, 25 );

this signifies that they were not to profane holy things, for "fat" signifies divine good and "blood" divine truth. In Matthew the Lord teaches that once converted a man must continue in good and truth to the close of life:

> Jesus said: Whosoever perseveres to the end, shall be saved (10:20; similarly Mk 13:13).

232. (4) *The Lord therefore does not admit man interiorly into truths of wisdom and at the same time into goods of love except as man can be kept in them to the close of life.* To demonstrate this we must proceed by steps for two reasons; one, because it concerns human salvation, and the other, because a knowledge of the laws of permission (to be considered in the next chapter) depends on a knowledge of this law. It concerns human salvation, because, as has just been said, one who first acknowledges what is divine in Word and church and subsequently departs from them profanes what is holy most grievously. In order, then, that this arcanum of divine providence may be revealed so that the rational man can see it in his own light, it is to be unfolded as follows:

1. Evil and good cannot exist together in man's interior being, consequently neither can the falsity of evil and the truth of good.
2. Good and the truth of good can be introduced into man's interior being only so far as evil and the falsity of evil there have been removed.
3. If good with its truth were introduced there before or further than evil with its falsity is removed, man would depart from the good and go back to his evil.
4. When man is in evil many truths may be introduced into his understanding and kept in memory, and yet not be profaned.
5. But the Lord in His divine providence takes the greatest care that they are not received from the understanding by the will sooner or more largely than man as of himself removes evil in the external man.

## XII. MAN IS NOT ADMITTED INWARDLY INTO TRUTHS OF FAITH AND GOODS OF CHARITY EXCEPT AS HE CAN BE KEPT IN THEM TO THE CLOSE OF LIFE

6. Should it welcome them sooner or in larger measure, the will would adulterate good and the understanding would falsify truth by mingling them with evils and falsities.
7. The Lord therefore admits man inwardly into truths of wisdom and goods of love only so far as man can be kept in them to the close of life.

233. In order, then, that this arcanum of divine providence may be disclosed so that the rational man will see it in his light, the points made will be explained one by one.

(a). *Evil and good cannot exist together in man's interior being, consequently neither can the falsity of evil and the truth of good.* By man's interiors the internal of his thought is meant. Of this he knows nothing until he comes into the spiritual world and its light, which happens on death. In the natural world it can be known only by the enjoyment of his love in the external of his thought, and from evils themselves as he examines them in himself. For the internal of thought in man is so closely connected with the external of thought that they cannot be separated (of this more may be seen above). We say "good and truth of good," and "evil and falsity of evil" because good cannot exist apart from its truth nor evil apart from its falsity. They are bedfellows or partners, for the life of good is from its truth and the life of truth is from its good; the same is to be said of evil and its falsity.

[2] The rational man can see without explanation that evil with its falsity and good with its truth cannot exist in man's interiors at the same time. For evil is the opposite of good and good the opposite of evil; two opposites cannot coexist. Implanted in all evil, moreover, is a hatred for good, and implanted in all good the love of protecting itself against evil and removing it from itself. Consequently one cannot be where the other is. If they were together conflict and combat would start and destruction ensue, as the Lord teaches also in these words:

> Every kingdom divided against itself is desolated, and every city or house divided against itself does not stand . . . Whoever is not with me is against me, and whoever does not gather with me disperses (Mt 25:30);

and in another place,

> No one can serve two masters at the same time: for either he will hate the one and love the other . . . (Mt 6:24).

Two opposites are impossible in one substance or form without its being torn apart and destroyed. If one should advance and approach the other, they would keep apart like two enemies, one retiring to his camp or fort, and the other posting himself outside. This happens with evil and good in a hypocrite; he harbors both, but the evil is inside and the good outside and so the two are separate and not mingled. It is plain then that evil with its falsity and good with its truth cannot coexist.

[3] (b). Good and the truth of good can be introduced into man's interiors only so far as evil and the falsity of evil there have been removed. This is a necessary consequence from what has preceded, for as evil and good cannot exist together, good cannot be introduced before evil has been removed. We say man's "interiors" and mean by these the internal of thought; and in these, now being considered, either the Lord or the devil must be present. The Lord is there after reformation and the devil before reformation. So far as man suffers himself to be reformed, therefore, the devil is cast out, but so far as he does not suffer himself to be reformed the devil remains. Anyone can see that the Lord cannot enter as long as the devil is there, and he is there as long as man keeps the door closed where man acts together with the Lord. The Lord teaches in the Apocalypse that He enters when that door is opened by man's mediation:

> I stand at the door, and knock; if anyone hears my voice, and opens the door, I will come in to him, and sup with him, and he with Me (3:20).

The door is opened by man's removing evil, fleeing and turning away from it as infernal and diabolical. Whether one says "evil" or "the devil," it is one and the same, in turn whether

## XII. MAN IS NOT ADMITTED INWARDLY INTO TRUTHS OF FAITH AND GOODS OF CHARITY EXCEPT AS HE CAN BE KEPT IN THEM TO THE CLOSE OF LIFE

one says "good" or "the Lord," for within all good is the Lord and within all evil is the devil. From these considerations the truth of this proposition is plain.

[4] (c). *If good with its truth were introduced before or further than evil with its falsity is removed, man would depart from the good and go back to his evil.* This is because evil would be the stronger, and what is stronger conquers, eventually if not then. As long as evil is stronger, good cannot be introduced into the inner chambers but only into the entry hall; for evil and good, as we said, cannot exist together, and what is in the entry hall is removed by its enemy in the chamber. Thus good is receded from and evil is returned to, which is the worst kind of profanation.

[5] Furthermore, it is the enjoyment of man's life to love himself and the world above all else. This enjoyment cannot be removed in a moment, but only gradually. In the measure in which it remains in man, evil is stronger in him and can be removed only as self-love becomes a love of uses, or as the love of ruling is not for its own sake but for the sake of uses. Uses then make the head, and self-love or the love of ruling is at first the body under the head and finally the feet, on which to walk. Who does not see that good should be the head, and that when it is, the Lord is there? Good and use are one. Who does not see that when evil is the head, the devil is there? As civil and moral good and, in its external form, spiritual good, too, are still to be received, who does not see that these then constitute the feet and the soles of the feet, and are trodden on?

[6] Inasmuch, then, as man's state of life is to be inverted so that what is uppermost may be lowermost, and the inversion cannot be instantaneous, for the chief enjoyment of his life, coming of self-love and the love of ruling, can be diminished and turned into a love of uses only gradually, the Lord cannot introduce good sooner or further than this evil is removed; done earlier or further, man would recede from good and return to his evil.

[7] (d). *When man is in evil many truths may be introduced into his understanding and kept in memory, and still not be profaned.* This is because the understanding does not flow into the will, but the will into the understanding. As the understanding does not flow into the will, many truths can be received by the understanding and held in memory and still not be mingled with the evil in the will, and the holy thus not profaned. Moreover, it is incumbent on everyone to learn truths from the Word or from preaching, to lay them up in the memory and to think about them. For by truths held in the memory and entering into the thought, the understanding is to teach the will, that is, the man, what he should do. This is therefore the chief means of reformation. Truths that are only in the understanding and thence in the memory are not in man but outside him.

[8] Man's memory may be compared to the ruminatory stomach of certain animals in which they put their food; as long as it is there, it is not in but outside their body; as they draw it thence and consume it, it becomes part of their life, and their body is nourished. The food in man's memory is not material but spiritual, namely truths, rightly knowledges; so far as he takes them thence by thinking, which is like ruminating, his spiritual mind is nourished. It is the will's love that has the desire and the appetite, so to speak, and that causes them to be taken thence and to be nourishing. If that love is evil, it desires or has an appetite for what is unclean, but if good, for what is clean, and sets aside, rejects and casts out what is unsuitable; this is done in various ways.

[9] (e). *But the Lord in His divine providence takes the greatest care that truths are not received from the understanding by the will sooner or more largely than man as of himself removes evil in his external man.* For what is from the will enters man, is appropriated to him, and becomes part of his life, and in that life, which is man's from the will, evil and good cannot exist together, for so he would perish. The two may, however, be in the understanding, where they are called falsities of evil and truths of good, and without being mingled; else man could not behold evil from good or know good from evil; but there they are

## XII. MAN IS NOT ADMITTED INWARDLY INTO TRUTHS OF FAITH AND GOODS OF CHARITY EXCEPT AS HE CAN BE KEPT IN THEM TO THE CLOSE OF LIFE

distinguishable and separated like the inner and outer sections of a house. When a wicked man thinks and speaks what is good, he is thinking and speaking externally to himself, but inwardly when he thinks and speaks what is evil; his speech, therefore, when he speaks what is good, comes off a wall, as it were. It can be likened to fruit fair outside but wormy and decayed inside, or to the shell, especially, of a serpent's egg.

[10] (f). *Should the will welcome truths sooner or in larger measure, it would adulterate good and the understanding would falsify truth by mingling them with evils and falsities.* When the will is in evil, it adulterates good in the understanding, and good adulterated in the understanding is evil in the will, for it confirms that evil is good and good is evil. So evil deals with all good, which is its opposite. Evil also falsifies truth, for truth of good is the opposite of the falsity of evil; this is done in the understanding by the will, and not by the understanding alone. Adulterations of good are depicted in the Word by adulteries and falsifications of truth by whoredoms. These adulterations and falsifications are effected by reasonings from the natural man which is in evil, and also by confirmations of appearances in the sense of the letter of the Word.

[11] The love of self, the head of all evils, surpasses other loves in the ability to adulterate goods and falsify truths, and it does this by misuse of the rationality which every man, wicked as well as good, enjoys from the Lord. By confirmations it can in fact make evil look exactly like good and falsity like truth. What can it not do when it can prove by a thousand arguments that nature created itself and then created human beings, animals and plants of every kind, and also prove that by influx from within itself nature causes men to live, to think analytically and to understand wisely? Self-love excels in ability to prove whatever it desires because a certain glamour of varicolored light overlays it. This glamour is the vainglory of that love in being wise and thus also of being eminent and dominant.

[12] And yet, when self-love has proved such things, it becomes so blind that it sees man only as a beast, and that man and beast both think, and if a beast could also speak, conceives it would be man in another form. If it were induced by some manner of persuasion to believe that something of the human being survives death, it then is so blind as to believe that the beast also survives; and that the something which lives after death is only a subtle exhalation of life, like a vapor, constantly falling back to its corpse, or is something vital without sight, hearing or speech, and so is blind, deaf and dumb, soaring about and cogitating. Self-love entertains many other insanities with which nature, in itself dead, inspires its fantasy. Such is the effect of self-love, which regarded in itself is love of the proprium. Man's proprium, in respect of its affections which are all natural, is not unlike the life of a beast, and in respect of its perceptions, inasmuch as they spring from these affections, is not unlike a bird of night. One who constantly immerses his thoughts in his proprium, therefore, cannot be raised out of natural light into spiritual light and see anything of God, heaven or eternal life. Since the love of the proprium is of this nature and yet excels in the ability to confirm whatever it pleases, it has a similar ability to adulterate the goods of the Word and falsify its truths, even while it is constrained by some necessity to confess them.

[13] (g). The Lord therefore does not admit man inwardly into truths of wisdom and goods of love except as man can be kept in them to the close of life. The Lord does this lest man fall into that most serious kind of profanation of which we have treated in this chapter. In view of that peril the Lord also tolerates evils of life and many heresies in worship, the tolerance of which will be the subject of the following chapter.

# XIII. LAWS ON PERMISSION ARE ALSO LAWS OF DIVINE PROVIDENCE

234. There are no laws of permission per se or apart from the laws of divine providence; rather they are the same. Hence to say that God permits something does not mean that He wills it, but that He cannot avert it in view of the end, which is salvation. Whatever is done for the sake of that end is in accord with the laws of divine providence. For divine providence, as was said, constantly travels in a different direction from that of man's will and against his will, always intent on its objective. At each moment of its activity or at each step in its progress, as it perceives man straying from that end, it directs, turns and disposes him according to its laws, leading him away from evil and to good. It will be seen in what follows that this cannot be done without the tolerance of evil. Furthermore, nothing can be permitted for no cause, and the cause can only be in some law of divine providence, explaining why it is permitted.

235. One who does not acknowledge divine providence at all does not acknowledge God at heart, but nature instead of God, and human prudence instead of divine providence. This does not appear to be so because man can think and speak in two ways. He can think and speak in one way from his inner self and in another from his outer self. This capability is like a hinge that lets a door swing either way, in one direction as one enters, in the other as one leaves; or like a sail which can take a ship one way or the other as the skipper spreads it. Those who have confirmed themselves in favor of human prudence to the denial of divine providence see nothing else as long as they are in this way of thinking, no matter what they see, hear or read, nor can they, for they accept nothing from heaven but only from themselves. As they draw their conclusions from appearances

and fallacies alone and see nothing else, they can swear that prudence is all. If they also recognize nature only, they become enraged at defenders of divine providence, except that they think when these are priests they are simply pursuing their teaching and office.

236. We will enumerate now some things that are tolerated and yet are in accord with laws of divine providence, by which, however, the merely natural man confirms himself in favor of nature and against God and in favor of human prudence and against divine providence. For instance he reads in the Word that:

1. Adam, wisest of men, and his wife allowed themselves to be led astray by the serpent, and God did not avert this in His divine providence.
2. Their first son, Cain, killed his brother Abel, and God did not speak to him and dissuade him but only afterwards cursed him.
3. The Israelites worshiped a golden calf in the wilderness and acknowledged it as the god that had brought them out of Egypt, yet Jehovah saw this from Mt. Sinai nearby and did not warn against it.
4. David numbered the people and as a consequence a pestilence befell them in which so many thousands of them perished; God sent the prophet Gad to him not before but after the deed and denounced punishment.
5. Solomon was allowed to establish idolatrous worship.
6. After him many kings were allowed to profane the temple and the sacred things of the church.
7. And finally that nation was permitted to crucify the Lord.

One who hails nature and human prudence sees nothing but what contradicts divine providence in these and many other passages of the Word. He can use them as arguments in denial of providence, if not in his outward thought nearest to speech, still in his inner thought, remote from it.

## XIII. LAWS ON PERMISSION ARE ALSO LAWS OF DIVINE PROVIDENCE

237. Every worshiper of self and nature confirms himself against divine providence:

1. When he sees such numbers of wicked in the world and so many of their impieties and how some glory in them, and sees the men go unpunished by God.
2. He confirms himself the more against divine providence when he sees plots, schemes and frauds succeed even against the devout, just and sincere, and injustice triumph over justice in the courts and in business.
3. He confirms himself especially on seeing the impious advanced to honors and becoming leaders in the state or in the church, abounding, too, in riches and living in luxury and magnificence, and on the other hand sees worshipers of God despised and poor.
4. He also confirms himself against divine providence when he reflects that wars are permitted and the slaughter of so many in them and the looting of so many cities, nations and families.
5. Furthermore, he reflects that victories are on the side of prudence and not always on the side of justice, and that it is immaterial whether a commander is upright or not.

Besides many other things of the kind, all of which are permissions according to laws of divine providence.

238. The same natural man confirms himself against divine providence when he observes how religion is circumstanced in various nations.

1. Some are totally ignorant of God; some worship the sun and moon; others idols and monstrous graven images, dead men also.
2. He notes especially that the Mohammedan religion is accepted by so many empires and kingdoms.
3. He notes that the Christian religion is found only in a very small part of the habitable globe, called Europe, and is divided there.

4. Also that some in Christendom arrogate divine power to themselves, want to be worshiped as gods, and invoke the dead.
5. And there are those who place salvation in certain phrases which they are to think and speak and not at all in good works which they are to do; likewise there are few who live their religion.
6. Besides there are heretical ideas; these have been many and some exist today, like those of the Quakers, Moravians and Anabaptists, besides others.
7. Judaism also persists.

As a result, one who denies divine providence concludes that religion in itself is nothing, but still is needed to serve as a restraint.

239. To these more arguments can be added today by which those who think interiorly in favor of nature and of human prudence alone can still further confirm themselves. For example:

1. All Christendom has acknowledged three Gods, not knowing that God is one in essence and in person and that He is the Lord.
2. It has not been known before this that there is a spiritual sense in each particular of the Word from which it derives its holiness.
3. Again, Christians have not known that to avoid evils as sins is the Christian religion itself.
4. It has also been unknown that the human being lives as such after death.

For men may ask themselves and one another, "Why does divine providence, if it exists, reveal such things for the first time now?"

240. All the points listed in nn. 236-239 have been put forward in order that it may be seen that each and all things which take place in the world are of divine providence; consequently divine providence is in the least of man's thoughts

## XIII. LAWS ON PERMISSION ARE ALSO LAWS OF DIVINE PROVIDENCE

and actions and thereby is universal. But this cannot be seen unless the points are taken up one by one; therefore they will be explained briefly in the order in which they were listed, beginning with n. 236.

241. *The wisest of human beings, Adam and his wife, allowed themselves to be led astray by the serpent, and God in His divine providence did not avert this.* This is because by Adam and his wife the first human beings created in the world are not meant, but the people of the Most Ancient Church, whose new creation or regeneration is described thus: their creation anew or regeneration in Genesis 1 by the creation of heaven and earth; their wisdom and intelligence by the Garden of Eden; and the end of that church by their eating of the tree of knowledge. For the Word in its bosom is spiritual, containing arcana of divine wisdom, and in order to contain them has been composed throughout in correspondences and representations. It is plain then that the men of that church, who at first were the wisest of men but finally became the worst through pride in their own intelligence, were led astray not by a serpent but by self-love, meant in Genesis by "the serpent's head," which the Seed of the woman, namely, the Lord, was to trample.

[2] Who cannot see from reason that other things are meant than those recorded literally like history? For who can understand that the world could be created as there described? The learned therefore labor over the explanation of the things in the first chapter, finally confessing that they do not understand them. So of the two trees placed in the garden or paradise, one of life and the other of knowledge, the latter as a stumbling-block. Again, that just by eating of this tree they transgressed so greatly that not only they but their posterity—the whole human race—became subject to damnation; further, how any serpent could lead them astray; besides other things, as that the woman was created out of a rib of her husband; that they recognized their nakedness after the fall and covered it with fig leaves; that coats of skin were given them to cover the body; and that cherubim with a flaming sword were stationed to guard the way to the tree of life.

[3] All this is representative, describing the establishment, state, alteration and finally destruction of the Most Ancient Church. The arcana involved, contained in the spiritual sense which fills the details, may be seen explained in Arcana Caelestia, on Genesis and Exodus, published at London. There it may also be seen that by the tree of life the Lord is meant as to His divine providence, and by the tree of knowledge man is meant as to his own prudence.

242. *Their first son, Cain, killed his brother Abel, and God did not speak to him and dissuade him, but only afterwards cursed him.* As the Most Ancient Church is meant by Adam and his wife, as we have just said, the two essentials of a church, love and wisdom or charity and faith are meant by their first sons, Cain and Abel. Love and charity are meant by Abel, and wisdom and faith and in particular wisdom separate from love, and faith separate from charity, are meant by Cain. Wisdom as well as faith when separate is of such a nature that it not only rejects love and charity, but also destroys them and thus kills its brother. It is well known in Christendom that faith apart from charity does so; see *Doctrine of the New Jerusalem about Faith.*

[2] The curse on Cain portends the spiritual state into which those come after death who separate faith from charity or wisdom from love. But lest wisdom or faith should perish, a mark was put on Cain lest he be slain, for love cannot exist without wisdom, nor charity without faith. As almost the same thing is represented by this as by eating of the tree of knowledge, it follows next after the account of Adam and his wife. Moreover, those in faith separate from charity are in intelligence of their own; those who are in charity and thence in faith are in intelligence from the Lord, thus in divine providence.

243. *The Israelites worshiped a golden calf in the wilderness and acknowledged it as the god that had brought them out of Egypt, yet Jehovah saw this from Mt. Sinai nearby and did not warn against it.* This occurred in the desert of Sinai near the mountain. It is in accordance with all the laws of divine providence recounted so far and with those to follow that

## XIII. LAWS ON PERMISSION ARE ALSO LAWS OF DIVINE PROVIDENCE

Jehovah did not restrain the Israelites from that atrocious worship. This evil was permitted them that they might not all perish. For the children of Israel were brought out of Egypt to represent the Lord's church; they could not represent it unless the Egyptian idolatry was first rooted out of their hearts. This could not be done unless it was left to them to act upon what was in their hearts and then to remove it on being severely punished. What further is signified by that worship, by the threat that they would be entirely rejected, and by the possibility that a new nation might be raised from Moses, may be seen in *Arcana Caelestia* on Exodus 32, where these things are spoken of.

244. *David numbered the people and as a consequence a pestilence befell them in which so many thousands of them perished; God sent the prophet Gad to him not before but after the deed and denounced punishment.* One who confirms himself against divine providence may have various thoughts about this also and ponder especially why David was not admonished first and why the people were so severely punished for the king's transgression. That he was not warned first is in accord with the laws of divine providence already adduced, especially with the two explained at nn. 129-153 and 154-174. The people were so severely punished for the king's transgression and seventy thousand smitten by the pestilence not on account of the king but on account of themselves, for we read

> The anger of Jehovah kindled still more against Israel; therefore He incited David against them saying, Go, number Israel and Judah (2 Sa 24:1).

245. *Solomon was allowed to establish idolatrous forms of worship.* For he was to represent the Lord's kingdom or church in all varieties of religion in the world. For the church established with the Israelitish and Jewish nation was a representative church; all of its judgments and statutes represented the spiritual things of a church, which are its internals. The people represented the church, the king the Lord, David the Lord to come into the world, Solomon the Lord after His coming. As the Lord after the glorification of His humanity had all power over heaven and earth (as He said, Mt 28:18), Solomon as

representative of Him appeared in glory and magnificence, was wise beyond all earthly kings, and also built the temple. Moreover, he permitted and set up the forms of worship of many nations, by which the various religions of the world were represented. His wives, who numbered seven hundred and his concubines who numbered three hundred (1 Kgs 11:13), had a similar signification, for "wife" in the Word signifies the church and "concubine" a form of religion. Hence it may be evident why it was granted Solomon to build the temple, by which the Divine Humanity of the Lord (Jn 2:19, 21) is signified and the church, too; and why he was allowed to establish idolatrous forms of worship and to take so many wives. See *Doctrine of the New Jerusalem about the Lord* (nn. 43, 44) that in many places in the Word the Lord who was to come into the world is meant by David.

246. *After Solomon many kings were allowed to profane the temple and the sacred things of the church.* This was because the people represented the church and the king was their head. The Israelitish and Jewish nation was of such a nature that they could not represent the church for long, for at heart they were idolaters; they therefore relapsed gradually from representative worship, perverting all things of the church, even to devastating it finally. This was represented by the profanations of the temple by the kings and by the people's idolatries; the full devastation of the church was represented by the destruction of the temple, the carrying off of Israel, and the captivity of Judah in Babylon. Such was the cause of this toleration; and what is done for some cause is done under divine providence according to one of its laws.

247. *That nation was permitted to crucify the Lord.* This was because the church with that nation was entirely devastated and had become such that they not only did not know or acknowledge the Lord, but hated Him. Still, all that they did to Him was according to laws of His divine providence. See in *Doctrine of the New Jerusalem about the Lord* (nn. 12-14) and in *Doctrine of the New Jerusalem about Faith* (nn. 34, 35) that the passion of the cross was the last temptation or battle by which

## XIII. LAWS ON PERMISSION ARE ALSO LAWS OF DIVINE PROVIDENCE

the Lord fully conquered the hells and fully glorified His Humanity.

248. So far the points listed at n. 236 have been explained, involving passages in the Word by which the naturally minded reasoner may confirm himself against divine providence. For, as was said, whatever such a man sees, hears or reads he can make into an argument against providence. Few persons, however, confirm themselves against divine providence from incidents in the Word, but many do so from things before their eyes, listed at n. 237. These are to be explained now in like manner.

249. *Every worshiper of self and of nature confirms himself against divine providence when he sees so many impious in the world and so many of their impieties and how some glory in them, yet sees the impious go unpunished by God.* All impieties and all gloryings in them are permissions, of which the causes are laws of divine providence. Each human being can freely, indeed very freely, think what he wills, against God as well as in favor of God. One who thinks against God is rarely punished in the natural world, for he is always in a state to be reformed then, but is punished in the spiritual world, which is done after death, for then he can no longer be reformed.

[2] That laws of divine providence are the causes of tolerance is clear from the laws set forth above, if you will recall and examine them. They are: that man shall act in freedom according to reason (of this law above, nn. 71-79); that he shall not be forced by external means to think and will, thus to believe and love what is of religion, but bring himself and sometimes compel himself to do so (nn. 129-153); that there is no such thing as one's own prudence, but there only appears to be and it should so appear, but divine providence is universal from being in the least things (nn. 191-213); divine providence looks to what is eternal, and to the temporal only as this makes one with the eternal (nn. 214-220); man is not admitted inwardly into truths of faith and goods of charity except as he can be kept in them to the close of life (nn. 221-233).

Divine Providence

[3] That the laws of divine providence are the causes of tolerance will also be evident from the following, for one thing from this: evils are tolerated because of the end, which is salvation. Again from this: that divine providence is continual with the wicked as well as with the good. And finally from this: the Lord cannot act contrary to the laws of His divine providence because to do so would be to act contrary to His divine love and wisdom, thus contrary to Himself. Brought together, these laws can make the causes manifest why impieties are tolerated by the Lord and are not punished while they exist in the thought only and rarely, too, while they exist in intention, thus in the will but not in act. Yet its own punishment follows every evil; it is as if its punishment were inscribed on an evil, and the impious man suffers it after death.

[4] These considerations also explain the next point, listed at n. 237: *The worshiper of self and of nature confirms himself still more against divine providence when he sees plots, schemes and frauds succeed even against the devout, just and sincere, and injustice triumph over justice in the courts and in business.* All the laws of divine providence have requirements; and as they are the causes why such things are permitted, it is plain that for man to live as a human being and be reformed and saved, these things can be removed from him by the Lord only through means. The Word and, in particular, the precepts of the Decalog are the means with those who acknowledge all kinds of murder, adultery, theft and false witness to be sins. With those who do not acknowledge such things as sins, they are removed by means of the civil laws and fear of their penalties and by means also of the moral laws and fear of disrepute and consequent loss of standing and wealth. By the latter means the Lord leads the evil, but only away from doing such things, not from thinking and willing them. But by the former means He leads the good, not only away from doing them, but from thinking and willing them, too.

250. *The worshiper of self and of nature confirms himself against divine providence on seeing the impious advanced to honors and becoming leaders in the state and in the church,*

## XIII. LAWS ON PERMISSION ARE ALSO LAWS OF DIVINE PROVIDENCE

*abounding, too, in riches and living in luxury and magnificence, and on the other hand sees worshipers of God despised and poor.* A worshiper of self and of nature believes that standing and riches are the greatest and the one felicity possible, thus felicity itself. If he has some thought of God as a result of worship begun in childhood, he calls them divine blessings, and as long as he is not elated by them he thinks that there is a God and worships Him. But in the worship there lurks a desire, of which he is unaware then, to be advanced by God to still higher standing and to still greater wealth. If he attains them, his worship tends more and more to externalities until it slips away and at last he makes little account of God and denies Him. The same thing occurs if he is cast down from the standing and loses the riches on which he has set his heart. What, then, are standing and riches to the wicked but stumbling blocks?

[2] To the good they are not, for these do not set their heart on them, but on the uses or goods for rendering which standing and wealth serve as means. Hence only a worshiper of self and of nature can confirm himself against divine providence because the impious are advanced to honors and become leaders in the state and in the church. Moreover, what is greater or less standing, or greater or less wealth? Is this not in itself imaginary? Is one person more blessed and happier than another for it? Is a great man's standing, or even a king's or an emperor's, not regarded in a year's time as a commonplace, no longer exalting his heart with joy but quite possibly becoming worthless to him? Have those with standing a larger measure of happiness than those with little standing or even the least standing, like farmers and their hands? May not these enjoy more happiness when it is well with them and they are content with their lot? What is more unquiet at heart, more often provoked, or more violently enraged than self-love? It happens as often as it is not honored to suit the haughtiness of its heart or as something does not succeed at its beck and wish. What, then, is standing except an idea, unless it attaches to the office or the use? Can the idea exist in any other thought than thought about self and the world, and does it not really mean that the world is all and eternity nothing?

## Divine Providence

[3] Something shall be said now why divine providence permits the impious at heart to be promoted to standing and to acquire wealth. The impious or the evil can render services as well as the pious or good, indeed with more fire, for they regard themselves in the use and their standing as the use. As self-love mounts, therefore, the lust of doing service for one's glory is fired. There is no such fire with the devout or good unless it is kindled incidentally to their standing. Therefore the Lord governs the impious at heart who have standing by their desire for a name and arouses them to perform uses to the community or their country, their society or city, and their fellow citizen or neighbor. With such persons this is the Lord's government which is called divine providence, for the Lord's kingdom is one of uses, and where only a few perform uses for uses' sake providence brings it about that worshipers of self are raised to higher offices, in which each is incited by his love to do good.

[4] Suppose an infernal kingdom in the world (though there is none) where self-love alone rules, which is itself the devil, would not everyone perform uses with the zeal of self-love and for the enhancement of his glory more than in another kingdom? The public good is borne on the lips of them all, but their own benefit in the heart. And as each relies on what rules him in order to become greater, and aspires to be greatest, how can he see that God exists? A smoke like that of a conflagration envelops him through which no spiritual truth can pass with its light. I have seen that smoke around the hells of such men. Light a lamp and inquire how many in present-day kingdoms aspire to eminence who are not loves of self and the world. Will you find fifty in a thousand who are loves of God, among whom, moreover, only a few aspire to eminence? Since so few are loves of God and so many are loves of self and the world and since the latter perform more uses by their ardor, how can one confirm himself against divine providence because the evil surpass the good in eminence and opulence?

[5] This is borne out also by these words of the Lord:

> The lord praised the unjust steward because he had acted prudently; for the sons of this age are more prudent in their

## XIII. LAWS ON PERMISSION ARE ALSO LAWS OF DIVINE PROVIDENCE

> generation than the sons of light in their generation. So I say to you, Make friends for yourselves of the unjust mammon that when you fail they may receive you into eternal habitations (Lu 16:8, 9).

The meaning in the sense of the letter is plain. But in the spiritual sense by the "mammon of injustice" are meant knowledges of good and truth which the evil possess and employ solely to acquire standing and wealth for themselves. It is of these knowledges that the good or the children of light are to make friends for themselves and it is these knowledges that will conduct them into eternal homes. The Lord also teaches that many are loves of self and the world, and few are loves of God, in these words:

> Wide is the gate, and broad is the way, which leads to destruction, and many there be who enter it, but narrow and strait is the way which leads to life, and there are few who find it (Mt 7:13, 14).

It may be seen above (n. 217) that eminence and riches are either curses or blessings, and with whom they are the one or the other.

Footnotes:

202-1 It is the doctrine of all churches in Christendom that God the Father, God the Son and God the Holy Spirit is infinite, eternal, uncreated and omnipotent, as may be seen in the Athanasian Creed.

231-1 Plural in the Hebrew, especially of blood that has been shed. "Both" is emphatic here, and for the significance of the plural see Arcana Caelestia, n. 374e and Apocalypse Explained, n. 329(27).

251. *The worshiper of self and of nature confirms himself against divine providence when he reflects that wars are permitted and the slaughter in them of so many men and the plundering of their wealth.* It is not by divine providence that wars occur, for they entail murder, plunder, violence, cruelty, and other terrible evils which are diametrically opposed to Christian charity. Yet they cannot but be permitted because the

life's love of mankind, since the time of the most ancient people, meant by Adam and his wife (n. 241), has become such that it wants to rule over others and finally over all, and also to possess the wealth of the world and finally all wealth. These two loves cannot be kept in fetters, for it is according to divine providence that everyone is allowed to act in freedom in accordance with reason, as may be seen above (nn. 71-97); and apart from permissions man cannot be led from evil by the Lord and consequently cannot be reformed and saved. For unless evils were allowed to break out, man would not see them, therefore would not acknowledge them, and thus could not be induced to resist them. Evils cannot be repressed, therefore, by any act of providence; if they were, they would remain shut in, and like a disease such as cancer and gangrene, would spread and consume everything vital in man.

[2] For from birth man is like a little hell between which and heaven there is perpetual discord. No one can be withdrawn from his hell by the Lord unless he sees he is in it and desires to be led out of it. This cannot be done apart from tolerations the causes of which are laws of divine providence. As a result, minor and major wars occur, the minor between owners of estates and their neighbors, and the major between sovereigns of kingdoms and their neighbors. Except for size the only difference is that the minor conflicts are held within limits by a country's laws and the major by the law of nations; each may wish to transgress its laws, but the minor cannot, and while the major can, still the possibility has limits.

[3] Hidden in the stores of divine wisdom are several causes why the major wars of kings and rulers, involving murder, looting, violence and cruelty as they do, are not prevented by the Lord, either at their beginning or during their course, only finally when the power of one or the other has been so reduced that he is in danger of annihilation. Some of the causes have been revealed to me and among them is this: all wars, although they are civil in character, represent in heaven states of the church and are correspondences. The wars described in the Word were all of this character; so are all wars at this day. Those in the Word are

## XIII. LAWS ON PERMISSION ARE ALSO LAWS OF DIVINE PROVIDENCE

the wars which the children of Israel waged with various nations, Amorites, Moabites, Philistines, Syrians, Egyptians, Chaldeans and Assyrians. Moreover, it was when the children of Israel, who represented the church, departed from their precepts and statutes and fell into evils represented by other peoples (for each nation with which the children of Israel waged war represented a particular evil), that they were punished by that nation. For instance, when they profaned the sanctities of the church by foul idolatries they were punished by the Assyrians and Chaldeans because Assyria and Chaldea signify the profanation of what is holy. What was signified by the wars with the Philistines may be seen in *Doctrine of the New Jerusalem about Faith* (nn. 50-54).

[4] Wars at the present day, wherever they may occur, represent similar things. For all things which occur in the natural world correspond to spiritual things in the spiritual world, and all spiritual things are related to the church. It is not known in the world which kingdoms in Christendom represent the Moabites, the Ammonites, the Syrians, the Philistines, the Chaldeans and the Assyrians or others, with whom the children of Israel waged war; yet there are nations that do so. Moreover, the condition of the church on earth and what the evils are into which it falls and for which it is punished by wars, cannot be seen at all in the natural world, for only externals are manifest here and these do not constitute the church. This is seen, however, in the spiritual world where internal conditions appear and in these the church itself consists. There all are united according to their various states. Conflicts between them correspond to wars, which on both sides are governed by the Lord correspondentially in accordance with His divine providence.

[5] The spiritual man acknowledges that wars on earth are ruled by the Lord's divine providence. The natural man does not, except that at a celebration of a victory he may thank God on his knees for having given the victory, and except for a few words on going into battle. But when he returns into himself he ascribes the victory either to the prudence of the general or to some counsel or incident in the midst of the fighting which escaped notice and yet decided the victory.

[6] It may be seen above (n. 212) that divine providence, which is called fortune, is in the least things, even in trivial ones, and if you acknowledge divine providence in these you will certainly do so in the issues of war. Success and happy conduct of war, moreover, are in common parlance called the fortune of war, and this is divine providence, to be found especially in a general's judgments and plans, although he may at the time and also afterwards ascribe all to his own prudence. This he may do if he will, for he has full freedom to think in favor of divine providence or against it, indeed in favor of God or against Him; but let him know that no judgment or plan is from himself; it comes either from heaven or from hell, from hell by permission, from heaven by providence.

252. *A worshiper of self and of nature confirms himself against divine providence when he thinks, as he sees it, that victories are on the side of prudence and not always on the side of justice, and that it is immaterial whether a commander is upright or not.* Victories seem to be on the side of prudence and not always on the side of justice, because man judges by the appearance and favors one side more than the other and can by reasoning confirm what he favors. Nor does he know that the justice of a cause is spiritual in heaven and natural in the world, as was said just above, and that the two are united in a connection of things past and of things to come, known only to the Lord.

[2] It is immaterial whether the commander is an upright man or not because, as was established above (n. 250), the evil as well as the good perform uses, and by their zeal more ardently than the good. This is so especially in war because the evil man is more crafty and cunning in devising schemes than a good man, and in his love of glory takes pleasure in killing and plundering those whom he knows and declares to be the enemy. The good man has prudence and zeal for defense and rarely for attacking. This is much the same as it is with spirits of hell and angels of heaven; the spirits of hell attack and the angels of heaven defend themselves. Hence comes this conclusion that it is allowable for one to defend his country and his fellow-citizens against

## XIII. LAWS ON PERMISSION ARE ALSO LAWS OF DIVINE PROVIDENCE

invading enemies even by iniquitous commanders, but not allowable to make oneself an enemy without cause. To have the seeking of glory for cause is in itself diabolical, for it comes of self-love.

253. The points made above (n. 237) by which the merely natural man confirms himself against divine providence have now been explained. The points which follow (n. 238) about the varieties of religion in many nations, which also serve the merely natural man for arguments against divine providence, are to be clarified next. For the merely natural man says in his heart, How can so many discordant religions exist instead of one world-wide and true religion when (as was shown above, nn. 27-45) divine providence has a heaven from mankind for its purpose? But pray, listen: all human beings who are born, however numerous and of whatever religion, can be saved if only they acknowledge God and live according to the precepts of the Decalog, which forbid committing murder, adultery, theft, and false witness because to do such things is contrary to religion and therefore contrary to God. Such persons fear God and love the neighbor. They fear God inasmuch as they think that to do such things is to act against God, and they love the neighbor because to murder, commit adultery, steal, bear false witness and covet the neighbor's house or wife is to act against one's neighbor. Heeding God in their lives and doing no evil to the neighbor, they are led by the Lord, and those whom He leads are also taught about God and the neighbor in accordance with their religion, for those who live in this way love to be taught, but those living otherwise have no such desire. Loving to be taught, they are also instructed by angels after death when they become spirits, and willingly receive such truths as the Word contains. Something about them may be seen in *Doctrine of the New Jerusalem about Sacred Scripture* (nn. 91-97 and 104-113).

254. *The merely natural man confirms himself against divine providence when he observes the religious conditions in various nations and notes that some people are totally ignorant of God, some worship the sun and moon, and some worship idols and graven images.* Those who argue from these facts against divine

providence are ignorant of the arcana of heaven; these arcana are innumerable and man is acquainted with hardly any of them. Among them is this: man is not taught from heaven directly but mediately (this may be seen treated above, nn. 154-174). Because he is taught mediately, and the Gospel could not through the medium of missionaries reach all who dwell in the world, but religion could be spread in various ways to inhabitants of the remote corners of the earth, this has been effected by divine providence. For a knowledge of religion does not come to a man from himself, but through another who has either learned it from the Word or by tradition from others who have learned it, for instance that God is, heaven and hell exist, there is a life after death, and God must be worshiped for man to be blessed.

[2] See in *Doctrine of the New Jerusalem about Sacred Scripture* (nn. 101-103) that religion spread throughout the world from the Ancient Word and afterwards from the Israelitish Word, and (nn. 114-118) that unless there had been a Word no one could have known about God, heaven and hell, life after death, and still less about the Lord. Once a religion is established in a nation the Lord leads that nation according to the precepts and tenets of its own religion, and He has provided that there should be precepts in every religion like those in the Decalog, that God should be worshiped, His name not be profaned, a holy day be observed, that parents be honored, murder, adultery and theft not be committed, and false witness not be spoken. A nation that regards these precepts as divine and lives according to them in religion's name is saved, as was just said (n. 253). Most nations remote from Christendom regard these laws not as civil but as divine, and hold them sacred. See in *Doctrine of the New Jerusalem [about Life] from the Precepts of the Decalog*, from beginning to end, that a man is saved by a life according to these precepts.

[3] Also among the arcana of heaven is this: in the Lord's sight the angelic heaven is like one man whose soul and life is the Lord. In each particular of his form this divine man is man, not only as to the external members and organs but as to the

## XIII. LAWS ON PERMISSION ARE ALSO LAWS OF DIVINE PROVIDENCE

more numerous internal members and organs, also as to the skins, membranes, cartilages and bones; but in that man all these, both external and internal, are not material but spiritual. Further, the Lord has provided that those who cannot be reached by the Gospel but only by some form of religion shall also have a place in this divine man, that is, in heaven, by constituting the parts called skins, membranes, cartilages and bones, and like others should be in heavenly joy. For it does not matter whether their joy is that of the angels of the highest heaven or of the lowest heaven, for everyone entering heaven comes into the highest joy of his own heart; joy higher still he does not endure; he would suffocate in it.

[4] A peasant and a king may serve for comparison. A peasant may reach the height of joy when he steps out in a new suit of homespun wool or seats himself at a table with pork, a piece of beef, cheese, beer and fiery wine on it. He would feel constricted at heart if he was clothed like a king in purple, silk, gold and silver, or if a table was set for him on which were delicacies and costly viands of many kinds with noble wine. It is plain from this that the last as well as the first find heavenly happiness, each in his measure, those outside Christendom also, therefore, provided they shun evils as sins against God because these are contrary to religion.

[5] Few are entirely ignorant of God. If they have lived a moral life they are instructed after death by angels and receive what is spiritual in their moral life (see *Doctrine of the New Jerusalem about Sacred Scripture*, n. 116). The same is true of those who worship sun and moon, believing that God is there. They know no better, therefore it is not imputed to them as a sin, for the Lord says,

> If you were blind (that is, if you did not know), you would have no sin (Jn 9:41).

But there are many who worship idols and graven images even in the Christian world. This, to be sure, is idolatrous, yet not with all. There are those for whom graven images serve as a means of exciting thought about God, for by an influx from heaven one who acknowledges God desires to see Him, and these, unable to raise the mind above the sensuous as those do who are inwardly spiritual, rouse it by means of statue or image. Those who do so and do not worship the image itself as God are saved if they also live by the precepts of the Decalog from religious principle.

[6] It is plain, then, that as the Lord desires the salvation of all, He has also provided that everyone who lives well may have a place in heaven. See in the work *Heaven and Hell*, published at London, 1758 (nn. 59-102 ), in *Arcana Caelestia* (nn. 5552-5569) and above (nn. 201-204) that heaven in the Lord's sight is like one man; that heaven accordingly corresponds to each and all things in man; and that there are also those who represent skin, membranes, cartilages and bones.

255. *The merely natural man confirms himself against divine providence when he sees the Mohammedan religion accepted by so many empires and kingdoms.* The fact that this form of religion is accepted by more kingdoms than Christianity is may be a stumbling-block to those who give thought to divine providence and at the same time believe that no one can be saved unless he has been born a Christian, thus where the Word is, by which the Lord is known. That form of religion is no stumbling-block, however, to those who believe that all things are of divine providence. These ask in what the providence consists and find it is in this, that Mohammedanism, acknowledges the Lord as Son of God, the wisest of men and a very great prophet who came into the world to teach men; most Mohammedans consider Him to be greater than Mohammed.

[2] That form of religion was called forth in the divine providence to destroy the idolatries of many nations. To make this fully known we will pursue some order; first, something on the origin of idolatries. Previously to that form of religion the worship of idols was general in the world. This was because the churches before the Lord's advent were all representative churches. The Israelitish church was of this character. In it the tabernacle, Aaron's garments, the sacrifices, all things of the

## XIII. LAWS ON PERMISSION ARE ALSO LAWS OF DIVINE PROVIDENCE

temple in Jerusalem, the statutes also, were representative. Moreover, the ancients had a knowledge of correspondences, which is the knowledge of representations—it was the chief knowledge of their wise men. This knowledge was cultivated especially in Egypt and was the origin of Egyptian hieroglyphics. By that knowledge the ancients knew what animals of every kind signified and what trees of every kind signified, as they did what mountains, hills, rivers and fountains signified, as well as sun, moon and stars. As all their worship was representative, consisting of sheer correspondences, they worshiped on mountains and hills and in groves and gardens, regarded fountains as sacred, and in adoration of God faced the rising sun. Furthermore, they made graven images of horses, oxen, calves and lambs, and of birds, fish and serpents, and placed them in their houses and elsewhere, arranged according to the spiritual things of the church to which they corresponded or which they represented. They placed similar objects in their temples, too, to put them in mind of the holy things they signified.

[3] Later, when the knowledge of correspondences had been lost, their posterity began to worship the graven images themselves, as holy in themselves, not knowing that their forefathers had seen no holiness in them, but only that they represented holy things by correspondences and thus signified them. So arose the idolatries which filled the whole world, Africa and Europe as well as Asia with its adjacent islands. In order that all these idolatries might be uprooted, of the Lord's divine providence it was brought about that a new religion, adapted to the genius of Orientals, should start up, in which there would be something from each Testament of the Word, and which would teach that the Lord had come into the world and was a very great prophet, wisest of all, and Son of God. This was done through Mohammed, from whom the religion is called the Mohammedan religion.

[4] Of the Lord's divine providence this religion was raised up and, as we said, adapted to the genius of Orientals, in order that it might destroy the idolatries of so many peoples and give them some knowledge of the Lord before they passed into the

spiritual world. This religion would not have been accepted by so many kingdoms or had the power to uproot idolatries, had it not suited and met the ideas and thinking of them all. It did not acknowledge the Lord as God of heaven and earth, for the Orientals acknowledged God the Creator of the universe, but could not comprehend that He came into the world and assumed human nature, quite as Christians do not comprehend this, who therefore separate His divine from His humanity in their thinking and place His divine near the Father in heaven and His humanity they know not where.

[5] Hence it may be seen that the Mohammedan religion arose under the Lord's divine providence and that all adherents of it who acknowledge the Lord as Son of God and live according to the precepts of the Decalog, which they also have, shunning evils as sins, come into a heaven called the Mohammedan heaven. This heaven, like others, is divided into three, the highest, middle and lowest. Those who acknowledge the Lord to be one with the Father and thus the one God are in the highest heaven; in the next heaven are those who renounce a plurality of wives and live with one; and in the lowest are those who are being initiated. More about this religion may be seen in *Continuation about the Last Judgment and the Spiritual World* (nn. 68-72), where the Mohammedans and Mohammed are treated of.

256. *The merely natural man confirms himself against divine providence when he sees that the Christian religion exists only in a small part of the habitable world, called Europe, and there is divided.* The Christian religion exists only in the small part of the habitable world called Europe because it was not adapted to the genius of Orientals as was a mixed one like the Mohammedan religion, as was just shown; and an unadapted religion is not received. For example, a religion which ordains that it is unlawful to take more than one wife is not received but rejected by those who for ages have been polygamists. This is true of other ordinances of the Christian religion.

## XIII. LAWS ON PERMISSION ARE ALSO LAWS OF DIVINE PROVIDENCE

[2] Nor is it material whether a smaller or a larger part of the world has received this religion, as long as there are people with whom the Word is. For those who are outside the church and do not possess the Word still have light from it, as was shown in *Doctrine of the New Jerusalem about Sacred Scripture*, nn. 104-113. It is a marvel that where the Word is reverently read and the Lord is worshiped from it, He is present with heaven. The reason is that He is the Word and the Word is divine truth which makes heaven. The Lord therefore says:

> Where two or three are gathered in my name, there am I in the midst of them (Mt 18:20).

Europeans can bring this about with the Word in many parts of the habitable globe, for they trade the world over and read or teach the Word everywhere. This seems like fiction and yet is true.

[3] The Christian religion is divided because it is from the Word and the Word is written in sheer correspondences and these in large part are appearances of truth in which, nevertheless, genuine truths lie concealed. As a church's doctrine is to be drawn from the sense of the letter of the Word which is of this character, disputes, controversies and dissensions were bound to arise over the understanding of the Word, but not over the Word itself or the Divine itself of the Lord. For it is acknowledged everywhere that the Word is holy and that the Lord possesses the divine, and these two are essentials of the church. Those, therefore, who deny the Divine of the Lord and are called Socinians have been excommunicated from the church, and those who deny the holiness of the Word are not regarded as Christians.

[4] To this let me add a remarkable item about the Word from which one may conclude that inwardly the Word is divine truth itself and inmostly the Lord. When a spirit opens the Word and touches his face or dress with it, just from the contact his face or garment shines as brightly as the moon or a star, in the sight of all, too, whom he meets. It is evidence that there is nothing holier in the world than the Word.

## Divine Providence

That the Word is written throughout in correspondences may be seen in *Doctrine of the New Jerusalem about Sacred Scripture*, nn. 5-26; that the church's doctrine is to be drawn from the sense of the letter of the Word and confirmed thereby, nn. 50-61; that heresies can be wrested from the sense of the letter of the Word, but that it is harmful to confirm them, nn. 91-97; that the church is from the Word and is such as is its understanding of the Word, nn. 76-79.

257. *The merely natural man confirms himself against divine providence because in many kingdoms where the Christian religion is accepted there are those who arrogate divine power to themselves, want to be worshiped as gods, and also invoke dead men.* To be sure, they say that they have not arrogated divine power to themselves and do not wish to be worshiped as gods. Yet they say that they can open and close heaven, remit and retain sins, and so save and condemn men, and this is what is divine itself. Divine providence has no other purpose than reformation and hence salvation; this is its unceasing activity with everyone. And salvation can be effected only by acknowledgment of the divine of the Lord and by confidence that He brings salvation as man lives according to His commandments.

[2] Who cannot see that the usurpation of divine power is the Babylon described in the Apocalypse and the Babel spoken of here and there in the Prophets? It is also Lucifer in Isaiah 14, as is plain from verses 4 and 22 of that chapter, where are the words:

> You shall speak this parable about the king of Babel (verse 4);

> (Then), I will cut off the name and remnant of Babel (verse 22);

it is plain from this that this Babel is Lucifer, of whom it is said:

> How you have fallen from heaven, O Lucifer, son of the morning! ... For you have said in your heart, I will ascend into heaven, I will exalt my throne above the stars of God; I

## XIII. LAWS ON PERMISSION ARE ALSO LAWS OF DIVINE PROVIDENCE

will also sit on the mount of the congregation, at the sides of the north; I will ascend above the heights of the clouds; I will be like the Most High (Isa 14:12-14).

It is well known that the same persons invoke the dead and pray to them for help. We make the assertion because such invocation was established by a papal bull, confirming the decree of the Council of Trent, in which it is openly said that the dead are to be invoked. Yet who does not know that only God is to be invoked, and not any dead person?

[3] It shall be told now why the Lord has permitted such things. Can one deny that He has done so for the sake of the end in view, namely salvation? For men know that there is no salvation without the Lord. Therefore it was necessary that the Lord should be preached from the Word and that the Christian Church should be established by this means. This could be done, however, only by leaders who would act with zeal and no others offered than those who burned with zeal out of self-love. At first this fire aroused them to preach the Lord and teach the Word. From this their first state Lucifer is called "the son of the morning" (14:12). But as they saw that they could dominate by means of the sanctities of the Word and the church, the self-love by which they were first aroused to preach the Lord broke out from within and finally exalted itself to such a height that they transferred all the Lord's divine power to themselves, leaving Him none.

[4] This could not be prevented by the Lord's divine providence, for if it had been they would have declared that the Lord is not God and that the Word is not sacred and would have made themselves Socinians and Arians, so would have destroyed the whole church. But, whatever its rulers are, the church continues among the people submissive to them. For all in this religion who approach the Lord and shun evils as sins are saved; therefore many heavenly societies are formed from them in the spiritual world. It has also been provided that there should be a nation among them that has not bowed to the yoke of such domination and that regards the Word as holy; this noble nation is the French nation.

[5] But what was done? When self-love exalted its dominion even to the Lord's throne, removing Him and setting itself on it, that love, which is Lucifer, could not but have profaned all things of the Word and the church. Lest this should happen, the Lord in His divine providence took care that they should recede from worship of Him, invoke the dead, pray to graven images of the dead, kiss their bones and kneel at their tombs, should ban the reading of the Word, appoint holy worship in masses not understood by the common people, and sell salvation for money. For if they had not done this, they would have profaned the sanctities of the Word and the church. For, as was shown in the preceding section, only those profane holy things who know them.

[6] Lest, too, they should profane the most Holy Supper it is of the Lord's divine providence that they divide it, giving the bread to the people and drinking the wine themselves. For the wine of the Supper signifies holy truth and the bread holy good; but divided the wine signifies truth profaned and the bread good adulterated. It is also of the Lord's divine providence that they should render the Holy Supper corporeal and material and give it the prime place in religion. Anyone who gives these particulars his attention and reflects on them in some enlightenment of his mind can see the amazing action of divine providence for the protection of the sanctities of the church and for the salvation of all who can be saved and are ready to be snatched from the fire, so to speak, from which they must be snatched.

258. The merely natural man confirms himself against divine providence because some among those who profess the Christian religion place salvation in certain phrases which they are to think and speak and not at all in good works which they are to do. We showed in *Doctrine of the New Jerusalem about Faith* that these are such as make faith alone saving and not the life of charity, thus such as separate faith from charity. It was also shown that these are meant in the Word by "Philistines," "dragon" and "goats."

## XIII. LAWS ON PERMISSION ARE ALSO LAWS OF DIVINE PROVIDENCE

[2] That such doctrine has been permitted is also of divine providence lest the divine of the Lord and the sanctity of the Word should be profaned. The divine of the Lord is not profaned when salvation is placed in these words: That God the Father may have mercy for the sake of the Son, who suffered the Cross and made satisfaction for us. For men do not then address the divine of the Lord but have in mind His human nature, which they do not acknowledge to be divine. Nor do they profane the Word, for they do not attend to the passages in which love, charity, deeds and works are mentioned. All this, they say, is involved in the faith expressed in the saying quoted. Those who confirm this tell themselves, "The law does not condemn me, neither then does evil, and good does not save because good done by me is not good." They are therefore like those who do not know any truth from the Word and consequently cannot profane it. Only those confirm the faith expressed in that saying who from self-love are in the pride of their own intelligence. Nor are these Christians at heart; they only desire to be looked on as such.

[3] It shall now be shown that the Lord's divine providence is nevertheless acting constantly to save those with whom faith separated from charity has become an article of religion. Although this faith has become an article of their religion, by the Lord's divine providence each knows that it is not faith that saves, but a life of charity with which faith makes one. For all churches in which that religion is accepted also teach that there is no salvation unless man examines himself, sees and acknowledges his sins, repents, desists from them, and begins a new life. This is read out with much zeal in the presence of all who come to the Holy Supper. In addition they are told that unless they do so, they mingle the holy with the profane and cast themselves into eternal condemnation. Indeed, in England they are told that unless they do so the devil will enter them as he did Judas and destroy them soul and body. It is plain, then, that everyone in the churches in which faith alone is accepted is nevertheless taught that evils are to be shunned as sins.

[4] Furthermore, everyone who is born a Christian is aware that evils are to be shunned as sins because the Decalog is put into the hands of every boy and girl and is taught by parents and teachers. The citizens of a kingdom and especially the common people are examined by the priest on the Decalog alone, which is recited from memory, for what they know of the Christian religion, and are also admonished to do what is commanded in it. At such times they are not told by the priest that they are not under the yoke of that law, or that they cannot do what is commanded because they cannot do anything good of themselves. Again, the Athanasian Creed has been accepted throughout the Christian world and what is said at its close is also acknowledged, namely, that the Lord will come to judge the living and the dead, and then those who have done good will enter everlasting life and those who have done evil will enter everlasting fire.

[5] In Sweden, where the religion of faith alone has been received, it is also plainly taught that faith is impossible apart from charity or good works. This is pointed out in an Appendix on things to be remembered, inserted in all copies of the Psalms, and called "Impediments or Stumbling Blocks of the Impenitent" (Obotferdigas Foerhinder), where are these words,

> Those who are rich in good works thereby show that they are rich in faith, because when faith is saving it acts through charity. For justifying faith is never found alone and separate from good works, quite as no good tree is without fruit, nor the sun without light and heat, nor water without moisture.

[6] These items have been adduced to make known that although a religious formula about faith alone has been accepted, nevertheless goods of charity, which are good works, are taught everywhere and that this is by the Lord's divine providence, lest the common people be led astray by the formula. I have heard Luther, with whom I have spoken at times in the spiritual world, execrate faith alone and heard him say that when he established it he was warned by an angel of the Lord not to do it; but that he thought to himself that if he did not reject works, separation from

## XIII. LAWS ON PERMISSION ARE ALSO LAWS OF DIVINE PROVIDENCE

Catholicism would not be accomplished. Therefore, contrary to the warning, he established that faith.

259. *The merely natural man confirms himself against divine providence in that there have been so many heresies in Christendom and still are, such as Quakerism, Moravianism, Anabaptism, and more.* For he may think to himself, If divine providence is universal in the least things and has the salvation of all for its object, it would have seen to it that one true religion should exist on the globe, not one divided and, still less, one torn by heresies. But use reason and think more deeply if you can. Can man be saved without being reformed first? For he is born into love of self and the world, and as these loves do not have any love of God and the neighbor in them except for the sake of self, he is also born into evils of every kind. Is there love or mercy in those loves? Does the man make anything of defrauding or defaming or hating another even to death, or of committing adultery with his wife, or of being cruel to him out of revenge, the while having the desire in mind to get the upper hand of all and to possess the goods of all others, thus regarding others in comparison with himself as insignificant and of little worth? To be saved, must he not first be led away from these evils and thus be reformed? As has been shown above in many places, this can be accomplished only in accordance with many laws of divine providence. For the most part these laws are unknown and yet they come of divine wisdom and at the same time of divine love, and the Lord cannot act contrary to them, for to do so would result in destroying man, not in saving him.

[2] Look over the laws which have been set forth, bring them together, and you will see. According to those laws there is no direct influx from heaven but one mediated by the Word, doctrine and preaching; and since the Word, to be divine, had to be composed wholly in correspondences, inevitably there are dissensions and heresies. The tolerance of them is also in accord with the laws of divine providence. Furthermore, when the church itself has taken for essentials what pertains only to the understanding, that is, to doctrine, and not what pertains to the will, that is, to life, and what pertains to life is not made the

essentials of a church, then man is in complete darkness for understanding and wanders like one blind, striking against things constantly and falling into pits. For the will must see in the understanding and not the understanding in the will, or what is the same, the life and its love must lead the understanding to think, speak and act, and not the reverse. Were the reverse true, the understanding might out of an evil and even diabolical love seize on what comes by the senses and demand that the will do it. What has been said may show whence dissensions and heresies come.

[3] Yet it has been provided that everyone, in whatever heresy he may be intellectually, may still be reformed and saved if he shuns evils as sins and does not confirm heretical falsities in himself. For by shunning evils as sins the will is reformed and through it the understanding is, which emerges for the first time then out of obscurity into light. There are three essentials of the church: acknowledgment of the divine of the Lord, acknowledgment of the holiness of the Word, and the life which is called charity. Everyone's faith is according to the life which is charity; from the Word he has a rational perception of what life should be; and from the Lord he has reformation and salvation. Had these three been regarded as the church's essentials, intellectual differences would not have divided it but only varied it as light varies colors in beautiful objects and as various insignia of royalty give beauty to a king's crown.

260. *The merely natural man confirms himself against divine providence in that Judaism still continues.* That is, after all these centuries the Jews have not been converted although they live among Christians and do not, in keeping with prophecies in the Word, confess the Lord and acknowledge Him to be the Messiah, who, as they think, was to lead them back to the land of Canaan; but they steadfastly persist in denying Him and yet it is well with them. Those who take this view, however, and thus call divine providence in question, do not know that by Jews in the Word all who are of the church and acknowledge the Lord are meant, and by the land of Canaan, into which it is said that they are to be led, the Lord's church is meant.

## XIII. LAWS ON PERMISSION ARE ALSO LAWS OF DIVINE PROVIDENCE

[2] But the Jews persist in denying the Lord because they are such that, if they received and acknowledged the divine of the Lord and the holy things of His church, they would profane them. Therefore the Lord said of them:

> He has blinded their eyes, and hardened their heart; that they should not see with their eyes, nor understand with their heart, and be converted, and I should heal them (Jn 12:40; Mt 13:14; Mk 4:12; Lu 8:10; Isa 6:9, 10).

It is said, "lest they should be converted, and I should heal them" because if they had been converted and healed they would have committed profanation, and according to the law of divine providence treated above (nn. 221-233) no one is admitted interiorly into truths of faith and goods of charity by the Lord except so far as he can be kept in them to the close of life; were he admitted, he would profane what is holy.

[3] This nation has been preserved and dispersed over much of the earth for the sake of the Word in its original language, which they hold more sacred than Christians do. The Lord's divine is in every particular of the Word, for it is divine truth joined with divine good coming from the Lord. By it the Lord is united with the church, and heaven is present, as was shown in *Doctrine of the New Jerusalem about Sacred Scripture* (nn. 62-69). The Lord and heaven are present wherever the Word is read as sacred. This is the end which divine providence has pursued in the preservation and in the dispersal of the Jews over much of the world. On the nature of their lot after death see *Continuation about the Last Judgment and the Spiritual World* (nn. 79-82).

261. These then are the objections listed above at n. 238 by which the natural man confirms himself against divine providence, or may do so. Still other objections, listed at n. 239, may serve the natural man for arguments against divine providence; they may occur to the minds of others, too, and excite doubts. They are the following.

262. *Doubt may be raised against divine providence in that the whole of Christendom worships one God under three persons, that is, three Gods, and has not known hitherto that*

*God is one in person and in essence, in whom is the Trinity, and that this God is the Lord.* One who reasons about divine providence may ask, Are not three persons three Gods if each person by himself is God? Who can think of it otherwise? In fact, who does? Athanasius himself could not; therefore it is said in the Creed which bears his name:

> Although in Christian verity we ought to acknowledge each Person as God and Lord, yet by Christian faith it is not allowable to affirm or to name three Gods or three Lords.

This can only mean that we ought to acknowledge three Gods and Lords, but it is not allowable to affirm or name three Gods and three Lords.

[2] Who can possibly have a perception of one God unless He is one in person? If it is said that such a concept is possible if one thinks of the three as having one essence, does one, indeed can one, have any other idea than that they are thus of one mind and agree, and yet are three Gods? Thinking more deeply, one asks oneself, How can the divine essence, which is infinite, be divided? Further, how can divine essence from eternity beget another and produce still another who proceeds from them both? It may be said that it is to be believed and not thought about; but who does not think about what he is told must be believed? How else can there be any acknowledgment which in its essence is faith? Was it not because of the concept of God as three persons that Socinianism and Arianism arose, which prevail in the hearts of more persons than you suppose? Belief in one God and that this God is the Lord makes the church, for in Him is the divine trinity. The truth of this may be seen in *Doctrine of the New Jerusalem about the Lord*, from beginning to end.

[3] But what is thought of the Lord today? Is it not thought that He is God and Man, God from Jehovah the Father of whom He was conceived and Man from the Virgin Mary from whom He was born? Who thinks that God and Man in Him, or His Divine and His Human, are one person, and are one as soul and body are? Does anyone know this? Ask the learned in the church and they will say that they have not known it. Yet it is part of the

## XIII. LAWS ON PERMISSION ARE ALSO LAWS OF DIVINE PROVIDENCE

doctrine of the church received throughout Christendom, as follows:

> Our Lord Jesus Christ, the Son of God, is God and Man; and although He is God and Man yet there are not two, but there is one Christ. He is one because the divine took to itself the human; indeed He is altogether one, for He is one Person, since as soul and body make one man, so God and Man is one Christ.

This comes from the Faith or Creed of Athanasius. The learned have not known it because on reading this they have thought of the Lord not as God but only as Man.

[4] When they are asked if they know from whom the Lord was conceived, whether from God the Father or from His own Divine, they reply that He was conceived from God the Father, for this is according to Scripture. Are the Father and He not one then, like soul and body? Who can think that He was conceived from two Divines, and if from His own that this was His Father? If you ask them further what their idea of the Lord's Divine and of His Human is, they will say that His Divine is from the essence of the Father and His Human from the essence of His mother, and that His Divine is with the Father. Then, when they are asked where His Human is, they have no answer, for they separate His Divine and His Human in their thinking and make His Divine equal to the Divine of the Father and His Human like the human of another man, unaware that in doing this they separate soul and body; nor do they see the flaw in this, that then a rational man would have been born from a mother alone.

[5] As a result of the fixed idea that the Lord's humanity was like that of another man, it has come about that a Christian can with difficulty be led to think of a Divine Human, even when it is said that the Lord's soul or life from conception was and is Jehovah Himself. Now sum up the reasons and consider whether there is any other God of the universe than the Lord alone, in whom is the Divine itself, Source of all, called the Father; the Divine Human, called the Son; and the proceeding Divine, called the Holy Spirit; and thus that God is one in person and essence, and that this God is the Lord.

[6] You may persist and remark that the Lord Himself spoke of three in Matthew:

> Go and make disciples of all nations, baptizing them in the name of the Father, the Son and the Holy Spirit (28:19).

But it is plain from the preceding verse and the one following that the Lord said this in order to make it known that the Divine Trinity was in Him, now glorified. For in the preceding verse He said that all power in heaven and on earth was given Him, and in the following verse that He would be with men to the end of the age, speaking of Himself alone and not of three.

[7] Now, why did divine providence permit Christians to worship the one God under three persons, that is, worship three Gods, and not know until now that God is one in essence and person, in whom is the Trinity and that this God is the Lord? Man and not the Lord was the cause. The Lord had taught it plainly in His Word, as is clear from all the passages cited in *Doctrine of the New Jerusalem about the Lord*, and has also taught it in the doctrine of all the churches, in which it is said that His Divine and His Human are not two but one Person united like soul and body.

[8] The first reason why men divided the Divine and the Human and made the Divine equal to the Divine of Jehovah the Father and the Human equal to the human of another man, was that the church after its rise fell away into Babylonianism. This took to itself the Lord's divine power, and in order that it should be called human and not divine power made the Lord's human like that of another man. When later the church was reformed and faith alone was received as the one means of salvation—faith that God the Father has mercy for the sake of the Son—the Lord's Human could be viewed in no other way. For no one can approach the Lord and acknowledge Him at heart as God of heaven and earth unless he lives by His precepts. In the spiritual world, where everyone is bound to speak as he thinks, no one can so much as mention the name Jesus if he has not lived as a Christian in the world; this is by divine providence lest His name be profaned.

## XIII. LAWS ON PERMISSION ARE ALSO LAWS OF DIVINE PROVIDENCE

263. To make what has just been said clearer I will add what was set forth in *Doctrine of the New Jerusalem about the Lord* (towards the end, nn. 60, 61), which is as follows:

"That God and Man in the Lord, according to the Creed, are not two but one Person, altogether one as soul and body are, appears clearly in many sayings of the Lord, as that the Father and He are one; that all things of the Father are His and all His the Father's; that He is in the Father and the Father in Him; that all things are given into His hand; that He has all power; that He is God of heaven and earth; that one who believes on Him has eternal life; and that the wrath of God abides on one who does not believe on Him; and further, that both the Divine and the Human were taken up into heaven; and that as to both He sits at the right hand of God, that is, is almighty; besides the numerous passages in the Word about His Divine Human which were quoted abundantly above. They all testify that God is one both in person and in essence, and in Him is the Trinity, and that this God is the Lord.

[2] "These things about the Lord are published now for the first time because it is foretold in the Apocalypse, chapters 21 and 22, that at the end of the former church a new church is to be established in which this will be the chief doctrine. This church is meant in those chapters by the New Jerusalem into which only one who acknowledges the Lord alone as God of heaven and earth can enter; this church is therefore called 'the Lamb's wife'. I can also report that all heaven acknowledges the Lord alone and that one who does not is not admitted to heaven, for heaven is heaven from the Lord. This very acknowledgment made in love and faith causes men to be in the Lord and Lord in them, as He teaches in John:

> In that day you will know that I am in my Father, and you in me and I in you (14:20);

again in the same:

> Abide in me, and I in you; ... I am the vine, and you are branches; he who abides in me and I in him, bears much

fruit; for without me you can do nothing; unless a man abides in me, he is cast out (15:4-6, also 17:22, 23).

[3] "This has not been seen from the Word before, because if it had been, it would not have been received. For the last judgment had not been accomplished yet, and prior to it the power of hell prevailed over the power of heaven. Man is in the midst between heaven and hell; had this been seen before, therefore, the devil, that is, hell, would have plucked it from men's hearts and furthermore would have profaned it. The predominance of hell was completely broken by the last judgment which has been accomplished now; since that judgment, thus today, every man who wishes enlightenment and wisdom is able to have it."

264. *A doubt may be raised against divine providence in that it has been unknown hitherto that in each particular of the Word there is a spiritual meaning from which it has its holiness.* One may raise this doubt about divine providence, asking, "why has this been revealed for the first time now, and why has it been revealed through any one at all and not through a church leader?" But it is at the Lord's good pleasure whether it should be a leader or a leader's servant; He knows the one and the other. However, that sense of the Word has not been disclosed before because

1. If it had been, the church would have profaned it and thereby profaned the holiness itself of the Word.
2. Neither were the genuine truths, in which the spiritual sense of the Word resides, revealed by the Lord until the last judgment was accomplished, and a new church, meant by the Holy Jerusalem, was about to be established by the Lord. These reasons will be examined separately.

[2] 1. *The spiritual sense of the Word was not disclosed earlier because if it had been, the church would have profaned it and thereby would have profaned the holiness itself of the Word.* Not long after it was established, the church was turned into Babylon, and later into Philistia. Babylon acknowledges the Word, to be sure, and yet esteems it lightly, asserting that the

## XIII. LAWS ON PERMISSION ARE ALSO LAWS OF DIVINE PROVIDENCE

Holy Spirit inspires its own highest judgment just as much as it did the prophets. They acknowledge the Word for the vicarship founded on the Lord's words to Peter, but esteem it lightly because it does not accord with their teaching. It is therefore taken from the people also and hidden in monasteries where few read it. If, therefore, the spiritual sense of the Word had been revealed, in which the Lord is present together with all angelic wisdom, the Word would have been profaned not only, as it is now, in its lowermost expression in the sense of the letter, but in its inmosts, too.

[3] Philistia, by which faith separated from charity is meant, would have profaned the spiritual sense of the Word also, because, as we have shown before, it puts salvation in certain formulas which are to be thought and spoken, and not in good works which are to be done. It thus makes saving what is not saving and also removes the understanding from what is to be believed. What would they do with the light in which the spiritual sense of the Word is? Would that not be turned into darkness? When the natural sense is, why not the spiritual sense? Does any one of them who has confirmed himself in faith separate from charity and in justification by this faith alone, want to know what good of life is, what love to the Lord and towards the neighbor is, what charity is and what the goods of charity are, what good works are and what it is to do them, or in fact what faith is essentially and what genuine truth is, constituting it? They compose volumes, establish in them only what they call faith, and declare that all the things just mentioned are present in that faith. It is clear from this that if the spiritual sense of the Word had been revealed earlier, it would come to pass according to the Lord's words in Matthew:

*If your eye is evil, your whole body will be full of darkness. If then the light that is in you is darkness, how great is that darkness ( 6:23).*

In the spiritual sense of the Word by "eye" the understanding is meant.

[4] 2. *Neither were the genuine truths in which the spiritual sense of the Word resides, revealed by the Lord until after the last judgment was accomplished, and a new church, meant by the Holy Jerusalem, was about to be established by the Lord.* The Lord foretold in the Apocalypse that after the last judgment was effected genuine truths were to be revealed, a new church was to be established, and the spiritual sense of the Word would be disclosed. In the small work, The Last Judgment, and later in the Continuation of that work, it was shown that the last judgment has been accomplished and that this is meant by the heaven and earth which would pass away (Apoc 21:1). That genuine truths are then to be revealed is foretold in these words in the Apocalypse:

*And he that sat upon the throne said, Behold, I make all things new (11:5; also 19:17, 18; 21:18-21; 22:1, 2).*

At 19:11-16 it was predicted that the spiritual sense of the Word was to be revealed; it is meant by "the white horse" on which He who sat was called the Word of God and was Lord of lords and King of kings (on this see the little work The White Horse). That by the Holy Jerusalem a new church is meant which was to be established then by the Lord may be seen in *Doctrine of the New Jerusalem about the Lord* (nn. 62-65).

[5] It is clear, then, that the spiritual sense of the Word was to be revealed for a new church which should acknowledge and worship the Lord alone, hold His Word sacred, love divine truths and reject faith separated from charity. More about this sense of the Word may be seen in *Doctrine of the New Jerusalem about Sacred Scripture* (nn. 5-26 and following numbers); what the spiritual sense of the Word is (nn. 5-26); that a spiritual sense exists in all of the Word in general and in detail (nn. 9-17); that by virtue of the spiritual sense the Word is divinely inspired and holy in every expression (nn. 18, 19); that until now the spiritual sense has been unknown, and why it was not revealed before (nn. 20-25); and that henceforth that sense will be open only to one who is in genuine truths from the Lord (n. 26).

## XIII. LAWS ON PERMISSION ARE ALSO LAWS OF DIVINE PROVIDENCE

[6] It may be evident from these propositions that it is by the Lord's divine providence that the spiritual sense has lain concealed from the world until the present day and been kept meanwhile in heaven with the angels, who draw their wisdom from it. This sense was known and treasured among ancient peoples who lived before Moses, but when their descendants converted the correspondences, of which their Word and hence their religion solely consisted, into various idolatries, and the Egyptians converted them into magic, by the Lord's divine providence this sense was closed up, first with the Israelites and then with Christians for the reasons given above, and is now opened for the first time for the Lord's new church.

265. *Doubt may arise against divine providence in that it has been unknown hitherto that to shun evils as sins is the Christian religion itself.* That this is the Christian religion itself was shown in *Doctrine of Life for the New Jerusalem*, from beginning to end; and as faith separated from charity is the one obstacle to its being received, that also was treated of. We say that it has not been known that to shun evils as sins is the Christian religion itself, for it is unknown to nearly everyone; yet everyone does know it, as may be seen above (n. 258). Nearly all are ignorant of it because faith separate has obliterated knowledge of it. For this faith declares that it alone saves and not any good work, that is, any good of charity; also that men are no longer under the yoke of the law, but are free. Those who have frequently heard such teaching no longer give thought to any evil of life or any good of life. Everyone, moreover, is inclined by nature to embrace such teaching, and once he has done so he no longer thinks about the state of his life. This is why it is not known that shunning evils as sins is the Christian religion itself.

[2] That this is unknown was disclosed to me in the spiritual world. I have asked more than a thousand newcomers from the world whether they knew that to shun evils as sins is religion itself. They said that they did not and that it was a new idea which they had not heard before, but had heard that they cannot of themselves do good and that they are not under the yoke of the law. When I inquired whether they knew that a man must

examine himself, see his sins, repent and begin a new life and that otherwise sins are not remitted, and if sins are not remitted, men are not saved; and when I reminded them that this was read out in a deep voice to them each time they observed the Holy Supper, they replied that they paid no attention to that but only to this, that they have remission of sins by the sacrament of the Supper and that faith effects the rest without their knowing it.

[3] I asked again, Why have you taught your children the Decalog? Was it not that they might know what evils are sins to be shunned? Was it only that they might know and believe, but do nothing? Why is it said that this is new? To this they could only reply that they know and yet do not know, and that they never think of the sixth 265-1 commandment when they commit adultery, or about the seventh when they steal or defraud secretly, and so on, and still less that such acts are contrary to divine law, thus contrary to God.

[4] When I recalled to them many things from the teachings of the churches and from the Word confirming the fact that to avoid and be averse to evils as sins is the Christian religion's very self and that one who does so has faith, they fell silent. They were convinced of it, however, when they saw that all were examined as to their life and judged according to their deeds, and no one was judged according to faith apart from life, for everyone has faith according to his life.

[5] Christendom in large part has not known this because by a law of divine providence everyone is left to act in freedom according to reason (on this, above, nn. 71-91 and nn. 101-128); and by another law no one is taught directly from heaven but by means of the Word and by doctrine and preaching from it; there are besides all the laws on permission which are also laws of divine providence. On these see above, n. 258.

274. *A doubt may be raised against divine providence in that it has not been known before that a man lives as a human being after death and that this has not been disclosed before.* It has been unknown because with those who do not shun evils as sins the belief lies hidden that man does not live after death. It is of

## XIII. LAWS ON PERMISSION ARE ALSO LAWS OF DIVINE PROVIDENCE

no moment therefore to them whether one says that man lives after death or will rise again on the day of the last judgment. If belief in resurrection happens to visit one, he tells himself, "I shall fare no worse than others; if I go to hell I shall have the company of many and also if I pass to heaven." Yet all in whom there is any religion have an implanted recognition that they will live as human beings after death. Only those infatuated with their own intelligence think that they survive as souls but not as human beings.

It may be seen from the following that anyone in whom is any religion has an implanted recognition that he lives after death as a human being:

1. Who thinks otherwise when he is dying?
2. What eulogizer, mourning the dead, does not exalt them to heaven and place them among the angels conversing with them and sharing their joy? Some men are deified.
3. Who among the common people does not believe that when he dies, if he has lived well he will enter a heavenly paradise, be arrayed in white, and enjoy eternal life?
4. What priest does not speak so to the dying? And when he speaks so he believes it, provided he does not think of the last judgment at the time.
5. Who does not believe that his little ones are in heaven and that after death he will see his wife, whom he has loved? Who thinks that they are spectres, still less souls or minds hovering in the universe?
6. Who contradicts when something is said about the lot or state of those who have passed from time into eternal life? I have told many what the state or lot of various persons is and have never heard anyone protest that their lot is not yet determined but will be at the time of the judgment.
7. When one sees angels in paintings or statuary does he not recognize them as such? Who thinks then that

they are bodiless spirits or airy entities or clouds, as do some of the erudite?
8. Papists believe that their saints are human beings in heaven and others elsewhere are; so do Mohammedans of their dead; more than others Africans do, and many other peoples do. Why then do not Reformed Christians believe it, who know it from the Word?
9. Moreover, as a result of the recognition implanted in everyone, some men aspire to the immortality of renown. The recognition is given that turn in them and makes heroes and brave men of them in war.
10. Inquiry was made in the spiritual world whether this knowledge is implanted in all men; it was found that it is in a spiritual idea attached to their internal thought, not in a natural idea attached to their external thought.

It is plain from all this that doubt should not be thrown on the Lord's divine providence on the supposition that only now has it been disclosed that the human being continues such after death. It is only the sensuous in man that wants to see and touch what is to be credited. One who does not raise his thinking above it is in the dark of night about the state of his own life.

# XIV. EVILS ARE TOLERATED IN VIEW OF THE END, WHICH IS SALVATION

275. If man were born into the love for which he was created, he would not be in evil, in fact would not know what evil is. For one who has not been in evil and is not in it, cannot know what it is; told that this or that is evil, he would not believe it. This is the state of innocence in which Adam and his wife Eve were; that state was signified by the nakedness of which they were not ashamed; the knowledge of evil subsequent to the fall is meant by eating of the tree of the knowledge of good and evil. The love for which the human being was created is love to the neighbor, to wish him as well as one does oneself and even better. He is in the enjoyment of this love when he serves his neighbor quite as parents do their children. This is truly human love, for in it is what is spiritual, distinguishing it from the natural love of brute animals. Were man born into this love, he would not be born into the darkness of ignorance as everyone is now, but into some light of the knowledge and hence of the intelligence soon to be his. To be sure, he would creep on all fours at first but come erect on his feet by an implanted striving. However much he might resemble a quadruped, he would not face down to the ground but forward to heaven and come erect so that he could look up.

276. When love of the neighbor was turned into self-love, however, and this love increased, human love was turned into animal love, and man, from being man, became a beast, with the difference that he could think about what he sensed physically, could rationally discriminate among things, be taught, and become a civil and moral person and finally a spiritual being. For, as was said, man possesses what is spiritual and is distinguished by it from the brute animal. By it he can know

what civil evil and good are, also what moral evil and good are, and if he so wills, what spiritual evil and good are also. When love for the neighbor was turned into self-love, however, man could no longer be born into the light of knowledge and intelligence but was born into the darkness of ignorance, being born on the lowest level of life, called corporeal-sensuous. From this he could be led into the interiors of the natural mind by instruction, the spiritual always attending on this. Why one is born on the lowest level of life known as corporeal-sensuous, therefore into the darkness of ignorance, will be seen in what follows.

[2] Anyone can see that love of the neighbor and self-love are opposites. Neighborly love wishes well to all from itself, but self-love wishes everyone to wish it well; neighborly love wants to serve everyone, but self-love wants all to serve it; love of the neighbor regards everyone as brother and friend, while love of self regards everyone as its servant, and if one does not serve it, as its enemy; in short, it regards only itself and others scarcely as human beings, esteeming them at heart less than one's horses and dogs. Thinking so meanly of others, it thinks nothing of doing evil to them; hence come hatred and vengeance, adultery and whoredom, theft and fraud, lying and defamation, violence and cruelty, and similar evils. Such are the evils in which man is by birth. That they are tolerated in view of the end, which is salvation, is to be shown in this order:

1. Everyone is in evil and must be led away from it to be reformed.
2. Evils cannot be removed unless they appear.
3. So far as they are removed they are remitted.
4. The toleration of evil is therefore for the sake of the end in view, namely, salvation.

277a. (1) *Everyone is in evil and must be led away from it to be reformed.* The church knows that there is hereditary evil in man and that as a result he is in the lust of many evils. Thence it is that he cannot do good of himself, for evil does only such good as has evil in it; the evil inwardly in it is that one does good

## XIV. EVILS ARE TOLERATED IN VIEW OF THE END, WHICH IS SALVATION

for one's own sake and thus only for the sake of appearances. It is known that hereditary evil comes from one's parents. It is said to come from Adam and his wife, but this is an error; for everyone is born into hereditary evil from his parent, and the parent from his parent, and so on; thus it is transmitted from one to another, is augmented and becomes an accumulation, and is passed to one's progeny. There is therefore nothing sound in man but all is evil. Who feels that it is evil to love himself above others? Who, then, knows that this is an evil, though it is the head of evils?

[2] Inheritance from parents, grandparents and great-grandparents is plain from much which is known in the world, from the fact, for instance, that households, families and even nations are distinguishable by the face; the face is also a type of the mind which in turn accords with the affections of one's love. Sometimes, too, the features of a grandfather recur in a grandson or a great-grandson. From the face alone I know whether a person is a Jew or not; likewise of what stock certain persons are; others no doubt know also. If the affections which spring from love are thus derived from parents and transmitted by them, evils are, for these spring from affections. But it shall be told how the resemblance comes about.

[3] Everyone's soul comes from his father and is only clothed with the body by one's mother. That the soul is from the father follows not only from what has been said above, but from many other indications, too; also from this, that the child of a black man or Moor by a white or European woman is black, and vice versa; and especially in that the soul is in the seed, for impregnation is by the seed, and the seed is what is clothed with a body by the mother. The seed is the primal form of the love in which the father is—the form of his ruling love with its nearest derivatives or the inmost affections of that love.

[4] These affections are enveloped in everyone with the honesties of moral life and with the goodnesses partly of civil and partly of spiritual life, which are the external of life even with the evil. An infant is born into this external life and is

therefore lovable, but coming to boyhood and adolescence he passes from that external to the inner life and at length to his father's ruling love. If this has been evil and not been moderated and bent by various means by his teachers, it becomes his ruling love as it was his father's. Still the evil is not eradicated, but put aside; of this in what follows. Plainly, then, everyone is in evil.

277b. It is plain without explanation that man must be led away from evil in order to be reformed. For one who is in evil in the world is in evil after he has left the world. Not removed in the world, evil cannot be removed afterwards. Where a tree falls, it lies. So, too, when a man dies his life remains such as it has been. Everyone is judged according to his deeds, not that these are recounted, but he returns to them and acts as before. Death is a continuation of life with the difference that man cannot then be reformed. For reformation is effected in full, that is, in what is inmost and outmost, and what is outmost is reformed suitably to what is inmost only while man is in the world. It cannot be reformed afterwards because as it is carried along by the man after death it falls quiescent and conforms to his inner life, that is, they act as one.

278. (2) *Evils cannot be removed unless they appear.* This does not mean that man must do evils in order for them to appear, but that he must examine himself, his thoughts as well as his deeds, and see what he would do if he did not fear the laws and disrepute—see especially what evils he deems allowable in his spirit and does not regard as sins, for these he still does. To enable him to examine himself, man has been given understanding, and an understanding separate from his will, in order that he may know, comprehend and acknowledge what is good and what is evil, likewise see the character of his will or what it loves and desires. To see this his understanding has been given higher and lower or interior and exterior thought, so as to see from the higher or interior what his will prompts in the lower or exterior thinking: he sees this quite as he does his face in a mirror. When he does and knows what is sin, he is able, on imploring the Lord's help, not to will it but to shun it, then to act contrary to it, if not freely, then by overcoming it through

## XIV. EVILS ARE TOLERATED IN VIEW OF THE END, WHICH IS SALVATION

fighting it, and finally to become averse to it and abominate it. Then first does he perceive and also sense that evil is evil and good is good. This, now, is self-examination—to see one's evils, acknowledge them, confess them and thereupon desist from them.

[2] But as few know that this is the Christian religion itself, and these alone have charity and faith and are led by the Lord and do good from Him, something will be said of those who fail to examine themselves but still think that they possess religion. They are

1. Those who confess themselves guilty of all sins but do not search out any one sin in themselves.
2. Those who neglect the search on religious principle.
3. Those who in absorption with the mundane give no thought to sins and hence do not know them.
4. Those who favor them and therefore cannot know them.
5. With all these, sins do not appear and therefore cannot be removed.
6. Finally, the reason, so far unknown, will be made plain why evils cannot be removed apart from their being searched out, appearing, being acknowledged, confessed and resisted.

278b. But these points will be considered one by one, for they are fundamentals of the Christian religion on man's part.

*First, of those who confess themselves guilty of all sins, but do not search out any one sin in themselves.* They say, "I am a sinner. I was born in sin. From head to foot there is nothing sound in me. I am nothing but evil. Good God, be gracious to me, pardon, cleanse and save me. Make me to walk in purity and in a right path"; and more of the kind. And yet the man does not examine himself and hence does not know any evil, and no one can shun what he is ignorant of, still less fight against it. After his confessions he also thinks that he is clean and washed, when nevertheless he is unclean and unwashed from the head to the sole of the foot. For the confession of all sins is the lulling of them all to sleep and finally blindness to them. It is like a generality devoid of anything specific, which amounts to nothing.

[2] Second: *Those who omit the search in consequence of their religion.* They are especially those who separate charity from faith. They say to themselves, "Why should I search out evil or good? Why evil, when it does not condemn me? Why good, when it does not save me? Faith alone, thought and uttered with trust and confidence, justifies and purifies from all sin, and when once I am justified, I am whole in the sight of God. I am indeed in evil, but God wipes it away the moment it is committed and it no longer appears"; and much else. But who does not see, if he opens his eyes, that these are empty words, without reality because nothing of good is in them? Who cannot think and speak so, with trust and confidence, too, even when he is thinking of hell and eternal condemnation? Does he want to know anything further about either truth or good? Of truth he says, "What is truth except that which confirms this faith?" and of good, "What is good except what is in me from this faith? And that it may be in me I will not do it as from myself, for that would be self-righteous and what is self-righteous is not good." So he neglects all until he does not know what evil is; what then is he to search out and see in himself? Is it not his state then that a pent-up fire of lusts of evil consumes the interiors of his mind and lays them waste even to the entrance? He is on guard only at the door to keep the fire from appearing. After death the door is opened and the fire appears for all to see.

[3] Third: *Those absorbed with the mundane give no thought to sins, hence do not know of any.* These love the world above all things and welcome no truth that would lead them away from any falsity in their religion. They tell themselves, "What is this to me? It is not to my way of thinking." So they reject truth on hearing it and if they listen to it smother it. They do much the same on hearing sermons; they retain some sayings but not any of the substance. Dealing in this way with truths they do not know what good is, for truth and good act as one; and from good which is not linked with truth one does not recognize evil except

## XIV. EVILS ARE TOLERATED IN VIEW OF THE END, WHICH IS SALVATION

as one calls it good also, which is done by rationalizing from falsities. It is these who are meant by the seed which fell among thorns, of whom the Lord said:

> Other seeds fell among thorns; and the thorns sprang up and choked them ... These are they who hear the Word, but the cares of this world and the deceitfulness of riches choke the Word so that it become unfruitful (Mt 13:7, 22; Mk 4:7, 18, 19; Lu 8:7, 14).

[4] Fourth: *Those who favor sins and therefore cannot know them.* These acknowledge God and worship Him with the usual ceremonials and assure themselves that a given evil, which is a sin, is not a sin. For they color it with fallacies and appearances and thus hide its enormity. Then they indulge it and make it their friend and familiar. We say that those who acknowledge God do this, for others do not regard an evil as a sin, for one sins against God. But let examples illustrate this. A man makes an evil not to be a sin when in coveting wealth he makes some kinds of fraud allowable by reasoning which he devises. So does the man who confirms himself in plundering those who are not his enemies in a war.

[5] Fifth: *Sins do not appear in these men, therefore cannot be removed.* All evil which does not come to sight nurses itself; it is like fire in wood under ashes or like matter in an unopened wound; for all evil which is repressed increases and does not stop until it destroys all. Lest evil be repressed, therefore, everyone is allowed to think in favor of God or against God and in favor of the sanctities of the church or against them, without being punished for it in the world. Of this the Lord says in Isaiah:

> From the sole of the foot even to the head there is no soundness; wound, and scar, and fresh bruise; they have not been pressed out, nor bound up, nor softened with oil.... Wash you, make you clean, remove the evil of your doings from before my eyes; cease to do evil, learn to do good. . . . Then if your sins have been as scarlet, they shall be white as snow; if they have been red like crimson, they shall be like wool. . . . But if you refuse and rebel, you shall be devoured by the sword (Isa 1:6, 16, 17, 18, 20).

To be devoured by the sword signifies to perish by falsity of evil.

[6] Sixth: *The cause, hidden so far, why evils cannot be removed apart from their being searched out, appearing, being acknowledged, confessed and resisted.* In preceding pages we have mentioned the fact that all heaven is arranged in societies according to affections of good, and all hell in societies according to the lusts of evil opposite to the affections of good. Each person as to his spirit is in some society, in a heavenly one if in an affection of good, but in an infernal one if in some lust of evil. While living in the world man does not know this and yet as to his spirit he is in some society; otherwise he cannot live; and by it he is governed by the Lord. If he is in an infernal society, he cannot be led out of it by the Lord except according to the laws of divine providence, among which is this also, that a man shall see that he is there, want to leave, and make the effort himself to do so. One can do this while in the world but not after death, for then he remains forever in the society in which he put himself in the world. It is for this reason that man is to examine himself, see and avow his sins, do repentance, and thereupon persevere to the close of life. I might substantiate this to full belief by much experience, but this is not the place to document the experience.

279. (3) So far as evils are removed they are remitted. It is an error of the age to believe

1. That evils are separated and in fact cast out from man when they are remitted; and
2. That the state of man's life can be changed in a moment, even to its opposite, so that from wicked he becomes good, and consequently can be led from hell and be transported straightway to heaven, and this by the Lord's sheer mercy.
3. But those who believe and suppose so, do not know at all what evil and good are and nothing at all about the state of man's life.

## XIV. EVILS ARE TOLERATED IN VIEW OF THE END, WHICH IS SALVATION

4. Moreover, they are wholly unaware that affections, which are of the will, are nothing other than changes and variations of the state of the purely organic substances of the mind; and that thoughts, which are of the understanding, also are; and that memory is the permanent state of these changes.

When one knows these things, one can see clearly that an evil can be removed only by successive stages, and that the remission of an evil is not complete removal of it. But all this has been said in summary form and unless the items are demonstrated may be assented to and yet not comprehended. What is not comprehended is as indistinct as a wheel spun around by the hand. The points made above are therefore to be demonstrated one by one in the order in which they were set forth.

[2] First: *It is an error of the age to believe that evils are separated and in fact cast out when they are remitted.* It has been granted me to learn from heaven that no evil into which man is born and which he has made actual in him is separated from him, but is removed so as not to appear. Earlier I shared the belief of most persons in the world that when evils are remitted they are cast out and are washed and wiped away as dirt is from the face by water. It is not like this with evils or sins. They all remain. When they are remitted on repentance, they are thrust from the center to the sides. What is in the center, being directly under view, appears as in the light of day, and what is to one side is in shadow and at times in the darkness of night. Inasmuch as evils are not separated but only removed, that is, thrust to one side, and as man can go from The center to the periphery, he can return, as it may happen, to his evils, which he supposed had been cast out. For the human being is such that he can go from one affection to another and sometimes to the opposite, and thus from one center into another; the affection in which he is at the time makes the center, for he is then in the enjoyment and light of it.

[3] Some who are raised after death into heaven by the Lord, for they have lived well, have carried with them, however, the

belief that they are clean and rid of sins, therefore are not in a state of guilt. In accord with their belief they are clothed at first in white garments, for white garments signify a state purified from evils. But after a time they begin to think, as they did in the world, that they are washed, as it were, from all evil, and to glory that they are no longer sinners like other men. This can hardly be kept from being an elation of mind and a contempt of others in comparison with oneself. In order, therefore, that they may be delivered from their imaginary belief, they are sent down from heaven and let back into the evils which they pursued in the world; they are also shown that they are in hereditary evils of which they had not known. When they have been led in this way to realize that their evils have not been separated from them but only put aside, thus that in themselves they are impure, indeed nothing but evil, and that they are withheld from evils and held in goods by the Lord, and that this only seems to be their doing, they are raised again into heaven by the Lord.

[4] Second: *It is an error of the age to believe that the state of man's life can be changed in a moment, so that from wicked he can become good, and consequently can be led from hell and transported at once to heaven, and this by the Lord's direct mercy.* Those who separate charity and faith and place salvation in faith alone, commit this error. For they suppose that merely to think and speak formulas of that faith, if it is done with trust and confidence, justifies and saves one. Many think it is done instantly, too, and if not previously, can be done in the last hour of one's life. These are bound to believe that the state of man's life can be changed in a moment and that he can be saved by direct mercy. But in the last chapter of this treatise it will be seen that the Lord's mercy is mediated, that man cannot become good in a moment from being wicked, and can be led from hell and transported to heaven only by the continual activity of divine providence from infancy to the very close of life. Here it need only be said that all the laws of divine providence have the salvation and reformation of the human being for their object, in other words, the inversion of his state, which by nativity is infernal, into the opposite, which is heavenly. This can only be

## XIV. EVILS ARE TOLERATED IN VIEW OF THE END, WHICH IS SALVATION

done progressively as man recedes from evil and its enjoyment and comes into good and its enjoyment.

[5] Third: *Those who believe in an instantaneous change do not know at all what evil and good are.* For they do not know that evil is the enjoyment of the lust of acting and thinking contrary to divine order, and good is the enjoyment of the affection for acting and thinking in accord with divine order. They do not know, either, that myriads of lusts enter into and compose each individual evil and myriads of affections enter into and compose each individual good, and that these myriads are in such order and connection in man's interiors that it is impossible to change one without changing all at the same time. Those who are ignorant of this may believe or suppose that evil, which seems to them to be a single entity, can be easily removed, and that good, which also seems to be a single entity, can be introduced in its place. Not knowing what evil and good are, they cannot but suppose that there is such a thing as instantaneous salvation and such a thing as direct mercy. That these are not possible will be seen in the last chapter of this treatise.

[6] Fourth: *Those who believe in instantaneous salvation and unmediated mercy do not know that affections, which are of the will, are nothing other than changes of state in the purely organic substances of the mind; that thoughts, which are of the understanding, are nothing other than changes and variations in the form of those substances; and that memory is the persisting state of the changes and variations.* Everyone acknowledges, on its being said, that affections and thoughts exist only in substances and their forms, which are the subjects; existing in the brain which is full of substances and forms, they are called purely organic forms. No one who thinks rationally can help laughing at the fancies of some that affections and thoughts do not have substantive bases, but are exhalations given shape by heat and light, like images apparently in the air or ether. For thought can no more exist apart from a substantial form than sight can apart from its form, the eye, or hearing apart from its form, the ear, or taste apart from its form, the tongue. If you

examine the brain, you will see innumerable substances and fibres, also, and see, too, that everything in it is organized. What more is needed than this ocular proof?

[7] But one may ask, What are affection and thought then? A conclusion can be reached from each and all things in the body. In it are many viscera, each fixed in its place, and all performing their several functions by changes and variations of state and form. It is well known that they are engaged in their own activities—the stomach, the intestines, the kidneys, the liver, the pancreas, the spleen, the heart and the lungs, each in its particular activity. All the activities are maintained from within, and to be actuated from within means that it is by changes and variations of state and form. It may be plain then that the activities of the purely organic substances of the mind are similar, the one difference being that those of the organic substances of the body are natural, but of the mind are spiritual; plainly, also, the two make one by correspondences.

[8] The nature of the changes and variations of state and form in the organic substances of the mind, which are affections and thoughts, cannot be shown to the eye. It may, however, be seen as in a mirror by the changes of state in the lungs on speaking and singing. There is correspondence, moreover; for the sound of the voice in speaking and singing, and the articulations of the sound which are the words of speech and the modulations of song, are produced by means of the lungs; sound corresponds to affection, and speech to thought. Sound and speech are produced also from affection and thought. This is done by changes and variations in the state and form of the organic substances of the lungs, and from the lungs through the trachea or windpipe in the larynx and glottis, and then in the tongue, and finally in the lips. The first changes and variations in the state and form of the sound occur in the lungs, the second in trachea and larynx, the third in the glottis by the different openings of its orifice, the fourth in the tongue by its various positions against palate and teeth, and the fifth in the lips by the various modifications of form in them. It may be evident, then, that these consecutive changes and variations in the state of organic forms produce the

## XIV. EVILS ARE TOLERATED IN VIEW OF THE END, WHICH IS SALVATION

sounds and their articulations which are speech and song. Inasmuch, then, as sound and speech are produced from no other source than the affections and thoughts of the mind (for they exist from them and are never apart from them), clearly the affections of the will are changes and variations in the state of the purely organic substances of the mind, and the thoughts of the understanding are changes and variations in the form of those substances, quite like those in the substances of the lungs.

[9] Since affections and thoughts are simply changes of state in the forms of the mind, memory is nothing other than the permanent state of those changes. For all changes and variations of state in organic substances are such that once they are habitual they become permanent. So the lungs are habituated to produce certain sounds in the trachea, to vary them in the glottis, articulate them by the tongue, and modify them by the mouth; once these organic activities have become habitual, they are settled in the organs and can be reproduced. These changes and variations are infinitely more perfect in the organs of the mind than in those of the body, as is evident from what was said in the treatise *Divine Love and Wisdom* (nn. 199-204), where we showed that all perfections increase and ascend by and according to degrees. More on this will be seen below (n. 319).

280. It is also an error of the age to suppose that when sins are remitted they are taken away. This is the error of those who believe that their sins are pardoned by the sacrament of the Holy Supper although they have not removed them from themselves by repentance. Those also commit this error who believe that they are saved by faith alone; those also who believe that they are saved by papal dispensations. All these believe in unmediated mercy and instant salvation. But when the statement is reversed it becomes truth, that is, when sins are removed they are also remitted. For repentance precedes pardon, and aside from repentance there is no pardon. Therefore the Lord bade His disciples:

> That they should preach repentance for the remission of sins (Lu 24:27, 47),

and John preached

> The baptism of repentance for the remission of sins (Lu 3:3).

The Lord remits the sins of all; He does not accuse and impute; but He can take sins away only in accordance with laws of His divine providence. For when Peter asked how often he was to forgive a brother sinning against him, whether seven times, the Lord said to him:

> That he should forgive not only seven times, but seventy times seven (Mt 18:21, 22).

What then will the Lord not do, who is mercy itself?

281. (4) *Thus the permission of evil is for the sake of the end, namely, salvation.* It is well known that man has full liberty to think and will but not to say and do whatever he thinks and wills. He may think as an atheist, deny God and blaspheme the sanctities of Word and church. He may even want to destroy them utterly by word and deed, but this is prevented by civil, moral and ecclesiastical laws. He therefore cherishes this impiety and wickedness inwardly by thinking, willing and even intending to do it, but not doing it actually. The man who is not an atheist also has full liberty to think many evil things, things fraudulent, lascivious, revengeful and otherwise insane; he also does them at times. Who can believe that unless man had full liberty, he not only could not be saved but would even perish utterly?

[2] Now let us have the reason for this. Everyone from birth is in evils of many kinds. They are in his will, and what is in the will is loved. For what a man wills inwardly he loves, what he loves he wills, and the will's love flows into the understanding where it makes its pleasure felt and thereupon enters the thoughts and intentions. If, therefore, he were not allowed to think in accord with the love in his will, which is hereditarily implanted in him, that love would remain shut in and never be seen by him. A love of evil which does not become apparent is like an enemy in ambush, like matter in an ulcer, like poison in the blood, or corruption in the breast, which cause death when they are kept

## XIV. EVILS ARE TOLERATED IN VIEW OF THE END, WHICH IS SALVATION

shut in. But when a person is permitted to think the evils of his life's love, even to intend doing them, they are cured by spiritual means as diseases are by natural means.

[3] It will be told now what man would be like if he were not permitted to think in accord with the enjoyment of his life's love. No longer would he be man, for he would lose his two faculties called liberty and rationality in which humanness itself consists. The enjoyment of those evils would occupy the interiors of his mind to such an extent that it would burst open the door. He could then only speak and commit the evils; his unsoundness would be manifest not only to himself but to the world; and at length he would not know how to cover his shame. In order that he may not come into this state, he is permitted to think and to will the evils of his inherited nature but not to say and commit them. Meanwhile he is learning civil, moral and spiritual things. These enter his thoughts and remove the unsoundness and he is healed by the Lord by means of them, only to the extent, however, of knowing how to guard the door unless he also acknowledges God and implores His aid for power to resist the unsoundness. Then, so far as he resists it, he does not let it into his intentions and eventually not even into his thoughts.

[4] Since man is free to think as he pleases to the end that his life's love may emerge from its hiding-place into the light of his understanding, and since he would not otherwise know anything of his own evil and consequently would not know how to shun it, it is also true that it would increase in him so much that recovery would become impossible in him and hardly be possible in his children, were he to have children, for a parent's evil is transmitted to his offspring. The Lord, however, provides that this may not occur.

282. The Lord could heal the understanding in every man and thus cause him to think not evil but good, and this by means of fears of different kinds, miracles, conversations with the dead, or visions and dreams. But to heal the understanding alone is to heal man only outwardly, for understanding with its thought is the external of man's life while the will with its affection is the

internal. The healing of the understanding alone would therefore be like palliative healing in which the interior malignity, closed in and kept from issuing, would destroy first the near and then the remote parts till all would become mortified. The will itself must be healed, not by the influx of the understanding into it, for that is impossible, but by means of instruction and exhortation from the understanding. Were the understanding alone healed, man would become like a dead body embalmed or covered by fragrant spices and roses which would soon get such a foul odor from the body that they could not be brought near anyone's nostrils. So heavenly truths in the understanding would be affected if the evil love of the will were shut in.

283. Man is permitted, as was said, to think evils even to intending them in order that they may be removed by means of what is civil, moral and spiritual. This is done when he considers that they are contrary to what is just and equitable, to what is honest and decorous and to what is good and true, contrary therefore to the peace, joy and blessedness of life. By these three means the Lord heals the love of man's will, in fear at first, it is true, but with love later. Still the evils are not separated from the man and cast out, but only removed in him and put to the side. When they are and good has the center, evils do not appear, for whatever has the central place is squarely under view and is seen and perceived. It should be known, however, that even when good occupies the center man is not for that reason in good unless the evils at the side tend downward or outward. If they look upward or inward they have not been removed, but are still trying to return to the center. They tend downward and outward when man shuns his evils as sins and still more when he holds them in aversion, for then he condemns them, consigns them to hell, and makes them face that way.

284. Man's understanding is the recipient of both good and evil and of both truth and falsity, but not his will. His will must be either in evil or in good; it cannot be in both, for it is the man himself and in it is his life's love. But good and evil are separate in the understanding like what is internal and what is external. Thus man may be inwardly in evil and outwardly in good. Still,

## XIV. EVILS ARE TOLERATED IN VIEW OF THE END, WHICH IS SALVATION

when he is being reformed, the two meet, and conflict and combat ensue. This is called temptation when it is severe, but when it is not severe a fermentation like that of wine or strong drink occurs. If good conquers, evil with its falsity is carried to the side, as lees, to use an analogy, fall to the bottom of a vessel. The good is like wine that becomes generous on fermentation and like strong drink which becomes clear. But if evil conquers, good with its truth is borne to the side and becomes turbid and noisome like unfermented wine or unfermented strong drink. Comparison is made with ferment because in the Word, as at Hosea 7:4, Luke 12:1 and elsewhere, "ferment" signifies falsity of evil.

## XV. DIVINE PROVIDENCE ATTENDS THE EVIL AND THE GOOD ALIKE

285. In every person, good or bad, there are two faculties one of which makes the understanding and the other the will. The faculty making the understanding is the ability to understand and think, therefore is called rationality. The faculty making the will is the ability to do this freely, that is, to think and consequently to speak and act also, provided that it is not contrary to reason or rationality; for to act freely is to act as often as one wills and according as one wills. The two faculties are constant and are present from first to last in each and all things which a man thinks and does. He has them not from himself, but from the Lord. It follows that the Lord's presence in these faculties is also in the least things, indeed the very least, of man's understanding and thought, of his will and affection too, and thence of his speech and action. If you remove these faculties from even the very least thing, you will not be able to think or utter it as a human being.

[2] It has already been shown abundantly that the human being is a human being by virtue of the two faculties, enabled by them to think and speak, and to perceive goods and understand truths, not only such as are civil and moral but also such as are spiritual, and made capable, too, of being reformed and regenerated; in a word, made capable of being conjoined to the Lord and thereby of living forever. It was also shown that not only good men but evil also possess the two faculties. These faculties are in man from the Lord and are not appropriated to him as his, for what is divine cannot be appropriated but only adjoined to him and thus appear to be his, and this which is divine with the human being is in the least things pertaining to him. It follows that the Lord governs the least things in an evil

## XV. DIVINE PROVIDENCE ATTENDS THE EVIL AND THE GOOD ALIKE

man as well as in a good man. This government of His is what is called divine providence.

286. Inasmuch as it is a law of divine providence that man shall act from freedom according to reason, that is, from the two faculties, liberty and rationality; and a law of divine providence that what he does shall appear to be from himself and thus his own; and also a law that evils must be permitted in order that man may be led out of them, it follows that man can abuse these faculties and in freedom according to reason confirm whatever he pleases. He can make reasonable whatever he will, whether it is reasonable in itself or not. Some therefore ask, "What is truth? Can I not make true whatever I will?" Does not the world do so? Anybody can do it by reasoning. Take an utter falsity and bid a clever man confirm it, and he will. Tell him, for instance, to show that man is a beast, or that the soul is like a small spider in its web and governs the body as that does by threads, or tell him that religion is nothing but a restraining bond, and he will prove any one of these propositions until it appears to be truth. What is more easily done? For he does not know what appearance is or what falsity is which in blind faith is taken for truth.

[2] Hence it is that a man cannot see this truth, namely, that divine providence is in the very least things of the understanding and the will, or what is the same, in the very least things of the thoughts and affections of every person, wicked or good. He is perplexed especially because it seems then that evils are also from the Lord, but it will be seen in what follows that nevertheless there is not a particle of evil from the Lord but that evil is from man in that he confirms in him the appearance that he thinks, wills, speaks and acts of himself. In order that these things may be seen clearly, they will be demonstrated in this order:

1. Divine providence is universal in the least things with the evil as well as the good, and yet is not in one's evils.

2. The evil are continually leading themselves into evils, but the Lord is continually leading them away from evils.
3. The evil cannot be fully withdrawn from evil and led in good by the Lord so long as they believe their own intelligence to be everything and divine providence nothing.
4. The Lord rules hell through opposites; and rules the evil who are in the world, in hell as to their interiors, but not as to their exteriors.

287. (1) *Divine providence is universal in the least things with the evil as well as the good, and yet is not in one's evils.* It was shown above that divine providence is in the least things of man's thoughts and affections. This means that man can think and will nothing from himself, but that everything he thinks and wills and consequently says and does, is from influx. If it is good, it is from influx out of heaven, and if evil, from influx out of hell; or what is the same, the good is from influx from the Lord and the evil from man's proprium. I know that it is difficult to grasp this, because what flows in from heaven or from the Lord is distinguished from what flows in from hell or from man's proprium, and yet divine providence is said to be in the least of man's thoughts and affections, even so far that he can think and will nothing from himself. It appears like a contradiction to say that he can also think and will from hell and from his proprium. Yet it is not, and this will be seen in what follows, after some things have been premised which will clarify the matter.

288. All the angels of heaven confess that no one can think from himself but does so from the Lord, while all the spirits of hell say that no one can think from any other than himself. These spirits have been shown many times that no one of them thinks or can think from himself, but that thought flows in; it was in vain, however; they would not accept the idea. But experience will teach, first, that everything of thought and affection even with spirits of hell flows in from heaven, but that the inflowing good is turned into evil there and truth into falsity, thus everything into its opposite. This was shown in this way: a truth

## XV. DIVINE PROVIDENCE ATTENDS THE EVIL AND THE GOOD ALIKE

from the Word was sent down from heaven, was received by those uppermost in hell, and by them sent to lower hells, and on to the lowest. On the way it was turned by stages into falsity and finally into falsity the direct opposite of the truth. Those with whom it was so changed thought the falsity of themselves seemingly and knew no otherwise; still it was truth, flowing down from heaven on the way to the lowest hell, which was thus falsified and perverted. I have heard of this several times. The same thing occurs with good; as it flows down from heaven, it is changed step by step into the evil opposite to it. Hence it was plain that truth and good, proceeding from the Lord and received by those who are in falsity and evil, are completely altered and so transformed that their first form is lost. The like happens in every evil person, for as to his spirit he is in hell.

289. I have often been shown that no one in hell thinks from himself but through others around him, and these do not, but through others still. Thoughts and affections make their way from one society to another, but no one is aware that they do not originate with himself. Some who believed that they thought and willed of themselves were dispatched to another society and held there, and communication was cut off with the societies around to which their thoughts usually extended. Then they were told to think differently from the spirits of this society, and compel themselves to think to the contrary; they confessed that they could not.

[2] This was done with a number and with Leibnitz, too, who was also convinced that no one thinks from himself, but from others, nor do these think from themselves, but all think by an influx from heaven, and heaven by an influx from the Lord. Some, pondering this, said that it was amazing, and that hardly anyone can be led to credit it, for it is utterly contrary to the appearance, but that they still could not deny it, for it was fully demonstrated. Nevertheless, astonished as they were, they said that they are not in fault then in thinking evil; also that it seems then as if evil is from the Lord; and, again, that they do not understand how the one Lord can cause all to think so diversely. The three points will be explained in what follows.

290. To the experiences cited this is also to be added. When it was granted me by the Lord to speak with spirits and angels, the foregoing arcanum was at once disclosed to me. For I was told from heaven that like others I believed that I thought and willed from myself, when in fact nothing was from myself, but if it was good, it was from the Lord, and if evil from hell. That this was so, was shown me to the life by various thoughts and affections which were induced on me, and gradually I was given to perceive and feel it. Therefore, as soon as an evil afterwards entered my will or a falsity into my thought, I investigated the source of it. I inquired from whom it came. This was disclosed to me, and I was also allowed to speak with those spirits, refute them, and compel them to withdraw, thus to take back their evil and falsity and keep it to themselves, and no longer infuse anything of the kind into my thought. This has occurred a thousand times. I have remained in this state for many years, and still do. Yet I seem to myself to think and will from myself like others, with no difference, for of the Lord's providence it should so appear to everyone, as was shown above in the section on it. Newly arriving spirits wonder at this state of mine, seeing as they do only that I do not think and will from myself, and am therefore like some empty thing. But I disclosed the arcanum to them, and added that I also think more interiorly, and perceive whether what flows into my exterior thought is from heaven or from hell, reject the latter and welcome the former, yet seem to myself, like them, to be thinking and willing from myself.

291. It is not unknown in the world that all good is from heaven and all evil from hell; it is known to everyone in the church. Who that has been inaugurated into the church's priesthood does not teach that all good is from God, and that man can receive nothing of himself except it be given him from heaven? And also that the devil infuses evils into the thoughts and leads astray and incites one to commit evils? Therefore a priest who believes that he preaches out of a holy zeal, prays that the Holy Spirit may teach him, and guide his thoughts and utterances. Some say that they have sensibly perceived being acted upon, and when a sermon is praised, reply piously that they

## XV. DIVINE PROVIDENCE ATTENDS THE EVIL AND THE GOOD ALIKE

have spoken not from themselves but from God. Therefore when they see someone speak and act well, they remark he was led to do so by God; on the other hand, seeing someone speak and act wickedly, they remark he was led to do so by the devil. That there is talk of the kind in the church is known, but who believes that it is so?

292. Everything that a man thinks and wills, and consequently speaks and does, flows in from the one Fountain of life, and yet that one Fountain of life, namely, the Lord, is not the cause of man's thinking what is evil and false. This may be clarified by these facts in the world of nature. Heat and light proceed from the sun of the world. They flow into all visible subjects and objects, not only into subjects that are good and objects that are beautiful, but also into subjects that are evil and objects that are ugly, producing varying effects in them. They flow not only into trees that bear good fruit but into trees that bear bad fruit, and into the fruits themselves, quickening their growth. They flow into good seed and into weeds, into shrubs which have a good use and are wholesome, and into shrubs that have an evil use and are poisonous. Yet it is the same heat and the same light; there is no cause of evil in them; the cause is in the recipient subjects and objects.

[2] The same warmth that hatches eggs in which a screech-owl, a horned owl, and a viper lie acts as it does when it hatches those in which a dove, a bird of paradise and a swan lie. Put eggs of both sorts under the hen and they will be hatched by her warmth, which in itself is innocent of harm. What has the heat in common then with what is evil and noxious? The heat flowing into a marsh or a dung-hill or into decaying or dead matter acts in the same way as it does when it flows into things flavorsome and fragrant, lush and living. Who does not see that the cause is not in the heat but in the recipient subject? The same light gives pleasing colors in one object and displeasing colors in another; indeed, it grows brighter in white objects and becomes dazzling, and dims in those verging on black and becomes dusky.

[3] There is what is similar in the spiritual world. There are heat and light in it from its sun, which is the Lord, and they flow from the sun into their subjects and objects. Now the subjects and objects are angels and spirits, in particular their volitional and mental life, and the heat is divine love going forth, and the light is divine wisdom going forth. The light and heat are not the cause of the different reception of them by one and another. For the Lord says,

> He makes the sun to rise on the evil and the good, and sends rain on the just and the unjust (Mt 5:45).

In the highest spiritual sense by the "sun" the divine love is meant, and by the "rain" the divine wisdom.

293. Let me add to this the view of the angels on will and understanding in man. This is that there cannot be a grain of will or of prudence in man that is his own. They say that if there were, neither heaven nor hell would continue in existence, and all mankind would perish. The reason they give is that myriads of human beings, as many as have been born since the creation of the world, constitute heaven and hell, of which the one is under the other in such an order that each is a unit, heaven one comely humanity, and hell one monstrous humanity. If the individual had a grain of will and intelligence of his very own, that unity could not exist, but would be torn apart. Upon this that divine form would perish, which can arise and remain only as the Lord is all in all and men are nothing besides. A further reason, they say, is that to think and will actually from one's own being is the divine itself, and to think and will from God, is the truly human. The very divine cannot be appropriated to anyone, for then man would be God. Bear the above in mind, and if you wish you will have confirmation of it by angels when on death you come into the spiritual world.

294. It was stated above (n. 289) that when some were convinced that no one thinks from himself but from others, nor the others from themselves, but all by influx through heaven from the Lord, they remarked in their astonishment that then they are not in fault when they do evil, also that then it seems

## XV. DIVINE PROVIDENCE ATTENDS THE EVIL AND THE GOOD ALIKE

evil comes from the Lord, nor do they comprehend how the Lord can cause them all to think so differently. Since these three notions cannot but flow into the thoughts of those who regard effects only from effects and not from causes, they need to be taken up and explained by what causes them.

[2] First: *They are not in fault then in doing evil.* For if all that a person thinks flows into him from others, the fault seems to be theirs from whom it comes. Yet the fault is the recipient's, for he receives what inflows as his own and neither knows nor wants to know otherwise. For everyone wants to be his own, to be led by himself, and above all to think and will from himself; this is freedom itself, which appears as the proprium in which every person is. If he knew, therefore, that what he thinks and wills flows in from another, it would seem to him that he was bound and captive and no longer master of himself. All enjoyment in his life would thus perish, and finally his very humanness would perish.

[3] I have often seen this evidenced. It was granted some spirits to perceive and sense that they were being led by others. Thereupon they were so enraged that they were reduced almost to mental impotence. They said that they would rather be kept bound in hell than not to be allowed to think as they willed and to will as they thought. This they called being bound in their very life, which was harder and more intolerable than to be bound bodily. Not being allowed to speak and act as they thought and willed, they did not call being bound. For the enjoyment of civil and moral life, which consists in speaking and acting, itself restrains and at the same time mitigates that.

[4] Inasmuch as man does not want to know that he is led to think by others, but wants to think from himself and believes that he does so, it follows that he himself is in fault, nor can he throw off the blame so long as he loves to think what he thinks. If he does not love it, he breaks his connection with those from whom his thought flows. This occurs when he knows the thought is evil, therefore determines to avoid it and desist from it. He is then also taken by the Lord from the society in that evil and

transferred to a society free of it. If, however, he recognizes the evil and does not shun it, fault is imputed to him, and he is responsible for the evil. Therefore, whatever a man believes that he does from himself is said to be done from the man, and not from the Lord.

[5] Second: *It then seems as if evil is from the Lord.* This may be thought to be the conclusion from what was shown above (n. 288), namely, that good flowing in from the Lord is turned into evil and truth into falsity in hell. But who cannot see that evil and falsity do not come of good and truth, therefore not from the Lord, but from the recipient subject or object which is in evil and falsity and which perverts and inverts what flows into it, as was amply shown above (n. 292). The source of evil and falsity in man has been pointed out frequently in the preceding pages. Moreover, an experiment was made in the spiritual world with those who believed that the Lord could remove evils in the wicked and introduce good instead, thus move the whole of hell into heaven and save all. That this is impossible, however, will be seen towards the end of this treatise, where instantaneous salvation and unmediated mercy are to be treated of.

[6] Third: *They do not comprehend how the one Lord can cause all to think so diversely.* The Lord's divine love is infinite, likewise His divine wisdom. An infinity of love and wisdom proceeds from Him, flows in with all in heaven, thence with all in hell, and from heaven and hell with all in the world. Thinking and willing therefore cannot lack in anyone, for what is infinite is limitless. The infinite things that issue from the Lord flow in not only universally but also in least things. For the divine is universal by being in least things, and the divine in least things constitutes what is called universal, as was shown above, and the divine in something least is still infinite. Hence it may be evident that the one Lord causes each person to think and will according to the person's nature and does so in accordance with laws of His providence. It was shown above (nn. 46-69) and also in the treatise *Divine Love and Wisdom* (nn. 17-22), that everything in the Lord, or proceeding from Him, is infinite.

## XV. DIVINE PROVIDENCE ATTENDS THE EVIL AND THE GOOD ALIKE

295. (2) *The evil are continually leading themselves into evils, but the Lord is continually leading them away from evils.* The nature of divine providence with the good is more readily comprehended than its nature with the evil. As the latter is now under consideration, it will be set forth in this order:

1. In every evil there are innumerable things.
2. An evil man of himself continually leads himself more and more deeply into his evils.
3. Divine providence with the evil is a continual tolerance of evil, to the end that there may be a continual withdrawal from it.
4. Withdrawal from evil is effected by the Lord in a thousand most secret ways.

296. In order, then, that divine providence with the evil may be seen clearly and therefore understood, the propositions just stated are to be explained in the order in which they were presented.

First: *In every evil there are innumerable things.* To man's sight an evil appears to be a single thing. Hatred does, and revenge, theft and fraud, adultery and whoredom, pride and presumption, and the rest. It is unknown that in every evil there are innumerable things, exceeding in number the fibres and vessels in the human body. For an evil man is a hell in least form, and hell consists of myriads and myriads of spirits, each of whom is in form like a man, but a monstrous one, in whom all the fibres and vessels are inverted. A spirit himself is an evil which appears to him as one thing, but in it are innumerable things, as numerous as the lusts of that evil. For everyone, from head to foot, is his own evil or his own good. Since an evil man is such, plainly he is one evil composed of countless different evils, all severally evils, and called lusts of evil. It follows that all these, one after another, must be cured and changed by the Lord for man to be reformed, and that it can be done only by the Lord's divine providence, step by step from man's first years to his last.

[2] Every lust of evil, when it is visually presented, appears in hell like some noxious creature, a serpent, a cockatrice, a viper, a horned owl, a screech-owl, or some other; so do the lusts of evil in an evil man appear when he is viewed by angels. All these forms of lust must be changed one by one. The man himself, who appears as to his spirit like a monstrous man or devil, must be changed to appear like a comely angel, and each lust of evil changed to appear like a lamb or sheep or pigeon or turtle dove, as affections of good in angels appear in heaven when they are visually represented. Changing a serpent into a lamb, or a cockatrice into a sheep, or an owl into a dove, can be done only gradually, by uprooting evil together with its seed and implanting good seed in its place. This can only be done, however, comparatively as is done in the grafting of trees, of which the roots with some of the trunk remain, but the engrafted branch turns the sap drawn through the old root into sap that produces good fruit. The branch to be engrafted in this instance is to be had only from the Lord, who is the tree of life; this is also in keeping with the Lord's words in John 15:1-7.

[3] Second: *An evil man from himself continually leads himself more deeply into his evils.* He does so "from himself" because all evil is from man, for, as was said, he turns good, which is from the Lord, into evil. He leads himself more and more deeply into evil for the reason, essentially, that as he wills and commits evil, he enters more and more interiorly and also more and more deeply into infernal societies. Hence the enjoyment of evil increases, too, and occupies his thoughts until he feels nothing more agreeable. One who has entered more interiorly and deeply into infernal societies becomes like one bound by chains. So long as he lives in the world, however, he does not feel his chains; they seem to be made of soft wool or smooth silken threads. He loves them, for they titillate; but after death, from being soft, those chains become hard, and from being pleasant become galling.

[4] That the enjoyment of evil grows is known from thefts, robberies, plunderings, revenge, tyranny, lucre, and other evils. Who does not feel a heightening of enjoyment in them as he

## XV. DIVINE PROVIDENCE ATTENDS THE EVIL AND THE GOOD ALIKE

succeeds in them and practices them uninhibited? A thief, we know, feels such enjoyment in thefts that he cannot desist from them, and, a wonder, he loves one stolen coin more than ten that are given him. It would be similar with adultery, had it not been provided that the power to commit this evil decreases with the abuse, but with many there still remains the enjoyment of thinking and talking about it, and if nothing more, there is still the lust of touch.

[5] It is not known, however, that this heightening of enjoyment comes from a man's entering into infernal societies more and more interiorly and deeply as he perpetrates evils from the will as well as from thought. If the evils are only in the thoughts, and not in the will, he is not yet in an infernal society having that evil; he enters it when the evils are also in the will. Then, if he also thinks the evil is contrary to the precepts of the Decalog and regards these precepts as divine, he commits the evil of set purpose and by so doing plunges to a depth from which he can be brought out only by active repentance.

[6] It is to be understood that everyone as to his spirit is in the spiritual world, in one of its societies, an evil man in an infernal society and a good man in a heavenly society; sometimes, when in deep meditation one also appears there. Moreover, as sound and, along with it, speech spread on the air in the natural world, affection and thought with it spread among societies in the spiritual world; there is correspondence, too, affection corresponding to sound and thought to speech.

[7] Third: *Divine providence with the evil is a continual tolerance of evil, to the end that there may be a continual withdrawal from it.* Divine providence with evil men is continual permission because only evil can issue from their life. For whether he is in good or in evil, man cannot be in both at once, nor by turns in one and the other unless he is lukewarm. Evil of life is not introduced into the will and through this into the thought by the Lord but by man, and this is named permission.

[8] Inasmuch as everything which an evil man wills and thinks is by permission, the question arises, what in this case

divine providence is, which is said to be in the least things with every person, evil or good. It consists in this, that it exercises tolerance continually for the sake of its objective, and permits what helps to the end and nothing more. It constantly observes the evils that issue by permission, separates and purifies them, and rejects what is unsuitable and discharges it by unknown ways. This is done principally in man's interior will and through it in his interior thought. Divine providence also sees to it constantly that what must be rejected and discharged is not received again by the will, since all that is received by the will is appropriated to the man; what is received by the thought, but not by the will, is set aside and banished. Such is the constant divine providence with the evil; as was said, it is a continual tolerance of evil to the end that there may be continual withdrawal from it.

[9] Of these activities man knows scarcely anything, for he does not perceive them. The chief reason why he does not, is that the evils come from the lusts of his life's love, and are not felt to be evils but enjoyments, to which one does not give thought. Who gives thought to the enjoyments of his love? His thought floats along in them like a skiff carried along by the current of a stream; and he perceives a fragrant air which he inhales with a deep breath. Only in one's external thought does one have a sense of the enjoyments, but even in it he pays no attention to them unless he knows well that they are evil. More will be said on this in what follows.

[10] Fourth: *Withdrawal from evil is effected by the Lord in a thousand most secret ways.* Only some of these have been disclosed to me, and only the most general ones. For instance, the enjoyments of lusts, of which man knows nothing, are let by clusters and bundles into the interior thoughts of his spirit and thence into his exterior thoughts, where they appear in a feeling of pleasure, delight or longing, and mingle with his natural and sensuous enjoyments. There the means to separation and purification and the ways of withdrawal and unburdening are to be found. The means are chiefly the enjoyments of meditation, thought and reflection on ends that are uses. Such ends are as numerous as the particulars and details of one's business or

## XV. DIVINE PROVIDENCE ATTENDS THE EVIL AND THE GOOD ALIKE

occupation. Just as numerous are the enjoyments of reflection on such an end as that one shall appear to be a civil and moral and also a spiritual person, no matter what interposes which is unenjoyable. These enjoyments, being those of one's love in the external man, are the means to the separation, purification, expulsion and withdrawal of the enjoyments of the lusts in the internal man.

[11] Take, for example, an unjust judge who regards gain or friendship as the end or use of his office. Inwardly he is constantly in those ends, but outwardly must act as one learned in the law and just. He is constantly in the enjoyment of meditation, thought, reflection and intent to bend and turn a decision and adapt and adjust it so that it may still seem to be in conformity with the laws and resemble justice. He does not know that his inward enjoyment consists in craftiness, defrauding, deceit, clandestine theft, and many other evils, and that this enjoyment, made up of so many enjoyments of the lusts of evil, governs each and all things of his external thought, in which he enjoys appearing just and sincere. Into the external enjoyment the internal enjoyment is let down, the two are mingled as food is in the stomach, and thereupon the internal enjoyments are separated, purified, and withdrawn. Still this is true only of the more grievous enjoyments of the lusts of evil.

[12] For in an evil man the only separation, purification and withdrawal possible is of the more grievous evils from the less grievous.

In a good man, however, separation, purification and withdrawal is possible not only of the more grievous evils but also of the less grievous. This is effected by the enjoyments of the affections of what is good and true, and of what is just and sincere, affections into which one comes so far as he regards evils as sins and therefore avoids and is averse to them, and still more as he fights against them. It is by these means that the Lord purifies all who are saved. He purifies them by external means also, such as fame and standing and sometimes wealth, but put into these means by the Lord are the enjoyments of affections of good and truth, by which they are directed and fitted to become enjoyments of love for the neighbor.

[13] If one saw the enjoyments of the lusts of evil assembled in some form, or perceived them distinctly by some sense, he would see and perceive that they are too numerous for definition. For hell in its entirety is nothing but the form of all the lusts of evil, and no one lust in it is quite similar to or the same as another, nor can be to eternity. Of these countless lusts man knows scarcely anything, and even less how they are connected with one another. Yet the Lord in His divine providence continually allows them to come forth, for them to be drawn away, and this is done in perfect order and sequence. For the evil man is a hell in miniature, and the good man a heaven in miniature.

[14] The withdrawal from evils, which the Lord effects in a thousand highly secret ways, may best be seen and concluded about from the secret activities of the soul in the body. Man knows that he examines the food he is about to eat, perceives what it is by its odor, hungers for it, tastes it, chews it, and by the tongue rolls it down into the esophagus and so into the stomach. But then there are the hidden activities of the soul of which he knows nothing, for he has no sensation of them. The stomach rolls about the food it receives, opens and breaks it up by solvents, that is, digests it, and offers fit portions to the little mouths opening in it and to veins which imbibe it. Some it sends to the blood, some to the lymphatic vessels, some to the lacteal vessels of the mesentery, and some down to the intestines. Then the chyle, conveyed through the thoracic duct from its cistern in the mesentery, is carried to the vena cava, and so to the heart. From the heart it is carried into the lungs, from them through the left ventricle of the heart into the aorta, and from this by its branches to viscera throughout the body and also to the kidneys. In each organ separation and purification of the blood are effected and removal of the heterogeneous, not to mention how the heart sends its blood up to the brain after purification in the lungs, which is done by the arteries called carotids, and how the brain returns the blood, now vivified, to the vena cava just above

## XV. DIVINE PROVIDENCE ATTENDS THE EVIL AND THE GOOD ALIKE

where the thoracic duct brings in the chyle, and so back again to the heart.

[15] These and countless other activities are secret operations of the soul in the body. Man has no sense of them, and unless he is acquainted with the science of anatomy, knows nothing of them. Yet similar activities take place in the interiors of the human mind. Nothing can take place in the body except from the mind, for man's mind is his spirit, and his spirit is equally man; the sole difference being that what is done in the body is done naturally, while what is done in the mind is done spiritually; there is all similarity. Plainly, then, divine providence operates with every man in a thousand hidden ways, and its incessant care is to cleanse him, since its purpose is to save him. Plainly, too, nothing more is incumbent on man than to remove evils in the outward man; the Lord sees to the rest, when He is implored.

297. (3) *The evil cannot be fully withdrawn from evil and led in good by the Lord so long as they believe their own intelligence to be everything and divine providence nothing.* It would seem that man could withdraw himself from evil provided he thought that this or that was contrary to the common good, or to what is useful, or to national or international law, and this an evil as well as a good man can do if by birth or through practice he is such that he can think clearly within himself, analysing and reasoning. But even then he is not capable of withdrawing himself from evil. The faculty of understanding and of perceiving, even abstractly, has indeed been given everyone by the Lord, to the evil as well as to the good, as has been shown above in many places, and yet man cannot deliver himself from evil by means of this faculty. For evil comes of the will, and the understanding influences the will only with light, enlightening and instructing. If the heat of the will, that is, man's love, is hot with the lust of evil, it is cold towards the affection of good, therefore does not receive the light but either repels or extinguishes it, or by some fabricated falsity turns it into evil. The light is then like winter light, which is as clear as the light in summer and remains as clear even when it flows into frozen trees. But this can be seen better in the following order:

1. When the will is in evil, one's own intelligence sees only falsity, and neither desires to see, nor can see, anything else.
2. If then one's own intelligence is confronted with truth, it either turns away from it or falsifies it.
3. Divine providence continually causes man to see truth, and also gives him affection for perceiving and receiving it.
4. Through this means man is withdrawn from evil, not by himself, but by the Lord.

298. For these things to be made apparent to the rational man, whether he is evil or good, thus whether he is in the light of winter or in the light of summer (for colors appear the same in them), they are to be explained in due order.

First: *When the will is in evil, one's own intelligence sees only falsity, and neither desires nor is able to see anything else.* This has often been demonstrated in the spiritual world. Everyone, on becoming a spirit, which takes place after death when he puts off the material body and puts on the spiritual, is introduced by turns into the two states of his life, the external and the internal. In the external state he speaks and acts rationally, quite as a rational and wise man does in the world; he can also instruct others in much that pertains to moral and civil life, and if he has been a preacher he can also give instruction in the spiritual life. But when he is brought from this external state into his internal state, and the external is put to sleep and the internal awakes, the scene changes if he is evil. From being rational he becomes sensuous, and from being wise he becomes insane. For he thinks then from the evil of his will and its enjoyments, thus from his own intelligence, and sees only falsity and does nothing but evil, believing that evil is wisdom and that cunning is prudence. From his own intelligence he believes himself to be a deity and with all his mind sucks up nefarious ways.

[2] I have often seen instances of such insanity. I have also seen spirits introduced into these alternating states two or three times within an hour, and it was granted them to see and also

## XV. DIVINE PROVIDENCE ATTENDS THE EVIL AND THE GOOD ALIKE

acknowledge their insanities. Nevertheless they were unwilling to remain in a rational and moral state, but voluntarily returned to their internal sensuous and insane state. They loved this more than the other because the enjoyment of their life's love was in it. Who can believe that an evil man is such beneath his outward appearance and that he undergoes such a transformation when he enters on his internal state? This one experience makes plain the nature of one's own intelligence when one thinks and acts from the evil of one's will. It is otherwise with the good. When they are admitted from their external state into their internal state, they become still wiser and still more moral.

[3] Second: *If then one's own intelligence is confronted with truth, it either turns away from it or falsifies it.* The human being has a volitional and an intellectual proprium. The volitional proprium is evil, and the intellectual proprium is falsity derived from evil; the latter is meant by "the will of man" and the former by "the will of the flesh" in John 1:13. The volitional proprium is in essence self-love, and the intellectual proprium is the pride coming of that love. The two are like married partners, and their union is called the marriage of evil and falsity. Into this union each evil spirit is admitted before he enters hell; he then does not know what good is; he calls his evil good, because that is what he feels to be enjoyable. He also turns away from truth then and has no desire to see it, because he sees the falsity which accords with his evil as the eye beholds what is beautiful, and hears it as the ear hears what is harmonious.

[4] Third: *Divine providence continually causes man to see truth and also gives him affection for perceiving and receiving it.* For divine providence acts from within and flows thence into the exteriors, that is, flows from what is spiritual into what is in the natural man, by the light of heaven enlightening his understanding and by the heat of heaven quickening his will. The light of heaven in essence is divine wisdom, and the heat of heaven in essence is divine love. From divine wisdom nothing can flow but truth, and from divine love nothing but good. With good the Lord bestows an affection in the understanding for seeing and also perceiving and receiving truth. Man thus

becomes man not only in external aspect but in internal aspect, too. Everyone desires to appear a rational and spiritual man, and knows he so desires in order that others may believe him to be truly man. If then he is rational and spiritual in external form only, and not at the same time in his internal form, is he man? Is he different from a player on the stage or from an ape with an almost human face? May one not know from this that only he is a human being who is inwardly what he desires others to think he is? One who acknowledges the one fact must admit the other. Man's own intelligence can induce the human form only on externals, but divine providence induces it on internals and thence on externals. When it has been so induced, a man does not only appear to be a man; he is one.

[5] Fourth: *Through this means man is withdrawn from evil, not by himself, but by the Lord.* When divine providence gives man to see truth and to be affected by it, he can be withdrawn from evil for the reason that truth points the way and dictates; doing what truth dictates, the will unites with truth and within itself turns it into good, for it becomes something one loves, and what is loved is good. All reformation is effected through truth, not without it, for without truth the will continues in its evil, and should it consult the understanding, is not instructed, rather the evil is confirmed by falsities.

[6] With regard to intelligence, this seems to the good man as well as to an evil man to be his and proper to him. Like an evil man, he is also bound to act from intelligence as if it were his own. But one who believes in divine providence is withdrawn from evil, and one who does not believe in it is not withdrawn; he believes who acknowledges that evil is sin and desires to be withdrawn from it, and he does not believe who does not so acknowledge and desire. The difference between the two kinds of intelligence is like that between what is believed to exist in itself and what is believed not to exist in itself but to appear as if it did. It is also like the difference between an external without an internal similar to it and an external with a similar internal. Thus it is like the difference between impersonations of kings, princes or generals by mimes and actors through word and

## XV. DIVINE PROVIDENCE ATTENDS THE EVIL AND THE GOOD ALIKE

bearing, and actual kings, princes or generals. The latter are such in fact as well as outwardly, but the former only outwardly, and when the exterior is laid off, are known only as comedians, actors or players.

299. (4) *The Lord governs hell by means of opposites, and those in the world who are evil He governs in hell as to their interiors but not as to their exteriors.* One who does not know the character of heaven and hell cannot know at all that of man's mind; his mind is his spirit which survives death. For the mind or spirit of man is altogether in form what heaven or hell is. The only difference is that one is vast and the other very small, or one is archetype and the other a copy. As to his mind or spirit, accordingly, the human being is either heaven or hell in least form, heaven if he is led by the Lord, and hell if he is led by his proprium. Inasmuch as it has been granted me to know what heaven and hell are, and it is important to know what the human being is in respect to his mind or spirit, I will describe both heaven and hell briefly.

300. All who are in heaven are nothing other than affections of good and thoughts thence of truth, and all who are in hell are nothing other than lusts of evil and imaginations thence of falsity. These are so arranged respectively that the lusts of evil and the imaginings of falsity in hell are precisely opposite to the affections of good and the thoughts of truth in heaven. Therefore hell is under heaven and diametrically opposite, that is, the two are like two men lying in opposite directions, or standing, invertedly, like men at the antipodes, only the soles of their feet meeting and their heels hitting. At times hell also appears to be so situated or inverted relatively to heaven, for the reason that those in hell make lusts of evil the head and affections of good the feet, while those in heaven make affections of good the head and lusts of evil the soles of the feet; hence the mutual opposition. When it is said that in heaven there are affections of good and thoughts of truth from them, and in hell lusts of evil and imaginations of falsity from them, the meaning is that there are spirits and angels who are such. For everyone is his affection

or his lust, an angel of heaven his affection and a spirit of hell his lust.

Footnotes

265-1 Swedenborg follows the numbering of the Commandments customary with Lutherans, as with Roman Catholics.

301. The angels of heaven are affections of good and thoughts thence of truth because they are recipients of divine love and wisdom from the Lord; for all affections of good are from the divine love and all thoughts of truth are from the divine wisdom. But the spirits of hell are lusts of evil and the imaginations thence of falsity because they are in self-love and their own intelligence, and all lusts of evil come of self-love and imaginations of falsity from one's own intelligence.

302. The ordering of affections in heaven and of lusts in hell is marvelous, and is known to the Lord alone. They are each distinguished into genera and species, and are so conjoined as to make a unit. As they are distinguished into genera and species, they are distinguished into larger and smaller societies, and as they are so conjoined as to make a unit, they are conjoined as all things in man are. Hence in its form heaven is like a comely man, whose soul is divine love and wisdom, thus the Lord, and hell in its form is like a monstrous man, his soul self-love and self-intelligence, thus the devil. No devil is sole lord there; self-love is so called.

303. But that the nature of heaven and of hell respectively may be better known, instead of affections of good let enjoyments of good be understood, and enjoyments of evil instead of lusts of evil, for no affections or lusts are without their enjoyments, and enjoyments make one's life. These enjoyments are distinguished and conjoined as we said affections of good and lusts of evil are. The enjoyment of his affection fills and surrounds each angel, the enjoyment common to a society of heaven fills and surrounds each society, and the enjoyment of all the angels together or the most widely shared enjoyment fills and

## XV. DIVINE PROVIDENCE ATTENDS THE EVIL AND THE GOOD ALIKE

envelops heaven as a whole. Similarly, the pleasure of his lust fills and envelops each spirit of hell, a common enjoyment every society in hell, and the enjoyment of all or the most widely shared enjoyment fills and envelops all hell. Since, as was said, the affections of heaven and the lusts of hell are diametrically opposite to each other, plainly a heavenly joy is so unenjoyable to hell that it is unbearable, and in turn an infernal joy is so unenjoyable to heaven that it is unbearable, too. Hence the antipathy, aversion and separateness.

304. As these enjoyments constitute the life of each individual and of all in general, they are not sensed by those in them, but the opposite enjoyments are sensed when brought near, especially if they are turned into odors; for every enjoyment corresponds to an odor and in the spiritual world may be converted into it. Then the general enjoyment in heaven is sensed as the odor of a garden, varied according to the fragrance of flowers and fruits; the general enjoyment in hell is sensed as the odor of stagnant water, into which filth of various sorts has been thrown, the odor varied according to the stench of the things decaying and reeking in it. While I have been given to know how the enjoyment of a particular affection of good is sensed in heaven, and the enjoyment of some lust of evil in hell, it would take too long to relate it here.

305. I have heard many newcomers from the world complain that they had not known that their destiny would be according to the affections of their love. To these, they said, they had given no thought in the world, much less to the enjoyments of the affections, for they loved what they found enjoyable. They had believed that each person's lot would be according to his thoughts from his intelligence, especially according to thoughts of piety and of faith. But they were answered, that they could have known, if they wished, that evil of life is unacceptable to heaven and displeasing to God, but acceptable to hell and pleasing to the devil, and the other way about, that good of life is acceptable to heaven and pleasing to God, but unacceptable to hell and displeasing to the devil; consequently that evil in itself is malodorous and good is fragrant. As they might have known

this if they wished, why did they not shun evils as infernal and diabolical, but indulge in them merely because they were enjoyable? Aware now that the enjoyments of evil smell so foully, they might also know that those full of them cannot enter heaven. Upon this reply they betook themselves to those who were in similar enjoyments, for only there could they breathe.

306. From the idea of heaven and hell just given, it may be evident what the nature of man's mind is. For, as was said, man's mind or spirit is either a heaven or a hell in least form, that is, his interiors are nothing other than affections and thoughts thence, distinguished into genera and species, like the larger and smaller societies of heaven or hell, and so connected as to act as a unit. The Lord governs them as He does heaven or hell. That the human being is either heaven or hell in least form may be seen in the work *Heaven and Hell*, published at London in 1758.

307. Now to the subject proposed, that the Lord governs hell by means of opposites, and those in the world who are evil He governs in hell as to their interiors but not as to their exteriors. On the first point, that the Lord governs hell through opposites, it was shown above (nn. 288, 289) that the angels of heaven are not in love and wisdom, or in the affection of good and thence in thought of truth from themselves, but from the Lord, likewise that good and truth flow from heaven into hell where good is turned into evil and truth into falsity because the interiors of the minds of those in heaven and in hell respectively are turned in opposite directions. Inasmuch then as all things in hell are the opposite of all things in heaven, the Lord governs hell by means of opposites.

[2] The second point, *that the Lord governs in hell those in the world who are evil*. This is for the reason that the human being as to his spirit is in the spiritual world and in some society there, in an infernal society if he is evil, in a heavenly one if he is good. For his mind, which in itself is spiritual, cannot be anywhere but among spiritual beings, of whom he becomes one after death. This has also been stated and demonstrated above. A man is not there, however, in the same way as a spirit is who has

## XV. DIVINE PROVIDENCE ATTENDS THE EVIL AND THE GOOD ALIKE

been assigned to the society, for man is constantly in a state to be reformed, and therefore, if he is evil, is transferred by the Lord from one infernal society to another according to his life and the changes in it. But if he permits himself to be reformed, he is led out of hell and elevated to heaven, and there, too, he is carried from one society to another until his death, after which this does not take place as he is then no longer in a state to be reformed, but remains in the state which is his from his life. When a person dies, therefore, he is assigned his place.

[3] Thirdly, *the Lord governs the evil who are in the world in this way as to their interiors, but in another way as to their exteriors.* The Lord governs the interiors of man's mind in the manner just stated, but governs the exteriors in the world of spirits, which is between heaven and hell. The reason is that commonly man is different in externals from what he is in internals. He can feign outwardly to be an angel of light and yet inwardly be a spirit of darkness. His external is therefore governed in one way, and his internal in another; as long as he is in the world, his external is governed in the world of spirits, and his internal in either heaven or hell. On death one also enters the world of spirits first, therefore, and comes into his external, which he puts off there; having put it off, he is conducted to the place assigned as his. What the world of spirits is and its nature may be seen in the work *Heaven and Hell*, published at London in 1758, nn. 421-535.

## XVI. DIVINE PROVIDENCE APPROPRIATES NEITHER EVIL NOR GOOD TO ANYONE, BUT ONE'S OWN PRUDENCE APPROPRIATES BOTH

308. Almost everyone believes that man thinks and wills, hence speaks and acts, from himself. Who of himself can believe otherwise? For the appearance that he does is so strong that it differs not at all from actually thinking, willing, speaking and acting from oneself, which is impossible. In *Angelic Wisdom about Divine Love and Wisdom* it was shown that there is only one life and that men are recipients of life; also that the human will is the receptacle of love, and the human understanding the receptacle of wisdom; love and wisdom are the one life. It was also demonstrated that by creation and steadily therefore by divine providence this life appears in the human being quite as though it sprang from him and hence was his own, but that this is the appearance so that man can be a receptacle. It was also shown above (nn. 288-294) that no one thinks from himself but from others, nor the others from themselves, but all from the Lord, an evil person as well as a good person. We showed further that this is well known in Christendom, especially to those who not only say but also believe that all good and truth, all wisdom and thus all faith and charity are from the Lord, also that all evil and falsity are from the devil or hell.

[2] One can only conclude from all this that everything which a man thinks and wills flows into him. And since all speech flows from thought as an effect from its cause, and all action flows similarly from the will, it follows that everything which one speaks and does also flows in, albeit derivatively or indirectly. It is undeniable that all which one sees, hears, smells,

## XVI. DIVINE PROVIDENCE APPROPRIATES NEITHER EVIL NOR GOOD TO ANYONE, BUT ONE'S OWN PRUDENCE APPROPRIATES BOTH

tastes or feels flows in; why not then what he thinks and wills? Can there be any difference other than this, that entities in the natural world flow into the organs of the external senses or of the body, while entities in the spiritual world flow into the organic substances of the internal senses or of the mind? Hence as the organs of the external senses or of the body are receptacles of natural objects, so the organic substances of the internal senses or of the mind are receptacles of spiritual objects. As this is man's situation, what then is his proprium? It cannot consist in his being such or such a receptacle, for then it would only be the man's manner of reception, not the life's proprium. No one understands by proprium anything else than that he lives of himself and consequently thinks and wills of himself; but that there is no such proprium and indeed cannot be with anyone follows from what was said above.

309. But let me relate what I have heard from some in the spiritual world. They were of those who believe that one's own prudence is everything and divine providence nothing. I remarked that man has no proprium unless you want to call it his proprium that he is such or such a subject or organ or form. This is not the proprium that is meant, however, for it is only descriptive of the nature of man. No man, I said, has any proprium as the word is commonly understood. At this those who ascribed everything to their own prudence and who may be called the very picture of proprietorship, flared up so that flames seemed to come from their nostrils as they said, "You speak paradox and insanity! Would man not be an empty nothing then? Or an idea or fancy? Or a graven image or statue?"

[2] To this I could only reply that it is paradox and insanity to believe that man has life of himself, and that wisdom and prudence, likewise the good of charity and the truth of faith, do not flow in from God but are in man. To attribute them to oneself every wise person calls insane and also paradoxical. Those who attribute them to themselves are like tenants of another's house and property who persuade themselves by living there that it is their own; or like stewards and administrators who consider all

Divine Providence

that their master owns to be theirs; or like servants in business to whom their master gave talents and pounds to trade with, but who rendered no account to him but kept all as theirs and thus behaved like robbers.

[3] It may be said of such that they are insane, indeed are nothing and empty, likewise are idealists, since they do not have in them from the Lord good which is the esse itself of life, thus do not have truth, either. They are also called "dead" therefore and "nothing and empty" (Isa 40:17, 23), and elsewhere "makers of images," "graven images" and "statues." More about them in what follows, to be done in this order:

1. What one's own prudence is, and what prudence not one's own is.
2. By his own prudence man persuades himself and confirms in himself that all good and truth are from him and in him; similarly all evil and falsity.
3. All that a man is persuaded of and confirms remains with him as his own.
4. If man believed, as is the truth, that all good and truth are from the Lord, and all evil and falsity from hell, he would not appropriate good to himself and consider it merited, nor appropriate evil to himself and make himself responsible for it.

310. (1) *What one's own prudence is, and what prudence not one's own is.* Those are in prudence of their own who confirm appearances in themselves and make them truths, especially the appearance that one's own prudence is all and divine providence nothing—unless it is something universal, which it cannot be without singulars to constitute it, as was shown above. They are also in fallacies, for every appearance confirmed as truth becomes a fallacy, and so far as they confirm themselves by fallacies they become naturalists and to that extent believe nothing that they cannot perceive by one of the bodily senses, particularly that of sight, for this especially acts as one with thought. They finally become sensuous. If they confirm themselves in favor of nature instead of God, they close the

## XVI. DIVINE PROVIDENCE APPROPRIATES NEITHER EVIL NOR GOOD TO ANYONE, BUT ONE'S OWN PRUDENCE APPROPRIATES BOTH

interiors of their mind, interpose a veil as it were, and then do their thinking below it and not at all above it. Such sense-ridden men were called serpents of the tree of knowledge by the ancients. It is also said of them in the spiritual world that as they confirm themselves they at length close the interiors of their mind "to the nose," for the nose signifies perception of truth, of which they have none. What their nature is will be told now.

[2] They are more cunning and crafty than others and are ingenious reasoners. They call cunning and craftiness intelligence and wisdom, nor do they know otherwise. They look on those who are not like themselves as simple and stupid, especially those who worship God and acknowledge divine providence. In respect of the interior principles of their minds, of which they know little, they are like those called Machiavellians, who make murder, adultery, theft and false witness, viewed in themselves, of no account; if they reason against them it is only out of prudence not to appear to be of that nature.

[3] Of man's life in the world they think it is like that of a beast, and of his life after death that it is like a vital vapor which, rising from the body or the grave, sinks back again and dies. From this madness comes the notion that spirits and angels are airy entities, and with those who have been enjoined to believe in everlasting life that the souls of men also are. They therefore do not see, hear or speak, but are blind, deaf and dumb, and only cogitate in their particle of air. The sense-ridden ask, "How can the soul be anything else? The external senses died with the body, did they not? They cannot be resumed before the soul is reunited with the body." Inasmuch as they could comprehend the state of the soul after death only sensuously and not spiritually, they have fixed upon the state described; otherwise their belief in everlasting life would have perished. Above all, they confirm self-love in themselves, calling it the fire of life and the incentive to various uses in the kingdom. Being of this nature, they are their own idols, and their thoughts, being fallacies and from fallacies, are images of falsity. Indulging in the enjoyments of lusts, they are satans and devils; those who confirm lusts of evil

in themselves are satans, and those who live them are called devils.

[4] It has also been granted me to know the nature of the most crafty sensuous men. Their hell is deep down at the back, and they want to be inconspicuous. Therefore they appear to hover about there like spectres, which are their fantasies, and they are called genii. Some were sent out from that hell once for me to learn what they are like. They immediately addressed themselves to my neck below the occiput and thus entered my affections, not wanting to enter my thoughts, which they adroitly avoided. They altered my affections one by one with a mind to bend them imperceptibly into their opposites, which are lusts of evil; and as they did not touch my thought at all they would have bent and inverted my affections without my knowledge, had not the Lord prevented it.

[5] Such do they become who do not believe that there can be any divine providence, and who search only for cupidities and cravings in others and thus lead them along until they dominate them. They do this so secretly and artfully that one does not know it, and they remain the same on death; therefore they are cast down into that hell as soon as they enter the spiritual world. Seen in heaven's light they appear to be without a nose, and it is remarkable that although they are so crafty they are more sense-ridden than others.

[6] The ancients called a sensuous man a serpent, and such a man is more cunning and crafty and a more ingenious reasoner than others; therefore it is said,

> The serpent was more crafty than any beast of the field (Ge 3:1),

and the Lord said:

> Be prudent as serpents and simple as doves (Mt 10:16).

The dragon, too, called "that old serpent" and the "devil" and "satin," is described as

> Having seven heads and ten horns, and on his heads seven crowns (Apoc 12:3, 9).

## XVI. DIVINE PROVIDENCE APPROPRIATES NEITHER EVIL NOR GOOD TO ANYONE, BUT ONE'S OWN PRUDENCE APPROPRIATES BOTH

Craftiness is signified by the seven heads; the power to persuade by fallacies is meant by the ten horns; and holy things of the Word and the church which have been profaned are signified by the seven crowns.

311. From the description of one's own prudence and of those who are in it, the nature of prudence not one's own and of those who are in it may be seen. Those have prudence not their own who do not confirm in themselves that intelligence and wisdom are from man. They ask, "How can anyone be wise of himself or do good of himself?" When they speak so, they see in themselves that it is so, for they think interiorly. They also believe that others think similarly, especially the learned, for they are unaware that any-one can think only exteriorly.

[2] They are not in fallacies by any confirmation of appearances. They know and perceive, therefore, that murder, adultery, theft and false witness are sins and accordingly shun them on that account. They also know that wickedness is not wisdom and cunning is not intelligence. When they hear ingenious reasoning from fallacies they wonder and smile to themselves. This is because with them there is no veil between interiors and exteriors, or between the spiritual and the natural things of the mind, as there is with the sensuous. They therefore receive influx from heaven by which they see these things.

[3] They speak more simply and sincerely than others and place wisdom in life and not in talk. Relatively they are like lambs and sheep while those who are in their own prudence are like wolves and foxes. Or they are like those living in a house who see the sky through the windows while those who are in prudence of their own are like persons living in the basement of a house who can look out through the windows only on what is down on the ground. Again they are like persons standing on a mountain who see those who are in prudence of their own as wanderers in valleys and forests.

[4] Hence it may be plain that prudence not one's own is prudence from the Lord, in externals appearing similar to

prudence of one's own, but totally unlike it in internals. In internals prudence not one's own appears in the spiritual world as man, while prudence which is one's own appears like a statue, which seems living only because those who are in such prudence still possess rationality and freedom or the capacity to understand and to will, hence to speak and act, and by means of these faculties can make it appear that they also are men. They are such statues because evils and falsities have no life; only goods and truths do. By their rationality they know this, for if they did not they would not feign goods and truths; hence in their simulation of them they possess a vital humanness.

[5] Who does not know that a man is what he is inwardly? Consequently that he is a man who is inwardly what he wishes to appear to be outwardly, while he is a copy who is a man outwardly only and not inwardly. Think, as you speak, in favor of God and religion, of righteousness and sincerity, and you will be a man, and divine providence will be your prudence; you will perceive in others that one's own prudence is insanity.

312. (2) *By his own prudence man persuades himself and confirms in himself that all good and truth are from him and in him; similarly all evil and falsity.* Rest the argument on the parallel between natural good and truth and spiritual good and truth. Ask what truth and good are to the sight of the eye. Is not what is called beautiful truth to it, and what is called enjoyable good to it? For enjoyment is felt in beholding what is beautiful. What are truth and good to the hearing? Is not what is called harmonious truth to it, and what is called pleasing good to it? For pleasure is felt in hearing harmonies. It is the same with the other senses. What natural good and truth are is plain, then. Consider now what spiritual good and truth are. Is spiritual truth anything other than beauty and harmony in spiritual matters and objects? And is spiritual good anything other than the enjoyment and pleasure of perceiving the beauty and harmony?

[2] Let us see now whether anything different is to be said of the one from what is said of the other, that is, of the spiritual from what is said of the natural. Of the natural we say that what

## XVI. DIVINE PROVIDENCE APPROPRIATES NEITHER EVIL NOR GOOD TO ANYONE, BUT ONE'S OWN PRUDENCE APPROPRIATES BOTH

is beautiful and enjoyable to the eye flows in from objects, and what is harmonious and pleasing to the ear flows in from musical instruments. Is something different to be said in relation to the organic substances of the mind? Of these it is said that the enjoyable and pleasing are in them, while it is said of eye and ear that they flow in. If you inquire why it is said that they flow in, the one answer possible is that distance appears between the objects and the organs. But when one asks why it is said that in the other case they are indwelling, the one possible answer is that no distance appears between the two. Consequently, it is the appearance of distance that results in believing one thing about what one thinks and perceives, and another thing about what one sees and hears. But this becomes baseless when one reflects that the spiritual is not in space as the natural is. Think of sun or moon, or of Rome or Constantinople: do you not think of them apart from distance (provided the thought is not joined to the experience gained by sight or hearing)? Why then persuade yourself that because there is no appearance of distance in thought, that good and truth, as also evil and falsity, are indwelling, and do not flow in?

[3] Let me add to this an experience which is common in the spiritual world. One spirit can infuse his thoughts and affections into another, and the other not know that it is not his own thinking and affection. This is called in that world thinking from and in another. I have witnessed it a thousand times and also done it a hundred times; and it seemed to occur at a considerable distance. As soon as the spirits learned that another was introducing the thoughts and affections, they were indignant and turned away, recognizing then, however, that to the internal thought or sight no distance is apparent unless it is disclosed, as it may be, to the external sight or the eye; as a result it is believed that there is influx.

[4] I will add to this experience an everyday experience of mine. Evil spirits have often put into my thoughts evils and falsities which seemed to me to be in me and to originate from me, or seemed to be my own thought. Knowing them to be evils

and falsities, I searched out the spirits who had introduced them, and they were detected and driven off. They were at a great distance from me.

It may be manifest from these things that all evil with its falsity flows in from hell and all good with its truth flows in from the Lord, and that both appear to be in man.

313. The nature of men who are in prudence of their own, and the nature of those in prudence not their own and hence in the divine providence, is depicted in the Word by Adam and his wife Eve in the Garden of Eden where were two trees, one of life and the other of the knowledge of good and evil, and by their eating of the latter tree. It may be seen above (n. 241) that in the internal or spiritual sense of the Word by Adam and Eve, his wife, the Most Ancient Church of the Lord on this earth is meant and described, which was more noble and heavenly than subsequent churches.

[2] Following is what is signified by other particulars. The wisdom of the men of that church is signified by the Garden of Eden; the Lord in respect to divine providence is signified by the tree of life, and man in respect to his own prudence is meant by the tree of knowledge; his sensuous life and his proprium, which in itself is self-love and pride in one's own intelligence, and thus is the devil and satan, is signified by the serpent; and the appropriation of good and truth with the thought that they are not from the Lord and are not the Lord's, but are from man and are his, is signified by eating of the tree of knowledge. Inasmuch as good and truth are what is divine with man (for everything of love is meant by good, and everything of wisdom by truth), if man claims them as his, he cannot but believe that he is as God. Therefore the serpent said:

In the day you eat of it, your eyes will be opened, and you will be as God, knowing good and evil (Ge 3:5).

> So do those in hell believe, who are in self-love and thence in the pride of their own intelligence.

## XVI. DIVINE PROVIDENCE APPROPRIATES NEITHER EVIL NOR GOOD TO ANYONE, BUT ONE'S OWN PRUDENCE APPROPRIATES BOTH

[3] Condemnation of self-love and self-intelligence is meant by the condemnation of the serpent; the condemnation of the volitional proprium is meant by the condemnation of Eve and the condemnation of the intellectual proprium by the condemnation of Adam; sheer falsity and evil are signified by the thorn and thistle which the earth would produce for Adam; the loss of wisdom is signified by the expulsion from the Garden; the Lord's care lest holy things of the Word and the church be violated is meant by guarding the way to the tree of life; moral truths, veiling men's self-love and conceit, are signified by the fig leaves with which Adam and Eve covered their nakedness; and appearances of truth, in which alone they were, are signified by the coats of skin with which they were later clothed. Such is the spiritual understanding of these particulars. Let him who wishes remain in the sense of the letter, only let him know that it is so understood in heaven.

314. The nature of those who are infatuated with their own intelligence can be seen from their fancies in matters of interior judgment, as, for example, about influx, thought and life. Their thinking about influx is inverted. They think that the sight of the eye flows into the internal sight of the mind or into the understanding, and that the hearing of the ear flows into the internal hearing, which also is the understanding. They do not perceive that the understanding from the will flows into the eye and the ear, and not only constitutes those senses but also employs them as its instruments in the natural world. As this is not according to the appearance, they do not perceive even if it is only said that the natural does not flow into the spiritual, but the spiritual into the natural. They still think, "What is the spiritual except a finer natural?" And again, "When the eye beholds something beautiful or the ear hears something melodious, of course the mind, which is understanding and will, is delighted." They do not know that the eye does not see of itself, nor the tongue taste, nor the nose smell, nor the skin feel of itself, but that it is the man's mind or spirit which has the perceptions in the sensation and which is affected according to its nature by the

sensation. Indeed, the mind or spirit does not sense things of itself, but does so from the Lord; to think otherwise is to think from appearances, and if these are confirmed, from fallacies.

[2] Regarding thought, they say that it is something modified in the air, varied according to topic, and widened by cultivation; thus that the ideas in thoughts are images appearing, meteor-like, in the air; and that the memory is a tablet on which they are imprinted. They do not know that thought goes on in purely organic substances just as much as sight and hearing do. Only let them examine the brain, and they will see that it is full of such substances; injure them and you will become delirious; destroy them and you will die. But what thought and memory are see above at n. 279 end.

[3] Regarding life, they know it only as an activity of nature, which makes itself felt in different ways, as a live body bestirs itself organically. If it is remarked that nature is alive then, they deny this, and say it enables to life. If one asks, "Is life not dissipated then on the death of the body?" they reply that life remains in a particle of air called the soul. Asked "What then is God? Is He not life itself?" they keep silence and do not want to utter what they think. Asked, "Would you grant that divine love and wisdom are life itself?" they answer, "What are love and wisdom?" For in their fallacies they do not see what these are or what God is.

These things have been adduced that it may be seen how man is infatuated by prudence of his own because he draws all conclusions then from appearances and thus from fallacies.

316. By one's own prudence one is persuaded and confirmed that all good and truth are from man and in man, because a man's own prudence is his intellectual proprium, flowing in from self-love, which is his volitional proprium; proprium inevitably makes everything its own; it cannot be raised above doing so. All who are led by the Lord's divine providence are raised above the proprium and then see that all good and truth are from the Lord, indeed see that what in the human being is from the Lord is always the Lord's and never man's. He who believes otherwise is

## XVI. DIVINE PROVIDENCE APPROPRIATES NEITHER EVIL NOR GOOD TO ANYONE, BUT ONE'S OWN PRUDENCE APPROPRIATES BOTH

like one who has his master's goods in his care and claims them himself or appropriates them—he is no steward, but a thief. As man's proprium is nothing but evil, he also immerses the goods in his evil, by which they are destroyed like pearls thrown into dung or into acid.

317. (3) *All that a man is persuaded of and confirms remains with him as his own.* Many believe that no truth can be seen by man without confirmations of it, but this is false. In civic and economic matters in a kingdom or republic what is useful and good can be seen only with some knowledge of its numerous statutes and ordinances; in judicial matters only with knowledge of the law; and in natural subjects, like physics, chemistry, anatomy, mechanics and others, only on acquaintance with those sciences. But in purely rational, moral and spiritual matters, truths appear in light of their own, if man has become somewhat rational, moral and spiritual through a suitable education. This is because everyone as to his spirit, which is what thinks, is in the spiritual world and is one among those there, consequently is in spiritual light, which enlightens the interiors of his understanding and, as it were, dictates. For spiritual light in essence is the divine truth of the Lord's divine wisdom. Thence it is that man can think analytically, form conclusions about what is just and right in matters of judgment, see what is honorable in moral life and good in spiritual life, and see many truths, which are darkened only by the confirmation of falsities. Man sees them almost as readily as he sees another's disposition from his face or perceives his affections from the sound of his voice, with no further knowledge than is implanted in one. Why should not man in some measure see from influx the interiors of his life, which are spiritual and moral, when there is no animal that does not know by influx all things necessary to it, which are natural? A bird knows how to build its nest, lay its eggs, hatch its young and recognize its food, besides other wonders which are named instinct.

318. How this state is changed, however, by confirmations and consequent persuasions will be told now in this order:

1. There is nothing that cannot be confirmed, and falsity is confirmed more readily than truth.
2. Truth does not appear when falsity has been confirmed, but falsity is apparent from confirmed truth.
3. The ability to confirm whatever one pleases is not intelligence but only ingenuity, to be found in the worst of men.
4. Confirmation may be mental and not at the same time volitional, but all volitional confirmation is also mental.
5. Confirmation of evil both volitional and intellectual causes man to believe that one's own prudence is everything and divine providence nothing, but not confirmation solely intellectual.
6. Everything confirmed by the will and at the same time by the understanding, remains to eternity, but not what has been confirmed only by the understanding.

[2] Touching the first, *that there is nothing that cannot be confirmed, and that falsity is confirmed more readily than truth.* What, indeed, cannot be confirmed when atheists confirm that God is not the Creator of the universe but that nature is her own creator; that religion is only a restraint and is for simple and common folks; that man is like the beast and dies like one; that adultery and secret theft, fraud and deceitful schemes are allowable, and that cunning is intelligence and wickedness is wisdom. Everyone confirms his heresy. Volumes are filled with confirmations of the two heresies prevalent in Christendom. Assemble ten heresies, however abstruse, ask an ingenious man to confirm them, and he will confirm them all. If you regard them then solely from the confirmations of them, will you not be seeing falsities as truth? Since all that is false lights up in the natural man from its appearances and fallacies, but truth lights up only in the spiritual man, plainly falsity can be confirmed more readily than truth.

## XVI. DIVINE PROVIDENCE APPROPRIATES NEITHER EVIL NOR GOOD TO ANYONE, BUT ONE'S OWN PRUDENCE APPROPRIATES BOTH

[3] For it to be known that everything false and everything evil can be confirmed even to the point that what is false seems true and what is evil seems to be good, take for example the confirmation that light is darkness and darkness is light. A man may ask: "What is light `in itself'? Is not light only something which appears in the eye according to the eye's condition? What is light when the eye is closed? Do not bats and owls have eyes to see light as darkness and darkness as light? I have heard it said that some persons see in like manner, and that infernal spirits, despite being in darkness, see one another. Does one not have light in his dreams in the middle of the night? Is darkness not light, therefore, and light darkness?" It can be replied, "What of that? Light is light as truth is truth, and darkness is darkness as falsity is falsity."

[4] Take a further example: confirmation that the crow is white. May its blackness not be said to be only a shading which is not the real fact? Its feathers are white inside, its body, too; and these are the stuff of which the bird is made. As its blackness is a shading, the crow turns white as it grows old—some such have been seen. What is black in itself but white? Pulverize black glass and you will see that the powder is white. When you call the crow black, therefore, you are speaking of the shadow and not of the reality. The reply can be, "What of it? All birds should be called white then."

Contrary as they are to sound reason, these arguments have been recited to show that it is possible to confirm falsity that is directly opposite to truth and evil that is directly opposite to good.

[5] Second: *Truth does not appear when falsity has been confirmed, but falsity is apparent from truth confirmed.* All falsity is in darkness and all truth in light. In darkness nothing is seen, nor indeed is it known what anything is except by contact with it, but it is different in the light. In the Word falsities are therefore called darkness, and those who are in falsities are said to walk in darkness and in the shadow of death. In turn, truths

are called light in it, and those who are in truths are said to walk in the light and to be the children of light.

[6] There is much to show that when falsity has been confirmed, truth does not appear, but when truth has been confirmed, falsity is apparent. For instance, who would see a spiritual truth unless the Word taught it? Would there not be darkness that could be dispelled only by the light in which the Word is, and only with one who wishes to be enlightened? What heretic can see his falsities unless he welcomes the genuine truth of the church? Until then he does not see them. I have talked with those who confirmed themselves in faith apart from charity and who were asked whether they saw the frequent mention in the Word of love and charity, works and deeds, and keeping the Commandments, and the declaration that the man who keeps the Commandments is blessed and wise, but the man who does not is foolish. They said that on reading these things they saw them only as matters of faith, and passed them by with their eyes closed, so to speak.

[7] Those who have confirmed themselves in falsities are like men who see streaks on a wall, and at twilight fancy that they see the figure of a horseman or just of a man, a visionary image which is dissipated when the daylight floods in. Who can sense the spiritual uncleanness of adultery except one who is in the cleanliness of chastity? Who can feel the cruelty of vengeance except one who is in good from love to the neighbor? What adulterer or what avenger does not sneer at those who call enjoyment in such acts as theirs infernal but the enjoyments of marital love and neighborly love heavenly? And so on.

[8] Third: *The ability to confirm whatever one pleases is not intelligence but only ingenuity, to be found in the worst of men.* Some show the greatest dexterity in confirmation, who know no truth and yet can confirm both truth and falsity. Some of them remark, "What is truth? Is there such a thing? Is not that true which I make true?" In the world they are believed to be intelligent, and yet they are only daubing a wall. 318-1 Only those are intelligent who perceive truth to be truth and who

## XVI. DIVINE PROVIDENCE APPROPRIATES NEITHER EVIL NOR GOOD TO ANYONE, BUT ONE'S OWN PRUDENCE APPROPRIATES BOTH

confirm it by verities constantly perceived. Little difference may be seen between the latter and the former because one cannot distinguish between the light of confirmation and the light of the perception of truth. Those in the light of confirmation seem also to be in the light of the perception of truth. Yet the difference is like that between illusory light and genuine. In the spiritual world illusory light is such that it turns into darkness when genuine light flows in. There is such illusory light with many in hell; on being brought out into genuine light they see nothing at all. It is evident, then, that to be able to confirm whatever one pleases is only ingenuity, which the worst of men may have.

[9] Fourth: *Confirmation may be mental and not at the same time volitional, but all volitional confirmation is also mental.* Let an example serve to illustrate this. Those who confirm faith separate from charity and yet live the life of charity, and in general those who confirm a falsity of doctrine and yet do not live according to it, are in intellectual confirmation but not at the same time volitional. On the other hand, those who confirm falsity of doctrine and live according to it are in volitional and at the same time in intellectual confirmation. For the understanding does not flow into the will, but the will into the understanding. Hence it is plain what falsity of evil is, and what falsity not of evil is. Falsity which is not of evil can be conjoined with good, but falsity of evil cannot be. For falsity which is not of evil is falsity in the understanding but not in the will, while falsity of evil is falsity in the understanding which comes of evil in the will.

[10] Fifth: *Confirmation of evil, both volitional and intellectual, but not confirmation only intellectual, causes man to believe that his own prudence is everything and divine providence nothing.* Many confirm their own prudence in themselves on the strength of appearances in the world, and yet do not deny divine providence; theirs is only intellectual confirmation. But in others, who deny divine providence at the same time, there is volitional confirmation; this, together with

317

## Divine Providence

persuasion, is found chiefly in worshipers of nature and also in worshipers of self.

[11] Sixth: *Everything confirmed by the will and at the same time by the understanding remains to eternity, but not what is confirmed only by the understanding.* For what pertains to the understanding alone is not within man but outside him; it is only in the thought. Nothing enters man and is appropriated to him except what is received by the will; then it comes to be of his life's love. This, it will be shown in the next number, remains to eternity.

319. Everything confirmed by both the will and the understanding remains to eternity because everyone is his own love, and love attaches to the will; also because everyone is his own good or his own evil, for that is called good or evil which belongs to the love. Since man is his own love he is also the form of his love, and may be called the organ of his life's love. It was stated above (n. 279) that the affections of man's love and his resulting thoughts are changes and variations of the state and form of the organic substances of his mind. What these changes and variations are and their nature will be explained now. Some idea of them may be obtained from the alternating expansions and compressions or dilations and contractions in the heart and lungs, called in the heart systole and diastole, and in the lungs respirations. These are reciprocal extensions and retractions or expansions and contractions of their lobes. Such are the changes and variations in the state of the heart and lungs. Such changes and variations occur in the other viscera of the body and in their parts, too, by which the blood and the animal juices are received and transmitted.

[2] Similar changes and variations take place in the organic forms of the mind, which, as we showed above, are the substances underlying man's affections and thoughts. There is a difference. Their expansions and compressions or reciprocal activities in comparison have so much greater perfection that they cannot be described in words of natural language, but only in words of spiritual language, which can sound only as saying

## XVI. DIVINE PROVIDENCE APPROPRIATES NEITHER EVIL NOR GOOD TO ANYONE, BUT ONE'S OWN PRUDENCE APPROPRIATES BOTH

that the changes and variations are vortical gyrations in and out, after the manner of perpetually winding spirals wonderfully massed into forms receptive of life.

[3] Now to tell the nature of these purely organic substances and forms in the evil and in the good respectively: in the good the spiral forms travel forward, in the evil backward; the forward-traveling are turned to the Lord and receive influx from Him; the retrogressive are turned towards hell and receive influx from hell. It should be known that in the measure in which they turn backward these forms are open behind and closed in front; and on the other hand in the measure in which they turn forward, they are open in front and closed behind.

[4] This can make plain what kind of form or organ an evil man is and what kind of form or organ a good man is, and that they are turned in opposite directions. As the turning once established cannot be twisted back it is plain that man remains to eternity such as he is at death. The love of man's will is what effects this turning, or is what either converts or inverts, for, as was said above, each person is his own love. Hence, on death, everyone goes the way of his love, the man in a good love to heaven, and the man in an evil love to hell, nor does he rest except in that society where his ruling love is. Marvelous it is that each knows the way; it is as though he scents it.

320. (4) If man believed, as is the truth, that all good and truth are from the Lord and all evil and falsity from hell, he would not appropriate good to himself and consider it merited, nor evil and make himself responsible for it. This is contrary to the belief of those who have confirmed in themselves the appearance that wisdom and prudence come from man and do not flow in according to the state of the organization of the mind, treated of above (n. 319). It must therefore be demonstrated, and to be done clearly, it will be done in this order:

> 1. One who confirms in himself the appearance that wisdom and prudence are from man and thus in him as his, must take the view that otherwise he would

not be a man, but either a beast or a statue; yet the contrary is true.
2. To believe and think, as is the truth, that all good and truth are from the Lord and all evil and falsity from hell, seems impossible, yet is truly human and hence angelic. 3. So to believe and think is impossible to those who do not acknowledge the divine of the Lord and that evils are sins, but possible for those who make these two acknowledgments. 4. Those who make the two acknowledgments alone reflect on the evils in themselves, and so far as they flee them and are averse to them, they send them back to hell from which they come. 5. So divine providence appropriates neither evil nor good to anyone, but one's own prudence appropriates both.

321. These propositions will be explained in the order proposed. First: *One who confirms in himself the appearance that wisdom and prudence are from man and thus in him as his, must take the view that otherwise he would not be a man, but either a beast or a statue; yet the contrary is true.* It comes from a law of divine providence that man is to think as it were from himself and act prudently as of himself, but still acknowledge that he does so from the Lord. It follows that one who thinks and acts prudently as of himself and acknowledges at the same time that he does so from the Lord, is a man, but that person is not who confirms in himself the idea that all he thinks and does is from himself. Neither is he a man who, knowing that wisdom and prudence are from God, keeps awaiting influx. This man becomes like a statue, the other like a beast. One who waits for influx is obviously like a statue; he is sure to stand or sit motionless, his hands dropped, his eyes closed or, if open, unblinking, and neither thinking nor breathing. What life has he then?

[2] Plainly, too, one who believes that everything he thinks and does is from himself is not unlike a beast. For he thinks only from the natural mind which man has in common with beasts, and not from the spiritual, rational mind which is the truly

## XVI. DIVINE PROVIDENCE APPROPRIATES NEITHER EVIL NOR GOOD TO ANYONE, BUT ONE'S OWN PRUDENCE APPROPRIATES BOTH

human mind; for this mind acknowledges that God alone thinks from Himself and that man does so from God. Therefore one who thinks only from the natural mind knows no difference between man and animal except that man speaks and a beast makes sounds, and he believes they die alike.

[3] Something further is to be said about those who await influx. They receive none, except for a few who desire it with the whole heart. These at times receive some response through a living perception in thought or by tacit utterance but rarely by an explicit one, and this then is that they should think and act as they determine and are able, and that one who acts wisely is wise and one who acts foolishly is foolish. They are never instructed what to believe or do, in order that human rationality and liberty may not perish, that is, in order that everyone shall act in freedom according to reason in all appearance as of himself. Those who are told by influx what they are to believe or do are not being instructed by the Lord, nor by any angel of heaven, but by some spirit, an Enthusiast, Quaker or Moravian, and are being misled. All influx from the Lord is effected by enlightenment of the understanding and by an affection of truth, and passes by the latter into the former.

[4] Second: *To believe and think, as is the truth, that all good and truth are from the Lord and all evil and falsity from hell, seems impossible, yet is truly human and hence angelic.* To believe and think that all good and truth are from God seems possible, if no more is said, for it falls in with a theological belief contrary to which it is not allowable to think. But to believe and think also that all evil and falsity are from hell seems impossible, for in that belief man would not think at all. But man still thinks as from himself though it is from hell, for the Lord grants to everyone that his thought, wherever it is from, shall appear to be his own in him. Else man would not live as a human being, nor could he be led out of hell and brought into heaven, that is, be reformed, as we have shown many times.

[5] Therefore the Lord also grants man to know and consequently to think that when he is in evil he is in hell, and that if he thinks evil he thinks from hell. He likewise grants him to think of the means by which he can escape from hell and not think from hell, but enter heaven and in heaven think from the Lord, and He grants man the freedom to choose. From all this it may be seen that man can think evil and falsity as if from himself and also think that this or that is evil or false; consequently that it is only an appearance that he does so of himself, an appearance without which he would not be man. To think from truth is what is human itself and consequently angelic itself; it is a truth that man does not think from himself, but is granted by the Lord to think from himself to all appearance.

[6] Third: *So to believe and think is impossible to those who do not acknowledge the divine of the Lord and that evils are sins, but possible to those who make the two acknowledgments.* It is impossible to those who do not acknowledge the divine of the Lord, for the Lord alone gives man to think and will; and those who do not acknowledge the divine of the Lord, being separated from Him believe that they think for themselves. It is impossible also to those who do not acknowledge evils to be sins, for they think then from hell, and in hell everyone supposes that he thinks from himself. That it is possible, however, to those who make the two acknowledgments can be seen from what was set forth fully above (nn. 288-294).

[7] Fourth: *Only those who live in the two acknowledgments reflect on the evils in themselves, and so far as they shun and are averse to them, they send them back to hell from which they come.* All know or can know that evil is from hell and good is from heaven. Who then cannot know that so far as man shuns and is averse to evil he shuns and is averse to hell? He can know then, too, that so far as he shuns and is averse to evil, he wills and loves what is good, and consequently is so far released from hell by the Lord and led to heaven. Every rational person may see these things provided he knows that heaven and hell exist, where good and evil have their respective origins. If, now, he reflects on the evils in him, which is the same thing as examining

## XVI. DIVINE PROVIDENCE APPROPRIATES NEITHER EVIL NOR GOOD TO ANYONE, BUT ONE'S OWN PRUDENCE APPROPRIATES BOTH

himself, and shuns them, he disengages himself from hell, puts it behind him, and brings himself into heaven, where he beholds the Lord before him. Man does this, we say, but he does it as of himself and from the Lord now. When a man acknowledges this truth out of a good heart and in a devout faith, it lies inwardly hidden in all that he thinks and does afterwards as of himself. It is like the prolific force in a seed which remains in it even until new seed is produced, and like the pleasure in one's appetite for food the wholesomeness of which one has learned; in a word, like heart and soul in all he thinks and does.

[8] Fifth: *So divine providence appropriates neither evil nor good to anyone, but one's own prudence appropriates both.* This follows from all that has been said. Good is the objective of divine providence; it purposes good in all its activity, therefore. Accordingly, it does not appropriate good to anyone, for then this would become self-righteous; nor does it appropriate evil to anyone, for so it would make him responsible for evil. But man does both by his proprium, for this is nothing but evil. The proprium of the will is self-love and that of the understanding is the pride of self-intelligence, and of these comes man's own prudence.

## XVII. EVERY MAN CAN BE REFORMED, AND THERE IS NO PREDESTINATION [as commonly understood]

322. Sound reason dictates that all are predestined to heaven and none to hell, for all are born human beings and consequently God's image is in them. God's image in them consists in their ability to understand truth and to do good. The ability to understand truth comes from the divine wisdom, and the ability to do good from the divine love. This ability, which is God's image, remains in any sane person and is not eradicated. Hence it is that he can become a civil and moral man, and one who is civil and moral can also become spiritual, for the civil and moral is a receptacle of what is spiritual. He is called a civil man who knows and lives according to the laws of the kingdom of which he is a citizen; he is called a moral man who makes those laws his ethics and his virtues and from reason lives by them.

[2] Let me say how civil and moral life is the receptacle of spiritual life. Live these laws not only as civil and moral laws but also as divine laws, and you will be a spiritual man. There is hardly a nation so barbarous that it has not by law prohibited murder, adultery, theft, false witness and damage to what is another's. The civil and moral man keeps these laws that he may be, or seem to be, a good citizen. If he does not consider them divine laws also he is only a civil and moral natural man, but if he considers them divine also, he becomes a civil and moral spiritual man. The difference is that the latter is a good citizen both of an earthly kingdom and of a heavenly, while the former is a good citizen only of the earthly kingdom and not of the heavenly. They are distinguishable by the good they do. The good done by civil and moral natural men is not in itself good, for man and the world are in it; the good done by civil and moral

## XVII. EVERY MAN CAN BE REFORMED, AND THERE IS NO PREDESTINATION [as commonly understood]

spiritual men is in itself good, because the Lord and heaven are in it.

[3] From all this it may be seen that every person, because he is born able to become a civil and moral natural being, is also born able to become a civil and moral spiritual man. He has only to acknowledge God and not commit evils because they are against God, but do good because good is siding with God. Then spirit enters into his civil and moral actions and they live; otherwise there is no spirit in them and hence they are not living. Therefore the natural man, however much he acts like a civil and moral being, is spoken of as dead, but the spiritual man is spoken of as living.

[4] Of the Lord's divine providence every nation has some religion, and primary in every religion is the acknowledgment that God is, else it is not called a religion. Every nation that lives its religion, that is, does not do evil because this is contrary to its God, receives something spiritual in its natural life. Who, on hearing a Gentile say he will not do this or that evil because it is contrary to his God, does not say to himself, "Is this person not saved? It seems, it cannot be otherwise." Sound reason tells him this. On the other hand, hearing a Christian say, "I make no account of this or that evil. What does it mean to say that it is contrary to God?" one says to himself, "This man is not saved, is he? It would seem, he cannot be." Sound reason dictates this also.

[5] Should someone say, "I was born a Christian, have been baptized, have known the Lord, read the Word, observed the Sacrament of the Supper," what does this amount to when he does not count as sins murder, or the revenge breathing it, adultery, stealing, false witness, or lying, and different sorts of violence? Does such a person think of God or of eternal life? Does he think they exist? Does sound reason not dictate that such a man cannot be saved? This has been said of a Christian, for a Gentile in his life gives more thought to God from religion

than a Christian does. But more is to be said on these points in what follows in this order:

1. The goal of creation is a heaven from mankind.
2. Of divine providence, therefore, every man can be saved, and those are saved who acknowledge God and live rightly.
3. Man himself is in fault if he is not saved.
4. Thus all are predestined to heaven, and no one to hell.

323. (1) *The goal of creation is a heaven from mankind.* It has been shown above and in the work, *Heaven and Hell* (London, 1758), that heaven consists solely of those who have been born as human beings. Since heaven consists of no others, it follows that the purpose of creation is a heaven from mankind. This has been shown above (nn. 27-45), it is true, but will be seen more clearly still with explanation of the following:

1. Everyone is created to live forever.
2. Everyone is created to live forever in a blessed state.
3. Thus every person has been created to enter heaven.
4. The divine love cannot but will this, and the divine wisdom cannot but provide it.

324. One can see from these points that divine providence is none other than predestination to heaven and cannot be altered into anything else. We must now demonstrate, therefore, in the order proposed, that the goal of creation is a heaven from the human race. First: Everyone has been created to live to eternity. In the treatise *Divine Love and Wisdom*, Parts III and V, it was shown that there are three degrees of life in man, called natural, spiritual and celestial, that they are actually in everyone, and that in animals there is only one degree of life, which is like the lowest degree in man, called the natural. The result is that by the elevation of his life to the Lord man is in such a state above that of animals that he can comprehend what is of divine wisdom, and will what is of divine love, in other words, receive what is divine; and he who can receive what is divine, so as to see and

## XVII. EVERY MAN CAN BE REFORMED, AND THERE IS NO PREDESTINATION [as commonly understood]

perceive it within him, cannot but be united with the Lord and by the union live to eternity.

[2] What would the Lord do with all the created universe if He had not also created images and likenesses of Himself to whom He could communicate His divine? What would He exist for, otherwise, except to make this and not that or bring something into existence but not something else, and this merely to be able to contemplate from afar only incidents and constant changes as on a stage? What would there be divine in these unless they were for the purpose of serving subjects who would receive the divine more intimately and see and sense it? The divine is of an inexhaustible glory and would not keep it to itself, nor could. For love wants to communicate its own to another, indeed to impart all it can of itself. Must not divine love do this, then, being infinite? Can it impart and then take away? Would that not be to give what will perish, what in itself is nothing, coming to nothing when it perishes? What really is is not in it. But divine love imparts what really is or what does not cease to be, and this is eternal.

[3] In order that a man may live forever, what is mortal with him is taken away. This mortal of his is his material body, which is taken away by its death. His immortal, which is his mind, is thus laid bare and he becomes a spirit in human form; his mind is this spirit. Ancient sages and wise men perceived that man's mind cannot die. They asked how the mind could die when it is capable of wisdom. Few today know the interior idea they had in this. It was the idea, slipping into their general perception from heaven, that God is wisdom itself, of which man partakes, and God is immortal or eternal.

[4] Since it has been granted me to speak with angels, I will say something from experience. I have spoken with those who lived many ages ago, with some who lived before the Flood and some who lived after it, with some who lived at the time of the Lord and with one of His apostles, and with many who lived in the centuries since. They all seemed like men of middle age and said that they do not know what death can be unless it is

condemnation. Further, all who have lived well, on coming into heaven, come into the state of early manhood in the world and continue in it to eternity, even those who had been old and decrepit in the world. Women, too, although they had become shrunken and old, return into the bloom and beauty of their youth.

[5] That man lives after death to eternity is manifest from the Word, where life in heaven is called eternal life, as in Mt 19:29, 25:46; Mk 10:17; Lu 10:25, 18:30; Jn 3:15, 16, 36, 5:24, 25, 39, 6:27, 40, 68, 12:50; also called simply life (Mt 18:8, 9; Jn 5:40, 20:31). The Lord also told His disciples,

> Because I live, you will live also (Jn 14:19),

and concerning resurrection said that

> God is God of the living and not God of the dead, and that they cannot die any more (Lu 20:38, 36).

[6] Second: *Everyone is created to live forever in a blessed state.* This naturally follows. He who wills that man shall live forever also wills that he shall live in a blessed state. What would eternal life be without this? All love desires the good of another. The love of parents desires the good of their children, the love of the bridegroom and the husband desires the good of the bride and the wife, and love in friendship desires the good of one's friends. What then must divine love desire! What is good but enjoyment, and divine good but eternal blessedness? All good is so named for its enjoyableness or blessedness. True, anything one is given or possesses is also called good, but again, unless it is enjoyable, it is a barren good, not in itself good. Clearly, then, eternal life is also eternal blessedness. This state of man is the aim of creation; that only those who come into heaven are in that state is not the Lord's fault but man's. That man is in fault will be seen in what follows.

[7] Third: *Thus every person has been created to come into heaven.* This is the goal of creation, but not all enter heaven because they become imbued with the enjoyments of hell, the opposite of heavenly blessedness. Those who are not in the

## XVII. EVERY MAN CAN BE REFORMED, AND THERE IS NO PREDESTINATION [as commonly understood]

blessedness of heaven cannot enter heaven, for they cannot endure doing so. No one who comes into the spiritual world is refused ascent into heaven, but when one ascends who is in the enjoyment of hell his heart pounds, his breathing labors, his life ebbs, he is in anguish and torment and writhes like a snake placed near a fire. This happens because opposites act against each other.

[8] Nevertheless, having been born human beings, consequently with the faculties of thought and volition and hence of speech and action, they cannot die, but they can live only with those in a similar enjoyment of life and are sent to them, those in enjoyments of evil to their like, as those in enjoyments of good are to their like. Indeed, everyone is granted the enjoyment of his evil provided that he does not molest those who are in the enjoyment of good. Still, as evil is bound to molest good, for inherently it hates good, those who are in evil are removed lest they inflict injury and are cast down to their own places in hell, where their enjoyment is turned into joylessness.

[9] But this does not alter the fact that by creation and hence by birth man is such that he can enter heaven. For everyone who dies in infancy enters heaven, is brought up there and instructed as one is in the world, and by the affection of good and truth is imbued with wisdom and becomes an angel. So could the man become who is brought up and instructed in the world; the same is in him as in an infant. On infants in the spiritual world see the work *Heaven and Hell*, London, 1758 (nn. 329-345).

[10] This does not take place, however, with many in the world because they love the first level of their life, called natural, and do not purpose to withdraw from it and become spiritual. The natural degree of life, in itself regarded, loves only self and the world, for it keeps close to the bodily senses, which are to the fore, also, in the world. But the spiritual degree of life regarded in itself loves the Lord and heaven, and self and the world, too, but God and heaven as higher, paramount and controlling, and self and the world as lower, instrumental and subservient.

[11] Fourth: *Divine love cannot but will this, and divine wisdom cannot but provide it.* It was fully shown in the treatise *Divine Love and Wisdom* that the divine essence is divine love and wisdom, and it was also demonstrated there (nn. 358-370) that in every human embryo the Lord forms two receptacles, one of the divine love and the other of the divine wisdom, the former for man's future will and the latter for his future understanding, and that in this way the Lord has endowed each human being with the faculty of willing good and the faculty of understanding truth.

[12] Inasmuch as man is endowed from birth with these two faculties by the Lord, and the Lord then is in them as in what is His own with man, it is manifest that His divine love cannot but will that man should come into heaven and His divine wisdom cannot but provide for this. But since it is of the Lord's divine love that man should feel heavenly blessedness in himself as his own, and this cannot be unless man is kept in the appearance that he thinks, wills, speaks and acts of himself, the Lord can therefore lead man only according to the laws of His divine providence.

325. (2) *Of divine providence, therefore, every man can be saved, and those are saved who acknowledge God and live rightly.* It is plain from what has been demonstrated above that every human being can be saved. Some persons suppose that the Lord's church is to be found only in Christendom, because only there is the Lord known and the Word possessed. Still many believe that the Lord's church is general, that is, extends and is scattered throughout the world, existing thus with those who do not know the Lord or possess the Word. They say that those men are not in fault and are without means to overcome their ignorance. They believe that it is contrary to God's love and mercy that any should be born for hell who are equally human beings.

[2] Inasmuch as many Christians, if not all, have faith that the church is common to many—it is in fact called a communion—there must be some very widely shared things of the church that

## XVII. EVERY MAN CAN BE REFORMED, AND THERE IS NO PREDESTINATION [as commonly understood]

enter all religions and that constitute this communion. These most widely shared factors are acknowledgment of God and good of life, as will be seen in this order:

1. Acknowledgment of God effects a conjunction of God and man; denial of God causes disjunction.
2. Each one acknowledges God and is conjoined with Him in accord with the goodness of his life.
3. Goodness of life, or living rightly, is shunning evils because they are contrary to religion, thus to God.
4. These are factors common to all religions, and by them anyone can be saved.

326. To clarify and demonstrate these propositions one by one. First: *Acknowledgment of God brings conjunction of God and man; denial of God results in disjunction.* Some may think that those who do not acknowledge God can be saved equally with those who do, if they lead a moral life. They ask, "What does acknowledgment accomplish? Is it not merely a thought? Can I not 'acknowledge God when I learn for certain that God there is? I have heard of Him but not seen Him. Let me see Him and I will believe." Such is the language of many who deny God when they have an opportunity to argue with one who acknowledges God. But that an acknowledgment of God conjoins and denial disjoins will be clarified by some things made known to me in the spiritual world. In that world when anyone thinks of another and desires to speak with him, the other is at once present. The explanation is that there is no distance in the spiritual world such as there is in the natural, but only an appearance of distance.

[2] A second phenomenon: as thought from some acquaintance with another causes his presence, love from affection for another causes conjunction with him. So spirits move about, converse as friends, dwell together in one house or in one community, meet often, and render one another services. The opposite happens, also; one who does not love another and still more one who hates another does not see or encounter him; the distance between them is according to the degree in which

love is wanting or hatred is present. Indeed, one who is present and recalls his hatred, vanishes.

[3] From these few particulars it may be evident whence presence and conjunction come in the spiritual world. Presence comes with the recollection of another with a desire to see him, and conjunction comes of an affection which springs from love. This is true also of all things in the human mind. There are countless things in the mind, and its least parts are associated and conjoined in accord with affections or as one thing attracts another.

[4] This is spiritual conjunction and it is the same in things large and things small. It has its origin in the conjunction of the Lord with the spiritual world and the natural world in general and in detail. It is manifest from this that in the measure in which one knows the Lord and thinks of Him from knowledge of Him, in that measure the Lord is present, and in the measure in which one acknowledges Him from an affection of love, in that measure the Lord is united with him. On the other hand, in the measure of one's ignorance of the Lord, in that measure He is absent; and so far as one denies Him, so far is He separated from one.

[5] The result of conjunction is that the Lord turns man's face towards Himself and thereupon leads him; the disjunction results in hell's turning man's face to it and it leads him. Therefore all the angels of heaven turn their faces towards the Lord as the Sun, and all the spirits of hell avert their faces from the Lord. It is plain from this what the acknowledgment of God and the denial of God each accomplish. Those who deny God in the world deny Him after death also; they have become organized as described above (n. 319); the organization induced in the world remains to eternity.

[6] Second: *Everyone acknowledges God and is conjoined with Him according to the goodness of his life.* All who know something of religion can know God; from information or from the memory they can also speak about God, and some may also think about Him from the understanding. But this only brings

## XVII. EVERY MAN CAN BE REFORMED, AND THERE IS NO PREDESTINATION [as commonly understood]

about presence if a man does not live rightly, for despite it all he can turn away from God and towards hell, and this takes place if he lives wickedly. Only those who live rightly can acknowledge God with the heart, and these the Lord turns away from hell and towards Himself according to the goodness of their life. For these alone love God; for in doing what comes from Him they love what is divine. The precepts of His law are divine things from Him. They are God because He is His own proceeding divine. As this is to love God, the Lord says:

> He who keeps my commandments is he who loves me ... But he who does not keep my commandments does not love me (Jn 14: 21, 24).

[7] Here is the reason why there are two tables of the Decalog, one having reference to God and the other to man. God works unceasingly that man may receive what is in His table, but if man does not do what he is bidden in his own table he does not receive with acknowledgment of heart what is in God's table, and if he does not receive this he is not conjoined. The two tables were joined, therefore, to be one and are called the tables of the covenant; covenant means conjunction. One acknowledges God and is conjoined to Him in accord with the goodness of his life because this good is like the good in the Lord and consequently comes from the Lord. So when man is in the good of life there is conjunction. The contrary takes place with evil of life; it rejects the Lord.

[8] Third: *Goodness of life, or living rightly, is shunning evils because they are contrary to religion, thus to God.* That this is good of life or living rightly is fully shown in *Doctrine of Life for the New Jerusalem*, from beginning to end. To this I will only add that if you do good aplenty, build churches for instance, adorn them and fill them with offerings, spend money lavishly on hospitals and hostels, give alms daily, aid widows and orphans, diligently observe the sanctities of worship, indeed think and speak and preach about them as from the heart, and yet do not shun evils as sins against God, all those good deeds are not goodness. They are either hypocritical or done for merit, for

evil is still deep in them. Everyone's life pervades all that he does. Goods become good only by the removal of evil from them. Plainly, then, shunning evils because they are contrary to religion and thus to God is living rightly.

[9] Fourth: *These are factors common to all religions, and anyone can be saved by them.* To acknowledge God, and to refrain from evil because it is contrary to God, are the two acts that make religion to be religion. If one is lacking, it cannot be called religion, for to acknowledge God and to do evil is a contradiction; so it is, too, to do good and yet not acknowledge God; one is impossible apart from the other. The Lord has provided that there should be some religion almost everywhere and that these two elements should be in it, and has also provided that everyone who acknowledges God and refrains from doing evil because it is against God shall have a place in heaven. For heaven as a whole is like one man whose life or soul is the Lord. In that heavenly man are all things to be found in a natural man with the difference which obtains between the heavenly and the natural.

[10] It is a matter of common knowledge that in the human being there are not only forms organized of blood vessels and nerve fibres, but also skins, membranes, tendons, cartilages, bones, nails and teeth. These have a smaller measure of life than those organized forms, which they serve as ligaments, coverings or supports. For all these entities to be in the heavenly humanity, which is heaven, it cannot be made up of human beings all of one religion, but of men of many religions. Therefore all who make these two universals of the church part of their lives have a place in this heavenly man, that is, heaven, and enjoy happiness each in his measure. More on the subject may be seen above (n. 254).

[11] That these two are primary in all religion is evident from the fact that they are the two which the Decalog teaches. The Decalog was the first of the Word, promulgated by Jehovah from Mount Sinai by a living voice, and also inscribed on two tables of stone by the finger of God. Then, placed in the ark, the

## XVII. EVERY MAN CAN BE REFORMED, AND THERE IS NO PREDESTINATION [as commonly understood]

Decalog was called Jehovah, and it made the holy of holies in the tabernacle and the shrine in the temple of Jerusalem; all things in each were holy only on account of it. Much more about the Decalog in the ark is to be had from the Word, which is cited in *Doctrine of Life for the New Jerusalem* (nn. 53-61). To that I will add this. From the Word we know that the ark with the two tables in it on which the Decalog was written was captured by the Philistines and placed in the temple of Dagon in Ashdod; that Dagon fell to the ground before it, and afterward his head, together with the palms of the hands, torn from his body, lay on the temple threshold; that the people of Ashdod and Ekron to the number of many thousands were smitten with hemorrhoids and their land was ravaged by mice; that on the advice of the chiefs of their nation, the Philistines made five golden hemorrhoids, five golden mice and a new cart, and on this placed the ark with the golden hemorrhoids and mice beside it; with two cows that lowed before the cart along the way, they sent the ark back to the children of Israel and by them cows and cart were offered in sacrifice (1 Sa 5 and 6).

[12] To state now what all this signified: the Philistines signified those who are in faith separated from charity; Dagon signified that religiosity; the hemorrhoids by which they were smitten signified natural loves which when severed from spiritual love are unclean, and the mice signified the devastation of the church by falsification of truth. The new cart on which the Philistines sent back the ark signified a new but still natural doctrine (chariot in the Word signifies doctrine from spiritual truths), and the cows signified good natural affections. Hemorrhoids of gold signified natural loves purified and made good, and the golden mice signified an end to the devastation of the church by means of good, for in the Word gold signifies good. The lowing of the kine on the way signified the difficult conversion of the lusts of evil of the natural man into good affections. That cows and cart were offered up as a burnt offering signified that so the Lord was propitiated.

[13] This is how what is told historically is understood spiritually. Gather all into a single conception and make the

application. That those who are in faith severed from charity are represented by the Philistines, see *Doctrine of the New Jerusalem about Faith* (nn. 49-54), and that the ark was the most holy thing of the church because of the Decalog enclosed in it, see *Doctrine of Life for the New Jerusalem* (nn. 53-61).

327. (3) *Man himself is in fault if he is not saved.* As soon as he hears it any rational man acknowledges the truth that evil cannot issue from good nor good from evil, for they are opposites; consequently only good comes of good and only evil of evil. When this truth is acknowledged this also is: that good can be turned into evil not by a good but by an evil recipient; for any form changes into its own nature what flows into it (see above, n. 292). Inasmuch as the Lord is good in its very essence or good itself, plainly evil cannot issue from Him or be produced by Him, but good can be turned into evil by a recipient subject whose form is a form of evil. Such a subject is man as to his proprium. This constantly receives good from the Lord and constantly turns it into the nature of its own form, which is one of evil. It follows that man is in fault if he is not saved. Evil is indeed from hell but as man receives it from hell as his and appropriates it to himself, it is the same whether one says that evil is from man or from hell. But whence there is an appropriation of evil until finally religion perishes will be told in this order:

1. Every religion declines and comes to an end in the course of time.
2. It does so through the inversion of God's image in man.
3. This takes place through a continual increase of hereditary evil over the generations.
4. Nevertheless the Lord provides that everyone may be saved.
5. It is also provided that a new church shall succeed in place of the former devastated church.

328. These points are to be demonstrated in the order given. First: *Every religion declines and comes to an end in the course*

## XVII. EVERY MAN CAN BE REFORMED, AND THERE IS NO PREDESTINATION [as commonly understood]

*of time.* There have been several churches on this earth, one after another, for wherever mankind is, a church is. For, as was shown above, heaven, which is the goal of creation, is from mankind, and no one can enter heaven unless he is in the two universal marks of the church which, as was shown just above (n. 326), are the acknowledgment of God and living aright. It follows that there have been churches on this earth from the most ancient times to the present. These churches are described in the Word, but not historically except the Israelitish and Jewish church. There were churches before it which are only described in the Word under the names of nations and persons and in a few items about them.

[2] The first, the Most Ancient Church, is described under the names of Adam and his wife Eve. The next church, to be called the Ancient Church, is described by Noah, his three sons and their posterity. This church was widespread and extended over many of the kingdoms of Asia: the land of Canaan on both sides of the Jordan, Syria, Assyria and Chaldea, Mesopotamia, Egypt, Arabia, Tyre and Sidon. These had the Ancient Word (*Doctrine of the New Jerusalem about Sacred Scripture*, nn. 101-103). That this church existed in those kingdoms is evident from various things recorded about them in the prophetical parts of the Word. This church was markedly altered by Eber, from whom arose the Hebrew church, in which worship by sacrifices was first instituted. From the Hebrew church the Israelitish and Jewish church was born and solemnly established for the sake of the Word which was composed in it.

[3] These four churches are meant by the statue seen by Nebuchadnezzar in a dream, the head of which was of pure gold, the breast and arms of silver, the belly and thighs of brass, and the legs and feet of iron and clay (Da 2:32, 33). Nor is anything else meant by the golden, silver, copper and iron ages mentioned by ancient writers. Needless to say, the Christian church succeeded the Jewish. It can be seen from the Word that all these churches declined in the course of time, eventually coming to an end, called their consummation.

[4] The consummation of the Most Ancient Church, brought about by the eating of the tree of knowledge, meaning by the pride of one's own intelligence, is depicted by the Flood. The consummation of the Ancient Church is depicted in the various devastations of nations mentioned in the historical as well as the prophetical Word and especially by the expulsion of the nations from the land of Canaan by the children of Israel. The consummation of the Israelitish and Jewish church is understood by the destruction of the temple at Jerusalem and by the carrying away of the people of Israel into permanent captivity and of the Jewish nation to Babylon, and finally by the second destruction of the temple and of Jerusalem at the same time, and by the dispersion of that nation. This consummation is foretold in many places in the Prophets and in Daniel 9:24-27. The gradual devastation of the Christian church even to its end is pictured by the Lord in Matthew (24), Mark (13) and Luke (21), but the end itself in the Apocalypse. Hence it may be manifest that in the course of time a church declines and comes to an end; so does a religion.

[5] Second: *Every religion declines and comes to an end through the inversion of God's image in man.* It is known that the human being was created in the image and after the likeness of God (Ge 1:26), but let us say what the image and the likeness of God are. God alone is love and wisdom; man was created to be a receptacle of both love and wisdom, his will to be a receptacle of divine love and his understanding a receptacle of the divine wisdom. These two receptacles, it was shown above, are in man from creation, constitute him, and are formed in everyone in the womb. Man's being an image of God thus means that he is a recipient of the divine wisdom, and his being a likeness of God means that he is a recipient of the divine love. Therefore the receptacle called the understanding is an image of God, and the receptacle called the will is a likeness of God. Since, then, man was created and formed to be a receptacle, it follows that he was created and formed that his will might receive love from God and his understanding wisdom from God. He receives these when he acknowledges God and lives according to His precepts,

## XVII. EVERY MAN CAN BE REFORMED, AND THERE IS NO PREDESTINATION [as commonly understood]

receiving them in lesser or larger measure as by religion he has some knowledge of God and of His precepts, consequently according to his knowledge of truths. For truths teach what God is and how He is to be acknowledged, also what His precepts are and how man is to live according to them.

[6] The image and likeness of God have not been destroyed in man, but seem to have been; they remain inherent in his two faculties called liberty and rationality, of which we have treated above at many places. They seem to have been destroyed when man made the receptacle of divine love, namely, his will, a receptacle of self-love, and the receptacle of divine wisdom, namely, his understanding, a receptacle of his own intelligence. Doing this, he inverted the image and likeness of God and turned these receptacles away from God and towards himself. Consequently they have become closed above and open below, or closed in front and open behind, though by creation they were open in front and closed behind. When they have been opened and closed contrariwise, the receptacle of love, the will, receives influx from hell or from one's proprium; so does the receptacle of wisdom, the understanding. Hence worship of men arose in the churches instead of the worship of God, and worship by doctrines of falsity instead of worship by doctrines of truth, the latter arising from man's own intelligence, and the former from love of self. Thence it is evident that religion falls away in the course of time and is ended by the inversion of God's image in man.

[7] Third: *This takes place as a result of a continual increase of hereditary evil over the generations.* It was said and explained above that hereditary evil does not come from Adam and his wife Eve by their having eaten of the tree of knowledge, but is derived and transmitted successively from parents to offspring. Thus it grows by continual increase from generation to generation. When evil increases so among many, it spreads to many more, for in all evil there is a lust to lead astray, in some burning with anger against goodness—hence a contagion of evil. When the contagion reaches leaders, rulers and the prominent in the church, religion has become perverted, and the means of

restoring it to health, namely truths, become corrupted by falsifications. As a result there is a gradual devastation of good and desolation of truth in the church on to its end.

[8] Fourth: *Nevertheless the Lord provides that everyone may be saved.* He provides that there shall be religion everywhere and in it the two essentials for salvation, acknowledgment of God and ceasing from evil because it is contrary to God. Other things, which pertain to the understanding and hence to the thinking, called matters of faith, are provided everyone in accord with his life, for they are accessory to life and if they have been given precedence, do not become living until they are subsidiary. It is also provided that those who have lived rightly and acknowledged God are instructed by angels after death. Then those who were in the two essentials of religion while in the world accept such truths of the church as are in the Word, and acknowledge the Lord as God of heaven and of the church. This last they receive more readily than do Christians who have brought with them from the world an idea of the Lord's human nature parted from His divine. It is also provided by the Lord that all are saved who die as infants, no matter where they have been born.

[9] Furthermore, every person is given the opportunity after death of amending his life if possible. All are instructed and led by the Lord by means of angels. Knowing now that they live after death and that heaven and hell exist, they at first receive truths. But those who did not acknowledge God and shun evils as sins when in the world soon show a distaste for truths and draw back, and those who acknowledged truths with the lips but not with the heart are like the foolish virgins who had lamps but no oil and begged oil of others, also went off and bought some, but still were not admitted to the wedding. "Lamps" signify truths of faith and "oil" signifies the good of charity. It may be evident then that divine providence sees to it that everyone can be saved and that man is himself in fault if he is not saved.

[10] Fifth: *It is also provided that a new church shall succeed in place of a former devastated church.* It has been so from the

## XVII. EVERY MAN CAN BE REFORMED, AND THERE IS NO PREDESTINATION [as commonly understood]

most ancient days that on the devastation of a church a new one followed. The Ancient Church succeeded the Most Ancient; the Israelitish or Jewish Church followed the Ancient; after this came the Christian Church. And this, it is foretold in the Apocalypse, will be followed by a new church, signified in that book by the New Jerusalem descending from heaven. The reason why a new church is provided by the Lord to follow in place of a former devastated church may be seen in *Doctrine of the New Jerusalem about Sacred Scripture* (nn. 104-113).

329. (4) Thus all are predestined to heaven, and no one to hell. In the work *Heaven and Hell* (London, 1758) we showed at nn. 545-550 that the Lord casts no one into hell; the spirit himself does this. So it happens with every evil and impious person after death and also while he is in the world, with the difference that while he is in the world he can be reformed and can embrace and avail himself of the means of salvation, but not after departure from the world. The means of salvation are summed up in these two: that evils are to be shunned because they are contrary to the divine laws in the Decalog and that it be acknowledged that God exists. Everyone can do both if he does not love evils. For the Lord is constantly flowing into his will with power for shunning evils and into his understanding with power to think that God there is. But no one can do the one without doing the other; the two are joined together like the two tables of the Decalog, one relating to God and the other to man. In accordance with what is in His table the Lord enlightens and empowers everyone, but man receives power and enlightenment so far as he does what he is bidden in his table. Until then the two tables appear to be laid face to face and to be sealed, but as man acts on the biddings in his table they are unsealed and opened out.

[2] Today is not the Decalog like a small, closed book or document, opened only in the hands of children and the young? Tell someone farther along in years, "Do not do this because it is contrary to the Decalog" and who gives heed? He may give heed if you say, "Do not do this because it is contrary to divine laws," and yet the precepts of the Decalog are the divine laws

themselves. Experiment was made with a number in the spiritual world, who at mention of the Decalog or Catechism rejected it with contempt. This is because in the second table, which is man's, the Decalog teaches that evils are to be shunned, and one who does not do so, whether from impiety or from the religious tenet that deeds effect nothing, only faith does, hears mention of the Decalog or Catechism with disdain, as though it was a child's book he heard mentioned, no longer of use to adults.

[3] These things have been said in order that it may be known that a knowledge of the means by which one can be saved is not lacking to anyone, nor power if he wants to be saved. It follows that all are predestined to heaven and no one to hell. Since, however, a belief in a predestination not to salvation but to damnation has prevailed with some, and this belief is damaging and cannot be broken up unless one's reason sees the insanity and cruelty in it, it is to be dealt with in this order:

1. Predestination except to heaven is contrary to divine love and its infiniteness.
2. Predestination other than to heaven is contrary to divine wisdom and its infiniteness.
3. That only those born in the church are saved is an insane heresy.
4. That any of mankind are condemned by predestination is a cruel heresy.

330. That it may be apparent how damaging the belief is in predestination as this is commonly understood, these four arguments are to be taken up and confirmed. First: *Predestination except to heaven is contrary to divine love and its infiniteness.* In the treatise *Divine Love and Wisdom* we demonstrated that Jehovah or the Lord is divine love, is infinite, and is the esse of all life; also that the human being was created in God's image after God's likeness. As everyone is formed in the womb by the Lord into that image and after that likeness, as was also shown, the Lord is the heavenly Father of all human beings and they are His spiritual children. So Jehovah or the

## XVII. EVERY MAN CAN BE REFORMED, AND THERE IS NO PREDESTINATION [as commonly understood]

Lord is called in the Word, and so human beings are. Therefore He says:

> Do not call your father on earth your father, for One is your Father, who is in the heavens (Mt 23:9).

This means that He alone is the Father with reference to the life in us, and the earthly father is father of the covering on life, which is the body. In heaven, therefore, no one but the Lord is called Father. And from many passages in the Word it is clear that those who do not pervert that life are said to be His sons and to be born from Him.

[2] Plainly, then, the divine love is in every man, an evil man as well as a good man, and the Lord who is divine love cannot act otherwise than a father on earth does with his children, infinitely more lovingly because divine love is infinite. Furthermore, He cannot withdraw from anyone because everyone's life is from Him. He appears to withdraw from those who are evil, but it is they who withdraw, while He still in love leads them. Thus the Lord says:

> Ask, and it shall be given you; seek and you will find; knock and it shall be opened to you . . . What man of you, if his son shall ask bread, will give him a stone? If you, then, who are evil, know how to give good things to your children, how much more shall your Father, who is in heaven, give good things to those who ask Him (Mt 7:7-11),

and in another place,

> He makes His sun to rise on the evil and the good, and sends rain on the just and unjust (Mt 5:45).

It is also known in the church that the Lord desires the salvation of all and the death of no one. It may be seen from all this that predestination except to heaven is contrary to divine love.

[3] Second: *Predestination other than to heaven is contrary to divine wisdom, which is infinite.* By its divine wisdom divine love provides the means by which every man can be saved. To

say that there is any predestination except to heaven is therefore to say that divine love cannot provide means to salvation, when yet the means exist for all, as was shown above, and these are of divine providence which is boundless. The reason that there are those who are not saved is that divine love desires man to feel the felicity and blessedness of heaven for himself, else it would not be heaven to him, and this can be effected only as it seems to man that he thinks and wills of himself. For without this appearance nothing would be appropriated to him nor would he be a human being. To this end divine providence exists, which acts by divine wisdom out of divine love.

[4] But this does not do away with the truth that all are predestined to heaven and no one to hell. Were the means to salvation lacking, it would; but, as was demonstrated above, the means to salvation have been provided for everyone, and heaven is such that all of whatever religion who live rightly have a place in it. Man is like the earth which produces fruits of every kind, a power the earth has as the earth. That it also produces evil fruits does not do away with its capability of producing good fruits; it would if it could only produce evil fruits. Or, again, man is like an object which variegates the rays of light in it. If the object gives only unpleasing colors, the light is not the cause, for its rays can be variegated to produce pleasing colors.

[5] Third: *That only those who have been born in the church are saved is an insane heresy.* Those born outside the church are human beings equally with those born within it; they have the same heavenly origin, and like them they are living and immortal souls. They also have some religion by virtue of which they acknowledge God's existence and that they should live aright. One who acknowledges God and lives aright becomes spiritual in his measure and is saved, as we showed above. It may be protested that they have not been baptized, but baptism does not save any who are not washed spiritually, that is, regenerated, of which baptism is a sign and reminder.

[6] It is also objected that the Lord is not known to them and that there is no salvation without Him. But salvation does not

## XVII. EVERY MAN CAN BE REFORMED, AND THERE IS NO PREDESTINATION [as commonly understood]

come to a person because the Lord is known to him, but because he lives according to the Lord's precepts. Moreover, the Lord is known to everyone who acknowledges God, for He is God of heaven and earth, as He Himself teaches (Mt 28:18 and elsewhere). Furthermore, those outside the church have a clearer idea about God as Man than Christians have, and those who have a concept of God as Man and live rightly are accepted by the Lord. They also acknowledge God as one in person and essence, differently from Christians. They also give thought to God in their lives, for they regard evils as sins against God, and those who do this regard God in their lives. Christians have precepts of religion from the Word, but few draw precepts of life from it.

[7] Roman Catholics do not read the Word, and the Reformed who are in faith apart from charity do not attend to those utterances in it which concern life, only to those which concern faith, and yet the Word as a whole is nothing else than a doctrine of life. Christianity obtains only in Europe; Mohammedanism and Gentilism are found in Asia, the Indies, Africa and America, and the people in these parts of the globe are ten times more numerous than those in the Christian part, and in this part few put religion in life. What then is more mad than to believe that only these latter are saved and the former condemned, and that a man has heaven on the strength of his birth and not on the strength of his life? So the Lord says:

> I say to you, many will come from the east and the west, and recline with Abraham, Isaac and Jacob in the kingdom of heaven; but the children of the kingdom shall be cast out (Mt 8:11, 12).

[8] Fourth: *That any of mankind are condemned by predestination is a cruel heresy.* For it is cruel to believe that the Lord, who is love itself and mercy itself, suffers so vast a throng of persons to be born for hell or so many myriads of myriads to be born condemned and doomed, that is, to be born devils and satans, and that He does not provide out of His divine wisdom that those who live aright and acknowledge God should not be cast into everlasting fire and torment. The Lord is still the

Creator and the Savior of all men and wills the death of no one. It is cruel therefore to believe and think that a vast multitude of nations and peoples under His auspices and care should be handed over as prey to the devil by predestination.

## XVIII. THE LORD CANNOT ACT CONTRARY TO THE LAWS OF DIVINE PROVIDENCE BECAUSE TO DO SO WOULD BE TO ACT CONTRARY TO HIS DIVINE LOVE AND WISDOM, THUS CONTRARY TO HIMSELF

331. It was shown in *Angelic Wisdom about Divine Love and Wisdom* that the Lord is divine love and wisdom, and that these are being itself and life itself from which everything is and lives. It was also shown that they proceed from Him, so that the proceeding divine is the Lord Himself. Paramount in what proceeds is divine providence, for this is constantly in the end for which the universe was created. The operation and progress of the end through means is what is called divine providence.

[2] Inasmuch as the proceeding divine is the Lord Himself and paramount in it is divine providence, to act contrary to the laws of His divine providence is to act contrary to Himself. One can also say that the Lord is providence just as one says that God is order, for divine providence is the divine order with reference primarily to the salvation of men. As order does not exist without laws, for they constitute it, and each law derives from order that it, too, is order, it follows that God, who is order, is also the law of His order. Similarly it is to be said of divine providence that as the Lord is providence Himself, He is also the law of His providence. Hence it is clear that the Lord cannot act contrary to the laws of His divine providence because to do so would be to act contrary to Himself.

[3] Furthermore, there is no activity except on a subject and on the subject by means; action is impossible except on a subject and on it by means. Man is the subject of divine providence; divine truths by which he has wisdom, and divine goods by

## Divine Providence

which he has love, are the means; and by these means divine providence pursues its purpose, which is the salvation of man. For he who wills the purpose, wills the means. Therefore when he who wills the purpose pursues it, he does so through means. But these things will become plainer on being examined in this order:

    a. The activity of divine providence to save man begins at his birth and continues to the close of his life and afterwards to eternity.
    b. The activity of divine providence is maintained steadily out of pure mercy through means.
    c. Instantaneous salvation by direct mercy is impossible.
    d. Instantaneous salvation by direct mercy is the flying fiery serpent in the church.

332. (1) The *activity of divine providence to save man begins at his birth and continues to the close of his life and afterwards to eternity.* It was shown above that a heaven from mankind is the very purpose of the creation of the universe; that this purpose in its operation and progress is the divine providence for the salvation of man; and that all which is external to man and available to him for use is a secondary end in creation—in brief, all that is to be found in the three kingdoms, animal, vegetable and mineral. When all this constantly proceeds according to laws of divine order fixed at the first of creation, how can the primary end, which is the salvation of the human race, fail to proceed constantly according to laws of its order, which are the laws of divine providence?

[2] Observe just a fruit tree. It springs up first as a slender shoot from a tiny seed, grows gradually into a stalk, spreads branches which become covered with leaves, and then puts forth flowers and bears fruit, in which it deposits fresh seed to provide for its perpetuation. This is also true of every shrub and of every herb of the field. Do not each and all things in tree or shrub proceed constantly and wonderfully from purpose to purpose

## XVIII. THE LORD CANNOT ACT CONTRARY TO THE LAWS OF DIVINE PROVIDENCE BECAUSE TO DO SO WOULD BE TO ACT CONTRARY TO HIS DIVINE LOVE AND WISDOM, THUS CONTRARY TO HIMSELF

according to the laws of their order of things? Why should not the supreme end, a heaven from the human race, proceed in similar fashion? Can there be anything in its progress which does not proceed with all constancy according to the laws of divine providence?

[3] As there is a correspondence of man's life with the growth of a tree, let us draw the parallel or make the comparison. His infancy is relatively like the tender shoot of the tree sprouting from seed out of the ground; his childhood and youth are like the shoot grown to a stalk with its small branches; the natural truths with which everyone is imbued at first are like the leaves with which the branches are covered ("leaves" signify precisely this in the Word); man's first steps in the marriage of good and truth or the spiritual marriage are like the blossoms which the tree puts forth in the springtime; spiritual truths are the petals in these blossoms; the earliest signs of the spiritual marriage are like the start of fruit; spiritual goods, which are goods of charity, are like the fruit (they are also signified in the Word by "fruits"); the procreations of wisdom from love are like the seed and by them the human being becomes like a garden or paradise. Man is also described in the Word by a tree, and his wisdom from love by a garden; nothing else is meant by the Garden of Eden.

[4] True, man is a corrupt tree from the seed, but still a grafting or budding with shoots taken from the Tree of Life is possible, by which the sap drawn from the old root is turned into sap producing good fruit. The comparison was drawn for it to be known that when the progression of divine providence is so constant in the growth and rebirth of trees, it surely must be constant in the reformation and rebirth of human beings, who are of much more value than trees; so the Lord's words:

> Are not five sparrows sold for two farthings, yet not one of them is forgotten by God? But even the hairs of your head are all numbered; fear not therefore; you are of more value than many sparrows. Which of you moreover can by taking

thought add a cubit to his stature? ... if then you are unable to do what is least, why do you take thought for the rest? Consider the lilies, how they grow . . . If then God so clothed the grass, which is in the field today and is cast into an oven tomorrow, how much more will he clothe you, 0 men of little faith? (Lu 12: 6, 7, 25-28).

333. The activity of divine providence for man's salvation is said to begin with his birth and continue to the close of his life. For this to be understood, it should be known that the Lord sees what a man's nature is and foresees what he wills to be and thus what he will be. For him to be man and thus immortal, his freedom of will cannot be taken away. The Lord therefore foresees his state after death and provides for it from the man's birth to the close of his life. With the evil He makes the provision by permitting and withdrawing from evils, in the case of the good by leading to good. Divine providence is thus continually acting for man's salvation, but more cannot be saved than are willing to be saved, and those are willing who acknowledge God and are led by Him. Those are not willing who do not acknowledge God and who lead themselves. The latter give no thought to eternal life and to salvation, the former do. The Lord sees the unwillingness but still He leads such men, and does so in accordance with the laws of His divine providence, contrary to which he cannot act, for to act contrary to them would be to act contrary to His divine love and wisdom, and this is to act contrary to Himself.

[2] Inasmuch as the Lord foresees the states of all after death, and also foresees the places in hell of those who do not desire to be saved and the places in heaven of those who do desire to be saved, it follows that He provides their places for the evil by the permitting and withdrawing of which we spoke, and their places for the good by leading them. Unless this was done steadily from birth to the close of life neither heaven nor hell would remain standing, for apart from this foresight and providence neither would be anything but confusion. It may be seen above (nn. 202, 203) that everyone has his place provided for him by the Lord through this foresight.

## XVIII. THE LORD CANNOT ACT CONTRARY TO THE LAWS OF DIVINE PROVIDENCE BECAUSE TO DO SO WOULD BE TO ACT CONTRARY TO HIS DIVINE LOVE AND WISDOM, THUS CONTRARY TO HIMSELF

[3] A comparison may throw light on this. If a javelin thrower or a marksman should aim at a target, from which a line was drawn straight back for a mile and should err in aim by only a finger's breadth, the missile or the bullet at the end of the mile would have deviated very far from the line. So would it be if the Lord did not, at every moment and even the least fraction of a moment, look to what is eternal in foreseeing and making provision for one's place after death. But this the Lord does: the entire future is present to Him, and the entire present is to Him eternal. That divine providence looks in all it does to what is infinite and eternal, may be seen above, nn. 46-49, 214 ff.

334. As was said also, the activity of divine providence continues to eternity, for every angel is being perfected in wisdom to eternity, each, however, according to the degree of affection of good and truth in which he was when he left this world. It is this degree that is perfected to eternity; what is beyond that is outside the angel and not in him, and what is external to him cannot be perfected in him. This perfecting is meant by the "Good measure, pressed down and shaken together and running over" which will be given into the bosom of those who forgive and give to others (Lu 6:37, 38), that is, those who are in the good of charity.

335. (2) *The activity of divine providence is maintained steadily out of pure mercy through means.* Divine providence has means and methods. Its means are the things by which man becomes man and is perfected in will and understanding; its methods are the ways this is accomplished. The means by which man becomes man and is perfected in understanding are collectively called truths. In the thought they become ideas, are called objects of the memory, and in themselves are forms of knowledge from which information comes. All these means, viewed in themselves, are spiritual, but as they exist in what is natural, they seem by reason of their covering or clothing to be natural and some of them seem to be material. They are infinite in number and variety, and more or less simple or composite,

and also more or less imperfect or perfect. There are means for forming and perfecting natural civil life; likewise for forming and perfecting rational moral life; as there are for forming and perfecting heavenly spiritual life.

[2] These means advance, one kind after another, from infancy to the last of man's life, and thereafter to eternity. As they come along and mount, the earlier ones become means to the later, entering into all that is forming as mediate causes. From these every effect or conclusion is efficacious and therefore becomes a cause. In turn what is later becomes means; and as this goes on to eternity, there is nothing farthest on or final to make an end. For as what is eternal is without end, so a wisdom that increases to eternity is without end. If there were an end to wisdom for a wise man, the enjoyment of his wisdom would perish, which consists in the perpetual multiplication and fructification of wisdom. His life's enjoyment would also perish; in its place an enjoyment of glory would succeed, in which by itself there is no heavenly life. The wise man then becomes no longer like a youth but like an old man, and at length like a decrepit one.

[3] Although a wise man's wisdom increases forever in heaven, angelic wisdom cannot approximate the divine wisdom so much as to touch it. It is relatively like what is said of a straight line drawn about a hyperbola, always approaching but never touching it, and like what is said about squaring a circle. Hence it may be plain what is meant by the means by which divine providence acts in order that man may be man and be perfected in understanding, and that these means are called by the common term truths. There are an equal number of means by which man is formed and perfected as to his will. These are called collectively goods. By them man comes to have love, by the others wisdom. The conjunction of love and wisdom makes the man, for what he is is in keeping with the nature of this conjunction. This conjunction is what is called the marriage of good and truth.

## XVIII. THE LORD CANNOT ACT CONTRARY TO THE LAWS OF DIVINE PROVIDENCE BECAUSE TO DO SO WOULD BE TO ACT CONTRARY TO HIS DIVINE LOVE AND WISDOM, THUS CONTRARY TO HIMSELF

336. The methods by which divine providence acts on and through the means to form and perfect the human being are also infinite in number and variety. They are as numerous as the activities of divine wisdom from divine love to save man, and therefore as numerous as the activities of divine providence in accordance with its laws, treated of above. That these methods are most secret was illustrated above by the activities of the soul in the body, of which man knows so little it is scarcely anything—how, for instance, eye, ear, nose, tongue and skin sense things; how the stomach digests; how the mesentery elaborates the chyle and the liver the blood; how the pancreas and the spleen purify the blood, the kidneys separate it from impure humors, the heart collects and distributes it, and the lungs purify it and pass it on; how the brain refines the blood and vivifies it anew; besides innumerable other things which are all secret, and of which one can scarcely know. Clearly, the hidden activities of divine providence can be entered into even less; it is enough to know its laws.

337. Divine providence acts in all things out of pure mercy. For the divine essence is itself pure love; this love acts through divine wisdom and its activity is what is called divine providence. This pure love is pure mercy because

1. It is active with all men the world over, who are such that they can do nothing of themselves.
2. It is active with the evil and unjust and the good and just alike.
3. It leads the former in hell and rescues them from it.
4. It strives with them there perpetually and fights for them against the devil, that is, against the evils of hell.
5. To this end pure love came into the world and endured temptations even to the last of them, which was the passion of the Cross.

6. It acts continually with the unclean to make them clean and with the unsound to make them sound in mind.

Thus it labors incessantly out of pure mercy.

338. (3) *Instantaneous salvation by direct mercy is impossible.* We have just shown that the activity of divine providence to save man begins at his birth and continues to the close of his life and afterwards to eternity; also that this activity is continually pursued out of pure mercy through means. It follows that there is neither instantaneous salvation nor unmediated mercy. But as many, not thinking from the understanding about things of the church or of religion, believe that they are saved by immediate mercy and hence that salvation is instantaneous, and yet this is contrary to the truth and in addition is a pernicious belief, it is important that it be considered in due order:

1. Belief in instantaneous salvation by direct mercy has been assumed from man's natural state.
2. This belief comes from ignorance of the spiritual state, which is completely different from the natural state.
3. The doctrines of all churches in Christendom, viewed interiorly, are opposed to instantaneous salvation by direct mercy, but external men of the church nevertheless maintain the belief.

[2] First: *Belief in instantaneous salvation by direct mercy has been assumed from man's natural state.* From his state the natural man does not know otherwise than that heavenly joy is like worldly joy and that it flows in and is received in the same way; that, for example, it is like a poor man's becoming rich and from a sad state of poverty coming into a happy one of plenty, or like a lowly person's being raised to honors and passing thus from contempt to renown; or like one's going from a house of mourning to happy nuptials. As these states can be changed in a day and as there is a like idea of man's state after death, it is plain

## XVIII. THE LORD CANNOT ACT CONTRARY TO THE LAWS OF DIVINE PROVIDENCE BECAUSE TO DO SO WOULD BE TO ACT CONTRARY TO HIS DIVINE LOVE AND WISDOM, THUS CONTRARY TO HIMSELF

whence it comes that instantaneous salvation by direct mercy is believed in.

[3] In the world, moreover, many can join in one group or in one civic community and enjoy the same things, yet all differ in mind; this is true of the natural state. The reason is that the external of one person can be accommodated to that of another, no matter how unlike their internals are. From this natural situation it is also concluded that salvation is merely admission among angels in heaven, and that admission is by direct mercy. It is also believed, therefore, that heaven can be given to the evil as well as to the good, and that their association then is similar to that in the world, with the difference that it is filled with joy.

[4] Second: *This belief comes from ignorance of the spiritual state, which is altogether different from the natural state.* The spiritual state, which is man's state after death, has been treated of in many places above. It has been shown that everyone is his own love, that no one can live with others than those who are in a like love, and that if he comes among others he cannot breathe his own life. For this reason everyone comes after death into a society of his own people, that is, who are in a like love, and recognizes them as relatives and friends, and what is remarkable, on meeting and seeing them it is as if he had known them from infancy. Spiritual relationship and friendship bring this about. What is more, in a society no one can dwell in any other house than his own. Everyone in a society has his own home, which he finds prepared for him as soon as he enters the society. He may be in close company with others outside his home, but he cannot dwell elsewhere. Again, in somebody else's apartment one can sit only in his own place; seated elsewhere he becomes frustrated and mute. And it is remarkable that on entering he knows his own place. This is as true in temples he enters and in any companies in which people gather.

[5] It is plain from this that the spiritual state is altogether different from the natural state, and is such that no one can be

anywhere but where his ruling love is to be found. For there the enjoyment of one's life is, and everyone desires to be in the enjoyment of his life. A man's spirit cannot be anywhere else because that enjoyment constitutes his life, his very breathing, in fact, and his heartbeat. It is different in the natural world; there man's external is taught from infancy to simulate in look, speech and bearing other enjoyments than those of his internal man. Accordingly, no conclusion can be formed about man's state after death from his state in the natural world. For after death everyone's state is spiritual and is such that he cannot be anywhere except in the enjoyment of his love, an enjoyment that he has acquired in the natural world by his life.

[6] Hence it is quite plain that no one who is in the enjoyment of hell can be admitted into the enjoyment of heaven, commonly called heavenly happiness, or what is the same, no one who is in the enjoyment of evil can be admitted into the enjoyment of good. This can be concluded still more plainly from the fact that after death no one is denied going up to heaven; he is shown the way, has the opportunity given him, and is admitted, but as soon as he enters heaven and inhales its enjoyment, he begins to feel constricted in his chest and racked at heart, and falls into a swoon, in which he writhes as a snake does brought near a fire. Then with his face turned away from heaven and towards hell, he flees headlong and does not stop until he is in a society of his own love. Hence it may be plain that no one reaches heaven by direct mercy. Consequently, just to be admitted is not enough, as many in the world suppose. Nor is there any instantaneous salvation, for this presupposes unmediated mercy.

[7] When some who had believed in the world in instantaneous salvation by direct mercy became spirits, they wanted their infernal enjoyment or enjoyment of evil changed by both divine omnipotence and divine mercy into heavenly enjoyment or enjoyment in the good. As they ardently desired this, permission was given for it to be done by angels, who proceeded to remove their infernal enjoyment. But as this was the enjoyment of their life's love and consequently their life, they thereupon lay as if dead, devoid of all feeling and movement; nor

## XVIII. THE LORD CANNOT ACT CONTRARY TO THE LAWS OF DIVINE PROVIDENCE BECAUSE TO DO SO WOULD BE TO ACT CONTRARY TO HIS DIVINE LOVE AND WISDOM, THUS CONTRARY TO HIMSELF

could any life be breathed into them except their own, because all things of mind and body which had been turned backward could not be reversed. They were therefore revived by letting in the enjoyment of their life's love. They said afterwards that in that state they had experienced something dreadful and horrible, which they did not care to divulge. There is a saying in heaven, therefore, that it is easier to change an owl into a turtle-dove or a serpent into a lamb than an infernal spirit into an angel of heaven.

[8] Third: *The doctrines of all churches in Christendom, viewed interiorly, are opposed to instantaneous salvation by direct mercy, but still some external men of the church maintain the idea.* Viewed interiorly, the doctrines of all the churches teach life. Is there a church whose doctrine does not teach that man ought to examine himself, see and acknowledge his sins, confess them, repent and then live a new life? Who is admitted to Holy Communion without this admonition and precept? Inquire and you will be assured of it. Is there a church whose doctrine is not based on the precepts of the Decalog? The precepts of the Decalog are precepts of life. What man of the church, in whom there is anything of the church, does not, on hearing it, acknowledge that he who lives rightly is saved and he who lives wickedly is condemned? In the Athanasian Creed, which is also the doctrine received in the whole Christian world, it is therefore said:

> The Lord will come to judge the quick and the dead; and then those who have done good will enter into eternal life, and those who have done evil into everlasting fire.

[9] It is clear, then, that the doctrines of all churches, when viewed interiorly, teach life, and teaching life they teach that salvation is according to the life. Man's life is not breathed into him in a moment but is formed gradually, and it is reformed as the man shuns evils as sins, consequently as he learns what sin is, recognizes and acknowledges it, does not will it but desists

from it, and also learns the helps that come with a knowledge of God. By all these means man's life is formed and reformed, and they cannot be given on the instant. For hereditary evil, in itself infernal, has to be removed, and good, in itself heavenly, implanted in its place. Because of his hereditary evil man may be compared to an owl as to the understanding and to a serpent as to the will, but when he has been reformed, he may be compared to a dove as to the understanding and to a sheep as to the will. Instantaneous reformation and hence salvation would be like changing an owl at once into a dove or a serpent at once into a sheep. Who that knows anything about man's life does not see the impossibility of this? Salvation is impossible unless the owl and serpent nature is removed and the nature of the dove and sheep implanted instead.

[10] Moreover, it is common knowledge that every intelligent person can become more intelligent than he is, and every wise man wiser than he is, and that intelligence and wisdom in man may increase and do so in some men from infancy to the close of life, and that man is thus continually perfected. Why should not spiritual intelligence and wisdom increase as well? These rise by two degrees above natural intelligence and wisdom, and as they ascend become angelic intelligence and wisdom, which are ineffable. These in turn increase to eternity with the angels. Who cannot understand, if he will, that what is being perfected to eternity cannot possibly be made perfect in an instant?

339. Thence it is evident now that all who give thought to salvation for their life's sake do not think of an instantaneous salvation by immediate mercy. Their thought is about the means to salvation, on and by which the Lord acts in accord with the laws of His divine providence, and thus by which man is led by the Lord out of pure mercy. Those, however, who do not think of salvation for their life's sake presume an instantaneousness in salvation and an immediacy in mercy, as do those who, separating faith from charity (charity is life), presume that faith can be instantaneous, at the final hour of death, if not earlier. Those do this, too, who believe remission of sins without any repentance to be absolution from sins and thus salvation, when

## XVIII. THE LORD CANNOT ACT CONTRARY TO THE LAWS OF DIVINE PROVIDENCE BECAUSE TO DO SO WOULD BE TO ACT CONTRARY TO HIS DIVINE LOVE AND WISDOM, THUS CONTRARY TO HIMSELF

attending the Holy Supper. So again those do who trust to indulgences of monks, their prayers for the dead, and the dispensations they grant by the authority which they claim over the souls of men.

340. (4) *Instantaneous salvation by unmediated mercy is the flying fiery serpent in the church.* By a flying fiery serpent evil aglow with infernal fire is meant, as it is by the flying fiery serpent in Isaiah:

> Rejoice not, all Philistia, that the rod which smote you is broken, for out of the serpent's root shall come forth a basilisk, whose fruit is a flying fiery serpent (14:29).

Evil of the kind is flying about in the church when belief is put in instantaneous salvation by immediate mercy, for this

1. abolishes religion;
2. induces security; and
3. charges condemnation to the Lord.

[2] First: *It abolishes religion.* Two things are the essentials and at the same time the universals of religion, namely, acknowledgment of God, and repentance. Neither has meaning for those who believe that they are saved out of mercy alone no matter how they live. What need then to do more than cry, "Have mercy on me, O God"? In all else pertaining to religion they are in darkness, even loving the darkness. In regard to the first essential of the church, which is an acknowledgment of God, they only think, "What is God? Who has seen Him?" If told that God is, and is one, they say that He is one; if told there are three, they also say there are three, but the three must be called one. Such is their acknowledgment of God.

[3] Touching the church's second essential, namely, repentance, they give this no thought, nor thought to any sin, and finally do not know that there is such a thing as sin. Then they hear and drink in with pleasure that the law does not condemn them because a Christian is not under its yoke. If only you say,

## Divine Providence

"Have mercy on me, 0 God, for the sake of the Son," you will be saved. This is repentance in their life. If, however, you take away repentance, or what is the same thing, separate life from religion, what is left except the words, "Have mercy on me"? They are therefore sure to maintain that salvation is instantaneous, accomplished by these words, even if uttered at the hour of death, if not before. What does the Word become to them then but an obscure and cryptic utterance issuing from a tripod in a cave, or like an incomprehensible response from the oracle of an idol? In a word, if you remove repentance, that is, sever life from religion, what is human nature then but evil aglow with infernal fire or a flying fiery serpent in the church? For without repentance man is in evil, and evil is hell.

[4] Second: *By the belief in instantaneous salvation out of pure mercy alone security of life is induced.* Security of life arises either from the belief of the impious man that there is no life after death, or from the belief of one who separates life from salvation. Although the latter may believe in eternal life, he still thinks, "whether I live rightly or wickedly, I can be saved, for salvation is by outright mercy, and God's mercy is universal, for He does not desire the death of anyone." If it occurs to him that mercy should be implored in the words of the traditional faith, he can think that this can be done, if not earlier, just before death. Everyone who feels this security, makes light of adultery, fraud, injustice, acts of violence, blasphemy and revenge, and gives a free rein to body and spirit for committing all these evils; nor does he know what spiritual evil, or the lust of evil, is. Should he hear something about it from the Word, it is like something falling on ebony and rebounding, or falling into a ditch and being swallowed up.

[5] Third: *By this belief condemnation is charged to the Lord. If the Lord can save anybody out of pure mercy, who is not going to conclude that if man is not saved, it is not he but the Lord who is in fault?* If it is asserted that faith is the medium of salvation, what man cannot have this faith? For it is only a thought, and this can be imparted, along with confidence, in any state of the spirit withdrawn from the mundane. Man may also declare "I

## XVIII. THE LORD CANNOT ACT CONTRARY TO THE LAWS OF DIVINE PROVIDENCE BECAUSE TO DO SO WOULD BE TO ACT CONTRARY TO HIS DIVINE LOVE AND WISDOM, THUS CONTRARY TO HIMSELF

cannot acquire this faith of myself." Hence if it is not vouchsafed him and he is condemned, what else can he think except that the Lord is in fault who could have given him the faith but would not? Would this not amount to calling the Lord unmerciful? Moreover, in the fervor of his belief he may ask, "How can God see so many condemned in hell when He can save them all in an instant from pure mercy?" And more such things, which can only be called an atrocious indictment of the Divine. From the above it may be evident that belief in instantaneous salvation out of sheer mercy is the flying fiery serpent in the church.

[6] Excuse the addition of what follows to fill the remainder of the sheet.

Certain spirits were permitted to ascend from hell who said to me, "You have written much from the Lord; write something from us, too." I asked, "What shall I write?" They said, "Write that every spirit, good or evil, has his own enjoyment; a good spirit is in the enjoyment of his good, and an evil spirit in the enjoyment of his evil." I then asked, "What is your enjoyment?" They answered that it was the enjoyment of committing adultery, stealing, defrauding and lying. Again I inquired, "What is the nature of those enjoyments?" They replied, "By others they are perceived as offensive odors from excrement and as the putrid smell from dead bodies and as the reeking stench from stagnant urine." I then said, "Do you find them enjoyable?" "Most enjoyable," they said. I remarked, "Then you are like unclean beasts which live in such filth." They replied to this, "If we are, we are; but such things are delightful to our nostrils."

[7] I asked, "What more shall I write from you?" They said, "Write this. Everyone is allowed to be in his own enjoyment, even the most unclean, as it is called, provided he does not infest good spirits and angels, but as we could not but infest them, we were driven off and cast into hell, where we suffer fearful things." I asked, "Why did you infest the good?" They replied that they could not help it; a fury seems to seize them when they

see an angel and feel the divine sphere around him. Then I said, "So you are also like savage beasts!" On hearing this, a fury came over them which appeared like the fire of hate, and lest they inflict some injury, they were drawn back into hell. On enjoyments sensed as odors or as stenches in the spiritual world, see above (nn. 303-305, 324).

Footnotes

318-1 Cf. Ezekiel 13:10, 11 and *Arcana Caelestia* n. 739(2), Apocalypse Explained nn. 237(5) and 644(25). Tr.

CPSIA information can be obtained
at www.ICGtesting.com
Printed in the USA
BVHW041158151118
533219BV00009B/74/P